Gender in the Middle Ages

Volume 25

FINANCING QUEENSHIP IN LATE FIFTEENTH CENTURY ENGLAND

Gender in the Middle Ages

ISSN 1742-870X

Series Editors
Jacqueline Murray
Diane Watt

Editorial Board
Clare Lees
Katherine J. Lewis
Liz Herbert McAvoy

This series investigates the representation and construction of masculinity and femininity in the Middle Ages from a variety of disciplinary and interdisciplinary perspectives. It aims in particular to explore the diversity of medieval genders, and such interrelated contexts and issues as sexuality, social class, race and ethnicity, and orthodoxy and heterodoxy.

Proposals or queries should be sent in the first instance to the editors or to the publisher, at the addresses given below; all submissions will receive prompt and informed consideration.

Professor Jacqueline Murray
jacqueline.murray@uoguelph.ca

Professor Diane Watt
d.watt@surrey.ac.uk

Boydell & Brewer Limited, PO Box 9, Woodbridge, Suffolk IP12 3DF, UK
editorial@boydell.co.uk

Previously published volumes in the series are listed at the end of this book.

FINANCING QUEENSHIP IN LATE FIFTEENTH CENTURY ENGLAND

Michele L. C. Seah

THE BOYDELL PRESS

© Michele L. C. Seah 2025

All Rights Reserved. Except as permitted under current legislation
no part of this work may be photocopied, stored in a retrieval system,
published, performed in public, adapted, broadcast,
transmitted, recorded or reproduced in any form or by any means,
without the prior permission of the copyright owner

The right of Michele L. C. Seah to be identified as the author of this work has
been asserted in accordance with sections 77 and 78 of the Copyright, Designs and
Patents Act 1988

First published 2025
The Boydell Press, Woodbridge

ISBN 978-1-83765-046-0

The Boydell Press is an imprint of Boydell & Brewer Ltd
PO Box 9, Woodbridge, Suffolk IP12 3DF, UK
and of Boydell & Brewer Inc.
668 Mt Hope Avenue, Rochester, NY 14620–2731, USA
website: www.boydellandbrewer.com

A CIP catalogue record for this book is available
from the British Library

Our Authorised Representative for product safety in the EU is Easy
Access System Europe – Mustamäe tee 50, 10621 Tallinn,
Estonia, gpsr.requests@easproject.com

The publisher has no responsibility for the continued existence or accuracy of
URLs for external or third-party internet websites referred to in this book, and
does not guarantee that any content on such websites is, or will remain, accurate
or appropriate

CONTENTS

List of Illustrations	vii
Acknowledgements	ix
List of Abbreviations and Notes	xi
Simplified Genealogy	xiv
Introduction	1
1 The Queen's Resources	15

PART I LANDS AND ESTATES: A MAJOR SOURCE OF REVENUE

2 Surveying the Queen's Lands	51
3 Managing the Queen's Lands	89

PART II USING THE QUEEN'S RESOURCES: THE 'SERVICE' ECONOMY

4 The Queen's Household	135
5 The Queen's Affinity	179
Conclusion	209

Appendices

1 The Queens' Lands and Holdings – A Composite List	215
2 The Queens' Fee-farms – A Composite List	235
3 Extant Manorial Documents Consulted	243
Select Bibliography	257
Index	273

ILLUSTRATIONS

MAPS

1.	Composite Distribution of Margaret of Anjou's Landholdings	61
2.	Composite Distribution of Elizabeth Woodville's Landholdings	63
3.	Composite Distribution of Elizabeth of York's Landholdings	65
4.	Composite Distribution of Philippa of Hainault's Landholdings	69

TABLES

1.	Queen's Gold Claims in Margaret of Anjou's Household Account for 1452–53 (TNA DL28/5/8)	41
2.	Distribution of Writs for Queen's Gold for Elizabeth Woodville	41
3.	Records of Queen's Gold Owed to Elizabeth Woodville	42
4.	Distribution of Writs for Queen's Gold for Elizabeth of York	45
5.	Annual Fees for Stewards of Lands	103
6.	Annual Fees for Receivers	108
7.	Fifteenth-Century Household Ordinances	141
8.	The Queens' Household Officials and Personnel	157
9.	The Queens' Ladies	170

ACKNOWLEDGEMENTS

The research in this book builds on previously published work, as below, and I would like to thank the publishers for their kind permission in allowing me to re-use some of the material:

Michele Seah and Katia Wright, 'The Medieval English Queen as Landholder: Some Reflections on Sources and Methodology', in *Women and Economic Power in Premodern Royal Courts*, ed. Cathleen Sarti (Leeds: ARC Humanities Press, 2020), 9–33.

Michele Seah, '"My Lady Queen, the Lord of the Manor": The Economic Roles of Late Medieval Queens', *Parergon* 37, no. 2 (2020): 9–36.

 This book has been a long time in the making and could not have been finished without all the support I received along the way. I owe so many people thanks and more for their help and advice that it is quite impossible to name them all individually. Please know that even if I have not mentioned you by name, that does not mean that I value your help any less.

 I would, however, like to acknowledge a huge debt of gratitude to Dr Camilla Russell, who laboured tirelessly long ago to instil in a would-be historian critical thinking and good research and writing habits. Her support, encouragement, and belief in me have been unwavering. Her own work ethic and outlook on life remain inspirational.

 The many scholars I have met at conferences and seminars, especially the royal studies and queenship historians, have wholeheartedly welcomed me and my work. I have greatly benefitted from their knowledge and advice and can only hope I return in kind. Thank you all; you are my tribe and you re-inspire me every time we meet and re-connect. Special mention must go to Katia Wright, who early on agreed to collaborate with me on an essay for a book collection. Thank you for all our fruitful discussions on everything 'queens', especially queens' lands.

 Last but by no means least, my love and heartfelt appreciation go to my parents, whose life choices have shaped my own, and to my husband and children, Peng, Anne, Liz, and Nick. You have always been in my corner, and I could not have stayed the course without you. This work is for you as much as it is for me.

ABBREVIATIONS AND NOTES

BIHR	*Bulletin of the Institute of Historical Research*
BJRL	*Bulletin of the John Rylands Library*
BL	London: The British Library
CChR	*Calendar of the Charter Rolls*
CCR	*Calendar of the Close Rolls*
CIPM	*Calendar of Inquisitions Post Mortem*
CPR	*Calendar of the Patent Rolls*
The Chamber Books	*The Chamber Books of Henry VII and Henry VIII, 1485–1521*, eds. M. M. Condon, S. P. Harper, L. Liddy, S. Cunningham and J. Ross. https://www.tudorchamberbooks.org
EcHR	*The Economic History Review*
EHR	*The English Historical Review*
ERO	Chelmsford, Essex: Essex Record Office
EETS	Early English Text Society
Foedera	*Rymer's Foedera*, 5 vols. (volumes 8–12), ed. Thomas Rymer (London: Apud Joannem Neulme, 1739–1745), British History Online, http://www.british-history.ac.uk/rymer-foedera/
HALS	Hertford, Hertfordshire: Hertfordshire Archives and Local Studies
HHLA	Hatfield, Hertfordshire: Hatfield House Library and Archives
Johnstone I	Hilda Johnstone, 'The Queen's Household', in *Chapters in the Administrative History of Mediaeval England: The Wardrobe, the Chamber and the Small Seals*, Vol. V, ed. T. F. Tout (Manchester: Manchester University Press, 1930)

Abbreviations and Notes

Johnstone II	Hilda Johnstone, 'The Queen's Household', in *The English Government at Work, 1327–1336*, vol. I, eds. James F. Willard, William A. Morris, et al., (Cambridge, Mass.: The Mediaeval Academy of America, 1940)
LP	*Letters and Papers, Foreign and Domestic, Henry VIII, Volume I, 1509–1514*, ed. J. S. Brewer (London: H. M. Stationery Office, 1920), British History Online, http://www.british-history.ac.uk/letters-papers-hen8/vol1
Materials for a History	*Materials for a History of the Reign of Henry VII*, 2 vols, ed. William Campbell (London: Longman, 1877)
ODNB	*Oxford Dictionary of National Biography*, https://www.oxforddnb.com
PROME	Parliament Rolls of Medieval England, eds. Chris Given-Wilson, Paul Brand, Seymour Phillips, Mark Ormrod, Geoffrey Martin, Anne Curry and Rosemary Horrox (Woodbridge: Boydell Press, 2005), British History Online, http://www.british-history.ac.uk/no-series/parliament-rolls-medieval
Queen's Book	*The Chamber Books of Henry VII and Henry VIII, 1485–1521*, eds. M. M. Condon, S. P. Harper, L. Liddy, S. Cunningham and J. Ross, TNA E36/210, https://www.tudorchamberbooks.org/edition/manuscript/E36_210/folio
RP	*Rotuli Parliamentorum, ut et petitiones, et placita in Parliamento tempore Edwardi R.I. [ad finem Henrici R.VII.]*, 6 vols. (London, House of Lords Record Office, 1767–77)
SJC	Cambridge: St John's College Archives
SR	*Statutes of the Realm*, 11 vols. (London: Great Britain Record Commission, 1810–28)
TNA	London: The National Archives
TRHS	*Transactions of the Royal Historical Society*
WAM	London: Westminster Abbey Library, Muniment Collection

Abbreviations and Notes

Contemporary spellings of names and places are retained in quotes and in tabulations of primary source information. However, the spellings are modernised in the body of the text. For example, Marleburgh is written as Marlborough in the main text.

All translations are my own except where stated otherwise.

Where currency is concerned, marks are always converted to pounds, shillings, and pence in brackets. All figures except where specified are rounded to the nearest unit.

Calendars of Charter Rolls, Close Rolls and Patent Rolls are referenced by the chronological period covered.

Regnal dates in primary source material have been converted to present-day dates in the main text. For example, the regnal year 23 Henry VI is equivalent to the period 1 September 1444–31 August 1445.

Simplified Genealogy

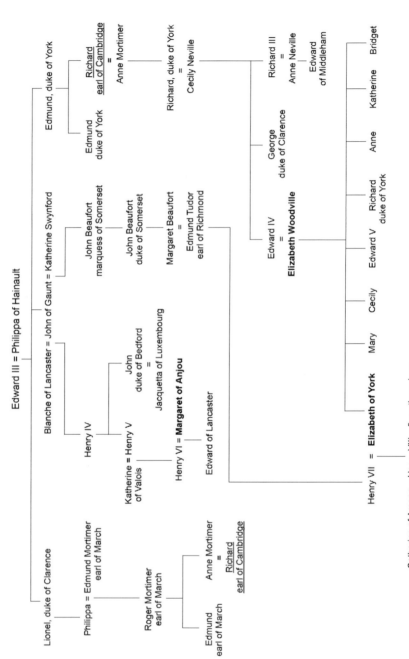

INTRODUCTION

Between the years 1450 and 1509, England endured a tremendous amount of upheaval and unrest springing from the civil wars we know today as the Wars of the Roses.[1] The feuds, revolts and other related violence that occurred during this conflict resulted in a startlingly large number of monarchic changes. In this relatively short amount of time, there were five different kings of England – Henry VI (r.1422–61, 1470–71), Edward IV (r.1461–83), Edward V (r.1483), Richard III (r.1483–85) and Henry VII (r.1485–1509). Except for the twelve-year-old Edward V, each of these kings was married. Consequently, there were four different queens consort – Margaret of Anjou (c.1430–82; r.1445–61, 1470–71), Elizabeth Woodville (c.1437–92; r.1464–83), Anne Neville (c.1456–85; r.1483–85), and Elizabeth of York (c.1466–1503; r.1486–1503). In a father–son monarchic changeover, the queen consort's successor would typically have been her daughter-in-law, the wife of the new king. None of these queens was related to each other in this manner.[2]

Margaret of Anjou, a niece of the French king, Charles VII (r.1422–61), was married to the Lancastrian king of England, Henry VI, in 1445 as part of diplomatic efforts by England to resolve the long-standing war with France. Henry, however, lost the throne to the Yorkists in battle in 1461. Although he regained his crown (and Margaret her title as queen consort) in October 1470 with the help of Richard Neville, earl of Warwick – who had famously changed sides from the Yorkists to the Lancastrians – he lost it again after only six months. This short period is known as Henry VI's Readeption. The first Yorkist king, Edward IV (who had taken the crown in 1461), conclusively defeated the Lancastrian army in May 1471 and re-claimed the crown, killing Margaret and Henry's only son, Edward of Lancaster. Although Henry was murdered shortly after in the Tower of London, possibly on Edward IV's

---

[1] For general information about the Wars of the Roses, see John Gillingham, *The Wars of the Roses: Peace and Conflict in 15th Century England* (London: Weidenfeld & Nicolson, 1981); Michael Hicks, *The Wars of the Roses* (New Haven: Yale University Press, 2010); A. J. Pollard, *The Wars of the Roses* (Basingstoke: Macmillan Education, 1988).

[2] Elizabeth Woodville was the mother of Elizabeth of York – a highly unusual situation for queens consort.

orders, Margaret survived for another eleven years in confinement and, later, exile in France, where she lived out her final days.[3]

Margaret's successor as queen was Elizabeth Woodville, an English-born widow of a Lancastrian knight, who secretly married Edward IV in 1464. The reasons for this clandestine marriage were not clear to contemporaries, lacking as Elizabeth did any obvious diplomatic or political usefulness. After Edward died in April 1483, Elizabeth lived on for almost ten years and with mixed fortunes. Their eldest son became Edward V but his reign lasted less than three months, after which he and his younger brother, Richard, were removed to the Tower of London by their uncle Richard, duke of Gloucester. Since the brothers were never seen again and Gloucester was crowned as Richard III in 1483, Elizabeth experienced the same fate as Margaret in seeing the end to her immediate family's claim to the throne occur in her own lifetime.

Richard III's wife, Anne Neville, was the younger daughter of the previously mentioned earl of Warwick who had been killed in battle over a decade before his daughter was crowned alongside her husband. Anne predeceased Richard, dying only a few months before he lost the battle, his life and his crown at Bosworth Field to Henry Tudor (Henry VII) in 1485. Their only son, Edward, had predeceased his parents.

The last queen of fifteenth-century England was Elizabeth of York. In her case, the political turmoil of the age produced another unusually placed queen consort. The daughter of a king would not typically have become the queen consort of a future occupant of the same throne. However, this Elizabeth was the eldest daughter of a previous king, Edward IV, and his queen, Elizabeth Woodville. She married the Tudor king, Henry VII, in 1486, a year after he wrested the crown from Richard III. Elizabeth of York's usefulness as a prospective queen to Henry lay in her parentage; as the eldest daughter of Edward IV, her marriage was meant to join the Yorkist and Tudor bloodlines and end the civil conflict.

Each of these queens is an important subject of investigation in her own right, with biographical narrative being a favoured vehicle by which to illuminate these women to the wider academic and general population.[4]

---

[3] The question of who ordered the murder of Henry VI at the Tower of London remains unresolved. Helen E. Maurer, *Margaret of Anjou: Queenship and Power in Late Medieval England* (Woodbridge: Boydell Press, 2003), 208.

[4] Examples of biographical work include the following. For Margaret of Anjou: Bonita Cron, 'Margaret of Anjou: Tradition and Revision' (unpublished MA thesis, Massey University, 1999); Maurer, *Margaret of Anjou*; Diana Dunn, 'Margaret [Margaret of Anjou]', in *ODNB* (2004). For Elizabeth Woodville: David Baldwin, *Elizabeth Woodville: Mother of the Princes in the Tower* (Stroud: Sutton, 2002); Arlene Okerlund, *Elizabeth Wydeville: The Slandered Queen* (Stroud: Tempus, 2005); Michael Hicks, 'Elizabeth [*née* Elizabeth Woodville]', in *ODNB* (2004). For Anne Neville: Michael Hicks, *Anne Neville: Queen to Richard III* (Stroud: Tempus, 2006); Michael Hicks, 'Anne [*née* Anne Neville]', in *ODNB* (2004). For Elizabeth

Introduction

Most of the narratives surrounding this group of queens take little account of the material bases of their queenships, reflecting a broader lack of attention on economic resources and finances in queenship studies up until relatively recently.[5] Yet such resources were the practical foundations upon which the queen's role and life rested and, if nothing else, provided revenues upon which the queens depended. Their income and financial sources enabled them to dispense patronage, exercise power, establish and maintain political and social networks, and make a variety of contributions in social and cultural terms to the society they lived in. The lack of research into these resources leaves a gap in our understanding of how they functioned in their world. We stand in danger of either downplaying or totally dismissing their specific economic roles, assuming such a role is even thought of in relation to these individuals. There are vital questions to be addressed in relation to ideas about queens as economic players in society. How involved were these queens in administrative matters? Did they function as landholders in the same manner as other great lords who possessed vast estates and widely dispersed lands? How do we relate their economic roles and possession of economic resources to issues of queenly authority, power and agency?

This book addresses the lacuna in studies of queenly economic resources, focusing on three of the above-mentioned fifteenth-century queens, Margaret of Anjou, Elizabeth Woodville and Elizabeth of York.[6] It examines the structural and organisational aspects of the economic resources available to these queens and some major ways that they used and benefitted from these

---

of York: Nancy Lenz Harvey, *Elizabeth of York: Tudor Queen* (London: A. Barker, 1973); Arlene Okerlund, *Elizabeth of York* (New York: Palgrave Macmillan, 2009); Rosemary Horrox, 'Elizabeth [Elizabeth of York]', in *ODNB* (2004). For grouped collections: Lisa Hilton, *Queens Consort: England's Medieval Queens* (London: Weidenfeld & Nicolson, 2008); David Loades, *The Tudor Queens of England* (London; New York: Continuum, 2009); *Later Plantagenet and the Wars of the Roses Consorts: Power, Influence and Dynasty*, eds. Aidan Norrie, Carolyn Harris, J. L. Laynesmith, Danna R. Messer and Elena Woodacre (Cham: Palgrave Macmillan, 2023); *Tudor and Stuart Consorts: Power, Influence, and Dynasty*, eds. Aidan Norrie, Carolyn Harris, J. L. Laynesmith, Danna R. Messer and Elena Woodacre (Cham: Palgrave Macmillan, 2022).

5 Attila Bárány notes that research on the economic relations and finances of medieval queens in Europe has fared a little better than in the case of late-medieval English queens. Attila Bárány, 'Medieval Queens and Queenship: A Retrospective on Income and Power', in *Annual of Medieval Studies at the CEU* (CEU, Budapest, 2013), 165–6 (This paper was prompted by a conference on queenship and questions of income and patronage held in 2004 at the Department of Medieval Studies, Central European University, Budapest); Theresa Earenfight, *Queenship in Medieval Europe* (Basingstoke: Palgrave Macmillan, 2013), 243.

6 Anne Neville, Richard III's queen, has not been included, primarily because the lack of pertinent sources makes it difficult to include her in discussions within the scope of this book.

resources. The study further aims to identify commonalities and differences within the group. This provides the scope to explore the broader question of queenship and its foundations. In doing so, it aims to capture the spirit of the current trends in queenship studies that look beyond individuals towards the practical foundations of queenship itself. Another benefit of this study is that the process of extending our knowledge of the exercise of medieval queenship in the economic arena unquestionably adds to our understanding of the economic and administrative landscape of late medieval England. It expands what we know of the nuances of the power and authority of the queen in relation to her subjects.

These specific queens make interesting case studies partly because of the particular period during which each of them lived their lives as queen consort. The earlier brief outline of the conditions surrounding each of these reigns illustrates how atypical the period was for the English realm. Margaret of Anjou, Elizabeth Woodville and Elizabeth of York each became queen in the aftermath of conflict and dynastic change. Moreover, their backgrounds and political allegiances were quite different, and they lived their lives as queen consort amid events disruptive to government and monarchy. These differences form a crucial part of the framework for this study and prompt us to consider the impact of different backgrounds and political disruption on the broader issue of economic resources for late medieval English queens.

Most research on Margaret and the two Elizabeths has not so far included much more than brief forays into their households and finances. Many scholars of Margaret of Anjou, such as Helen Maurer, have been primarily concerned with the queen's political role and reputation, eschewing extensive discussion or analysis of the queen's household and connections unless warranted.[7] However, Diana Dunn's reassessment of Margaret from various perspectives includes a short discussion of the queen's household organisation, finances and social connections as a backdrop to her investigation.[8] This relative paucity is repeated in the cases of the two queens Elizabeth. David Baldwin's biography of Elizabeth Woodville discusses her finances and household management generally, while Retha Warnicke's monograph on Elizabeth of York and her six daughters-in-law devotes a chapter to their incomes and expenditures, although the comparative analysis employed necessarily dilutes the focus on Elizabeth herself.[9] An unpublished study by Derek Neal also deals with queenly landholdings, households and social

---

[7] See Maurer, *Margaret of Anjou*.

[8] Diana Dunn, 'Margaret of Anjou: Queen Consort of Henry VI: A Reassessment of Her Role, 1445–53', in *Crown, Government and People in the Fifteenth Century*, ed. Rowena Archer (Stroud: Sutton, 1995), 107–43.

[9] Baldwin, *Elizabeth Woodville*, Chapter 5; Retha Warnicke, *Elizabeth of York and Her Six Daughters-in-Law: Fashioning Tudor Queenship, 1485–1547* (Cham: Palgrave Macmillan, 2017), Chapter 3, Income and Expenditures.

relationships in some detail.[10] Neal focuses on the two queens Elizabeth and includes some significant structural exploration of the queens' landholdings.

Most scholars who have delved into late medieval English queens' income and expenditure have drawn upon the publications of A. R. Myers on the household accounts of Margaret of Anjou and Elizabeth Woodville, as well as one of Margaret's jewel accounts.[11] These publications are invaluable as a source of primary material for these queens and operate as key foundational works for this study. Myers also makes significant contributions to analytical research with his general summaries of the queens' income and expenses, observations on the continuity of their sources of income, and discussions of their household personnel. In addition to Myers' work, Hilda Johnstone's research on queenly households is still considered crucial. Her articles examine the organisation, finances and functions of the households of the Plantagenet queens from 1236 until 1399, and more specifically the households of Edward II's queen, Isabella of France (c.1295–1358; r.1308–27), and her daughter-in-law, Philippa of Hainault (c.1310–69; r.1328–69), consort to Edward III.[12] These articles chart the development of the queen's household in medieval England under the Plantagenets and provide a valuable comparative point for the group of queens in this book.

Naturally, this study cannot proceed without acknowledging current issues and debates on questions of power, agency, and gender. Power is a term with variable meanings and exists in many forms. Scholars grappling with this concept tend to start with the theories of Michel Foucault, who defines power in a neutral manner, seeing it as omnipresent and embedded everywhere.[13] For Theresa Earenfight, power is 'the ability to exercise mastery over people, to organize people to cooperate, and to persuade people to act'.[14] Lisa Benz

---

[10] J. L. Laynesmith, *The Last Medieval Queens: English Queenship 1445–1503* (Oxford; New York: Oxford University Press, 2004), Chapter 5; Derek Neal, 'The Queen's Grace: English Queenship, 1464–1503,' (unpublished MA thesis, McMaster University, 1996), Chapter 4.

[11] A. R. Myers, 'The Household of Queen Elizabeth Woodville, 1466–7', *BJRL* 50, no. 1 (1967), 207–35 and *BJRL* 50, no. 2 (1968), 443–81, repr. in *Crown, Household and Parliament in Fifteenth Century England*, ed. Cecil H. Clough (London: Hambledon Press, 1985), 251–318; A. R. Myers, 'The Household of Queen Margaret of Anjou, 1452–3', *BJRL* 40, no. 1 (1957), 79–113 and *BJRL* 40, no. 2 (1958), 391–451, repr. in *Crown, Household and Parliament*, 135–209; A. R. Myers, 'The Jewels of Queen Margaret of Anjou', *BJRL* 42, no. 1 (1959), 113–31, repr. in *Crown, Household and Parliament*, 211–30. Hereafter, references are to the reprints.

[12] Johnstone I, 231–89; Johnstone II, 250–99.

[13] Michel Foucault, *The History of Sexuality, Volume 1: An Introduction*, trans. Robert Hurley (London: Allen Lane, 1979), 92–6.

[14] Theresa Earenfight, 'A Lifetime of Power: Beyond Binaries of Gender', in *Medieval Elite Women and the Exercise of Power, 1100–1400: Moving Beyond the Exceptionalist Debate*, ed. Heather J. Tanner (Cham: Palgrave Macmillan, 2019), 271.

St John observes that power may be defined as 'the ability to get people to do things or make things happen'.[15] It is, in essence, the capacity to gain compliance, yet its effectiveness may be backed up by other elements such as coercion, stress, threat or force.[16] I should add that an emphasis on coercion or force often leads to the conclusion that it is 'hard' power that is at play: power that is exercised without regard for or consideration of the wellbeing of any individuals who may be involved in such events and that is focused only on obtaining the desired result. Conversely, 'soft' power is typically perceived as possessing more indirect and subtler attributes, manifesting in less public ways with less overtly applied pressure and more covert manipulation. Interestingly, different terms such as 'authority', 'influence' and 'agency' have been used to describe variants of power, with each conveying subtle differences in meaning. 'Authority' provides the official legitimate rationale for the exercise of power, but 'influence' and 'agency' have been and often are used to indicate that soft power is being employed.[17] Unsurprisingly, such variability of meaning for the term 'power' suggests that queenly power could be manifested in many different ways, some of which might be indirect and less explicit, thus perhaps not obviously present or discernible.

At this point we should relate economic resources to power by acknowledging that they provided queens with material forms of what Pierre Bourdieu called capital, in this case, economic capital.[18] Possession and/or access to, if not outright ownership of, economic resources gave queens the wherewithal to use this capital as they saw fit. Consideration of the meanings of power and some of its variants steers us towards asking exactly how the queens' economic capital assisted in the exercise of power in its different forms. Such investigations have the potential to shed light on the queen's application of power (or for that matter, agency) in different ways, including economic, social and political. Queens had the ability to effect change and influence response and their use of their economic capital underwrote their actions. In so doing, they transformed their economic capital into many other forms, including social, political and symbolic.

---

[15] Lisa Benz St John, *Three Medieval Queens: Queenship and the Crown in Fourteenth-Century England* (New York: Palgrave Macmillan, 2012), 17.

[16] Maurer, *Margaret of Anjou*, 5.

[17] For additional discussion on distinctions to be drawn between 'power', 'authority' and 'influence', see Louise Lamphere, 'Strategies, Cooperation and Conflict among Women in Domestic Groups', in *Woman, Culture and Society*, eds Michelle Zimbalist Rosaldo and Louise Lamphere (Stanford: Stanford University Press, 1974), 99; Michelle Zimbalist Rosaldo, 'Woman, Culture and Society: A Theoretical Overview', in *Woman, Culture and Society*, 21.

[18] Pierre Bourdieu, 'The Forms of Capital', in *Handbook of Theory and Research for the Sociology of Education*, ed. J. G. Richardson (New York: Greenwood Press, 1986), 243.

Introduction

Discussions about power often take on a different tenor when gender comes into the equation. Here I ascribe to the term 'gender' the earliest meaning offered by theorists of modern feminism, that is, gender as biological and sexual identity.[19] Arguably, it is precisely the reason that gender appears to constantly enter into discussions of power that so many different types of power have emerged. Marie Kelleher was not alone in querying the meaning of power in relation to women and finding many forms.[20] Lois Huneycutt's examination of medieval women's power also categorised it into different types, including authority, autonomy and influence.[21] The crux of the matter is that, since Joan Wallace Scott's analysis of gender as a category of study, research on gender and power appears to have coalesced around ideas of hard and soft power. The former is overwhelmingly associated with men and public interactions, while the latter is consigned to the domain of women and behind-the-scenes machinations.[22] Soft power is deemed to be indirect power; therefore, it tends to be labelled alternatively as influence or agency. Although agency, for example, can be defined differently from power, this suggests that agency and, by extension, women's or soft power have tended to be looked upon as somehow being less public or important than hard power.[23] Queenship scholars, too, have grappled with this notion, some recently calling for power to be looked at more broadly than has been done in the past, others suggesting that power should be looked at in terms of what it is based upon and 'what people are actually doing, rather than on the identity of the person exercising that power'.[24]

Agency stands out as a key concept in women's and gender studies. When we say that a person possesses agency, we usually mean that the individual has 'the capacity to act, make choices, and intentionally shape their own lives and the world around them to some degree'.[25] This is an apparently simple

---

[19] Joan W. Scott, 'Gender: A Useful Category of Historical Analysis', *The American Historical Review* 91, no. 5 (1986): 1054.

[20] Marie A. Kelleher, 'What Do We Mean by "Women and Power"?', *Medieval Feminist Forum: A Journal of Gender and Sexuality* 51, no. 2 (2016): 104–15.

[21] Lois L. Huneycutt, 'Power: Medieval Women's Power through Authority, Autonomy, and Influence', in *A Cultural History of Women in the Middle Ages*, ed. Kim M. Phillips (London: Bloomsbury Publishing PLC, 2013), 153–78.

[22] Earenfight, 'A Lifetime of Power', 272–3.

[23] Kelleher, 'What Do We Mean by "Women and Power"?', 110; Heather J. Tanner, Laura L. Gathagan and Lois L. Huneycutt, 'Introduction', in *Medieval Elite Women and the Exercise of Power, 1100–1400: Moving Beyond the Exceptionalist Debate*, ed. Heather J. Tanner (Cham: Palgrave Macmillan, 2019), 10.

[24] Earenfight, 'A Lifetime of Power', 275; Lois L. Huneycutt, 'Queenship Studies Comes of Age', *Medieval Feminist Forum: A Journal of Gender and Sexuality* 51, no. 2 (2016): 15.

[25] Merry E. Wiesner-Hanks, 'Women's Agency: Then and Now', *Parergon* 40, no. 2 (2023): 10.

definition that underscores actions, tasks, behaviours. Yet scholars such as Merry Wiesner-Hanks have recently challenged us to expand our thinking about agency and, based on concepts with roots in the social sciences, to consider 'whether women's agency might have been a matter of norms as well as actions'.[26] For the queens in this study, we need to think beyond their actions, even as we historicise and contextualise them. We must, in fact, consider expectations and perceptions as well. The question is not just 'what did the queens do' but also 'how were they perceived by others while in the process of doing'.

It is also worth asking whether we can ignore gender altogether in this study. Earenfight in her examination of Catherine of Aragon's actions at different stages of her life in England from 1501 to 1536 posits that it is possible to investigate queenly power without allowing gender to dictate its parameters or qualify its reach.[27] I suggest, however, that research into economic resources and queens cannot be conducted without gendered perspectives, given the legal and economic frameworks within which medieval women (including queens) lived and operated. It is also telling that gender often features as an important site of difference in wide-ranging research on theories and ideas in relation to money and finances.[28] Gender, therefore, constantly informs the analysis in this study. Queens ostensibly lived lives that were circumscribed within the same societal frameworks as other medieval women. Their gender, grounded in biological difference but transformed into the social constructs enveloping a queen consort, should have constrained or limited their operations in the economic world just as it did for other medieval women.[29] The question is whether it did so in the case of the queens in this study, and a challenge for this book is to situate its exploration clearly within considerations of gender whilst not allowing gender to wholly circumscribe or limit the analysis.

The core sources for this study comprise the estate archives consisting of household and manorial records. Notwithstanding the existence of myriad noble estate studies, there is a general scarcity in extant records of estate archives with the dearth of records being particularly acute for the households of these queens. Of the many possible types of household accounts that might have been assembled when Margaret of Anjou was queen consort, only a very few have survived as far as is known.[30] A single account compiled by

[26] *Ibid.*, 9–10.
[27] Earenfight, 'A Lifetime of Power', especially 277–89.
[28] For instance, consider Viviana A. Zelizer, 'The Social Meaning of Money: "Special Monies"', *American Journal of Sociology* 95, no. 2 (1989): 342–77.
[29] S. H. Rigby, *English Society in the Later Middle Ages: Class, Status, and Gender* (New York: St. Martin's Press, 1995), 243.
[30] Any large medieval English household would have produced various kinds of accounts such as cash, corn and stock accounts, diet accounts and wardrobe

Introduction

her receiver-general, William Cotton, for the year 1452–53 remains extant.[31] Five other accounts have also survived, all of them produced by the queen's treasurer of the chamber, who also functioned as the master of jewels during that period. These five accounts are referred to as the queen's jewel accounts.[32] The sources for the households of Elizabeth Woodville and Elizabeth of York are similarly sparse. One receiver-general's account survives for Elizabeth Woodville and a Privy Purse expense account, drawn up by Elizabeth of York's most senior official for the final year of her life, is the only known extant household record for this queen.[33] The lack of similar accounts for comparison in the case of each queen means, at the very least, that general conclusions for any queen must be qualified accordingly.

Each of these accounts provides a wealth of information, relevant for but not limited to the queens' revenues, expenditure, and household organisation and personnel. However, there are issues to consider when using these documents. In the case of the accounts compiled by the receivers-general of Margaret and Elizabeth Woodville as well as Elizabeth of York's Privy Purse expense account, all three are not strictly comparable. They are not laid out in precisely the same format, with the first two being the most similar in arrangement. Margaret's household account notably includes lists of wages paid to personnel who made up her general household staff, namely, esquires, yeomen, grooms and pages. Such lists are not present in the accounts for Elizabeth Woodville or Elizabeth of York.

Additionally, these accounts do not apply to the same stages of the queens' reigns. The account for Margaret dates from her eighth year as queen, while Elizabeth Woodville's account was drawn up only a year or so after her dower

---

accounts. The term 'household account' is used here in a general sense to encompass all these different types of documents. C. M. Woolgar, *Household Accounts from Medieval England, Part 1* (Oxford; New York: Oxford University Press, 1992), 7.

[31] TNA DL28/5/8, first transcribed and published by Myers in 1957 and reprinted in 1985 in Myers, 'The Household of Queen Margaret of Anjou', 155–209.

[32] TNA E101/409/14, E101/409/17, E101/410/2, E101/410/8, E101/410/11. The last manuscript was transcribed and published by Myers in 1959 and reprinted in 1985 in Myers, 'The Jewels of Queen Margaret of Anjou', 213–30.

[33] TNA E36/207, first transcribed and published by Myers in 1967 and reprinted in 1985 in Myers, 'The Household of Queen Elizabeth Woodville', 260–318. TNA E36/210 was first published in a slightly different format as *The Privy Purse Expenses of Elizabeth of York,* ed. Nicholas Harris Nicolas (London: Pickering, 1830). A new online version was made available to the research community in 2018 by the Tudor Chamber Books project. This constitutes an important development since technological advances have made it possible for the project team to transcribe manuscript sections that were previously considered illegible. The online version contains a significant amount of additional information that is not in the 1830 printed version. It is referred to throughout this study as Queen's Book (see Abbreviations).

was settled. Elizabeth of York's expense account covers the last year of her life, after she had been queen for seventeen years.[34] Clearly the specific needs and experiences of each queen varied at different times, a newly established queen cannot as a matter of course be regarded on exactly the same footing as one who had been queen for several years.

In the case of manorial records for these queens, there are added drawbacks. Research on noble estates generally relies on specific sources – the written records that comprise the archive of the estate and central government records produced by the Chancery, the Exchequer and the royal courts.[35] Among the records regularly produced by officials as part of administering an estate were surveys, financial accounts, manorial court rolls, and land valors, each of which had its particular uses and limitations.[36] As with present-day financial records, these different manorial documents must be read and interpreted with careful reference to each other, taking into account the aims of the compiling official. For instance, the receiver-general's account should be analysed in conjunction with the accounts of the local receivers, if possible, because they were complementary. Local receivers administered the finances of holdings within their jurisdictions whilst the receiver-general received only the surplus profits of the holdings. Thus, neither type of record presents a complete picture of revenues and expenditure incurred.[37] In the same way, land valors and accounts of arrears should be read together. As its name suggests, the account of arrears recorded debts owed and often included notes of cancellation or arrangements made for payments by instalment. Land valors were reports of the expected revenues and possible charges on the estates. This means that the monetary amounts recorded in the valors are not necessarily what the queen's receiver-general actually received in cash. They are primarily useful as a guide to the queen's potential revenues and present an overall view of the queen's landed holdings and revenue sources. Clearly, therefore, strictly accurate estimates of income are possible only when a land valor is read alongside its corresponding account of arrears.[38]

[34] Laynesmith, *The Last Medieval Queens*, 224–5.
[35] R. H. Hilton's exploration of the types of sources useful for medieval agrarian and estate studies discusses those sources that are especially relevant for the late fourteenth and fifteenth centuries. R. H. Hilton, 'The Content and Sources of English Agrarian History before 1500', *The Agricultural History Review* 3, no. 1 (1955): 14–18.
[36] Surveys recorded what the estate tenants owed to their lord. For more information on different types of surveys, see Hilton, 'The Content and Sources', 15.
[37] C. D. Ross and T. B. Pugh, 'Materials for the Study of Baronial Incomes in Fifteenth-Century England', *EcHR* 6, no. 2 (1953): 19.
[38] For more information on the uses and limitations of land valors, see R. R. Davies, 'Baronial Accounts, Incomes, and Arrears in the Later Middle Ages', *EcHR* 21, no. 2 (Aug. 1968): 214–18; Ross and Pugh, 'Materials for the Study of Baronial Incomes', 192–3.

Introduction

Besides the limitations of the different types of manorial documents, there are problems related to the quantity of such records for the queens in this study. For a variety of reasons, including the lack of value attached to documents of this kind, estate records for most, if not all, of the queens' lands have not survived in a consistent manner for the period between the 1440s and 1510s. In fact, the survival rate of the estate records of our queens appears at first sight to be abysmal. These records seem to have, at best, a sparse and inconsistent survival rate with the added challenge of being stored in many different regional archives.[39] Yet it is not necessarily true that records relating to estates and lands belonging to the queens have not survived in reasonable numbers. For this study, organised and detailed searches of the archives have yielded some useful and unexpected finds. As a case in point, there is, among the Duchy of Lancaster records for the south parts of England, an essentially complete series of receivers' accounts for the lands and estates granted to and owned by Elizabeth Woodville during her tenure as queen. These records are not labelled in the archive catalogue as being related to queens' lands and were found only when examined individually.[40] Nonetheless, despite occasional fortuitous discoveries, the inconsistent survival rate for manorial documents remains a daunting obstacle for research into the queens' holdings.

The core sources are supplemented by a diverse range of documents, such as Chancery and Exchequer records, Parliament Rolls, extant correspondence by the queens, and literary and didactic works from the period such as chronicles and treatises on estate administration. In addition, household ordinances produced during the reigns of Henry VI, Edward IV and Henry VII are most informative for the light they shed on the theoretical general workings of royal households in fifteenth-century England.[41] The ordinances articulate contemporary attempts to lay down broad general operating rules and define the members of the household as well as their duties and privileges. They are not necessarily completely accurate but, rather, provided views of how contemporaries regarded the makeup and regular operation of royal households. Their usefulness for such viewpoints is unquestionable even though they should be interpreted with caution.

This book is not biographical in nature nor is it a wide-ranging examination of the ideology of late medieval queenship. It is grounded firmly in practical matters, with a key aim being to increase our knowledge and comprehension of the financial and economic foundations of a late medieval queen's ability

---

[39] This statement is based on a general search of manorial records catalogued by The National Archives (including those located in regional archives) using keywords such as 'queen' or the names of individual queens of the fifteenth century.
[40] TNA DL29/711/11460-11476. See Appendix 3 for more examples of such documents discovered during the research for this study.
[41] See Table 7 for a list of ordinances consulted in this study.

to exercise power or agency. It does this, firstly, by examining the nature of the economic assets made available to and used by the three queens consort in this study. Secondly, it focuses on two major entities that depended on the availability of economic resources: the queens' households and affinities. The objective in the second instance is to showcase these entities as tangible major examples of how the queens used their economic resources, no matter what form they were in or whether these resources were legally owned by them.

Chapter One begins with a survey of the range of income sources available to the queens and clarifies their form and nature. In the process, it assesses the importance of each source type in monetary terms and thus its usefulness to each queen. It sets the stage for the later chapters in the book while questioning whether any one queen had more economic resources at her disposal than the others and what, if any, comparisons can be made with earlier English queens. The next two chapters examine one of the most important economic resources available to the queens in this study, lands and estates, which provided both monetary benefits as well as other less perceptible benefits. Chapter Two undertakes a comparative survey of the lands and estates owned by the queens. It outlines the particular social and economic context of the period in order to place our study of resources in a holistic framework that takes account of the multitude of factors that may affect lives and societies. Chapter Three continues the exploration of these assets by extensively investigating the queens' administrative structures for their holdings. This chapter delves into the administration of the queen's lands and estates, illuminating how the queen's administrative machinery functioned and discussing the people that made it happen. These two chapters enable us to, among other things, gain a fuller sense of the queens' roles as landholders and administrators.

Two major entities that relied on the queens' economic resources were their households and affinities. As P. D. A. Harvey comments, the 'spending' half of a queen's administration was the household.[42] This observation may be applied to the queen's affinities as well. The household and the affinity were both crucial elements of the queen's life and position, and their maintenance was a primary use of queenly financial wealth. Since the household lay at the centre of the queen's life and position, it forms the initial focus of our exploration of the benefits of queens having economic resources and is examined in Chapter Four. We need to understand the composition of the queen's household and how it functioned if we are to extend our knowledge and appreciation of the queen as an administrator. Household and estate administration were not mutually exclusive, and the queen's households and estates were not such independent and separate entities that administration did not overlap. Lastly, Chapter Five investigates the queens' affinities. In social terms, the core of the queen's affinity was her household and administration.

[42] P. D. A. Harvey, *Manorial Records* (London: British Records Association, 1999), 3.

Introduction

No study of economic resources should neglect the human aspect, and the affinities are the perfect vehicles to situate the queens' resources within the social context of their worlds. This chapter treats that human aspect as a vital feature of this analysis of the benefits of having financial sources and rounds out this study by increasing our comprehension of this linkage between the queens and their economic resources.[43]

This study is designed to be more qualitative than quantitative in its examination of the topic at hand. Rather than focusing on the minutiae of the incomes and expenditures of the queens, it aims to highlight and appraise broader issues in relation to their economic resources and finances. This must be done so that we can extend our understanding of the foundations of queenly exercise of power and agency and better appreciate the significance of the queen consort in the economic landscape of her world. Ultimately, the objectives of this book speak to issues of gender and power that cannot but have impacts on ideas of late medieval queenship in England.

---

[43] As scholars of royal and elite households and affinities will attest, entire books have been written on the many different aspects of these entities, from the physical and locational to the social aspects. It is not possible for me to address all facets of these entities in two individual chapters and, thus, there is far less focus on aspects related to specific expenditure.

1

THE QUEEN'S RESOURCES

... when anyone promises 100 or 200 m.[marks] to the king, he is likewise obligated to pay the queen one mark of gold for the 100 m. of silver promised to the king, or two marks of gold for 200 m. of silver, and so on.[1]

While working on the English queen's household in the thirteenth and fourteenth centuries, Johnstone devised a framework that outlines three categories for the methods used to provide for a late medieval queen consort.[2] In this framework, one of the queen's primary sources of revenue was a traditional payment to the queen that seems to have first been mentioned in a treatise from the twelfth century.[3] This treatise, concerned with matters relating to the Royal Exchequer and commonly known as the *Dialogus de Scaccario*, was written during the reign of Henry II (c.1133–89; r. 1154–89) by the king's treasurer, Richard FitzNigel. In his discussion on the obligations and fees due to the king, FitzNigel stated, as in the above quotation, that whoever owed certain payments to the king was also bound to pay a requisite sum to the queen as her prerogative. This sum was set at one mark of gold to be paid to the queen for every one hundred marks of silver to the king. Proportionally, since a mark of gold was understood to be equal to ten marks of silver, this meant that a 10 per cent levy was imposed on the payer in addition to what was already payable to the king.[4] This payment was known as queen's gold

---

[1] One mark was equivalent to 13*s* 4*d*. This translation is from Richard FitzNigel, *Dialogus de Scaccario: The Dialogue of the Exchequer; Constitutio Domus Regis: Disposition of the King's Household*, ed. and trans. Emilie Amt & S. D. Church (Oxford: Oxford University Press, 2007), 182–3.

[2] Johnstone I, 264–5.

[3] For more information about the treatise and its author, see Richard FitzNigel, *De Necessariis Observantiis Scaccarii Dialogus commonly called Dialogus de Scaccario*, eds. Arthur Hughes, C. G. Crump and C. Johnson (Oxford: Clarendon Press, 1902), 1–53.

[4] William Prynne, *Aurum Reginae; or A Compendious Tractate, and Chronological Collection of Records in the Tower, and Court of Exchequer Concerning Queen-gold* (London: Ratcliffe, 1668), 2; Kristen Geaman, 'Queen's Gold and Intercession: The Case of Eleanor of Aquitaine', *Medieval Feminist Forum: A Journal of Gender and Sexuality* 46, no. 2 (2010): 12.

and may well have been enjoyed only by medieval queens in England and its neighbours in the British Isles.[5]

Queen's gold made up one category of sources in Johnstone's framework. It was paid to queens consort in England and Ireland, while in Wales, queens were entitled to *amobr*, or amobrage.[6] Johnstone goes on to discuss in detail two more categories of revenues – lands and estates granted in dower, and supplementary grants. In the process she surveyed no fewer than seven queens from the thirteenth and fourteenth centuries, and her work has long been positioned as a foundational point of comparison by later scholars of medieval English queens. This chapter lays the foundations for the rest of this book, taking its starting point from Johnstone's research. It aims to determine whether Johnstone's framework and analysis of the queens' resources also applies to the queens in this study and, while doing so, it surveys the range of resources accessible to them and analyses the importance to each queen of each type of resource in financial or monetary terms.

DOWER GRANTS AS THE BASIS OF THE QUEEN'S RESOURCES

Queens were often awarded grants by the king after their marriages, which usually enabled them to gain some financial independence. For some medieval queens, this would have been in addition to any assets or wealth that they brought to the marriage. None of the queens in this study, however, possessed large amounts of inherited wealth. Foreign-born consorts were usually sought for their political and diplomatic links, and Margaret of Anjou was no exception. In Maurer's words, Margaret, like others before her, was chosen to be a king's wife at least partially for 'the protection of English territorial interests in France'.[7] The new queen's dowry was paltry, consisting of 20,000 francs and her mother's hollow claims to the kingdom of Majorca, but she brought strategically important political links with various parts of France.[8] Elizabeth Woodville, as is well known, was a widow when she married Edward IV and, being domestic-born, was clearly not chosen for her political associations. She brought two manors as dower from her first marriage, and

---

[5] Amalie Fößel's brief comparison of the income of English and German medieval queens did not find any payment for German queens that was comparable to the queen's gold enjoyed by English queens. Amalie Fößel, 'The Queen's Wealth in the Middle Ages', *Majestas* 13 (2005): 34–5.

[6] Amobrage was a sum paid by a woman on her marriage and varied with the rank of the person. Johnstone I, 264–5.

[7] Maurer, *Margaret of Anjou*, 17.

[8] Carole Levin, 'Margaret of Anjou: Passionate Mother', in *Later Plantagenet and the Wars of the Roses Consorts: Power, Influence and Dynasty*, eds Aidan Norrie, Carolyn Harris, J. L. Laynesmith, Danna R. Messer and Elena Woodacre (Cham: Palgrave Macmillan, 2023), 196.

The Queen's Resources

both were probably held by her new husband in her name as per the law and custom of the period.[9] In Elizabeth of York's case, there is no mention or evidence of a dowry. However, it appears that she was considered her father's heiress, or at least co-heiress with her sisters, because of the disappearance of her brothers in the mid-1480s.[10] Nevertheless, scholars tend to agree that Elizabeth of York was married to Henry VII for political reasons. Henry's hereditary claim to the English throne was tenuous to say the least and his marriage to Elizabeth, whose birth technically made her own claim much stronger, reinforced his hold on the crown.[11] It is fair to assume that such political benefits took precedence over any material wealth Elizabeth might have had claim to. In the absence of substantial inherited wealth, the earliest grants made to Margaret and the two Elizabeths upon their marriages were clearly the primary foundation of their economic resources.

Interestingly, scholars often refer, seemingly without question, to these initial grants as 'dower' grants, a term I shall continue to use in this study but which requires more extensive comparison with the terms 'dowry' and 'jointure'. Some scholars, in fact, appear to use the terms 'dower' and 'dowry' interchangeably when discussing the grants made to Margaret of Anjou and Elizabeth Woodville.[12] Yet the specific wording of the grants made to all three queens is far from precise. The most common feature in each of the grants is the phrase '*ad terminum vite*' or 'for the term of life'.[13] But in Margaret of Anjou's 1446 dower grant the phrase '*in dotem*' or '*in dotis*' meaning dower (or possibly also dowry) is used quite liberally as well, often in conjunction with '*ad terminum vite*'.[14] This suggests that the resources being granted to Margaret constituted her dower and that she was meant to hold them for as long as she was alive, that is, while she was queen consort and if she became queen dowager as well. In comparison, *dotem* and *dotis* are not frequently found in the grants made to Elizabeth Woodville and Elizabeth of York.[15]

---

[9] Evidence shows that at least one of the two manors, Woodham Ferrers, was held by Edward IV 'in possession and title of his consort, Elizabeth, queen of England …' CPR 1461–67, 533.

[10] See CPR 1494–1509, 8, for a grant made on 12 Sept 1494 to James Ormond that references lands and tenements that previously formed part of the earldom of March and are 'now in the king's hands in right of Elizabeth, the Queen Consort'.

[11] Okerlund, *Elizabeth of York*, 41, 44.

[12] For example, Laynesmith, *The Last Medieval Queens*, 234–6; Maurer, *Margaret of Anjou*, 18; Myers, 'The Household of Queen Elizabeth Woodville', 253–4, 266; Myers, 'The Household of Queen Margaret of Anjou', 137–9, 151–2; Neal, 'The Queen's Grace', 109–10.

[13] TNA C66/482, 512, 513, 563, 572; CPR 1446–52, 56; CPR 1461–67, 430, 433, 445, 480–2; CPR 1485–94, 369; RP v. 118–20; 'Edward IV: June 1467', in PROME, v-627, v-628.

[14] RP v. 118–20.

[15] See TNA C66/563 for the grant of her former dower properties by Henry VII back

Financing Queenship in Late Fifteenth Century England

Similar ambiguity has been noted in grants made to queens in the fourteenth century.[16] For instance, in the grants made to Philippa of Hainault, Edward III's queen, she is noted variously as holding land 'in dower and for life', 'during her lifetime' and 'in dower'.[17]

Concerning Elizabeth of York, the situation is further complicated by the fact that it is not clear whether this queen's resources were granted to her as dower or as jointure. The two were not technically the same, dower being a common-law mechanism for the provision of a widow while jointure was a legal instrument created in the marriage contract to provide, among other things, support for a widow. The first grants to this queen were made in 1486 and do not mention either of these terms even though the grants to her mother, Elizabeth Woodville, were considered her dower. Conversely, the grant of the reversion of Cecily Neville's estates to Elizabeth of York in 1492 is titled 'An Acte for the Quenes Joynture', which suggests that Elizabeth of York was being granted Cecily Neville's estates as jointure rather than dower.[18] Nevertheless, the muddled understanding may not have mattered in practice since these grants were made to the queens for the terms of their lives. In principle, at least, the queens' administrative machinery and officials were empowered to take over administration of their granted possessions while their husbands were alive, and the revenues from those possessions became accessible to them and available for their use.

What, then, were Margaret of Anjou, Elizabeth Woodville and Elizabeth of York each granted for their dowers? After her marriage to Henry VI in 1445, Margaret of Anjou's dower, granted in 1446, was set by Parliament at 10,000 marks (£6666 13s 4d) *per annum*.[19] In summary, the dower was assigned in the following manner: £2000 in the form of lands and estates, £1000 as a cash annuity from Duchy of Lancaster estates, and a total of £3666 13s 4d from other sources – £1000 of customs revenue from the port of Southampton, £1008 15s 5d from the revenues of the Duchy of Cornwall and £1657 17s 11d directly from the Royal Exchequer.[20] These grants constituted the principal sources of her revenues.

---

to Elizabeth Woodville, which mentions the word '*dotis*'.

[16] For more extensive research on the language used in the grants for thirteenth- and fourteenth-century queens, see Katia Wright, 'The Queen's Lands: Examining the Role of Queens as Female Lords in Fourteenth Century England' (unpublished PhD thesis, University of Winchester, 2022), 113–17.

[17] CPR 1330–34, 420; CPR 1334–38, 123; CPR 1348–50, 323.

[18] SR, vol. II, 595.

[19] In present-day values, 10,000 marks would be roughly equivalent to almost £4.3 million, a very large sum by any measure both in the medieval and present-day periods.

[20] RP v. 118–20.

The Queen's Resources

The precedent for such a large dower, compared with the queens who came after her, lay in the arrangements for her immediate predecessors. The dowers of Margaret of France, Isabella of France, Philippa of Hainault and Anne of Bohemia, successive queens consort from 1299 to 1394, were each valued at £4000–4500.[21] In contrast, Anne of Bohemia's immediate successor, Isabella of Valois (second queen to Richard II), was granted a dower amounting to 10,000 marks (£6666 13s 4d). The reason for this deviation appears to be because Isabella brought a very large dowry of 800,000 gold francs (£130,000) as part of an Anglo–French peace treaty.[22] This should have meant that the size of Isabella's dower was atypical and not to be repeated for future queens. Nevertheless, she was the first queen consort to be granted a dower of that size and the resulting precedent held for the next three queens of the fifteenth century, Joan of Navarre, Katherine of Valois and Margaret of Anjou, with each being granted the same dower amounts.[23] In Katherine of Valois' case, the Treaty of Troyes, which was negotiated in 1420 between England and France and sealed by the marriage between Katherine and Henry V, stipulated a dower of 10,000 marks for the soon-to-be queen. It also included a clause asserting that the queens of England had long been accustomed to receiving such a dower.[24] This is remarkable given that the conventions of the preceding century had obviously regarded £4500 as a more suitable dower for queens, as evidenced by the grants made to the above-mentioned queens before Isabella of Valois.

Notwithstanding this discussion of the exact overall amount, the key point is where Margaret's dower was to come from. The combination of landed and non-landed resources as sources of revenue is clearly referenced in the extant household account for Margaret, which recorded her overall revenues for the accounting year. This is entirely in keeping with two of the categories outlined in Johnstone's framework, while the remaining category, queen's gold, is also listed in Margaret's household account as a source of revenue.[25]

The dower grants for Elizabeth Woodville, in comparison, were quite different from those of Margaret of Anjou. On their marriage in 1464, Edward IV provided for his consort by granting her a range of lands and estates as

---

[21] Kristen L. Geaman, *Anne of Bohemia* (Abingdon; New York: Routledge, 2022), 90; Wright, 'The Queen's Lands', 51, 56, 67, 75.

[22] Nigel Saul, *Richard II* (New Haven: Yale University Press, 2008), 227; Katia Wright, 'A Dower for Life: Understanding the Dowers of England's Medieval Queens', in *Later Plantagenet and the Wars of the Roses Consorts: Power, Influence, Dynasty*, eds Aidan Norrie, Carolyn Harris, J. L. Laynesmith, Danna Messer, and Elena Woodacre (New York: Palgrave Macmillan, 2022), 152.

[23] Elena Woodacre, *Joan of Navarre: Infanta, Duchess, Queen, Witch?* (Abingdon; New York: Routledge, 2022), 147; Wright, 'The Queen's Lands', 76, 179.

[24] 'Rymer's Foedera with Syllabus: May 1420', in *Foedera*, vol. 9, 891–910; Myers, 'The Household of Queen Margaret of Anjou', 136.

[25] Johnstone I, 264–5.

well as fee-farms in dower rather than making grants that combined landed sources, cash and annuities.[26] The original dower grants of 1465 and 1466 did not specify projected revenues or incomes from individual lands but they did record the values of individual fee-farms.[27] In total, the initial grants of fee-farms amounted to approximately £874. This sum was later augmented by two additional grants in 1467 of the fee-farms of the towns of Huntingdon and Godmanchester. The fee-farms were set at £63 and £120, respectively, taking her total projected revenue from fee-farm grants to approximately £1056. They were large sums compared with the other fee-farms and thus lucrative additions to Elizabeth Woodville's overall financial sources. As with Margaret, Elizabeth, too, was able to obtain additional monetary and non-monetary grants, although not on the same scale as her predecessor. Lastly, evidence from her household account shows that she also counted queen's gold among her sources of revenue.

Elizabeth of York was similarly granted a dower that was based on landed estates and fee-farms but she did not formally receive her grants until 26 November 1487, almost two years after her marriage to the king.[28] What is most unusual is that this queen's dower lands had in fact previously been granted in 1465 to her mother, Elizabeth Woodville, as part of her original dower as queen consort. Almost two decades later, in late 1483, Richard III stripped the older Elizabeth of her entitlements as queen dowager, alleging that his brother's marriage to her was invalid due to a prior betrothal contracted by Edward IV.[29] However, in March 1486, the new Tudor king, Henry VII, reinstated Edward IV's widow as queen dowager and re-granted to her most, but not all, of the lands and fee-farms initially granted as her dower.[30] Elizabeth Woodville did not enjoy the revenues from her restored dower for long since she retired to Bermondsey Abbey in early 1487.[31] The records clearly state that all previous lands and holdings, including fee-farms, that were granted to Elizabeth Woodville by Henry VII were now granted to

---

[26] See Appendix 1 for the lands granted and Appendix 2 for the fee-farms granted to Elizabeth Woodville as queen consort.

[27] CPR 1461–67, 430, 433, 445, 480–2; 'Edward IV: June 1467', in PROME, v-627, v-628.

[28] *Materials for a History*, vol. II, 148–9.

[29] Hicks, 'Elizabeth [*née* Elizabeth Woodville]', ODNB (2004).

[30] CPR 1485–94, 75–7; *Materials for a History*, vol. I, 338, 347–50. Appendix 2 also indicates which fee-farms granted to Elizabeth Woodville as queen consort were restored to her as queen dowager in 1486–87 by Henry VII.

[31] The question of whether Elizabeth Woodville's decision to retire to Bermondsey Abbey was voluntary or the result of coercion by the king or any others has not been definitively settled. See Baldwin, *Elizabeth Woodville: Mother of the Princes in the Tower* and Okerlund, *Elizabeth Wydeville: The Slandered Queen*.

his wife, Elizabeth of York.[32] The individual amounts in fee-farms granted were, therefore, the same for Elizabeth of York as they had been when granted to Elizabeth Woodville by her son-in-law, the king. This scenario was unusual but recalls past periods when a king had to provide for more than one queen. Edward I's mother, Eleanor of Provence (c.1223–91; r.1236–72), became queen dowager when her husband, Henry III, died in 1272. Thus, Edward I (r.1272–1307) had to provide for both his mother as queen dowager and his wife, Eleanor of Castile (c.1241–90; r.1272–90), as queen consort.[33] Henry VII, happily for him, did not need to face this issue after all.

Clearly, therefore, like her mother, Elizabeth of York enjoyed revenues that were principally based on landed sources. Also in her case, the grants did not specify what the expected revenues were from each specific land or property. She was initially granted far fewer lands, estates and fee-farms than the elder Elizabeth, but she did receive some supplementary grants of money and other non-landed items. She regarded queen's gold as her legitimate entitlement, although, naturally, the more significant question is how effectively she was able to collect it.

An important point is that the monetary total of Margaret of Anjou's dower was specified, whereas the dowers of the two queens Elizabeth were not. Specified dower amounts resulted in expectations of the amount of yearly revenue that the queen would receive. Hence, many of the later grants made to Margaret of Anjou must be assessed against the chief need to ensure that the queen obtained all that she was entitled to in dower revenue. This issue did not arise for the queens after Margaret because of the major change of not specifying set dower sums for them. While it is possible to arrive at estimates for the dowers for the two queens Elizabeth, not stipulating an exact dower amount obviated the need for the queen's dower revenue to reach a minimum level. This inference is supported by the lack of later grants that were specifically mooted as being intended to fill gaps in dower revenue. It does not, of course, mean that these queens did not receive later additions to the various sources of revenues they initially received, additions that almost certainly augmented their incomes and added to their economic resources.

It is also crucial to consider how the rapid monarchic changes during the latter half of the fifteenth century affected the situation in relation to the dowers of the queens in this study. Conventionally, the previous queen consort would, as queen dowager, have been able to access a dower for her upkeep for the remainder of her life. Any lands or properties granted while she was queen consort should have reverted to the Crown when her time in the position ended but could have been allocated to her as part of her dower

---

[32] *Materials for a History*, vol. II, 148–9.
[33] The lands of the queens of the late thirteenth and fourteenth centuries have been researched by Katia Wright in Wright, 'The Queen's Lands'.

at the discretion of the new king. As it happens, this process appears to be at odds with the terminology used and hence the understanding implicit in the grants made to all three queens in this study, that is, the queens received their grants 'for the terms of their lives', both as consorts and as dowagers. Certainly, even if they were re-granted their exact dowers once they ceased to be consort, 'grant for life' was evidently not synonymous with 'management for life' of their holdings. However, this issue did not apply to any of these queens.

In Margaret of Anjou's case, she ceased to be queen consort when Henry VI lost his throne in 1461 to Edward IV. Yet Margaret was not a widow, since Henry had not died but was imprisoned by Edward. In addition, both Margaret and her husband were subjected to an attainder by Edward and his government and, consequently, she was not considered the rightful queen dowager.[34] Even after 1471, when the period of Henry VI's Readeption ended and Margaret was widowed on Henry's death, there was no possibility that the Yorkists would have considered Margaret to be entitled to her dower lands as queen dowager because she remained attainted in their eyes. Margaret was, accordingly, not in any position to claim a dower.

The situation for Elizabeth Woodville in 1483–85 after Edward IV died was likewise fraught. Elizabeth expected to remain queen dowager on Edward V's accession, enjoying ownership of and access to any lands granted to her as dower. However, the events that culminated in Elizabeth's brother-in-law Richard, duke of Gloucester, becoming Richard III, forestalled this scenario. Elizabeth's lands reverted to the Crown soon after she ceased to be queen consort and remained so instead of being re-granted to her as queen dowager. As previously mentioned, she was, however, re-granted many of the initial dower lands by her new son-in-law, Henry VII.[35] The subsequent stabilisation of the Tudor dynasty may well have seen the conventional situation with respect to dowers and dowager queens reassert itself from the time of Elizabeth of York as queen consort. But Elizabeth predeceased her husband and did not become queen dowager, a scenario that remained unchanged until Elizabeth's son, Henry VIII (r.1509–47), died, leaving his sixth wife, Kateryn Parr, a widow.

In summary, the economic resources available to the queens in this study may be categorised in a similar manner as Johnstone did for the thirteenth- and fourteenth-century queens.[36] As their predecessors did, Margaret of Anjou, Elizabeth Woodville and Elizabeth of York counted queen's gold, lands and estates granted in dower, and supplementary grants as the basis of their economic wealth. I suggest, however, that the following categories are

---

[34] Maurer, *Margaret of Anjou*, 202.

[35] It is highly probable that Henry recognised Elizabeth Woodville as queen dowager in part because he had married her daughter, Elizabeth of York, soon after he became king. CPR 1485–94, 75–7.

[36] Johnstone I, 264–5.

more distinct and appropriate for these fifteenth-century queens: land-related sources, non-land sources in the form of grants, allowances and gifts, and queen's gold. What follows is analysis of each of these types of resources in turn. The primary questions that I will address relate to their importance and significance in monetary or financial terms. What benefits did the queens gain and what continuities or differences can we perceive in the fifteenth century with regards to expected and received queenly revenues?

LAND-RELATED SOURCES

For all three queens, their landed resources were initially based on the lands and fee-farms granted to them as part of their dowers when they became queen but were subsequently augmented with later grants and acquisitions. Each queen theoretically gained significant monetary benefits from her land-based possessions. To briefly recap, Margaret of Anjou was granted £2000, or about 30 per cent of her overall dower revenue, in the form of income from landed sources. The rest took the form of cash annuities or subsidies and revenue from other non-landed sources. Conversely, both Elizabeth Woodville and Elizabeth of York were granted dowers in the form of lands and fee-farm grants. The younger Elizabeth's initially granted dower in fact comprised the lands and fee-farms that her mother, Elizabeth Woodville, surrendered when she retired to Bermondsey Abbey in 1487 and in its turn was a subset of the older queen's original dower.

In Margaret's case, the bulk of her landed income was the projected revenue from the dower lands (as specified in the grants themselves), whilst only a very small amount was to come from fee-farms.[37] As time passed, increases in the latter resulted in changes in Margaret's landed interests. In 1447, only a year after her dower was granted, she was given a further £82 in fee-farm grants and in 1451 she was given the fee-farm of the town of Bristol, worth approximately £102. A further two separate groups of fee-farms worth £75 and £326 13s 4d were granted in 1447 and 1453, respectively.[38] The group of grants totalling £75 was stated to have been made 'in part recompense of her yearly dower', which suggests that Margaret very early on experienced difficulties in collecting some of her dower revenues.[39] The other group of grants given in 1453 was part of a different package that was meant to compensate the queen for the loss of

---

[37] RP v. 118–20. The grant generally specified the income to be obtained from the groups of lands of each county or shire. The value of the lands assigned is slightly less than £2000. A single fee-farm grant of 40 marks (£26 13s 4d) from Gunthorp was made to the queen as part of her dower.

[38] See Appendix 2 for fee-farms granted to Margaret of Anjou.

[39] This group of fee-farms totalling £75 was granted in 1447 but the queen sued for livery only in 1453. CPR 1452–61, 339–40.

revenues to the value of approximately £400 from the lordship of Pembroke, which the king re-granted elsewhere.[40] The extra fee-farm grants were not, therefore, intended to increase the queen's overall income. Neither did changes in her landholdings alter her projected revenue from landed sources since the additional properties she acquired, such as the lordship of Berkhamsted and the manors of Gillingham, Odiham and Feckenham, were also granted to her in recompense of her expected income from the Pembroke lands.

Closer analysis of Margaret's extant household account reveals disparities between the expected and the actual landed revenues received. Her income for the accounting year Sept 1452 – Aug 1453 was recorded by auditors as £7563 12s 1d.[41] However, this amount did not comprise only the expected revenues for the year in question but included queen's gold paid in arrears and payments for arrears from customs from the port of Southampton and from Duchy of Cornwall revenues.[42] The account shows that her landed income for the accounting year encompassed just over £2000 for the assigned lands and approximately £450 for fee-farm grants, that is, just over half of her total income for the actual accounting year.[43]

Like many others before her, Margaret was not able to collect all the income that she expected and was owed.[44] While receipts of revenues from landed sources were generally reliable, there were significant exceptions. These were the county of Pembroke, the manor of Pleasaunce at Greenwich and the manor of Feckenham in Worcestershire.[45] For Pembroke, the queen received no income at all.[46] In restitution, the king granted her other lands and fee-farms

---

[40] 'Henry VI: March 1453', in PROME, v-262. See Appendix 2 for the fee-farms granted in recompense to Queen Margaret for the loss of revenues from the Pembroke lands.

[41] Myers, 'The Household of Queen Margaret of Anjou', 181.

[42] Ibid., 137–8, 166–70.

[43] Ibid., 156–72. The income for the accounting year totalled approximately £4700. Of this amount, £1000 was paid as the expected cash annuity from Duchy of Lancaster estates, £887 from Duchy of Cornwall revenues and £333 as the queen's share from attainted estates, predominantly those belonging to Humphrey, duke of Gloucester.

[44] For example, Eleanor of Provence and Katherine of Valois did not receive the total income that was due to them. Johnstone I, 282; Myers, 'The Household of Queen Margaret of Anjou', 137; Robert Somerville, *The History of the Duchy of Lancaster*, vol. I (London: Chancellor and Council of the Duchy of Lancaster, 1953), 208. See also Woodacre, *Joan of Navarre*, Chapter Five, for Joan's difficulties in collecting her expected revenues.

[45] The manors of Pleasaunce and Feckenham had been owned by Gloucester before they were granted to Margaret. Feckenham was granted in 1453 but the grant for the manor of Pleasaunce has not been located. Since this manor is listed in the 1452–53 household account, it would have been granted between 1446 and 1453.

[46] Myers, 'The Household of Queen Margaret of Anjou', 160–1, 163.

and allowed her to claim the arrears from Pembroke.[47] As yet, no records have been found showing whether Margaret was able to collect these arrears. The queen was also unable to collect her dues from the manors of Pleasaunce and Feckenham, although the existence of only one extant household account does not confirm that she was never able to do so. Where her fee-farms were concerned, the queen was entitled to about £600 in 1452–53. Instead, she received only £450, which included payments in arrears of about £80, therefore about £230, or nearly 40 per cent, was not forthcoming.

There is more than one possible reason why the queen suffered delays in receiving her dues from the Pembroke lands between 1451 and 1453. One reason could have been residual tenant and gentry loyalty to Humphrey, duke of Gloucester and earl of Pembroke. The Pembroke lands granted to Margaret had reverted to the Crown when the duke was attainted for treason and put to death in the winter of 1446. The duke of Suffolk was Gloucester's principal enemy, and the queen was closely associated with Suffolk at this time. As such, she may have been viewed with hostility as the new owner of the Pembroke lands by the late duke's affinity on those estates, a stance that may have partially manifested in the form of difficulties in collecting revenue. It may not have been such a bad bargain for the queen to exchange the Pembroke lands for lordships and manors such as Gillingham and Odiham, from which she was rather more successful in collecting her dues, at least for the year 1452–53.[48] Gillingham and Odiham had long been among the lands typically assigned to queens in dower and, seen in that light, it may have been considered appropriate to substitute those for the Pembroke lands.[49] It is tantalising to contemplate the possibility that she may even have been able to collect her revenues from Gillingham and Odiham more successfully precisely because of their historical royal association.[50]

Nonetheless, if this was a typical accounting year, the landed sources of income appear to have been reasonably dependable, in particular the receipts of revenue from estates granted to her from the Duchy of Lancaster. This may have been a happy consequence of the fact that William Cotton, the queen's

---

[47] 'Henry VI: March 1453', in PROME, v-261–2.
[48] The queen's household account shows that she received £46 from Gillingham and £20 from Odiham in this year but nothing for the arrears owed her from the Pembroke lands. Myers, 'The Household of Queen Margaret of Anjou', 160–1.
[49] See Louise Tingle, *Chaucer's Queens: Royal Women, Intercession and Patronage in England, 1328–1394* (Basingstoke: Palgrave Macmillan, 2021), 96–7, in relation to queens from the fourteenth century. The thirteenth-century queen of Edward I, Eleanor of Castile, was known to have been granted the castle and town of Odiham as part of her dower. John Carmi Parsons, *Eleanor of Castile: Queen and Society in Thirteenth-Century England* (New York: St Martin's Press, 1995), Appendix I Queen Eleanor's Lands.
[50] There are few surviving relevant manorial documents for either Gillingham or Odiham that can be used to test such a possibility.

receiver-general at the time, was also the receiver-general for the Duchy of Lancaster. Then, too, it probably helped that her auditors, John Walsh and Nicholas Sharp, also served as officials in the Duchy of Lancaster administration. Such arrangements clearly benefitted Margaret where the collection of her landed revenues was concerned.

The original grants of dower to Elizabeth Woodville did not specify projected revenues or incomes from individual lands but they did specify the values of individual fee-farms. Additionally, a number of land valors and accounts for Elizabeth's lands provide some indication as to the revenues the queen could expect from her holdings.[51] The amounts vary for each year but gross revenues in total were generally recorded as £6000–6500, with the exception of the land valor for 1464–65, which recorded gross revenues of about £5200. From the gross amounts, payments for a variety of expenses including wages, annuities and repairs had to be made before income could be allocated to the queen.[52] Expenses, however, varied from year to year, meaning that the queen's chamber could not be sure of a set income every year. For example, land valors for 1464–65 and 1471–72 both show the queen's chamber expected to receive between £3000 and £3300 in net income. However, the gross revenues were £5185 and £6449.[53] Clearly, far larger amounts were expended on necessary estate expenses, wages, allowances, annuities, and the like in the latter year than in the former. This may simply be an indication that more extra-chamber expenses were met before funds were remitted to the queen, although this premise is difficult to assess without additional valors or accounts with which to compare. Where the fee-farms were concerned, the land valors show that by the 1470s, the queen could regularly expect about £830 in gross revenue, from which fees and wages were paid before the remainder was remitted to her chamber. As her fee-farms totalled £1056 for at least some of the years during which she was queen, this meant that there were almost certainly periods when she faced a shortfall of more than £200 in fee-farm income.[54]

In general, we can draw a more accurate picture of how much projected revenue the queen actually received into her household by comparing a land valor with the corresponding household account for that year. For the year 1466–67, such comparison is possible because both a land valor and a household account are extant.[55] Gross revenues for this year were recorded

---

[51] TNA DL29/735/12052, 12053, 12056, 12057; DL29/736/12059, 12064.
[52] Myers, 'The Household of Queen Elizabeth Woodville', 254.
[53] TNA DL29/735/12052; DL29/736/12059.
[54] Whether these shortfalls in fee-farm revenue were commonly experienced by noble landholders during this period is a question that requires research beyond the scope of this study.
[55] TNA DL29/735/12053 and E36/207, the latter published as Myers, 'The Household of Queen Elizabeth Woodville', 251–318.

in the valor as £6110, with about £4300 being apportioned to the queen, comprising £3600 in land revenues and £700 in fee-farms. In comparison, the household account records totals of roughly £3800 in land revenue and nearly £700 in fee-farms, £60 of which were arrears.[56] This suggests that there were arrears paid in land revenue that were not anticipated in the valor. What is also clear is that revenue in fee-farms fell short of what was expected. In this year, Elizabeth expected to receive about £873 in fee-farms, thus her household account points to a shortfall of about £233 (26 per cent) as there were several entities from which she received nothing, such as the town of Tamworth and the wapentake of Goscote.[57] This was less of a proportionate shortfall in fee-farm revenue than Margaret of Anjou experienced in 1452 but could be one reason why she was later granted the additional fee-farms of Huntingdon and Godmanchester in July 1467.[58] Interestingly, as the other land valors show, fee-farm revenue for the queen continued to fall short by about 20 per cent each year.

While her overall total in dower revenue might have been less than Margaret's, Elizabeth Woodville derived much more of her income from landed sources and appears to have been able to collect them in timely fashion. In addition, she managed to acquire more interests in properties besides her dower lands, either as sole or shared holdings. Moreover, she was known to have purchased lands in her own standing as queen, an action for which no records have yet been found to show that Margaret did the same. Elizabeth bought the Fitzlewis manors of West Thorndon, Feldhous and Gyngraff in Essex, worth 1000 marks in total (£666 13s 4d), from Richard, duke of Gloucester, and sold them to Thomas, archbishop of Canterbury, sometime before 1482.[59] She gained shares in some grants of groups of properties – the sixty-five properties that made up the Huse quitclaim, the attainted Tresham lands, the manors of the earl of Wiltshire during the minority of his heir, and a group of manors and a hundred in Oxfordshire.[60] These additional grants were made only after 1466, meaning that, lacking further evidence to compare with the extant household account for Elizabeth Woodville, it is difficult to say with certainty how much she benefitted financially. Even so, it is reasonable to presume that the queen would have gained a significant amount of extra income from these additional holdings. It should be noted that there was an extra grant of reversion of land to this queen that did not eventuate in the

---

[56] The household account records an auditor's note of the sum of all receipts as being £4540 18s 11d ½. Myers, 'The Household of Queen Elizabeth Woodville', 287.
[57] Ibid., 278–9.
[58] It is surely not a coincidence that the fee-farm amounts of Huntingdon and Godmanchester totalling £183 almost exactly matched the shortfall in fee-farm income Elizabeth Woodville experienced in the accounting year 1466–67.
[59] CCR 1476–85, 295.
[60] CCR 1476–85, 30; CPR 1467–77, 543, 562.

queen's favour despite her attempts to manoeuvre herself into just such a position, that is, the 1469 grant to the queen of the reversion of the lands of Anne, duchess of Exeter, in default of suitable heirs.[61] This was an inheritance to be coveted as many of the Exeter properties were located in counties where the queen owned nothing. It is clear, therefore, that this queen took an active interest in private land-related transactions.

The lands and fee-farms that Elizabeth of York was initially granted as her dower were the same as those surrendered by Elizabeth Woodville in 1487. Furthermore, they were a subset of Elizabeth Woodville's own dower as queen consort since Henry VII had not re-granted all her dower in 1486. Later, the queen gained other properties, such as the lordship of Brettes in Westham, Essex in 1489 for the duration of the heir's minority and the manor of Fotheringhay in Northamptonshire, formerly owned by her grandfather, Richard, duke of York, in 1495.[62] While no records of any transactions in the private land market involving this queen have been found, this does not mean that no such transactions occurred. Additionally, there do not appear to be any surviving records of income accruing to Elizabeth in relation to other properties she was supposed to have owned in her own right, such as a Shropshire property she inherited from her presumed-deceased brother, Edward V.[63]

By far the largest augmentation to the queen's overall landholdings and revenues was the grant made in early 1492 of lands in reversion on the death of her paternal grandmother, Cecily Neville, the former duchess of York.[64] The duchess died in May 1495 and her lands then passed to her granddaughter. This inheritance was a highly substantial boost to the queen's economic resources. Besides the additional monetary benefits, these new lands brought with them non-monetary benefits that could be utilised and exploited. It was also quite a remarkable occurrence that draws attention to the unique nature of her position. Due to the disappearance of her brothers, Edward V and Richard, the young duke of York, Elizabeth of York was the heiress of her father and, consequently, of her grandmother, Cecily Neville. No other queen consort in late medieval England had ever gained such an inheritance; her doing so highlighted the fact that she was a domestically born queen consort whose natal ties were to England.

---

[61] Suitable heirs referred to heirs born to her current heir, who was a daughter, also named Anne, and any other 'heirs of the body of the duchess'. CPR 1467–77, 137–8. See Neal, 'The Queen's Grace', 112–13 for discussion of the Exeter inheritance and Elizabeth Woodville's attempts to benefit from this inheritance.
[62] CPR 1485–94, 293; CPR 1494–1509, 14.
[63] CIPM Henry VII, vol. III, 376 (entry 666).
[64] CPR 1485–94, 369–70. See Appendix 1 for the lands of Cecily Neville that passed to Elizabeth of York.

The Queen's Resources

As with Elizabeth Woodville, the expected values of or projected revenues from Elizabeth of York's lands were not stated in any of the grants, though it is logical to assume that having fewer lands than her mother meant that Elizabeth of York should have received less landed revenue overall. The younger Elizabeth was obviously granted £762 in fee-farm income, as each fee-farm originally owned by Elizabeth Woodville was re-granted to her daughter. Again, land valors allow us some insight into what Elizabeth of York's revenues should have been. Two valors, for the accounting years 1488–89 and 1489–90, recorded gross revenues for the lands originally owned by Elizabeth Woodville when she was queen dowager (and now belonging to Elizabeth of York) as £2164 and £2235.[65] Of the revenue amounts, £1650 and £1834 were earmarked for the queen's chamber, being the theoretical income available for her use after accounting for expenses such as fees, repairs and annuities. A third valor, this time from 1496–97, recorded gross revenues of £2192 for the same lands, with the queen's chamber meant to receive £1215.[66] A second separate valor for 1496–97 recorded gross revenues of £1399 for the lands formerly owned by Cecily Neville and now owned by the queen.[67] Those lands yielded £1150 for the queen's use, taking her total for the year to £2365. Undoubtedly, the York lands granted to the queen vastly improved her theoretical financial status in terms of potential income. Regrettably, the lack of corresponding household accounts for the above years means that we are unable to ascertain whether the queen in fact received her estimated landed revenues.

Our principal source for Elizabeth of York's household is her extant Privy Purse expense account for 1502–03, which was the last year of her life. This document has been likened to a chamber account in structure and types of information recorded, especially in relation to expenditure.[68] Importantly, though, it also lists receipts of revenue from several sources and records her total income for this year as approximately £3585. Closer inspection of the details shows that there are some lands that are not recorded in the account as revenue sources. Specifically, the holdings in Buckinghamshire, Suffolk and Surrey are missing.[69] This may be because the manuscript is damaged in some parts and the relevant information may be lost. But it is also possible that those lands were no longer owned by the queen at this time, for whatever reason.

Where the fee-farms are concerned, the valors of 1488–89 and 1489–90 both recorded the same expected amounts as the figure originally granted,

---

[65] TNA DL29/736/12067, 12068.
[66] WAM 12173.
[67] WAM 12172.
[68] Neal, 'The Queen's Grace', 121.
[69] Manorial documents do not survive for most of the manors in these counties for the relevant period. Some existing evidence survives for Banstead and Walton. However, these are court rolls that do not indicate whether the queen was still in possession of these manors in the year 1502–03.

that is, £762. However, by 1496–97 the amount due was about £752. On the one hand, it is unsurprising that the fee-farm income expected in 1496 was less than the original figure since the queen had, in 1495, authorised the diversion of £120 from her annual fee-farm income to her sister Anne and her husband, Lord Thomas Howard, heir to the earl of Surrey, to support the couple until he gained his inheritance.[70] On the other hand, the expected fee-farm income had not been reduced by exactly £120, which suggests that the queen had acquired other fee-farms either as compensation for the diverted income or as new gains. Regrettably, the valor for 1496–97 does not contain individual listings, so we cannot tell what the new fee-farms were. Even so, the Privy Purse expense account listed Halesowen among the fee-farms received and, given the evidence from the valors, this fee-farm had obviously been added to the queen's revenues sometime between 1490 and 1502. Then, too, by 1502, the fee-farms that had been diverted in 1495 were once again listed, meaning that they had now reverted to the queen.

Compared with the land valors for the previous years, Elizabeth of York's income of £3585 for 1502–03 was significantly higher. That this might not have been an anomaly is demonstrated by the 1506 account drawn up by the receiver-general of the late queen's properties that recorded a net income of £3360 for the benefit of the Crown. It is also worth pointing out that the amount of £3585 includes approximately £2050 in land revenues, £626 in fee-farms, £127 in 'fines' and £543 in a category called 'Money received of the quenes grace'.[71] Thus, the queen's landed revenue of £2676 was much closer to the amount she expected to receive in 1496–97, that is, £2365. This shows that the queen's landed income was relatively stable once the York lands became hers to use.

Landed resources were very important to all the queens in this study, bringing in significant proportions of their revenues and positioning them, in monetary terms, as major landholders. However, it is clear that Elizabeth Woodville was granted and could have expected to receive the most income from landed sources, both as revenue from dower lands and from fee-farm grants. Insofar as can be determined, she also gained the most in terms of shares in estate holdings in the years after her dower lands were granted. Her queenship marked a momentous change in the manner of assigning queens' dowers, specifically, a move towards greater reliance on landed sources for the queen's revenues, which became a trend that held in Elizabeth of York's case and through to the queens consort in the sixteenth century at least.[72]

[70] The diverted fee-farms were Norwich, Ipswich, Cambridge and the Abbey of Bury St. Edmunds. SR, vol. II, 610.
[71] Queen's Book, fols 1–17.
[72] An unpublished study by Andrea C. Silen-McMillin supports the contention that the queens consort of sixteenth-century England were primarily supported with lands and estates granted to them. Andrea C. Silen-McMillin, 'Assessing the Lands

The Queen's Resources

GRANTS, ALLOWANCES AND GIFTS

Non-landed resources comprised a variety of rights and gifts granted, such as lump sums of money and wardships. The monetary benefits were apparent but certain types of grants, like wardships, brought with them not just income but also other non-monetary and often less perceptible benefits. How important, therefore, was this category of resources to each of these queens and what do the conclusions imply for queenship generally?

More than the other queens in this study, Margaret of Anjou theoretically benefitted substantially from monetary grants of the non-landed variety as precise arrangements of this sort were included in her dower. More than two-thirds of the queen's dower was assigned in this form: £1000 as a cash annuity from the estates of the Duchy of Lancaster, £1000 from the customs of the port of Southampton, £1008 15s 5d from the revenues of the Duchy of Cornwall and £1657 17s 11d from the Royal Exchequer.[73] Since non-landed sources supplied 70 per cent of her dower revenues, this ostensibly was a very important category of resources for Margaret. Other cash grants that were later assigned to the queen included 500 marks (£333 6s 8d) as her share of estates that had reverted to the king.[74]

Wardships proved to be a lucrative and important resource.[75] The keeping of heirs and heiresses who by reason of their minority were not able to take up their inheritances on the deaths of their fathers was a prize because the queens typically benefitted in many different ways. Aside from being afforded the use of the revenues of the lands in wardship, the queens had the right to marry the children to whomever they pleased or were able to on-sell this right to others. Having such rights was of great advantage, financially and otherwise.[76]

---

of the Six Wives of Henry VIII with Particular Focus on Wiltshire' (unpublished MA thesis, University of Winchester, 2024).

[73] RP v. 120.
[74] 'Henry VI: March 1453', in PROME, v-262.
[75] Royal wardship was one of the king's feudal rights and referred to the king taking custody of the underaged heir or heirs and the lands of a deceased tenant-in-chief. It placed the lands and the marriage of the heir or heirs at his disposal, and he used it as a source of revenue and a means to exercise patronage. Wardships could be granted or sold to the queen and the nobility. See Henry E. Bell, *An Introduction to the History and Records of the Court of Wards and Liveries* (London: Cambridge University Press, 1953); Joel Hurstfield, *The Queen's Wards: Wardship and Marriage Under Elizabeth I* (Cambridge, Mass.: Harvard University Press, 1958); Sue Sheridan Walker, 'Royal Wardship in Medieval England', (unpublished PhD diss., University of Chicago, 1966); Scott L. Waugh, *The Lordship of England: Royal Wardships and Marriages in English Society and Politics, 1217–1327* (Princeton: Princeton University Press, 1988).
[76] Financial benefits were only one aspect of this feudal right. See Waugh, *The*

Financing Queenship in Late Fifteenth Century England

Although the right of wardship is believed not to have been exercised as often in the fifteenth century as it had been in the two centuries since King John's reign (r.1199–1216), it was by no means a dying practice and Margaret was certainly granted a number of wardships.[77] In 1446, she was given the keeping and marriage, that is, the wardship of Anne, the three-year-old heiress of Henry Beauchamp, duke of Warwick. She was also granted £200 a year to maintain the child in her own household.[78] Other wardships later granted to the queen included those of Elizabeth Ingaldesthorp, the underaged heiress of Edmund Ingaldesthorp, knight and tenant-in-chief, and Henry Ogard, the son and heir of Andrew Ogard, knight.[79] The case of Anne Beauchamp, in particular, illustrates how beneficial wardships could be to the queens. Ralph Griffiths notes that Margaret sold this wardship to the duke of Suffolk for a substantial monetary profit a few months after she acquired it.[80] Additionally, several men who served in her administration were appointed into the administration of the late duke's lands and properties.[81] This was not unusual as there were many king's men who similarly benefitted. What it indicates is that Margaret was just as assiduous as the king or any other lord in working to profit financially from the wardships she gained and to provide benefits to others associated with her.

Unfortunately, the main sources for her non-landed dower income proved to be problematic in that they often yielded few or no payments on a timely basis, with some exceptions. Margaret's extant household account records full payment only for the originally granted cash annuity from the estates of the Duchy of Lancaster and the additional annuity from attainted estates that had reverted to the king.[82] During this period, the receiver-general of the Duchy of Lancaster also served as receiver-general of Margaret's household. This circumstance not only benefitted the queen in the case of her landed revenues but also where her cash grants and annuities from the same duchy were

---

Lordship of England, Chapter 4 for an extensive discussion of how this right was exercised by the king and how he benefitted from it.

[77] Waugh, *The Lordship of England*, 6–7. Another fifteenth-century example was Joan of Navarre, consort to Henry IV from 1403 until 1413, who was granted several wardships. For example, CPR 1405–08, 193, 408; CPR 1408–13, 38, 148.

[78] CPR 1441–46, 436, 450.

[79] CPR 1452–61, 325, 583.

[80] Ralph A. Griffiths, *The Reign of King Henry VI: The Exercise of Royal Authority, 1422–1461* (London: Benn, 1981), 260.

[81] Examples include George Ashby, the queen's clerk of the signet who became steward of Warwick, Thomas Eyre, groom of the queen's chamber sharing the post of keeper of the park of Berkeswell, and John Wenlock, usher of the queen's chamber who was granted the constableship of Cardiff Castle. CPR 1441–46, 433, 437; Griffiths, *The Reign of King Henry VI*, 260, 363.

[82] Attainted estates were the forfeited holdings of a person who was sentenced to death for treason or a felony.

concerned. In contrast, she appears to have had much difficulty in collecting her portions of the customs of the Port of Southampton and from the Royal Exchequer and her portion of the revenues of the Duchy of Cornwall. The amounts recorded in her account as paid from the customs of Southampton were arrears owing from up to four years previously. There were no payments recorded for the current year, admittedly for the very good reason that, in 1450, Parliament had enacted a law specifying that the first £20,000 from these customs and subsidies was to go to the king before any others.[83] Arrears owed by the Duchy of Cornwall also remained unpaid even though a sizeable portion of the current year's dues was received.[84] By far the greatest deficits occurred from non-payment of income owing from the Royal Exchequer. The queen's account records that part payments were received from the Exchequer totalling £1037 5s 1d, but instead of paying the queen actual cash, Exchequer officials resorted to delivering tallies and assignments on the issues of a variety of holdings and fee-farms.[85] These methods were questionable since many of the said holdings and fee-farms were already supposed to have been assigned to the queen in recompense for her loss of the lordship of Pembroke.[86]

The queen and her officials attempted to collect her dues using diverse methods. One such method was her surrender of tallies worth £1500 in 1448 in exchange for the rights to ship wool and retain the customs and subsidies of any such transactions to the total of that value. Her rights to the arrears owing to her were also affirmed.[87] She was further granted the right to nominate individuals to the official posts of collectors of customs and subsidies at the ports of Southampton, London and Kingston-on-Hull. These rights gave the queen a much better chance of collecting what she was owed.[88] However, assigning such privileges to the queen meant that someone else lost these same privileges. For example, the rights to ship wool while retaining the customs and subsidies were traditionally the sole preserve of merchant groups such as the staplers at Calais. Gaining such benefits as these rights afforded may well have negatively influenced the queen's relationships with various

---

[83] 'Henry VI: March 1453', in PROME, v-259.
[84] Myers, 'The Household of Queen Margaret of Anjou', 168–9 (fol. 6a).
[85] Myers, 'The Household of Queen Margaret of Anjou', 171–2 (fol. 8a). The original function of tallies was as receipts for payments. Tallies could be issued for payment instead of cash, functioning as cheques payable to the recipient, who then had to collect a cash payment for what they were owed from the original debtor named on the tally. Hilary Jenkinson, 'Exchequer Tallies', *Archaeologia* 62, no. 2 (1911): 369–70; Rudolph Robert, 'A Short History of Tallies', in *Studies in the History of Accounting*, ed. A. C. Littleton (London: Sweet & Maxwell, 1956), 75–85.
[86] CCR 1447–54, 222–5; 'Henry VI: March 1453', in PROME, v-261–2.
[87] CPR 1446–52, 171–2; Myers, 'The Household of Queen Margaret of Anjou', 140.
[88] CPR 1446–52, 172.

communities.[89] Last but not least, a generous grant in 1453 allowed the queen, for the term of her life, all moveable possessions forfeited to the king as well as a number of royal prerogatives including the power to exclude royal officials and impose trading tolls.[90] Griffiths asserts that all these grants and allowances created for Margaret 'a virtual queenly franchise'.[91] While this is a valid observation, it is important to remember that the underlying objective of many of these later grants was to enable the queen to obtain what had been granted to her as dower in the first place.

While much of Elizabeth Woodville's revenues came in the form of income from landed sources, she was also granted several generous allowances. In 1465 the queen was allocated 500 marks (£333 6s 8d) *per annum* from several of the king's lordships in South Wales, including £100 from the lordship of Newport for the maintenance of the minors Henry, duke of Buckingham, and his brother Humphrey. The brothers were wards of the kings but were being brought up in the queen's household.[92] Another £400 a year from the Royal Exchequer was permitted in October 1468 to the queen for the upkeep of her young daughters, Elizabeth and Mary.[93] In 1475 the king arranged for the queen to receive an extra £2200 for the royal household expenses while he was away at war in France.[94] Much smaller monetary gains were also obtained, such as the 1469 grant of £60 from the revenues of the lands owned by Anne, duchess of Exeter, in the counties of Devon, Cambridge and Huntingdon, albeit only on the death of the duchess, which occurred much later in January 1476.[95] These grants demonstrate that the king was mindful of the extra expenses often needed in extreme or atypical circumstances, such as those occasioned by war or a new royal birth.

Notably, Elizabeth's extant household account for 1466–67 does not contain any records of non-landed income. Of particular interest is the absence of recorded receipts of the grants made for the upkeep of the above-mentioned king's wards, the duke of Buckingham and his younger brother. Was this income received directly into the queen's chamber rather than processed by the household receiver-general? Such an omission in the household account suggests that this might have been the case with grants of this nature even though the lack of alternative household records to compare with makes it difficult to assess this possibility.

---

[89] Griffiths, *The Reign of King Henry VI*, 260.
[90] CCR 1447–54, 390; 'Henry VI: March 1453', in PROME, v-260.
[91] Griffiths, *The Reign of King Henry VI*, 261.
[92] CPR 1461–67, 463–4; Myers, 'The Household of Queen Elizabeth Woodville', 308.
[93] CPR 1467–77, 110.
[94] CCR 1468–76, 5; BL Cotton MS Vespasian C XIV, fol. 272b.
[95] CPR 1467–77, 138.

The Queen's Resources

Elizabeth was also awarded several non-monetary grants that brought significant extra benefits beyond their face value. Among them were the rights to award the next vacant canonry in such locations as the free chapel of St Anthony's, London, and St Stephen's in Westminster Palace.[96] These rights did not directly benefit her financially, but they were still advantageous. Where wardships were concerned, there is little record of Elizabeth being awarded the keeping of noble heirs in their minority. Nevertheless, that does not mean that she did not benefit at all. For instance, the king held the wardship of the underaged heir of John, earl of Shrewsbury. This enabled him in 1474 to grant to his queen the right of appointment to the advowson of the chantry or priory of Flaunsworde in the lordship of Goodrich (Goderige).[97] Interestingly, Elizabeth potentially could have gained many other wardships with attendant benefits as a result of an Act of Parliament in 1483 that granted her 'the wardships and marriages of the heirs of the [tenants-in-chief]' of the Duchy of Lancaster.[98] Unhappily for her, the king died only a few months after this parliament met and Elizabeth lost her position as queen consort.

Compared with Margaret of Anjou or Elizabeth Woodville, Elizabeth of York does not appear to have been given large formal cash grants or even many non-monetary grants of significant value. She was allowed an annuity of £100 in 1487 from the Trussell lands during the minority of the heir, Edward, she was granted a £40 life annuity in 1490, and she shared in some grants to assign livings and positions at St Stephen's at Westminster Palace, among others.[99] She also appears not to have been granted any wardships, a rather unlikely circumstance; perhaps none were recorded in the extant documents related to this queen. Then, too, there is no record of allowances being made to the queen for the maintenance of underaged heirs and heiresses who were king's wards even though it is highly probable that their upbringing would have been entrusted to the queen and her household. It is possible that the king's administration used a different method to financially reimburse the queen for the maintenance of minors in her household. Alternatively, there may have been changes in accounting and record-keeping on the queen's side that we cannot now discern.

Some intriguing details, however, can be found in the last two categories of revenue listed in Elizabeth of York's Privy Purse expense account. One category consists of 'fines' totalling £127 that appear to be similar to fees, although one of the 'fines' is a part payment for trespass in the forest of

---

[96] CPR 1467–77, 115, 360, 604.
[97] CPR 1467–77, 414.
[98] 'Edward IV: January 1483', in PROME, vi-207–8.
[99] The queen shared in the grant of both the next prebend to St Stephen's chapel in 1486 and the next dean of the college of St Stephen in 1487. CPR 1485–94, 65, 206; *Materials for a History*, vol. II, 116, 218, 560.

Pewsham. The other recorded 'fines' are payments to the queen for farms and for the offices of forester of the forest of Gillingham and steward of the lordship of Gillingham.[100] The queen obviously saw fit to grant these individuals the posts and offices they presumably sought and it is clear that she gained financial benefits in return. The existence of such a category of revenue suggests that the queen used other methods to obtain income besides relying on her dower grants. The other category, with the heading 'Money received of the quenes grace', totalled £543 and was probably meant to record the queen's borrowings and debts. Records from the expense and receipt books of the King's chamber for the period 1485–1521 show ample evidence of loans being made by the king's chamber to the queen.[101] One of the largest was a sum of £2000, which the queen borrowed in 1497 to pay her debts.[102] Her liability to the king was noted by the king's treasurer of the Chamber, John Heron, and she undertook to repay the amount in four yearly instalments of £500.[103] Other chamber records show that the queen owed the king at least £100 at the beginning of 1502 and that another loan of £500 was made to the queen in April of the same year, the latter being made on the queen's surrendering 'certain plate' as collateral.[104] The details of the £500 loan of April 1502 appear to match a record in the last category of revenue in the queen's Privy Purse expense account.[105] The size and frequency of the cash loans suggest that these were probably important sources of revenue.

Besides the cash loans and the few formal grants and allowances, Elizabeth was the recipient of sundry gifts from the king, both in the form of cash and otherwise. Among these were such items as 100 marks (£66 13s 4d) 'for the maintenance of her state' and £6 'for one tun of wine, by way of reward', another 100 marks 'by way of reward', and money to purchase jewels.[106] The

---

[100] Queen's Book, fol. 12.

[101] These books are known as *The Chamber Books* and referred to as such in this book (see Abbreviations). They were digitised and made available to the research community in 2018 by the Tudor Chamber books project.

[102] *The Chamber Books*, TNA E101/414/6, fol. 60v, https://www.tudorchamberbooks.org/edition/folio/E101_414_6_fo_060v.xml.

[103] *The Chamber Books*, TNA E101/414/6, fol. 111r, https://www.tudorchamberbooks.org/edition/folio/SH_E101_414_6_fo_111r.xml, E101/414/16, fol. 119r, https://www.tudorchamberbooks.org/edition/folio/SH_E101_414_6_fo_119r.xml. Evidence from *The Chamber Books* (TNA E101/415/3, fol. 243r, BL Add MS 59899, fol. 185r) shows that the queen made the first two repayments of £500 each in 1499 and 1502, both payments being later than the times stated in the original undertaking made to John Heron in 1497.

[104] *The Chamber Books*, BL Add MS 21480, fol. 184v, https://www.tudorchamberbooks.org/edition/folio/LL_BL_AddMS_21480_fo184v.xml, TNA E101/415/3, fol. 93r, https://www.tudorchamberbooks.org/edition/folio/E101_415_3_fo_093r.xml.

[105] Queen's Book, fol. 14.

[106] *The Chamber Books*, BL Add MS 7099, fol. 40, https://www.tudorchamberbooks.

king also regularly sent his queen gifts of robes and sumptuous cloth for the making of gowns and such like.[107] Furthermore, there are a number of occasions where the king paid the queen's debts for services rendered by her tailor and physician, among others.[108] Judging by the evidence, Elizabeth regularly received gifts and allowances from the king. As proportions of her overall income, it is unlikely that the smaller gifts contributed significantly to her revenues. Still, rather than being purely indicative of the queen's chronic indebtedness, these gifts could just as easily signify a high level of affection between the king and his queen and/or a high degree of interconnectedness between the two royal households. Were it possible to examine any corresponding accounts for Margaret of Anjou and Elizabeth Woodville, there could well be evidence showing that those queens were the recipients of similar largesse from their respective husbands.

It appears that non-landed resources were theoretically a very important category to Margaret of Anjou but were generally less important than landed sources to both Elizabeth Woodville and Elizabeth of York. In comparison with Margaret, both Elizabeths appear to have had access to far fewer non-landed sources of revenue. What they did receive almost certainly provided them with significant other benefits, but overall they garnered far less in monetary terms than Margaret did for this category of queenly resources. Admittedly, in Elizabeth of York's case, there is ample evidence of the king's generosity to her on an ad-hoc basis, both in the form of regular loans of money as well as assorted gifts. Nonetheless, this category of resources was not a reliable or consistent source of money to either of the Elizabeths.

QUEEN'S GOLD

Queen's gold was, as already mentioned on p. 15, an acknowledged entitlement belonging to queens in late medieval England and collected in the form of a levy. Notwithstanding the apparently fixed amount of 10 per cent, FitzNigel, the twelfth-century writer of the *Dialogus de Scaccario*, suggested that it was debatable as to whether queen's gold accrued on sums lower than the hundred marks of silver for the king.[109] Although he failed to provide a definitive

---

org/edition/folio/7099_fo_040.xml; *Materials for a History*, vol. II, 296–7, 392.
[107] *Materials for a History*, vol. II, 176–7, 497–8.
[108] For example, *The Chamber Books*, BL Add MS 7099, fols 15 and 23, https://www.tudorchamberbooks.org/edition/folio/7099_fo_015.xml and https://www.tudorchamberbooks.org/edition/folio/7099_fo_023.xml; TNA E101/414/6, fol. 34r, https://www.tudorchamberbooks.org/edition/folio/E101_414_6_fo_034r.xml; TNA E101/414/16, fol. 66r, https://www.tudorchamberbooks.org/edition/folio/LL_E101_414_16_fo066r.xml.
[109] FitzNigel, *Dialogus de Scaccario*, 184–5.

answer to this question, the records show that since the early thirteenth century writs for queen's gold were frequently issued on king's sums lower than a hundred marks of silver.[110]

Payments due were based on an assortment of different 'fines' to the king, a full list of which was compiled by William Prynne in his seventeenth-century work on queen's gold.[111] Neal argues that the term 'fines' in the twelfth century should be considered analogous to the present-day understanding of 'fees' even though its contemporary meaning supposedly carried with it a voluntary rather than coercive or punitive connotation.[112] However, while the fine owed to the king might have been of a voluntary nature, queen's gold was an automatic obligation.[113] The payer was still liable for queen's gold accrued on a fine even if the king remitted the fine itself since only the queen, strictly speaking, could remit the owed payment of queen's gold.[114]

The origins and justification for the payment of queen's gold have long been a matter of conjecture.[115] Yet, whatever the truth of its origins, queen's gold was certainly established as a customary privilege of the fourteenth-century English queens, although it had become a formal payment that was no longer linked to any particular service.[116] Johnstone is convinced that queen's gold was a significant financial resource for medieval English queens but she does not claim that it was uniformly important for all of them. For instance, she suggests that queen's gold was of negligible importance for the thirteenth-century queen Eleanor of Provence, consort of Henry III (r.1216–72), based on the inconsequential sums of queen's gold payments recorded in her wardrobe accounts.[117] Margaret Howell's research demonstrates, in contrast, that Eleanor did in fact receive more queen's gold payments than Johnstone allowed for and, moreover, did not receive the revenue from lands granted to her in dower during her husband's lifetime. Hence, queen's gold counted

---

[110] Geaman, 'Queen's Gold and Intercession', 13.
[111] The list included such items as payments for licences, charters, custodies and exemptions. Prynne, *Aurum Reginae*, 6–7.
[112] Neal, 'The Queen's Grace', 118.
[113] FitzNigel, *Dialogus de Scaccario*, 184–5; Geaman, 'Queen's Gold and Intercession', 12–15.
[114] Louise Tingle demonstrates that in practice for the fourteenth-century English queens Philippa of Hainault and Anne of Bohemia the king did not hesitate to cancel writs issued for queen's gold claims and occasionally interfered in the queen's administration of this source of her revenue. Tingle, *Chaucer's Queens*, 85–6.
[115] For discussion of the precursors to and origins of queen's gold, see Geaman, 'Queen's Gold and Intercession', 15–17.
[116] Louise Tingle, '*Aurum Reginae*: Queen's Gold in Late Fourteenth-Century England', *Royal Studies Journal* 7, no. 1 (2020): 78.
[117] Johnstone I, 265.

as one of her most important resources.[118] Queen's gold was also a very important source of revenue to Eleanor of Provence's daughter-in-law, Eleanor of Castile (wife to Edward I), and formed significant portions of the revenues of queens consort in the fourteenth century such as Philippa of Hainault and Anne of Bohemia. For many of these queens, collecting their entitlements was sometimes a fraught and frustrating exercise. This meant that while queen's gold was a monetarily valuable resource for many queens before the fifteenth century it was not necessarily a *reliable* source of funds.[119]

By the later fifteenth century this specific right belonging to England's queens consort was long established and its appeal was obvious. If a queen could successfully collect all that was owed to her, this could indeed be a significant source of income. It was no wonder, then, that our fifteenth-century queens invoked its continuity and jealously guarded and claimed their entitlements. But how successful were they in collecting their queen's gold?

A person who incurred a payment of queen's gold would receive a writ of *fieri facias*, that is, a writ of execution to levy debts.[120] Such writs were issued through the Exchequer and are typically found today among the records of bills and writs used to initiate suits in the Exchequer of Pleas.[121] However, no writs for Margaret have yet been discovered nor did Prynne record any in his work on queen's gold.[122] The lack of evidence of writs for Margaret makes it extremely difficult to say with any certainty how many claims were made each year. Even so, there is other extant material that provides information on what this queen could expect to gain from this resource. The account prepared by her receiver-general, William Cotton, for the year 1452–53 recorded fifty-nine claims for queen's gold amounting to a total of £167 11s 4d (as listed in Table 1).[123] There is also an account of arrears pertaining to the year 1449–50 that includes queen's gold owed to Margaret. This document lists five separate debts for queen's gold, totalling £7 13s 4d, which corresponds to the first five

---

[118] Howell does not make specific statements about the total amounts of queen's gold received by Eleanor of Provence but argues that evidence other than her wardrobe account pointed to substantial figures of such income, making this an important category of resources for this queen. Margaret Howell, 'The Resources of Eleanor of Provence as Queen Consort', *EHR* 102, no. 403 (1987): 374–5, 380–1.

[119] See Tingle, '*Aurum Reginae*' for Philippa of Hainault and see Geaman, *Anne of Bohemia*, 92–3 for Anne of Bohemia.

[120] Tingle, '*Aurum Reginae*', 81.

[121] These records are known as the E5 series of documents stored at The National Archives.

[122] Prynne, *Aurum Reginae*, 67. Prynne confirmed that Queen Margaret was entitled to her queen's gold and that there were two clerks in the Exchequer, John Croke and William Essex, responsible for her claims. But he makes no mention of her writs and recorded none.

[123] Myers, 'The Household of Queen Margaret of Anjou', 172–81 (fols 8b–11a).

claims listed in Cotton's account.[124] These debts appear to originate from perhaps as far back as late 1446 and remained unpaid even in 1452.

There are salient points to be gleaned from examining the records in Cotton's account. Assuming that all outstanding queen's gold claims were documented here, only sixteen of the fifty-nine claims were paid in this accounting year. The amount paid totalled £53 16s 2d, meaning that the queen received only about one-third of what was owed to her overall. The other forty-three claims were recorded with nil amounts received. In other words, they remained unpaid and presumably would have been carried over to the next accounting year. Only twelve claims, that is, 20 per cent of the total number, were current; the rest were outstanding claims for all the years going back to mid-1446, about a year after the royal marriage took place. Of the claims made in the current accounting year, none except possibly one was paid that same year. Additionally, only five of the fourteen unpaid claims recorded from the previous year (1451–52) were paid. The high proportion of unpaid current claims coupled with the patchy payments for claims from previous years point to a pattern of non-timely and inconsistent payment, which is probably indicative of the opposition faced by queens in relation to queen's gold.

Myers asserts that the number of outstanding claims related to the years prior to 1452 is an indication of how tenacious the queen and her servants could be in maintaining her claims.[125] This assertion should be tempered by a consideration that bureaucratic automation, even in the fifteenth century, could conceivably have seen unpaid claims continually recorded unquestioned in the accounts. The fact that Cotton recorded unpaid claims from the years before 1452 tells us only that these claims had not been settled as yet. It sheds little light on how vigorously the queen's claims were pursued or why they remained unpaid. It is also possible that these claims continued to remain unpaid since the older the claim, the less likely it would ever be settled. All of this assumes as well that sheer forgetfulness or administrative negligence on the part of the queen's officials did not factor in the lack of records of payments. Notwithstanding, the fact that claims existed for all the years since 1446 shows that Margaret of Anjou evidently considered that she was entitled to claim queen's gold and issued writs accordingly. The lack of surviving writs makes it impossible to make worthwhile assertions as to how successful she was in collecting the claims. Nonetheless, she almost certainly did not find it easy to collect her entitlements and, consequently, queen's gold cannot have been a consistently reliable source of revenue for her.

---

[124] TNA SC6/1093/14. The queen's gold debts are listed at the end of the roll.
[125] Myers, 'The Household of Queen Margaret of Anjou', 142.

Table 1: Queen's Gold Claims in Margaret of Anjou's Household Account for 1452–53 (TNA DL28/5/8).

Year	No. of Claims	Paid	Unpaid	Paid amount	Unpaid amount
Sept 1446–Aug 47	5		5		£7 13s 4d
Sept 1447–Aug 48	2	2		£9 16s 5d	
Sept 1448–Aug 49	10	4	6	£8 13s 4d	£6 15s 5d
Sept 1449–Aug 50	3		3		£8
Sept 1450–Aug 51	7	3	4	£4 19s 1d	£10 7s 1d
Sept 1451–Aug 52	14	5	9	£7 14s	£27 13s 4d
Sept 1452–Aug 53	12		12		£44 6s
Unclear	6	2[126]	4[127]	£22 13s 4d	£9
Totals	**59**	**16**	**43**	**£53 16s 2d**	**£113 15s 2d**

Table 2: Distribution of Writs for Queen's Gold for Elizabeth Woodville.*

Year	No. of writs	Year	No. of writs
1465–66	43[128]	1474–75	15
1466–67	8	1475–76	10
1467–68	39	1476–77	16
1468–69	12	1477–78	17
1469–70	8	1478–79	11

[126] Although the dates for these two paid claims have not been confirmed, one of the claims is recorded among all the claims for the current accounting period. It is not unreasonable to presume that the amount paid of 53s 4d may be counted as a current paid claim.

[127] Two of these claims are listed among other claims pertaining to the regnal years 28 and 30 Henry VI. Tellingly, they are not listed among the queen's gold debts in the account of arrears, SC6/1093/14, which supports the possibility that the writs for these claims were issued as late as 28 Henry VI or even 30 Henry VI.

[128] There appear to be three writs issued for 1464–65 that have been recorded among the writs for 1465–66. I have not included them here.

1470–71	2	1479–80	14
1471–72	3	1480–81	15
1472–73	10	1481–82	9
1473–74	5	1482–83	12

* The figures are derived from TNA E5/564, E5/565 and E19/1/2, which comprise surviving records of writs issued for the period between regnal years 5 and 23 Edw IV, that is, March 1465 until April 1483. The records in E5/564 and E19/1/2 do not appear to duplicate despite some chronological overlap. I have not used Prynne's list of writs for Elizabeth Woodville because, although it is based on the material in E19/1/2, it appears to be incomplete and incorrect in some parts.

Table 3: Records of Queen's Gold Owed to Elizabeth Woodville.

Year	Record Reference[129]	Record Type	Amount Due
1464–65	DL29/735/12052	Land Valor	£121 8s
1465–66?	DL29/734/12048	Land Valor	£154 7s 4d
1466–67	DL29/735/12053	Land Valor	£37
1469–70	SC6/1094/8	Account of Arrears	£6 13s 4d[130]
1471–72?	DL29/736/12059	Land Valor	£20 12s 8d
1473–74	DL29/735/12057	Land Valor	£20 13s 4d
1478–79	DL29/736/12064	Land Valor	£19

In comparison with Margaret, not only is there an extant household account with information on queen's gold received by Elizabeth Woodville but there are a few extant sources recording writs issued for the queen and, for some years, the amounts that she could expect to collect.[131] We cannot be absolutely sure that the surviving sources have listed all the writs that were issued for each year but some initial analysis is at least possible. Looking at the distribution of writs in Table 2, we can discern some interesting points. Firstly, the largest numbers of writs issued in a year were for the earliest years that Elizabeth Woodville was queen. Although, as noted earlier, queen's gold

[129] All the records in this table are available at The National Archives, UK.
[130] Accounts of arrears tell us what the queen was still owed in queen's gold but nothing about how much she might have expected or did receive for the year.
[131] TNA E5/564, E5/565 and E19/1/2 contain surviving evidence for writs for queen's gold in Elizabeth Woodville's case. Prynne, *Aurum Reginae*, 68–104 also outlines writs issued for queen's gold for Elizabeth Woodville and this information is known to have been based on E19/1/2. However, the information in Prynne is incomplete and inaccurate in some parts. Some surviving land valors contain information on expected amounts of queen's gold.

was an automatic obligation, the difficulties encountered by so many of the earlier queens consort in collecting this revenue surely influenced this queen's decisions on whether or not to issue writs to claim her queen's gold. Thus, the large numbers of writs issued for the years 1465–66 and 1467–68 reflect Elizabeth Woodville's wish as a new queen to lay claim to all her entitlements. Next, the smallest numbers of writs issued were for the years 1470–72 and this is entirely understandable considering the political situation of the period. Edward IV lost his throne briefly to the previous Lancastrian king Henry VI in October 1470, re-gaining it only in May 1471 after defeating the Lancastrians in battle. Elizabeth had much to occupy her during this time of crisis, and, naturally, even allowing for some degree of autonomy on the part of her officials, there were only a handful of writs issued then. Lastly, for the last decade of Edward's reign (1474–83), the numbers appear remarkably stable and consistent, if much smaller, compared with the years 1465–66 or 1467–68. This corresponds to the relatively peaceful decade of Edward's reign following the events of 1470–72. Still, taken as a whole, if we consider that as recently as 1412, the then-queen consort, Joan of Navarre, had made thirty-six claims for queen's gold, the numbers for Elizabeth Woodville demonstrate a clear downward trend, signifying a decreased perception of the importance of queen's gold as a source of revenue.[132]

A similar drift can be observed in the amounts of queen's gold revenue that Elizabeth Woodville received. Her household account for 1466–67, compiled by John Forster, recorded nine separate queen's gold claims, all paid.[133] An additional entry for queen's gold, recorded in the account as a nil payment, was for a portion of one of the earlier claims and should not be counted as a separate claim in its own right. In total, the queen received £37 in queen's gold income, a lower amount than Margaret received in 1452. Yet extant land valors for Elizabeth Woodville show that at times the queen expected to receive much more.[134] The valor for 1466 shows an expected amount of £37 in queen's gold, which corresponds to the recorded paid total in Forster's account. However, the valor for the year 1464 recorded an expected amount of £121 8s, while £154 7s 4d was recorded in another valor, possibly for 1465. Unhappily for the queen, valors for much later years record much smaller amounts, as little as £19 in 1478, while in 1481 the queen's receiver of queen's gold, Thomas Stidolf, collected only £13 6s 8d.[135] Such a downward trend in expected and received queen's gold amounts, in combination with relatively lower numbers of writs issued, suggests that Elizabeth, too, experienced

---

[132] Woodacre, *Joan of Navarre*, 172.
[133] TNA E36/207, fols 15–16; Myers, 'The Household of Queen Elizabeth Woodville', 283–6.
[134] See Table 3 for queen's gold owed to the queen.
[135] TNA DL28/27/11A.

Financing Queenship in Late Fifteenth Century England

difficulty in claiming and collecting her entitled queen's gold. In short, this particular entitlement did not contribute a substantial amount to Elizabeth Woodville's overall economic wealth.

Additional issues, related to financial administration, emerge when we consider how to reconcile the information contained in the three types of sources available for Elizabeth Woodville's queen's gold: the sources for writs, the land valors and the account compiled by Forster. Of the claims listed in Forster's account, at least two and possibly up to six were current claims, while the remaining ones date from the previous accounting years.[136] Yet the details for the writs that were recorded for the year of Forster's account do not correspond with all of the six current claims in the account itself. This suggests that Forster recorded only paid claims in his account. There are recorded writs for claims that are not listed at all in Forster's account and since no other relevant sources have surfaced, we have no way of knowing whether those were paid or not. At face value, it is probable that these claims were unpaid and that those as well as any older unpaid claims were either written off or recorded elsewhere. Hence it is difficult to make any conclusions about the proportional rate of non-payments of queen's gold for this queen. The discrepancy between the writs and the claims also suggests that there may have been other writs issued for 1466–67 that were not recorded in the writ roll and are now lost to us.

For Elizabeth of York, only one surviving source for writs issued for queen's gold has yet been found.[137] There is, besides, very little in the way of evidence for how much she was able to collect. Elizabeth's officials clearly included a collector of queen's gold, as indicated by the writs issued and the existence of a sub-section titled 'Aurum Regine' (Queen's Gold) within the section for receipts of revenue in the queen's Privy Purse Expense account.[138] There are not, however, any entries recorded in this sub-section.[139] At first glance, it would seem either that no claims had been made for the year of this account or that no claims were paid. The first scenario is not likely judging from the

---

[136] The eight writs recorded for 1466–67 in TNA E19/1/2 were compared with the claims in Forster's account. According to Neal, Prynne listed ten writs for this year, which may or may not be accurate depending on whether Prynne had access to other now-lost sources that he did not mention.

[137] TNA E5/5/33 is labelled as containing writs for queen's gold for the year 1497–98. However, examination of the contents reveals that the writs in this document span the period 1496–1501 and were issued by a receiver with the last name of Elyott.

[138] This expense account was prepared by Richard Decons, the queen's keeper of the Privy Purse whose job it may also have been to collect queen's gold.

[139] Judging by the state of the original manuscript, it is possible that the manuscript at this juncture is now simply too damaged even for present-day techniques to recover any information. TNA E36/210 (Queen's Book), fol. 15.

fact that, as Table 4 shows, writs were issued for almost all the accounting years between 1496 and 1502. As in Elizabeth Woodville's case, the numbers of writs for Elizabeth of York are relatively low compared with queens from earlier centuries or even at the beginning of the fifteenth century, endorsing the 'downward trend' I previously highlighted. But they do confirm that this Elizabeth also considered queen's gold to be one of her entitlements and anticipated being able to claim and collect it. In addition, extant land valors show that the queen issued writs for her entitled payments during at least some of the years before 1496. Two valors for 1488 and 1489 record that the queen expected to receive £19 4s 8d and £31 10s 8d.[140]

Table 4: Distribution of Writs for Queen's Gold for Elizabeth of York.[141]

Year	No. of writs
1496–97	1
1497–98	10
1498–99	17
1499–1500	0
1500–01	10
1501–02	5

Again, a key question is whether she actually received any payments of queen's gold. One solitary extant receipt shows that John Mayer, the queen's receiver of queen's gold, collected 16s in 1501, which proves that Elizabeth was indeed able to collect at least some of her entitlements some of the time.[142] The question of how much she might have been able to collect at any time as queen consort is moot for now since no other receipts or relevant accounts have yet been found for the years that we have writs for. There is also no guarantee that records of queen's gold receipts were recorded in the corresponding household accounts. In the last years of her time as queen, Elizabeth Woodville's receipts of queen's gold were recorded not by her receiver-general but by her clerk of queen's gold, his accounts also including fee-farm receipts but no other land-based revenues.[143] Following this precedent, it is possible that Elizabeth of York's collectors of queen's gold also compiled their own separate accounts, recording specific claim details. It may be that the empty sub-section on queen's gold in the Privy Purse expense account was meant

---

[140] TNA DL29/736/12067, 12068.
[141] The figures are derived from TNA E5/5/33.
[142] TNA E101/123/10.
[143] Two such accounts survive, compiled by Thomas Stidolf, Elizabeth Woodville's clerk of queen's gold – TNA DL28/27/11 and DL28/27/11A.

to record only the total sum as tallied by the collector of queen's gold and paid to the Keeper of the Privy Purse, Richard Decons. To sum up, the sparse evidence that is available for Elizabeth of York's entitlements to queen's gold points to the likelihood that, even more than for either Margaret of Anjou or Elizabeth Woodville, queen's gold was not a financially valuable resource for Elizabeth of York.

Overall, the evidence in this study for queen's gold from the numbers of writs issued and the amounts either expected or collected by the queens suggests that this source of revenue had declined in importance, at least in part due to its vast unpopularity. Queens and their officials from as far back as the mid-thirteenth century did not find queen's gold an easy item to collect, coming up against persistent recalcitrance on the part of debtors.[144] Contemporary writings show that such attitudes persisted into the fifteenth century, queen's gold being regarded as an 'intolerable imposition' by all who incurred the obligation.[145] It is not difficult to understand why people were so opposed to paying this particular levy. Kristen Geaman makes a direct connection between a medieval queen's role as intercessor and the development of queen's gold. She concludes that such payments were originally justified as an acknowledgement of and reward for the queen's influence in intercession and linked the decline in importance of queen's gold as an economic resource to a parallel decline in the importance of queenly intercession. This may be true, but Geaman also points out that by the late fifteenth century queen's gold had become a standardised fee with no especial symbolic meaning attached to it.[146] It was by then merely a regular payment that accrued on the basis of another obligation. To contemporaries, queen's gold had no obvious justification behind it. This meant that those who incurred this obligatory payment could see no reason why they should be required to pay it and, consequently, it is unsurprising that many took steps to avoid incurring or paying such claims altogether.

Queen's gold provided earlier medieval queens such as Eleanor of Provence and Eleanor of Castile with significant, even major, portions of their income. But the amounts claimed by the fifteenth-century queens in this study were insignificant in raw monetary value and inconsequential in proportion to their overall financial resources. Did this diminution of queen's gold as an important source of income matter very much in the fifteenth century? Perhaps not in terms of the impact to their resources. Nonetheless, in terms of dignity and prestige, it is understandable that these queens would wish to

---

[144] Johnstone I, 266; Johnstone II, 264–5; Howell, 'The Resources of Eleanor of Provence', 378–9.

[145] *The Great Chronicle of London*, eds. A. H. Thomas and I. D. Thornley (Gloucester: Alan Sutton, 1983), 208, note on 430; Myers, 'The Household of Queen Margaret of Anjou', 141.

[146] Geaman, 'Queen's Gold and Intercession', 24.

continue to claim these entitlements. Even if queen's gold was not important in financial terms, questions remain as to its importance in other respects. What did the queens' insistence on their rights to queen's gold mean for their reputations and how did it relate to their relationships with members of their networks? Could it be that the overall administration of queen's gold was a factor in the development of animosity towards particular queens? In other words, did ill feelings possibly generated by Margaret of Anjou and Elizabeth Woodville's pursuance of their queen's gold debts spill over and poison their standing with regards to other matters, thus contributing even more to the continued decline of the importance of queen's gold?

CONCLUSIONS

This comparative analysis of the resources and revenues available to Margaret of Anjou, Elizabeth Woodville and Elizabeth of York has shown that Johnstone's framework of categories of revenue for thirteenth- and fourteenth-century queens generally still holds for these fifteenth-century queens. The three queens were able to use and gained revenue from landed and non-landed resources as well as queen's gold. However, the relative importance of each category to these queens had changed from earlier centuries. Looking at all three queens together, it is clear that landed sources became the most important resource in terms of stability and consistency in queenly revenues. Conversely, non-landed sources and queen's gold became much less important categories of revenue.

How did each of the queens in this study compare with the others in relation to their overall revenues and the importance of each type? Margaret of Anjou was theoretically entitled to the largest estimated total revenue of either of her successor queens. Yet she was probably not always substantially better off financially than either of the others since she was unable to collect all the revenues she expected and was owed. While Margaret's landed revenues made up only 30 per cent of her dower total, they were generally reliable sources that were paid in a timely fashion. In comparison, both Elizabeths possessed revenue sources that were predominantly grounded in landholdings. That they depended heavily on these resources is not in doubt since their non-landed resources did not contribute much proportionally to their overall revenues. In Elizabeth Woodville's case, there are indications that she probably found her landed sources to be reliable. The case is less certain for Elizabeth of York since there is less corroborating evidence to work with. I would suggest that she, too, was able to rely on reasonably consistent revenues from her landed sources. In terms of overall landed revenues, however, Elizabeth Woodville clearly enjoyed the largest amount of revenue from this type of resource.

Non-landed resources were, overall, much less financially important to each of these queens. Margaret of Anjou experienced the greatest difficulty in collecting her non-landed revenues even though the largest portion, about 70 per cent, of her total dower revenues were meant to come from non-landed grants. Some were dependable sources of revenue, but many others posed problems for the queen. The lag in payments or outright inability to collect her entitled revenue from these sources necessitated frequent recourse to yet more grants from other sources to make up for it. For Elizabeth Woodville and Elizabeth of York, non-landed resources appear to have been significantly less consistent but no doubt just as important in monetary terms in Elizabeth of York's case. However, certain types of non-landed grants were vitally important in non-financial terms. A case in point was wardships. Wardships did not just contribute revenue; they also provided non-financial benefits such as opportunities to exercise patronage.

In the case of queen's gold, these late fifteenth-century queens clearly believed that they were entitled to claim and collect it just as their predecessors did. Insofar as the existing sources show, the numbers of issued writs markedly declined when we look both from one queen to another and, for Elizabeth Woodville, throughout her life as queen. Coupled with the distinctly lower monetary amounts expected and probably collected as well, it is obvious that by the late fifteenth century the financial significance of queen's gold had become relatively negligible. This difference is even more stark in comparison with the previous two centuries when cash grants and queen's gold were highly important sources of revenue to queens such as Eleanor of Provence and Eleanor of Castile.

Major changes occurred in the types of resources made available to the queens as dowers and for the provision of revenues. The changes in how to provide for a queen consort, especially the move towards more landed sources, can be discerned to some extent even in the early fourteenth century. Land was granted to Eleanor of Provence in the thirteenth century to provide her with additional income to support her household and this set an early precedent for the general use of land endowments for the queen's provision.[147] This shift continued further as demonstrated by the changes in dower grants made to the two queens Elizabeth compared with Margaret. Landed resources were now used as the primary method of providing for a queen consort, the evidence suggesting that such resources provided the queens with higher levels of reliability and consistency in revenue collection. This change has important implications for our knowledge of how successive queens after Margaret of Anjou supported themselves and what this meant for perceptions of their queenships. If we are to understand and appreciate these implications, the next step is to explore their landed resources in much more detail.

[147] Howell, 'The Resources of Eleanor of Provence', 388.

PART I

LANDS AND ESTATES:
A MAJOR SOURCE OF REVENUE

2

SURVEYING THE QUEEN'S LANDS

> Who will beware in purchasing
> Consider the points here following:
> First see that the land be clear
> In title of the seller;
> And that it stand in no danger
> Of any woman's dower;
> See whether the tenure be bond or free;
> And see release of every feoffee;
> See that the seller be of age,
> And that it lie in no mortgage;
> See whether an entail thereof be found
> And whether it be in statute bound;
> Consider what service belongs thereto,
> And what rent out of it must go:[1]

Land was highly prized by the nobility and gentry of England and was central to their lifestyles and livelihoods. Many noble families reached the heights of power and influence almost solely on the back of their landed resources, which were of great importance and not to be squandered. To be sure, as the above anonymous advice shows, there were many pitfalls that could trip up a premodern investor and purchaser of land. Land could carry with it many encumbrances and defective land title was a major hazard in the land market of the fifteenth century. Nevertheless, K. B. McFarlane, in his study of the investments made by Sir John Fastolf, views such encumbrances as posing insufficient risk to discourage would-be landowners; advantages aplenty, it was inferred, awaited the judicious investor in land.[2] As McFarlane points out, 'land had for [Fastolf] immaterial attractions…it brought him vexation

---

[1] Lines 3–16, 'No. 576 "Anonymous advice to investors in land in the fifteenth century"', *English Historical Documents, Vol. IV, 1327–1485*, ed. A. R. Myers (London: Eyre & Spottiswoode, 1969), 1012–13. This is the modernised version of the advice discussed by K. B. McFarlane in his study of the investments made by Sir John Fastolf, as mentioned above. McFarlane, 'The Investment of Sir John Fastolf's Profits of War', *TRHS* 7 (1957): 91–116.
[2] McFarlane, 'The Investment of Sir John Fastolf's Profits of War', 111–12.

but prestige, and the sheer joy of ownership'.[3] Fastolf's attitude towards land encapsulated the mindset of the nobility and gentry in that regard. For them, land equalled wealth and provided the resources to fund their households, live their lives and exercise patronage in all its forms.[4]

Queens and their domestic situations, naturally, were not the same as noble families; the dynamics of queens owning lands and estates are not strictly analogous with that of the nobility. For this reason, a separate analysis needs to be undertaken for queens since, as will be discussed, their position as a landholder was unlike any other in the land. Obviously, lands and estates were not the only foundation of a queen's power and influence but they could be the primary basis of her practical resources, which in turn provided the necessary concrete material foundations for her claim to authority. The queen's role as landowner and the connections between her and her landholdings deserve to be explored on their own terms and placed within the wider political, economic and social context of the period. Doing so enables us to consider how embedded the queen was in the economic landscape of her time. How extensive a landholder was she and were her rights and responsibilities as a landholder the same as those of any other? What did it mean for the specific lands, firstly, to have a female owner (even if she was the queen) and, secondly, when the individual occupying the position of queen changed?

The unusual circumstances of the second half of the fifteenth century for the monarchy lends this issue added significance. The queens in this study owed their allegiance to different political sides and witnessed events that disturbed the conventional order of monarchic succession. Their experiences as queens were very different from the theory that was meant to underpin a monarchy based on bloodlines. Theoretically, a queen's property should have passed seamlessly from generation to generation within her own bloodlines. What was bestowed on her as queen consort should, on her death, have been returned to the Crown – with her son as the king – so that it could then be passed on to the new consort, the wife of the new king, and so on. The history of queens in the late medieval period in England shows that in reality this arrangement was haphazard at best. To recap, each new king after Henry VI in the fifteenth century was a new claimant to the throne. Correspondingly, each new queen consort after Margaret of Anjou marked the beginning of a new dynastic generation, a disruptive process that ended only with the accession of Henry VIII in 1509, the second son of Henry VII and Elizabeth of York. These chaotic circumstances make the findings in this chapter all the more noteworthy.

---

[3] *Ibid.*, 116.
[4] Kate Mertes, 'Aristocracy', in *Fifteenth-Century Attitudes: Perceptions of Society in Late Medieval England*, ed. Rosemary Horrox (Cambridge; New York: Cambridge University Press, 1994), 49.

Surveying the Queen's Lands

THE QUEEN'S LEGAL POSITION AS LANDHOLDER

The first step in this survey of queenly lands is to consider the queen's legal position as a landowner in fifteenth-century England. This is an important issue given that the queen was a married woman in the upper-most echelons of society and, despite her unique status, one might expect that she would be subject to the same legal frameworks as other elite women of the period where property was concerned. Amy Erickson's study of women and property in early modern England gives us some hint of the complexities that can arise when considering women's legal positions concerning property.[5] By the late medieval and early modern periods, England generally operated within four legal jurisdictions. These were common, ecclesiastical, manorial, and equity law, which covered all the different types of property.[6] In addition, there were two other major factors affecting women and property – the law and customs governing inheritance, and women's marital status.

This study deals with real property or freehold land and summarises the issue of the inheritance of such property as follows. The inheritance of freehold land was chiefly governed by common law, and in medieval and early modern England such land was passed down according to the rules of primogeniture. Eldest sons inherited the whole of their fathers' landholdings; hence, the land would not be partitioned but would be passed down intact if a son inherited his deceased father's property. Generally, only if there was no living son would a daughter or daughters inherit, being preferred over any living male descendants of their fathers' extended relatives. In such circumstances, the landholdings would be divided equally among the daughters, even though upon a daughter's marriage her inheritance was typically incorporated within the holdings and property of the family into which she married. Examples of aristocratic women who held property in their own right in medieval England include the de Clare sisters (Eleanor de Clare, Lady Despenser, Margaret de Clare, countess of Cornwall, and Elizabeth de Clare, Lady de Burgh), who inherited equal shares in the property of their brother, Gilbert de Clare, earl of Hertford, after he was killed at the Battle of Bannockburn in 1314, leaving no surviving children.[7] By the late medieval period, families could even

---

[5] For an overview of the framework of legal jurisdictions governing inheritance of property, see Amy Louise Erickson, *Women and Property in Early Modern England* (London; New York: Routledge, 1993), 24–30.

[6] The two principal types of property were personal and real property. Personal property referred to 'moveable goods', including money, clothing, furniture and debts. Real property referred to freehold land. However, there were two other types of land, copyhold and leasehold. The possible situations that could arise within the context of multiple legal jurisdictions and types of property are tabulated in Erickson, *Women and Property*, 24.

[7] For the de Clare sisters, see, for example, Kathryn Warner, *Edward II's Nieces, The Clare Sisters: Power Pawns of the Crown* (Barnsley: Pen and Sword, 2020).

employ several different legal devices, such as enfeoffment, to divert property to daughters and younger sons even though there was an eldest living son to inherit.[8] Gender, it seems, was not an overwhelming barrier to women owning lands and property.

Marital status was the more crucial issue affecting women and ownership. As Amy Froide states in a study using marital status as a category of analysis, it was 'an important differentiating factor between women'; women of different marital states possessed different positions at law with regard to any sort of property.[9] In terms of property ownership, therefore, there were generally two types of women: those who were married and those who were not. Technically, unmarried women could attain parity with men at law. They were termed *femme sole* and were accorded the legal ability to 'hold land, ... [and] own chattels'.[10] Theoretically, at least, they could own, purchase and dispose of any sort of property, draw up contracts, and initiate or defend any lawsuits.[11] It was marriage that changed their status at law. In principle, if not always in practice, women lost their separate identity once married and became subsumed into that of their husbands.

The common law, as per the doctrine of coverture, was clear regarding a married woman's legal existence; known now as a *femme couvert*, she no longer possessed one.[12] Once married, a woman was not allowed to conduct

---

[8] Enfeoffment refers to a legal process whereby legal title of estates or property is vested in a group of feoffees who undertake to observe the conditions on which the grant was made as well as run the estate according to the feoffor's (the grantor's) wishes. For more information concerning such legal devices, see R. R. Davies, *Lords and Lordship in the British Isles in the Late Middle Ages* (Oxford: Oxford University Press, 2009), especially Chapter Five: Land, Family, and Marriage.

[9] Amy Froide, 'Marital Status as a Category of Difference: Singlewomen and Widows in Early Modern England', in *Singlewomen in the European Past, 1250–1800*, eds Judith M. Bennett and Amy Froide (Philadelphia: University of Pennsylvania Press, 1999), 237.

[10] Sir Frederick Pollock and Frederic William Maitland, *The History of English Law Before the Time of Edward I* (London: Cambridge University Press, 1968), I, 482.

[11] Reality belied the apparent simplicity of the theoretical framework outlined here. Women were not always placed on equal footing with men in relation to property inheritance since there were different legal jurisdictions in operation and different categories of property, not all of which were necessarily subject to the same inheritance principles. Moreover, it would not be accurate to place women who had never married on the exact same footing as widows, since women who never married could still remain under the control of their fathers or other male family members. Nonetheless, inheritance law at least did not exclude women outright even if it did generally favour men.

[12] The term *femme couvert* refers to a woman whose legal existence has been 'covered' or subsumed by marriage. For more information about the doctrine of coverture, see the essays in *Married Women and the Law: Couverture in England and the Common Law World*, eds. Tim Stretton and Krista J. Kesselring (London:

business as unmarried women could. She was legally disallowed from signing contracts, engaging in lawsuits or even writing binding wills without her husband's consent. In addition, her property rights became significantly diminished. Any personal property she might have owned became the legal possessions of her husband as married women could not own or hold any such belongings, with the exception of paraphernalia. Nor did she, generally, have any reciprocal rights to her husband's personal property. Wives did not have legal rights to own, purchase or dispose of any holdings such as land owned within the family, either by selling or gifting. Moreover, her husband became the administrator of and profited from any inherited estates she brought to the marriage.

This stark theoretical state of affairs relating to women and property in the fifteenth century was in reality moderated by the system of marriage settlements. Such settlements were primarily concerned with matters involving money and property and were usually drawn up in the form of formal contracts by the male members of the families concerned.[13] By the late medieval period in England three main elements were involved – dowry, jointure and dower.[14] Dowry, also known as *maritagium* (marriage portion), was given as money or land by the father on his daughter's marriage and paid directly to the husband's family. It was not necessarily meant to benefit the wife herself.[15] Jointure was a mechanism that increasingly became more popular than dowry in the late medieval period and was created in the marriage contract. It typically involved property provided by the husband's family and was settled jointly on the couple but was also meant to support the wife should she be widowed.[16] The income from such property was delivered to the husband during the marriage. However, on his death, a jointure formed part of a widow's personal property and could be passed on to subsequent

---

McGill-Queen's University Press, 2013) and *Married Women and the Law in Premodern Northwest Europe*, eds. Cordelia Beattie and Matthew Frank Stevens (Woodbridge: Boydell Press, 2013).

[13] Only those segments of society that had money and property to dispose of would realistically concern themselves with marriage settlements.

[14] For studies on marriage settlements in the early medieval and later early modern periods, see the following: Penelope Nash, 'Shifting Terrain – Italy and Germany Dancing in Their Own Tapestry', *Journal of the Australian Early Medieval Association* 6 (2010): 53–73; Penelope Nash, 'Jane Austen and Medieval Women: What on Earth Do They Have in Common?', *Sensibilities* 56 (June 2018): 49–67; Janet L. Nelson, 'The Wary Widow', in *Property and Power in the Early Middle Ages*, eds W. Davies and P. Fouracre (Cambridge: Cambridge University Press, 1995), 82–113.

[15] Jennifer Ward, *English Noblewomen in the Later Middle Ages* (London; New York: Longman, 1992), 25.

[16] Barbara J. Harris, *English Aristocratic Women, 1450–1550: Marriage and Family, Property and Careers* (Oxford: Oxford University Press, 2002), 22–4.

husbands or heirs other than those fathered with the original husband.[17] Dower was the husband's gift to his wife upon their marriage and intended for her maintenance and that of any of their offspring should he predecease her.[18] Although the beginnings of dower can be traced back to the pre-Conquest period, by the fifteenth century in England dower had become a common law mechanism that automatically provided a widow with one-third of all her husband's freehold land.[19] However, she owned and profited from the lands only while she lived; on her death they passed to the heirs of her husband. For the women themselves, dower and jointure provided longer-term financial security, but it is important to note that they were not theoretically allowed to independently access the resources set aside for these purposes while their husbands were alive. Only as widows were they able to do so. In short, the key point is that a married woman did not have any legal title to dower lands or estates while her husband lived, nor did she have independent legal control or access to jointure lands, even though she shared legal title with her husband.[20]

If a married noblewoman was widowed, she automatically attained *femme sole* status as a (once-again) unmarried woman with all the attendant legal powers and benefits, particularly relating to landholdings and property. However, if she remarried, her renewed loss of autonomous legal rights could have serious consequences. Newly remarried widows lost ownership and control of their own lands to their new husbands. It was precisely this reasoning that led Henry VII to seek and obtain a special Act of Parliament in 1485 to give his mother, Margaret Beaufort, countess of Richmond and Derby, *femme sole* status so that she might retain direct control over her massive estate holdings rather than cede control to her third husband, Thomas Stanley, earl of Derby.[21]

With regard to property and landholdings, the position of queens should have been analogous to that of married noble and aristocratic women. They, too, should have been regarded as *femme couvert* with no independent access

---

[17] Ward, *English Noblewomen*, 26.
[18] Janet Senderowitz Loengard, '"Of the Gift of Her Husband": English Dower and Its Consequences in the Year 1200', in *Women of the Medieval World: Essays in Honor of John H. Mundy*, eds Julius Kirshner and Suzanne Wemple (Oxford; New York: Blackwell, 1985), 215.
[19] Erickson, *Women and Property*, 25, n. 14.
[20] An interesting contrast to the situation in England can be found in Shennan Hutton's work on women's economic activities in late medieval Ghent. Hutton demonstrates that women were able to perform economic activities without male supervision or representation in geographic regions other than England. This included owning and managing property in their own right, no matter what their marital status was. Shennan Hutton, *Women and Economic Activities in Late Medieval Ghent* (New York: Palgrave Macmillan, 2011).
[21] 'Henry VII: November 1485', in PROME, vi-284-5, vi-311-12; Harris, *English Aristocratic Women*, 19.

to dower or jointure. Yet medieval queens' access to their dowers developed along different paths from married women in general. By the fifteenth century, unlike most married medieval women, queens could as a matter of course obtain and make use of the revenues from their dowers. This points to a significant advantage for the queens in terms of having practical resources for building their bases of power and influence. But the question remains as to whether the queens were merely allowed to accept and keep the revenues for their own use or whether they were considered the legal owners of their estates. This is a significant issue because ownership of a landholding or property implied accessibility to the said item, control and usage of its resources, and a certain degree of freedom to alienate it as desired.

The queen's dower was originally meant to support her as dowager queen, even if the dower was granted while the queen was consort and not yet a widow. Yet the way that queenly dower was held throughout the medieval period was not static. Both pre-Conquest and Anglo-Norman queens could hold land and property in their own right, with full rights and access even to dower lands that had been granted to them.[22] By the twelfth century, however, dower was not automatically granted to queens consort; it was granted only if it was needed for additional income, as in the case of Matilda of Boulogne, wife to Stephen, twelfth-century king of England.[23] The situation changed yet again for thirteenth-century queens. Johnstone regards the thirteenth- and fourteenth-century queens starting with Eleanor of Provence as having access to their dowers as queen consort.[24] But the holding of queenly dower, specifically in the cases of Eleanor of Provence and Eleanor of Castile, was not as clear cut as Johnstone would have it.[25] Katia Wright demonstrates instead that after the Anglo-Norman period it was not until the fourteenth century during the reign of Edward III (his queen being Philippa of Hainault) that queens once again began to access their dower lands during their husbands' lifetimes.[26] Thereafter, this arrangement continued as the model for future queens in England. By the middle of the fifteenth century, there was a clear precedent for

---

[22] There are many examples for pre-Conquest queens in Marc Anthony Meyer, 'The Queen's "Demesne" in Later Anglo-Saxon England', in *The Culture of Christendom: Essays in Medieval History in Commemoration of Denis L. T. Bethell*, ed. Marc Anthony Meyer (London; Rio Grande: Hambledon Press, 1993), 75–113. For Anglo-Norman queens, see Margaret Howell, *Eleanor of Provence: Queenship in Thirteenth-Century England* (Oxford: Blackwell, 1998), 260.

[23] Heather J. Tanner, 'Queenship: Office, Custom, or Ad Hoc? The Case of Queen Matilda III of England (1135–1152)', in *Eleanor of Aquitaine: Lord and Lady*, eds Bonnie Wheeler and John Carmi Parsons (Basingstoke: Palgrave Macmillan, 2003), 136–8.

[24] Johnstone II, 253.

[25] Howell, 'The Resources of Eleanor of Provence', 380–4; Parsons, *Eleanor of Castile*, 122.

[26] Wright, 'The Queen's Lands', 115–16.

the practice of granting lands and property to queens as their dower for use during their lifetimes, including while their husbands were alive.

For the queens in this study, there exists a variety of evidence that points to the queen being regarded as the legal owner of her landholdings. In the first place, the queen could be and usually was given specific authority to deal with all matters concerning her dower properties and to benefit from the outgoings and profits, except that these properties were recognised as being hers only for the term of her life. As discussed in the previous chapter, the exact phrasing in the records could vary.[27] The wording of dower grants to the queens in this study most frequently includes the key phrase 'grant for life'. Occasionally the documents state that the queen was to 'have, hold and enjoy' various lands and estates, or, for instance, in the case of the grant of the manor of Greenwich to Elizabeth Woodville, the grant expressly states that the queen was 'to hold the same ... as the said duke held them'.[28] Regardless of the specific terminology used, these royal grants entirely emphasised the queen's authority over the lands and estates granted to her, besides clarifying her rights and responsibilities. Furthermore, in administrative terms, the queens were considered the legal lords of their landholdings. The above-mentioned grants note that the queen's officials had administrative autonomy without being subject to the king or anyone else, and evidence of the same assumption can be gleaned from court rolls. Some of the court rolls for the manor of Havering-atte-Bower, for instance, specify that the court of Queen Margaret was in session, while later rolls record Elizabeth Woodville as the lord of the manor court.[29]

The queens also appeared to regard themselves as wholly and legally lords of the landholdings granted to them. In a letter written by Margaret of Anjou to the Corporation of London, the queen unmistakably referred to the residents of Enfield as being her tenants when she complained about their treatment at the hands of officials from the city of London.[30] In a different letter by Margaret, there is clear reference to a knight called John Montgomery whom the queen considered to be her tenant-in-chief in Enfield.[31] Similarly, Elizabeth Woodville's letter to Sir William Stonor concerning his illegal deer-hunting in the forest of Barnwood, Buckinghamshire, confirms that the queen considered herself to be the lord of the forest and that her legal rights had been

---

[27] See pp. 17–18.

[28] The previous owner of Greenwich manor was Humphrey, duke of Gloucester. CPR 1461–67, 433–4; 'Henry VII: November 1487', in PROME, vi-387.

[29] For example, ERO D/DU 102/44–45 (Margaret of Anjou) and D/DU 102/47–50, 134 (Elizabeth Woodville).

[30] *The Letters of Margaret of Anjou*, eds. Helen Maurer and B. M. Cron (Woodbridge: Boydell Press, 2019), 90 (no. 52).

[31] *The Letters of Margaret of Anjou*, 63 (no. 36).

usurped. She was, in her own mind, well within her rights to demand that he cease and desist from such activity.[32]

Nevertheless, it is not necessarily correct to conclude that the queens of fifteenth-century England were accorded *femme sole* status *de jure* as well as *de facto*. The special Act of Parliament by which Margaret Beaufort, Henry VII's mother, attained *femme sole* status contained the phrase 'shall be vested and remain in her alone by the same entry, as if she were single and unmarried'.[33] This phrase is not found in any of the Acts granting the queens their dower lands and is indicative of the special status that the king's mother was being afforded. It also strongly suggests that, technically, the queens consort were not being legally accorded *femme sole* status by their dower grants even though they appear to have been acting autonomously after the fashion of the legal landowner.

This ambiguity in the legal status of the queens as landowners has implications for our understanding of what the queens were able to do in these roles. Landowners had rights and responsibilities in relation to their lands, tenants and the people who served them in their estates. The issue is whether the queens enjoyed those rights and were bound by those obligations. In practice, the queens of this study claimed ownership and administered their own dower and jointure lands even though their technical legal status appears to be debatable. They could also purchase or acquire additional lands in their own name and dispose of them as well. In this sense, therefore, the queen occupied a position more closely equivalent with that of a widowed noble or aristocratic woman.[34] While she might not legally be a *femme sole*, in practice and in relation to her landholdings, at least, she acted as one. She was the legal owner of all estates granted to her, she held and exercised all the responsibilities of the lord, and she could benefit from the revenues and agricultural produce, among other things, of those same estates. Thus, she was able to call upon those holdings and include them among the practical resources that she needed in either direct or indirect establishment of power and influence. In brief, the queens consort of this period were not disadvantaged either by their gender or by their status as married women where landownership was concerned.

There is an additional point that needs to be addressed: that is, what happened to ownership of the queen's lands during the period of Henry VI's Readeption. In the previous chapter, I discussed what happened to the queens' dowers during the frequent monarchic changes, from the Lancastrians to the Yorkists and later from the Yorkists to the Tudors. The Readeption involved even more complications for the queens' dowers and lands. As mentioned, Margaret had

---

[32] *Letters of the Queens of England, 1100–1547*, ed. Anne Crawford (Stroud: Sutton, 1994), 135.
[33] 'Henry VII: November 1485', in PROME, vi-284–5.
[34] St John, *Three Medieval Queens*, 84.

been attainted and was never considered to be the rightful queen dowager by Edward IV. It is possible that when Henry VI regained his throne in October 1470, a similar fate might eventually have befallen Elizabeth Woodville, who had sought sanctuary with her children in Westminster Abbey. As an attainted queen, she would not have been entitled to any dower whatsoever. But even if she had been considered the rightful queen dowager, any lands she might have been granted in dower would certainly have been different from the lands owned by Margaret as queen consort. So, during Henry VI's Readeption, Margaret of Anjou theoretically should have regained her queen's lands and Elizabeth Woodville should have relinquished ownership of hers. This change in ownership might be illustrated by examining the estate documents for lands that were granted to and owned by both queens, such as the manor of Pleshey in Essex. However, accounts for this period compiled by the Pleshey bailiff show that Elizabeth Woodville was still considered the landowner during this period and revenues were being received by the deputy of the Essex receiver, Roger Ree, who served Elizabeth rather than Margaret.[35] Clearly, therefore, the administrative changes in ownership of this particular manor, at least, had not taken place. This shows at the very least that a period of eight months was insufficient for any monarchic changes to effect corresponding changes in the estate administrative machinery for the queen's lands. Henry VI's second and final loss of his crown in May 1471 renders moot the question of any possible resolution to the problem, securing as it did the ascendancy of the Yorkists and Elizabeth Woodville's position as the royal consort.

GEOGRAPHICAL DISTRIBUTION AND EXTENT OF THE QUEENS' LANDS

Having considered the legality of the queens as landholders and landowners, I will now survey the extent and variety of the lands and estates owned by Margaret of Anjou, Elizabeth Woodville and Elizabeth of York. Bearing in mind the fact that not all the lands granted to each of these queens were owned for the entirety of the periods during which they were queen, a comparative examination of their landholdings from non-financial perspectives will provide additional insights into a number of issues. These include similarities and differences in the distribution of each queen's lands and each individual's possible spheres of influence and authority as well as bases for their political and social networks.

The grant made in 1446 endowed Margaret of Anjou with many holdings, some of which were from the estates of the Duchy of Lancaster, which had become part of the royal patrimony on the accession of Henry Bolingbroke

---

[35] See TNA DL29/43/840, DL29/44/841–2. The queen's name appears on the title of each of these documents.

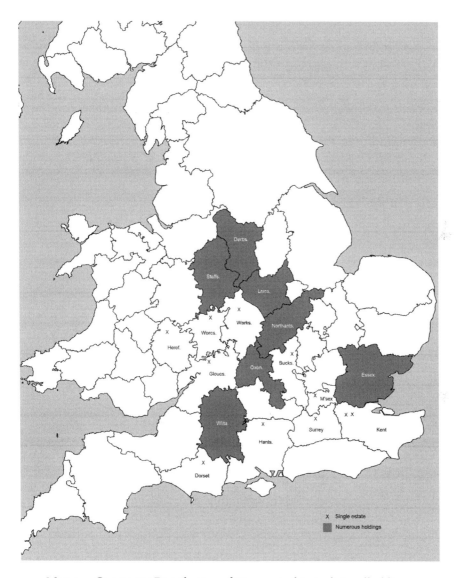

Map 1. Composite Distribution of Margaret of Anjou's Landholdings.

as Henry IV in 1399.[36] As the composite map in Map 1 shows, her holdings included a large number and variety in London and in the counties of Essex, Hertfordshire, Leicestershire, Middlesex and Staffordshire.[37] Margaret was also granted many holdings in Derbyshire, a number of individual manors in the counties of Buckinghamshire, Herefordshire and Surrey, the manor of Yarkhill in Herefordshire, and the castle and lordship of Kenilworth in Warwickshire. The queen received several manors in Oxfordshire as well, such as Haseley and Pyrton, which had been part of the lands in the 'south parts' of the Duchy of Lancaster.[38]

Later grants in 1447, 1452, 1454 and 1457 added a host of additional holdings in Berkshire, Dorset, Essex, Hampshire, Kent, Northamptonshire, Wiltshire, and Worcestershire to her considerably large estate. Some very important and valuable assets were included, such as the manor of Feckenham, the castles and lordships of Odiham in Hampshire, Rockingham in Northamptonshire, Marlborough and Devizes in Wiltshire, and the manor of Havering-atte-Bower in Essex.[39] In general, Margaret's holdings were predominantly located in the Midlands, but she did own substantial properties in the east and south-west of England, particularly in Essex and Wiltshire.

Elizabeth Woodville had been widowed already when she married Edward IV in 1464. Thus, from her first marriage to Sir John Grey, she owned the manors of Brington in Northamptonshire and Woodham Ferrers in Essex as her dower.[40] After she was crowned queen in 1465, she was given a significant number of lands and fee-farms, most of which were granted and confirmed between the years 1465–67. In his history of the Duchy of Lancaster, Robert Somerville outlines instances when the queen surrendered certain properties

[36] B. P. Wolffe, *The Royal Demesne in English History: The Crown Estate in the Governance of the Realm from the Conquest to 1509* (London: Allen and Unwin, 1971), 76.

[37] Appendix 1 contains a detailed composite listing of Margaret of Anjou's landed holdings. Appendix 2 contains a composite list of Margaret of Anjou's fee-farms.

[38] Lands in the 'south parts' of the Duchy of Lancaster were located in the counties of Hampshire, Wiltshire, Somerset, Dorset, Devon, Cornwall, Berkshire, Oxford, Hereford and Worcester. This group is different from the duchy's 'South Parts', that is, those located south of the River Trent. Somerville, *The History of the Duchy of Lancaster*, 99.

[39] Some of these holdings were granted to the queen in recompense for depriving her of the revenues of the earldom of Pembroke, which instead were granted to the king's half-brother Jasper Tudor when he was made earl of Pembroke. CPR 1446–52, 56, 559; CPR 1452–61, 339–40; 'Henry VI: March 1453', in PROME, v-261.

[40] Sir John Grey was a Lancastrian supporter who was killed in the second Battle of St Albans in 1461. Woodham Ferrers was held by Edward IV 'in possession and title of his consort, Elizabeth, queen of England ...' but no similar evidence has been found for the manor of Brington. CPR 1461–67, 533.

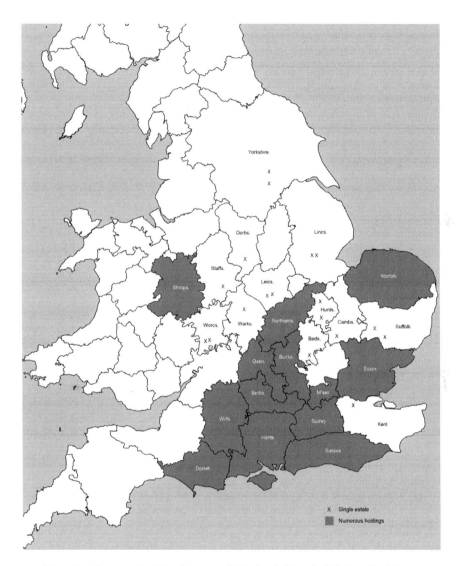

Map 2. Composite Distribution of Elizabeth Woodville's Landholdings.

and was compensated with others.[41] However, source evidence could not be found to substantiate his claims. In the case of Blaunch Appelton, for example, receivers accounts for the Essex/Hertford/Middlesex group of lands wholly contradict his claim that it was not regranted to the queen. On the whole, Elizabeth acquired more of the traditional queens' lands in the 'south parts' of the Duchy of Lancaster in the original grant of her dower than Margaret of Anjou did, although Margaret gained more such lands through later grants. Elizabeth was endowed with more lands, for example, in Wiltshire, Hampshire, Dorset and Berkshire than her predecessor. Overall, Edward IV's consort owned and possessed estates in a sizeable portion of England's southern and central regions, especially the Home Counties. She was granted nothing in the North, Somerset, Devon or Cornwall and possessed only a few properties in Kent, Dorset, Staffordshire and Suffolk.

The composite map in Map 2 illustrates the extent of Elizabeth's landholdings but it must be noted that some of them were acquired via other grants and commercial transactions.[42] She actively participated in the land market and also gained shares in properties that were subject to attainder or wardship. Elizabeth gained interests and was, therefore, able to extend her reach as landholder in counties such as Essex, Oxford and Northamptonshire, among others.[43] For example, her purchase of the Fitzlewis manors brought both financial advantages and opportunities to dispense patronage. Additionally, the quitclaim of December 1476 whereby William Huse gave a large group of people, including the queen, shares in sixty-five different properties and holdings would also have greatly benefitted Elizabeth.[44] Although she had to share the financial rewards, she obtained portions in a significant number of additional holdings in Derbyshire, Shropshire, Yorkshire, Surrey and Sussex. Derbyshire, Shropshire and Yorkshire were counties in which she had not previously owned any properties. In others, such as Sussex and Leicestershire, Elizabeth already owned properties that were close in proximity to some that were included in the Huse transfer. Examples of this included the queen's manor of East Grinstead, Sussex, and the town of Godmanchester, from which the queen received a fee-farm. The former was located within the hundred of Grinstead that was counted in the Huse transfer and the latter was located near the Huse-owned manors of Dysworth and Seagrave.

There were substantial benefits to be gained from these land transactions and shares in properties, not least since the queen's interests here were not the same as her interests in those lands granted to her. Unlike dower lands that were endowed only for the term of her natural life, the queen's interests

---

[41] Somerville, *The History of the Duchy of Lancaster*, 238–9.
[42] See Appendix 1 and Appendix 2 for a list of Elizabeth Woodville's landholdings and fee-farms, respectively.
[43] Neal, 'The Queen's Grace', 113–14.
[44] CCR 1476–85, 30.

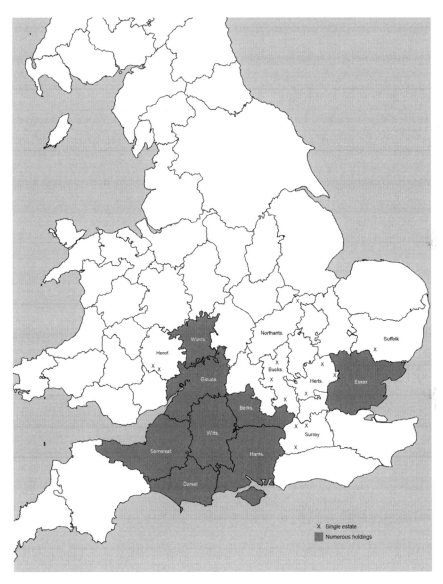

Map 3. Composite Distribution of Elizabeth of York's Landholdings.

in shared properties could be given to her 'heirs and assigns'.[45] There were, doubtless, financial benefits in the form of revenues from the lands and properties. Nonetheless, the queen would also have prized the non-financial benefits, such as opportunities for patronage, since these were resources she could use to provide for her dependants as she wished.

The circumstances surrounding the dower grants made to Elizabeth of York in 1487 meant that her dower lands essentially represented a subset of those re-granted to her mother Elizabeth Woodville, the queen dowager, by Henry VII in March 1486. Elizabeth of York received the majority of but not all her mother's lands and holdings when the queen dowager retired to Bermondsey Abbey. For example, in Berkshire, she received the holdings of Cookham and Bray, Swallowfield, Hamstead Marshall, Benham, Holbenham and Westbroke but not the manors of East Garston, Lambourn, Upper Lambourne, Hungerford, Wood Speen or Hinton. Likewise, Elizabeth received only some of her mother's dower lands in the counties of Wiltshire and Dorset and nothing at all in other counties such as Northamptonshire and Oxfordshire. Moreover, it appears that she never possessed any landholdings in other Midlands and Home Counties, such as Middlesex, Derbyshire, Oxfordshire, Staffordshire and Sussex.

However, as mentioned on p. 28, the queen's total landholdings were significantly enlarged in 1495 when she gained the lands of her grandmother, Cecily Neville, the dowager duchess of York. The 1492 grant of this inheritance by Henry VII to his queen stipulated that on the duchess' death, her lands on reverting to the Crown would be given to the queen consort.[46] Cecily Neville died three years later in 1495 and her granddaughter, the queen, was then given those lands, which were located in the counties of Berkshire, Dorset, Somerset, Gloucestershire, Hampshire, Herefordshire, Hertfordshire, Wiltshire and Worcestershire. With the addition of these York lands to her own holdings, Elizabeth of York became a significant landholder in the West Country counties of Somerset and Dorset (see Map 3), a key point of difference between this queen and the others in this study.

Closer comparison of these queens' landholdings reveals many similarities. In Essex, the manors and lordships of Bradwell, Havering-atte-Bower and Hadley, among many others, were granted to each of these queens as part of their dower lands. Each queen in turn was granted the manor of Hamstead Marshall in Berkshire, the manor of Walton in Surrey, the manor, town and barton of Gillingham in Dorset, the manor and forest of Feckenham in Worcestershire, and the manor and lordship of Odiham in Hampshire. The county of Wiltshire also contained many holdings that were regularly granted

---

[45] CPR 1467–77, 419, 543. No records have yet been found showing what assignments, if any, the queen made in later years in relation to these holdings.
[46] CPR 1485–94, 369–70.

to the queens as dower, including the castles and lordships of Marlborough and Devizes, as well as the forests of Savernake, Melksham and Pewsham. There are also holdings that were owned by both Margaret of Anjou and Elizabeth Woodville but not by Elizabeth of York. These were Crondon manor in Buckinghamshire, the manor of Pleasaunce in Greenwich, several important holdings in Northamptonshire, such as the castle and lordship of Rockingham, and some manors in Oxfordshire. There are unsurprisingly many similarities between the landholdings of the two queens Elizabeth, given the circumstances surrounding the grants by Henry VII to each of them.

Besides the similarities, there are also some marked differences between all these queens' landholdings. For instance, in Derbyshire, Margaret possessed more than a dozen manors, several wards and bailiwicks, and the castles and lordships of Melbourne and High Peak. In contrast, Elizabeth Woodville owned no more than four messuages and three hundred acres of land in Melton, Wylyngton, Assheborne and Howys in the same county (obtained as a share in the Huse quitclaim), and Elizabeth of York owned nothing at all. Likewise, in county Stafford, Margaret was granted the important castle, manor and honour of Tutbury in addition to a significant number of other manors, bailiwicks and wards; none of these was granted to her successors except the bailiwick of the Honour of Tutbury, which was endowed on Elizabeth Woodville.[47]

Conversely, Elizabeth Woodville was granted numerous holdings in East Anglia as well as in Sussex. Some of these had been owned by some fourteenth-century queens but not by Margaret of Anjou, nor were they subsequently granted to Elizabeth of York.[48] This made Elizabeth Woodville an economic power in the counties of Norfolk and Suffolk. The original dower grant made to Elizabeth Woodville was bolstered by later acquisitions and shares in the Tresham and Huse quitclaim properties, the former of which were concentrated in Northamptonshire and the latter in Shropshire, Surrey and Sussex. Elizabeth Woodville clearly held more lands overall in every county than Margaret of Anjou did, surely the reason why Margaret's expected revenues from those parts were so much lower than her successor's. The disparity in landownership between these two queens is conspicuous in the counties of Berkshire, Dorset, Sussex, Shropshire and Surrey. Where Elizabeth of York was concerned, the most obvious difference between her entire

---

[47] Tutbury was earmarked for George, duke of Clarence, and, therefore, was not available to be granted to the queens after Margaret of Anjou. I am indebted to Dr James Ross for drawing my attention to this fact.

[48] Examples include the manors of Aylsham and Fakenham, the hundreds of North and South Erpingham in Norfolk, and the manor of Soham in Cambridgeshire, all of which were owned by Isabella of France and Philippa of Hainault in the fourteenth century. Wolffe, *The Royal Demesne in English History*, Appendix A; Wright, 'The Queen's Lands', Appendix 2: Comparable Properties.

Financing Queenship in Late Fifteenth Century England

holdings and those of Elizabeth Woodville and Margaret of Anjou is that the younger Elizabeth received the lands of her grandmother, Cecily Neville, the dowager duchess of York. This resulted in her gaining many more lands in the West Country, that is, in the counties of Gloucestershire, Somerset, Dorset, Wiltshire and Worcestershire.

The findings thus far suggest some interesting possibilities about the correlation between the geographical distribution of the landholdings of the queens and their likely spheres of influence and authority. Of these queens, Margaret's power base in terms of lands lay predominantly in the Midland counties, chiefly in Derbyshire, Staffordshire and Leicestershire, although she also held much in Essex and Wiltshire, which contained many traditional queens' dower lands.[49] The elder Elizabeth possessed vast numbers of holdings in all the Home Counties except Kent and her interest was regarded as the 'main instrument of royal authority' in East Anglia, probably on the basis of her Norfolk and Suffolk possessions.[50] In addition, she controlled a large group of holdings, including dower lands and a share in the former Tresham properties, in Northamptonshire. It is interesting to note that Northamptonshire was not only her county of birth; she also held the manor of Brington there as dower from her first marriage.[51] It is not unreasonable to infer that Elizabeth Woodville intentionally pursued a policy of increasing her interests in counties such as Northamptonshire where she could build on her existing power base. Finally, by virtue of receiving the York lands, Elizabeth of York became an economic power in the West Country. This occurred despite the fact that her original grant of lands had been much smaller to begin with. As it was, while these lands were substantial in quantity, the fact remains that Elizabeth of York's possible economic impact as landholder and administrator as well as her potential sphere of influence was on the whole smaller than either Elizabeth Woodville or Margaret of Anjou.

At this juncture, it will be enlightening to briefly compare the landholdings of a fourteenth-century queen consort with those of the fifteenth-century queens of this study, with a view to gauging longer-term changes in the distribution and extent of queens' dower lands. For this, I use Philippa of Hainault since a composite picture of her landholdings can be easily constructed from Wright's work on the queen's lands in fourteenth-century England. There was a vital difference between the composition of fourteenth- and fifteenth-century queens' dower lands, that is, the inclusion of lands from the Duchy

---

[49] The queen's power base in the Midlands, especially in Coventry and Cheshire, was also bolstered by her ability to influence and exploit her connections with her son as Prince of Wales and his council. Griffiths, *The Reign of King Henry VI*, 781–2; Maurer, *Margaret of Anjou*, 106, 133–6.

[50] Rosemary Horrox, *Richard III: A Study of Service* (Cambridge: Cambridge University Press, 1991), 80.

[51] CCR 1461–68, 179; Myers, 'The Household of Queen Elizabeth Woodville', 261, n. 2.

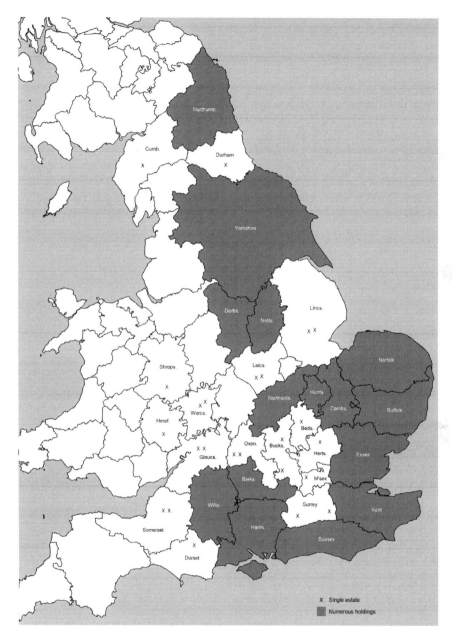

Map 4. Composite Distribution of Philippa of Hainault's Landholdings.

of Lancaster in the dower granted to queens in the fifteenth century from Katherine of Valois onwards. When Henry V died in 1422, his young son, Henry VI, found himself in the position of having to provide for a second queen dowager, his mother Katherine, since the widow of Henry IV, Joan of Navarre, was alive and technically also a queen dowager. Joan held the lands granted to her as dowager and Katherine had to be provided for, partly out of the lands of the duchy of Lancaster.[52] This formed a precedent for future queens of England and explains why there were Duchy of Lancaster lands among those granted to the queens in this study.

Nonetheless, as Map 4 shows, the contrast between Philippa's holdings and those of Margaret and the two Elizabeths is quite stark and cannot wholly be explained by the later inclusion of Duchy of Lancaster lands. Philippa's lands encompassed a far wider geographical area than any of the queens in this study and she had a foothold in far more counties.[53] She held many lands and properties in Yorkshire, Northamptonshire and the East Anglian counties of Norfolk, Suffolk and Cambridgeshire. This queen was a landholder in many other counties in the south and east of England as well, including Wiltshire, Berkshire, Hampshire, Essex and Kent. Closer inspection reveals that among her holdings were important lordships and manors such as Havering-atte-Bower, Odiham, Rockingham, Gillingham, Marlborough and Devizes. These specific holdings were all granted to the fifteenth-century queens of this study but, significantly, most of them (and a great many others listed as queens' lands in the fifteenth century) were granted to all the queens in the fourteenth century, except for Isabella of Valois, Richard II's second and very young queen consort. This points to a fluid group of landholdings that formed the core of the queens' dowers and provided continuity in queens' landholdings from the fourteenth into the fifteenth century.[54]

This comparison supports a contention that despite the differences in the fifteenth-century queens' landholdings, there are enough similarities to demonstrate a degree of continuity in the dower grants of lands to queens. This continuity is entirely in keeping with the tradition of queens being granted lands held by their predecessors. Edward II's queen, Isabella of France, received the bulk of the possessions of her predecessor, Margaret of France, and many of these were in turn granted to her daughter-in-law, Philippa of

---

[52] Woodacre, *Joan of Navarre*, 155.
[53] Map 4 was created using the list of lands owned by Philippa of Hainault in Wright, 'The Queen's Lands', Appendix 1: The Lands of Fourteenth-Century Queens.
[54] Elena Woodacre states that there was not a fixed group of lands owned by all English queens consort. However, the idea of continuous landholdings for successive queens has surfaced in Parsons' work on Eleanor of Castile and in Marc Anthony Meyer's article exploring the proposition that a 'queen's demesne' existed in pre-Conquest England. Meyer, 'The Queen's "Demesne"'; Parsons, *Eleanor of Castile*, 71; Woodacre, *Joan of Navarre*, 148.

Hainault. At a later stage, Philippa's lands were largely granted as dower to her eventual successor, Richard II's first queen, Anne of Bohemia. The upheavals of the accession of Henry IV following the deposition of Richard II upset this trajectory briefly but the king's decision to support a special act of resumption to help free the lands previously owned by Anne of Bohemia for the endowment of his new queen, Joan of Navarre, saw this trajectory resumed.[55]

A final point to note about the differences between Philippa's landholdings and those of the queens in this study concerns their overall distribution. Since Philippa's lands were more widely spread throughout England, it appears that this fourteenth-century queen at least had a far greater reach throughout the country than the late fifteenth-century queens did. This spread had shrunk by the time of Margaret of Anjou and it continued to shrink and shift its locus for her successors. By Elizabeth of York's time, there was a distinct concentration of dower and queenly lands in the south and south-western regions. It is clear that the locus of the queens' landholdings had progressively moved south in the period from the fourteenth century to the early sixteenth century.

Besides the changes in the spread of lands granted to the queens either in dower or for their maintenance, I want to emphasise in this study that the changes in the dowers granted to the two queens Elizabeth point to a change in the level of importance of lands granted to the queens. In monetary terms, Elizabeth Woodville and Elizabeth of York overwhelmingly depended on their landholdings as their primary source of revenue. In Margaret's case, landed sources theoretically made up only a third of her entitled revenues but, compared with many of her other revenue sources, they were reliable and consistent. Moreover, it is important to remember that the grants outlining which lands and estates were to be assigned to Margaret recorded the expected values of the individual holdings. Hence, as per the information in the grants, Margaret was informed about the values of the lands at the time they were granted to her and she possessed expectations as to the amounts that she was entitled to from each of her landed holdings. This was not the case for either Elizabeth. Neither of these queens should have expected specific amounts from any of their individual landholdings since no such values were categorically stated in their dower grants.

Margaret of Anjou's lands were not meant to provide her with all her entitled revenue, only about a third. But that was exactly the objective behind the granting of dower lands to Elizabeth Woodville and Elizabeth of York. After Margaret, there was a distinct and obvious move towards greater reliance on landed sources for the maintenance of the queens. This point takes on even greater significance in comparison with queens from before the latter half of the fifteenth century in England. Eleanor of Provence, for one, obtained greater monetary benefits from queen's gold than from her dower

---

[55] Wolffe, *The Royal Demesne in English History*, 56.

lands.[56] Anne of Bohemia, for another, received grants of substantial amounts of income from customs, making this type of resource an extremely valuable one for her.[57] Thus, these changes in the dower grants to queens after Margaret together with the shifts in geographical spread and extent of the lands granted to each queen indicate that methods for the financial maintenance of queens had shifted significantly, while not being completely overhauled.

FACTORS THAT INFLUENCED CHANGES IN THE QUEENS' DOWER GRANTS

There are a few factors that could have influenced these shifts and changes in how to provide for the queen consort's financial needs. The first and most obvious factor was the financial situation facing England in the fifteenth century, especially during the reigns of Henry VI and his successors. But there are other factors that warrant examination, such as the economic circumstances of the period, the backgrounds of the queens, and developments in the extent of royal authority.

Scholars of fifteenth-century English monarchy and government have long focused on the financial difficulties that dogged the country, causing widespread discontent. The reasons are complex and remain debatable but what matters here is that the financial situation is an obvious reason for the decisions made by the Yorkists and later the Tudors on how to provide for the queens consort.[58] Throughout his reign Henry VI and his government faced constant financial difficulties, and the demands placed on the royal funds by the need to adhere to the provisions of the queen's dower only made matters worse. The dynastic change of kings from Henry VI to Edward IV in 1461 was a jolt to the monarchic system generally but did not markedly improve the financial circumstances of the Crown. Edward IV's Yorkist regime simply inherited the difficult financial situation from the Lancastrians.

When Edward married Elizabeth Woodville in 1464, England acquired a new queen consort who needed to be provided with resources. Yet, the royal finances being what they were, it was simply not possible to follow precedent

---

[56] Howell, 'The Resources of Eleanor of Provence', 390.

[57] Geaman, *Anne of Bohemia*, Appendix 2: Anne's Dower and Grants; Wright, 'The Queen's Lands', 75.

[58] See Alex Brayson, 'Deficit Finance During the Early Majority of Henry VI of England, 1436–1444: The "Crisis" of the Medieval English "Tax State"', *The Journal of European Economic History* 49, no. 1 (2020): 10–13, for an overview of the scholarship on the causes of these financial difficulties. The focus of this article is a longer-term consideration of the reasons, especially from the point of view of structural aspects for the explosion in royal debt in the early fifteenth century that carried through to the end of the century.

and grant the queen as high a dower as that of Margaret of Anjou and some of her predecessors.[59] The Yorkists needed to ensure that the queen was reliably provided for but almost certainly sought to pre-empt any accusations of profligacy in the royal household.[60] Furthermore, Edward IV and his government may well have taken note of Margaret's difficulties in collecting her entitled income from non-landed sources.[61] Therefore, it was a question of finding the most suitable way of dowering Elizabeth Woodville that would serve the needs of the new king and government as well as avoid the problems that the previous queen had encountered.

The solution was to move away entirely from, firstly, stipulating a fixed dower revenue, and, secondly, including non-landed sources of any kind in the queen's dower. A fixed dower amount had resulted in a number of problems for Margaret of Anjou, not least the fact that unreliable collection of revenues from non-landed sources often resulted in additional grants (typically of lands or fee-farms) being awarded to make up for those losses. Elizabeth Woodville's dower was not set at any fixed amount and the sources allocated to her were wholly landed ones. This meant that it was not obvious to onlookers what sums the queen was being allocated in dower and thus it helped forestall any possible complaints that the Yorkists were being as extravagant with funds as the Lancastrians had been. It also meant that should any particular holding or estate be taken from the queen and granted elsewhere, there was no official obligation to replace it with something else to make up a stated shortfall. In any case, given the fact that Margaret's lands and estates turned out to be her most reliable and dependable sources of income, the granting of landholdings and landed sources to the new Yorkist queen was likely to provide her with generally reliable and consistent sources of revenue.

When Henry Tudor came to the throne in 1485 as Henry VII, his marriage to Elizabeth of York a year later provided England with a new queen consort who again needed to be provided for.[62] The fact that she was dowered with lands in the same manner as her mother, Elizabeth Woodville, makes it clear that the solution the Yorkists arrived at in the early 1460s for Edward's queen's dower was viewed favourably enough by the Tudor king to be adopted as well. Edward IV had managed to restore a degree of solvency to the government by the end of his reign. Yet the financial situation was still not so positive that the

---

[59] See Charles Ross, *Edward IV* (London: Methuen, 1974), Chapter 16 for an overview of the king's finances.

[60] See Griffiths, *The Reign of King Henry VI*, 310–19, for a discussion of the costs of Henry VI's household and its financial problems.

[61] Myers, 'The Household of Queen Margaret of Anjou', 140.

[62] The lack of relevant evidence pertaining to Anne Neville, Richard III's queen, means that we can only speculate as to how she might have been dowered, although it is reasonable to assume that Richard would have emulated his brother Edward IV in this regard.

new Tudor monarch could afford to return to the old methods of providing for the royal consort. Indeed, Henry VII continued to face on-going financial difficulties, though he was probably not in as dire financial straits as his three most recent predecessors. Hence, Elizabeth of York's dower, too, did not specify an exact amount of revenue and essentially was comprised of landed sources.

Economic issues may also have been relevant in decisions related to the queens' dowers. Late medieval England experienced several economic and social changes and one of these was in the use of land. Arable land, that is, land used to grow crops, began to be abandoned and reverted to pasture even before the advent of the Black Death in the mid-fourteenth century.[63] The reversion to pasture corresponded to an increase in growth in the enclosure of land for livestock farming, and economic historians such as Alan Baker have demonstrated that enclosure and conversion of arable land took the greatest hold in the southern counties, Home Counties and the Midlands.[64] The importance of this conclusion is accentuated by R. S. Schofield's revision of E. J. Buckatzsch's conclusions in his study of the geographical distribution of wealth during the later Middle Ages.[65] Schofield's analysis, among other things, establishes that by the end of the fifteenth century, lay wealth in the richest counties was increasingly linked to commodities such as wool and cloth and the rate of wealth increase in the southern and Midland counties of England was significantly higher than the rates in the northern and East Anglian counties.[66] In addition, the south-west and south-east counties in particular were increasing more rapidly in wealth than others in the south and Midlands.[67] A later survey by H. C. Darby, J. E. Glasscock, J. Sheail and G. R. Versey has re-visited the issue of wealth distribution in medieval England and does not significantly contradict Schofield's findings. The authors conclude that the main increases in wealth in the late medieval period occurred in, among other places, the south-west peninsula extending eastwards into Gloucestershire and Wiltshire, Essex and Suffolk counties, and the city of London and its surrounds.[68]

---

[63] Alan Baker, 'Changes in the Later Middle Ages', in *A New Historical Geography of England*, ed. H. C. Darby (Cambridge: Cambridge University Press, 1973), 207.

[64] Baker, 'Changes in the Later Middle Ages', 213–14.

[65] For Buckatzsch's work, see E. J. Buckatzsch, 'The Geographical Distribution of Wealth in England, 1086–1843', *EcHR* 3 (1950): 180–202.

[66] R. S. Schofield, 'The Geographical Distribution of Wealth in England, 1334–1649', *EcHR* 18, no. 3 (1965): 507–9.

[67] Schofield, 'The Geographical Distribution of Wealth in England', 509.

[68] H. C. Darby, R. E. Glasscock, J. Sheail, and G. R. Versey, 'The Changing Geographical Distribution of Wealth in England: 1086–1334–1525', *Journal of Historical Geography* 5, no. 3 (1979): 261.

What this suggests is that the variations in wealth distribution throughout different counties and regions may have been another factor influencing the Yorkist government's decisions about which lands to grant in dower to Elizabeth Woodville. It is possible that in the last two to three decades of the fifteenth century at least some of the traditional queens' lands in the southern parts of England were experiencing a higher growth rate than other regions and were, therefore, richer. Such lands may have yielded greater income but, just as importantly, forthcoming revenue may have been more reliable. In effect, the better economic situation of the southern regions may have influenced Edward IV and later Henry VII in their shift in focus to the south when looking at what lands to grant their consorts. They may have believed that the economic state of those lands was healthy enough that no other non-landed sources of revenue were needed for the maintenance of their queens.

The locality of each queens' landholdings undoubtedly mattered a great deal. Margaret of Anjou had a greater number of landholdings in the Midlands counties and was granted a much larger dower than either Elizabeth Woodville or Elizabeth of York. However, she experienced a great deal of difficulty in collecting certain portions of the income due to her.[69] Economic issues surely had as much impact as the traditional explanations of the financial difficulties of the Lancastrian monarchy and government. After all, the middle decades of the fifteenth century experienced economic misfortunes in myriad ways, including problems with England's overseas trade, slumping cloth exports and downward-trending wool and grain prices.[70] The military conflicts engendered by the Lancaster–York feud did not cause these misfortunes but the combination of political unrest, military strife and economic adversity must have contributed to the difficulties Margaret faced in collecting some of her landed revenues. Greater prosperity and economic growth in at least some of the traditional queens' lands in the southern parts of England could help explain why Elizabeth Woodville and Elizabeth of York seemed to experience fewer difficulties in collecting their revenues and hence appear to have been more effective at estate and household management.

It may also partially explain why Elizabeth Woodville was later re-granted a smaller number of dower lands by her new son-in-law, Henry VII, dower

---

[69] Myers, 'The Household of Queen Margaret of Anjou', 107, 115–16.

[70] For research demonstrating economic depression in, for example, Derbyshire in the late medieval period, see I. S. W. Blanchard, 'Economic Change in Derbyshire in the Late Middle Ages, 1272–1540' (unpublished PhD thesis, University of London, 1967). See also the following for research into the economic circumstances of fifteenth-century England: R. H. Britnell, 'The Economic Context', in *The Wars of the Roses*, ed. A. J. Pollard (London: Macmillan, 1995), 45, 47–8; John Hatcher, 'The Great Slump of the Mid-Fifteenth Century', in *Progress and Problems in Medieval England: Essays in Honour of Edward Miller*, eds Richard Britnell and John Hatcher (New York: Cambridge University Press, 1996), 237–72.

lands that were later granted to Elizabeth of York on the older Elizabeth's retirement into monastic life. Henry, mindful of his mother-in-law and her Woodville family's former pre-eminence in political terms, possibly sought to reduce the queen dowager's power base by curtailing the overall number of her lands and estates. Later, he may have also aimed to limit his own queen's capacity to build a power base of her own by granting her far fewer lands that could serve accordingly. Alternatively, he may have believed that the economic state of those lands granted to his consort was healthy enough to sustain a lifestyle and household befitting a queen and, therefore, saw no need to allocate more. As the evidence shows, this did not turn out to be the case and he granted Elizabeth the lands of her grandmother, Cecily Neville, lands that proved to be a significant boost to her overall income.[71]

Then there is the question of whether the backgrounds of Elizabeth Woodville and Elizabeth of York as domestic-born royal consorts might have been a factor influencing the change in the queens' dowers. The norm for post-Conquest England until the mid-fifteenth century was for the king to choose a foreign-born royal or highly placed noblewoman as his queen.[72] Thereafter, there were seven native-born English consorts – Elizabeth Woodville, Anne Neville, Elizabeth of York, Anne Boleyn, Jane Seymour, Katherine Howard and Kateryn Parr (the last four being four of Henry VIII's six queens). After these queens, the practice of English kings choosing foreign-born brides resumed and England would not have another English or British-born queen consort until the twentieth century (Elizabeth, wife of George VI). Warnicke's research on the Tudor queens of Henry VII and his son, Henry VIII, reveals that the mechanism for the queens' financial provision changed further when Henry VIII became king.[73] Unlike his father, Henry VIII granted jointures instead of dowers to all his queens, including Catherine of Aragon and Anne of Cleves, who were Spanish and Dutch, respectively. By this time, jointures had become more popular than dowers as a general way of providing for wives and were based on landed sources of revenue.[74] Thus, the method of providing for queens first begun by Edward IV had now become the norm, even for foreign-born royal consorts. This apparent parallel in the methods of providing for English married women generally as well as English royal consorts suggests that the domestic background of Elizabeth Woodville and

---

[71] SR, vol. II, 595–7.
[72] It is noted that Matilda of Scotland, consort to Henry I (r.1100–35), and Matilda of Boulogne, consort to Stephen (r.1135–54), were related to the West Saxon and Scottish royal families.
[73] Warnicke, *Elizabeth of York and Her Six Daughters-in-Law*, 69–70; Retha Warnicke, *The Marrying of Anne of Cleves: Royal Protocol in Tudor England* (Cambridge: Cambridge University Press, 2000), 153.
[74] Harris, *English Aristocratic Women*, 22–4.

her immediate successors did indeed influence the change in methods for providing for queens consort. The choice of domestic-born consorts did not involve additional political considerations of the sort that accompanied foreign-born queens such as Katherine of Valois and Margaret of Anjou. Having to provide for them consistently and reliably was probably the primary consideration and, seen in that light, it would have been quite natural for the methods of providing for aristocratic English married women to be extended to domestic-born English queens consort.

A final possible factor relates to the extent of royal authority. Prior to the 1460s, there were hardly any great magnates or noble families whose influence and power were of such magnitude that they could be considered regional authorities on par with the Crown. The Crown did not, as James Ross says, pursue 'a policy of the wholesale promotion of one peer in any region at the expense of others'.[75] Yet, from 1461 onwards, Edward IV, and to a lesser extent Richard III and Henry VII after him, began to promote certain nobles and their families in the regional areas. This policy of promotion created genuine regional powers but did so typically at the expense of other peers and, I contend, even at the expense of royal authority. Ross asserts that 'royal authority and aristocratic power ... were complementary' in the regions where this occurred.[76] However, I would suggest that the corollary of expanding the regional power of any one noble family was a retreat of royal influence in those same regions and there are several instances where local magnates held primary sway. These included the Neville family in the north, the Herberts in Wales and the Marches, Hastings in the Midlands, and the Staffords in the south-west.[77] Edward's brothers, George duke of Clarence and Richard duke of Gloucester (the future Richard III), also benefitted from this policy, particularly Gloucester, who was able to build a mighty affinity in the north and north-west. Unsurprisingly, it looks as if monarchic authority began to consolidate and centralise in the south and around London. Set against this backdrop, decisions about which landholdings to grant in dower to the queen must have manifested the same underlying objectives. It stands to reason that if the king meant to promote certain regional families, he would hardly then grant lands in those regions to his queen. The most obvious example here is the north, a region where the Nevilles held sway and where none of the queens in this study had any foothold.[78]

---

[75] James Ross, 'A Governing Elite? The Higher Nobility in the Yorkist and Early Tudor Period', in *The Yorkist Age*, eds H. W. Kleineke and C. Steer (Donington: Shaun Tyas, 2013), 97.
[76] Ross, 'A Governing Elite?', 114.
[77] Ross, *Edward IV*, 334.
[78] Ross, 'A Governing Elite?', 98.

This proposition is supported by an observation made by Simon Thurley in his work on the general spread of royal residences in late medieval and early modern England. Thurley has established that between the reigns of Henry II and Henry VIII, that is, between the twelfth and early sixteenth centuries, the spread of royal residences, presumably those belonging to both king and queen, became increasingly concentrated in a small geographical area and that there was in fact a decrease in the actual number of such dwellings. The gradual shrinking throughout these centuries in the physical area within which royal residences were to be found resulted in a marked concentration of royal dwellings within the vicinity of London and its surrounds.[79] This matching in the consolidation and concentration of royal authority and royal residences around London and the south of England marks out the shrinking of the extent of royal authority as yet another factor that may have influenced changes in the provision of queens' dowers and the spread of queens' landholdings.

The discussion so far infers that the kings (from Edward IV to Henry VII) and their advisors had clear intent and even strategic objectives in mind when trying to make decisions about the queens' dowers. Regrettably, I have not found direct evidence to support that idea. However, the fact that the changes in queens' dowers fit the changing circumstances of the period provides circumstantial support for the idea of intentional strategising. It is only logical to assume that it would have been the king and his advisors who engaged in those actions.

TYPES OF LANDHOLDINGS

The queens in this study were granted and acquired a variety of different holdings, many of which provided non-financial as well as financial benefits. Closer examination of the records shows that most of their holdings consisted of manors and lordships but there were other kinds, such as castles, forests and parks.

The most frequently granted type of holding, the 'manor', is problematic because it has not always had a concrete or static definition.[80] It was often included as part of a lordship, another commonly granted holding. However, the manor did not merely constitute a large physical building or house in the country surrounded by some land or perhaps a village, farmsteads and a church as per our current perceptions.[81] In medieval England, the term

---

[79] Simon Thurley, *The Royal Palaces of Tudor England: Architecture and Court Life 1460–1547* (New Haven, CT: Yale University Press, 1993), 2.

[80] A succinct introduction to the medieval English manor is found in Mark Bailey, *The English Manor, c.1200–c.1500* (Manchester: Manchester University Press, 2002), Chapter I.

[81] Mary Ellis, *Using Manorial Records* (London: PRO Publications, 1997), 6.

'manor', as it developed from the Anglo-Norman period, referred to the basic administrative unit of a landed estate, with or without a physical building serving as the owner's residence on the land.[82] It essentially encompassed the idea of a community but there was no set physical form for a manor.[83] A manor could be small or large in physical and geographic terms, that is, it could comprise a single village, parcels of land in several parishes or extend over several villages. Some manors might contain demesne lands with tenants on other parts of the estate or be made up of either demesne lands only or tenanted land only.[84] In fact, the emblematic picture of a manor is of a compact area that contained the lord's residence, that is, a physical house located at its centre and surrounded by buildings such as tenants' dwellings and a church.[85]

By the fifteenth century, the manor now included an additional defining feature. It encompassed 'landed property with tenants over whom the landlord exercised rights of jurisdiction in a private court'.[86] In other words, an estate or holding in the fifteenth century was a manor for administrative purposes only if there was a manorial court. Regardless of its form, however, this unit lay at the heart of the organisation and administration of a lord's estate holdings. The fact that manors could vary in size means that the absolute number of manors granted to each of the queens is not necessarily the best indicator of whether one queen had gained more than another had. Margaret and the younger queen Elizabeth both owned about seventy manors, while Elizabeth Woodville was the owner of more than a hundred manors. It would, nonetheless, be simplistic to conclude that, based on numbers alone, Elizabeth Woodville was a greater landholder than either her predecessor or her daughter.

What, then, did the queens gain from grants or acquisitions of manors besides the revenues? It depended partly on the size of the manors. The largest manors, such as Havering-atte-Bower or Gillingham, often yielded the most extensive and most lucrative seigniorial prerogatives. Advowsons, for instance, gave the lord of the manor the right to appoint the incumbent of a church and the churches on the largest manors were usually of greater significance than those on smaller manors. Some of the recorded grants of queens' dowers did not specify exactly what rights, privileges and fees accrued to the grantees, possibly because common law and tradition had established the entitlements of the lord of a manor. Others outlined in minute detail what the queens were entitled to claim and should receive as well as their

---

[82] Harvey, *Manorial Records*, 1.
[83] Ellis, *Using Manorial Records*, 1; Harvey, *Manorial Records*, 1–2.
[84] The manorial demesne is defined as the home farm with the manor house and its farm buildings serving as the centre. Harvey, *Manorial Records*, 1.
[85] Ellis, *Using Manorial Records*, 6.
[86] *Ibid.*, 2.

responsibilities.[87] As an example, the 1465 grant to Elizabeth Woodville of the manors and lordships of Langley Marish, Feckenham and Hadley clarified that she would receive 'the chattels of felons, fugitives and outlaws, knights' fees, advowsons, wards, marriages, reliefs, escheats, courts leet, views of frankpledge, hundreds, fairs, markets, parks, warrens, chaces and all other profits, liberties and franchises'.[88] In addition, the royal charters granted to Elizabeth Woodville in 1465 and 1467 and to Elizabeth of York in 1488 outlined in voluminous manner the queen's rights and responsibilities as landholders.[89] In comparison, a grant in 1465 to John Neville, earl of Northumberland, of a range of different manors and lordships also confirmed that the holdings were granted 'with advowsons, knights' fees, courts, markets, fairs, leets, views of frank-pledge, and other commodities ...'[90] This shows that it was normally anticipated that the queen should be regarded on a similar footing as any other noble landowner, with similar traditional benefits accruing to her but also bearing similar duties and responsibilities as any other lord did.

Castles were another type of holding that was frequently granted to the queens. Not all medieval castles looked exactly the same but, generally, they included 'the trappings of fortification [symbolic or otherwise]', which suggests that a castle was not a castle without certain physical features.[91] Nevertheless, as with manors, a grant of a castle typically brought with it both financial and non-financial gains. Margaret of Anjou, for example, received the grant of the 'castle, manor, town and lordship of Marleburgh ...with all appurtenant yearly rents, farms, sums of money and other rents of or for wastes rented, minute rents ...' in 1452.[92] Likewise, in 1466, Elizabeth Woodville was granted '...the castle and honour of Huntingdon with members and appurtenances in the counties of Huntingdon, Cambridge, Bedford, Buckingham and Northampton ... with courts leet, rents, views of frankpledge, liberties and other customs ...'[93] The long list of different types of revenue is indicative of the variety of financial sources that the queens could draw upon when granted a manor or castle. But again, castles afforded much more than just financial benefits to their owners. The largest and most important ones were well fortified and secure strongholds. Where our queens are concerned, the worth of castles in terms of physical security is demonstrated most markedly

---

[87] Manors came with standard rights but if the grant included holdings such as lordships, there were often more extensive rights and responsibilities accruing to the owners that sometimes were clarified in writing.
[88] CPR 1461–67, 445.
[89] CChR 1427–1516, 207–10, 217–18; *Materials for a History*, vol. II, 265–70.
[90] CPR 1461–67, 484.
[91] Robert Liddiard, 'Introduction', in *Late Medieval Castles*, ed. Robert Liddiard (Woodbridge: Boydell Press, 2016), 1.
[92] CPR 1446–52, 559.
[93] CPR 1461–67, 481.

Surveying the Queen's Lands

for Margaret of Anjou. As Margaret and the royal court retreated northward from London towards Coventry in the face of growing opposition from the Yorkists, they sought security in, among other places, Margaret's nearby castles of Tutbury and Kenilworth, both of which were key royal fortresses of considerable size and magnitude.[94]

What is more, as castles could also function as status symbols as well as strongholds for defence, the value of castles to queens in that respect is also evident.[95] Owning castles, which were grander and more imposing residences with greater comforts, said much about the status of their owners, while licences to crenellate indicated that the grantee was possessed of a lordly status.[96] Hence, castles tended to be owned by individuals or families within the highest echelons of society, the most important nobles and royals. It is no surprise, therefore, to see that Margaret of Anjou was granted a dozen and more castles. Elizabeth Woodville and Elizabeth of York were granted half that number of castles but the lower numbers for these queens appear meagre only in comparison with Margaret's.

The discussion thus far highlights another point, that is, that grants typically included a variety of types of holdings within a certain physical location or region. Manors, specifically, could be listed on their own on a dower grant. Examples of these include Hertingfordbury, Hertfordshire, which was granted to only Margaret of Anjou and Elizabeth Woodville, and the more substantial Hamstead Marshall, which was owned by all three queens.[97] Yet, more often than not, they were granted together with a castle, lordship, town, park or forest, to name just a few other types of holdings, and the dower grants of the queens in this study are replete with such cases. For instance, the castle, lordship and manor of Berkhamsted were granted to Margaret of Anjou together 'with the mills, parks, pastures and other appurtenances ...'[98]. Similarly, the castle, lordship, forest and manor of Rockingham was granted to

---

[94] The castle of Kenilworth had been extensively enlarged by John of Gaunt in the fourteenth century and was a favourite residence of the Lancastrian kings (Henry IV, V and VI), who assiduously maintained it. Tutbury was a principal castle inherited by Henry IV as duke of Lancaster and on which extensive work and additions were made by the same Lancastrian kings as well as by Queen Margaret herself after it had been granted to her as part of her dower. H. M. Colvin, ed., *The History of the King's Works, Volume II, The Middle Ages* (London: H. M. Stationery Office, 1963), 683–5, 847–9.

[95] Liddiard, 'Introduction', 6, 10–11.

[96] A licence to crenellate was a grant, usually from the monarch, that gave permission for a building to be fortified in the manner of a castle or to build a new building in the style of a castle. It allowed the grantee to install military-style defensive features as well.

[97] See Wright, 'The Queen's Lands', Appendix 1: The Lands of Fourteenth-Century Queens.

[98] CPR 1452–61, 339.

Margaret and re-granted to Elizabeth Woodville in its entirety except for the manor. Castles, in particular, tended to be granted with a lordship, town or at least a manor, and, as the examples show, there was a wide range of different fees and rights that belonged to the owner of such holdings. What this means is that the queens could have many different sources of revenue from any one location, and, generally, it could be said that the greater the number of types of holding, the greater the opportunities they had for reaping both financial and non-financial benefits.

Naturally, castles and manors were among the queens' principal and favoured residences. The manor of Sheen was a favourite residence of Edward IV and since he had granted it to his queen, Elizabeth Woodville, it is likely that she, too, often resided there.[99] Judging by the itinerary for the last year of her life, Elizabeth of York also appears to have visited Sheen frequently, by then renamed Richmond after Henry VII rebuilt the palace, which had been destroyed by fire in 1497. In Margaret of Anjou's case, quite a few of her extant letters, mainly those dated in the late 1440s, were written when the queen was in residence at her castle of Pleshey in Essex or her manor of Pleasaunce in Greenwich.[100] Even given the possibility that there are many lost letters that could have been written elsewhere, it is not unreasonable to presume that the queen favoured and frequently visited Pleshey and Greenwich. Indeed, the accounts of Robert Kettlewell, clerk of Works to Queen Margaret for the manor of Pleasaunce, show that the queen undertook a five-year programme of improvements to the manor, including significant structural extensions, additions, and commissions for repairs and the like.[101] Several gardens and wider landscaping projects on outdoor spaces were also included as part of the programme, as was the building of new stables. All this work is testament to the status of Pleasaunce as a favoured residence of the queen, a point supported by the fact that Margaret owned other castles, such as Marlborough and Devizes, which were not as well maintained or improved.[102] The owner of a residence was responsible for its upkeep and maintenance but whether or not he or she chose to do so is surely indicative of its importance to the said owner.

Two more types of holdings that were highly valued by the queens were forests and parks. Like the manor and castle, there are definitional difficulties with the term 'forest', which in the medieval period had a particular legal meaning as well as a more general or physical meaning attached to it.[103] In

[99] Unfortunately, few records survive in relation to any expenditure the queen might have incurred in the upkeep of Sheen.
[100] For example, see *The Letters of Margaret of Anjou*, 12–14, 34, 42, 48, 53, 67–8, 87–8 (nos 4, 5, 18, 20, 24, 29, 38, 50).
[101] Rachel M. Delman, 'The Queen's House before Queen's House: Margaret of Anjou and Greenwich Palace, 1447–1453', *Royal Studies Journal* 8, no. 2 (2021): 15–21.
[102] Colvin, ed., *The History of the King's Works, Vol. II*, 626–8, 734–8.
[103] For a general overview and discussion of medieval forests in England and

essence, a legal forest did not typically match the physical forest. A legal royal forest was 'land reserved for the use of the king'.[104] It could encompass not just physical woodland areas but also areas devoid of trees and woods or containing villages, farms and even towns.[105] The royal forest of Feckenham comprised, among other things, a park, a number of different estates with appurtenances such as markets, fairs and a fishpond, tenements, messuages and a mill.[106] Needwood Forest and Duffield Frith in the Honour of Tutbury included broad areas of pasture as well as extensive woodland spaces. These two forests were especially known for their quality timber and excellent grasslands, both items being important resources from which income might be earned.[107] Forest resources could be quite varied and the forest could make significant contributions to the economy of an entire region. The owners of forests could expect to enjoy revenue from a variety of sources depending on the area. These included the granting of royal licences to assart, sales of timber, agistment fees for the use of grassland as pasture for livestock, rents from leased pastures, pannage fees earned from tenants who pastured pigs in the woodland areas, and fees from forest courts, known as *wodemotes* and *swanimotes*.[108]

Margaret and the two queens Elizabeth were each in their turn granted the forests of Gillingham in Dorset, Feckenham in Worcestershire, and Savernake, Melksham, Pewsham and Chippenham in Wiltshire. The forest of Rockingham in Northamptonshire was granted to Margaret and Elizabeth Woodville but not to Elizabeth of York, although she obtained the forests of Exmoor, Rache and Mendip in Somerset as part of the York lands.[109] All of these forests, barring those on the York lands, were among the most traditional of queens' dowers, being regularly granted to them between the thirteenth and sixteenth centuries.[110] Again, the grants of forests rarely made any mention of specific rights that came with them. A rare exception was the grant of the forest as well as the castle, lordship and bailiwick of Rockingham to Elizabeth Woodville;

---

continental Europe, see Charles R. Young, *The Royal Forests of Medieval England* (Leicester: Leicester University Press, 1979).

[104] Chris Wickham, 'European Forests in the Early Middle Ages: Landscape and Land Clearance', reproduced in *Land and Power: Studies in Italian and European Social History, 400–1200*, ed. Chris Wickham (London: British School at Rome, 1994), 159.

[105] Young, *The Royal Forests of Medieval England*, 5.

[106] 'Parishes: Feckenham', in *A History of the County of Worcester*: vol. 3, (London: Victoria County History, 1913), 111–20. British History Online, http://www.british-history.ac.uk/vch/worcs/vol3/pp111-120.

[107] Jean Birrell, 'The Forest Economy of the Honour of Tutbury in the Fourteenth and Fifteenth Centuries', *University of Birmingham Historical Journal* 8 (1962): 114.

[108] 'Assarting' referred to the clearing of woodland for conversion to arable land.

[109] CPR 1485–94, 369–70; SR, vol. II, 595.

[110] 'Royal forests', in *A History of the County of Wiltshire*: vol. 4, ed. Elizabeth Crittall (London: Victoria County History, 1959), 391–433. British History Online, http://www.british-history.ac.uk/vch/wilts/vol4/pp391-433.

Financing Queenship in Late Fifteenth Century England

the forest grant included the prized 'supervision of vert and venison', that is, the rights to the timber and deer within the forest.[111] Nevertheless, notwithstanding any outlining of rights (or lack of it) in the forest grants, substantial amounts of revenue were a possible benefit of owning forests.

There were other non-financial benefits as well. One of the primary objectives of setting up forests in the first place was to protect those areas that were favourable for hunting. Extant household and expense accounts show ample evidence of the fact that the queens in this study hunted and very likely did so frequently, just as the nobility and their royal husbands did.[112] Owning forests facilitated these activities and the queens, like any other lord, claimed their rights to do so. Another significant advantage was having the resources of the forest available for their own food supplies. The queens and their households needed regular food supplies and forests, among other holdings, could supply many food items, including deer, game and fish. Household accounts for Margaret of Anjou and Elizabeth Woodville do not record much relevant detail but Elizabeth of York's Privy Purse Expense account does, clearly showing that such procurement by the queen's household did take place and probably on a regular basis. There are, for instance, regular entries of payments or reimbursements to household servants for the transport of bucks, does and other animals back to the household.[113]

The resources of the forest also facilitated the queens' capacity to reward supporters and servants with gifts. There are examples of gifts of deer that were regularly sent by the lords of the Honour of Tutbury to nearby households around the forests of the said Honour, and also of timber used by the lords to reward local officials.[114] The queens emulated that practice by bestowing gifts of the same ilk to their supporters. Elizabeth of York sent gifts of bucks, one to the duchess of Suffolk and another to John Vandelf and Lybart goldsmiths, presumably to show her favour.[115] On different occasions, she gave officers and keepers of her stables cash amounts and deer.[116] Timber, too, could be utilised for rewards, as a letter from Henry VI to his wife, Margaret of Anjou, demonstrates.[117]

These same non-financial benefits can be applied to parks. As we see from grants such as the 1465 grant to Elizabeth Woodville, manors or lordships could include one or more parks.[118] Parks were an important feature of the

---

[111] CPR 1461–67, 430.
[112] For example, see Queen's Book, fols 45, 61, 65, 87. These items refer to payments for the purchase of horses, arrows, and for wages for servants of the stables.
[113] For example, Queen's Book, fols 53, 54, 80, 82, 89.
[114] Birrell, 'The Forest Economy of the Honour of Tutbury', 117.
[115] Queen's Book, fol. 83.
[116] Queen's Book, fol. 49.
[117] *The Letters of Margaret of Anjou*, 59–60 (no. 32).
[118] CPR 1461–67, 445.

countryside in medieval England, and geographically, though not legally, they bore much resemblance to forests in that there were usually areas of woodland that served as sources of timber and within which could be found animals such as deer.[119] In a sense, therefore, many of the benefits discussed in relation to forests can be equally applied to parks. Still, a strikingly different feature of parks was the fact that they were secured private enclosures.[120] Parks were typically located at major residences and owning parks, more so than forests, provided queens with opportunities to host and entertain their followers as well as those whom they might wish to get to know better. If it is true that among the objectives of owning parks was the ability to showcase one's status for the purpose of creating good impressions, then parks were likely to have been as highly prized as forests.[121]

CONCLUSIONS

This exploration of the landholdings of the fifteenth-century queens in this study has shed light on a number of features related to the relationship between landownership and queenship. It has uncovered some apparent paradoxes as well. In the first instance, the queen as a landowner is a concept that does not appear to fit comfortably within the ideological and legal frameworks that shaped the lives of late medieval married English women and forbade their outright ownership of land. In practice, however, many women in the period effectively possessed estates and were recognised as doing so. In the second instance, the contemporary view held that there was nothing unusual about the queen being a landowner in the late fifteenth century since she was typically recognised and treated as such. Therein another paradox emerges because there existed several curbs on this role. Each time a new

---

[119] Different types of deer were found in medieval England, that is, red, fallow and roe deer. By the late medieval period the red and fallow deer were the most sought-after. However, fallow deer were most suited for rearing and hunting in parks and were far more numerous than red deer during this period. For more information on deer in medieval England, see Jean Birrell, 'Deer and Deer Farming in Medieval England', *The Agricultural History Review* 40, no. 2 (1992): 112–26; Jean Birrell, 'Procuring, Preparing and Serving Venison in Late Medieval England', in *Food in Medieval England: Diet and Nutrition*, eds C. M. Woolgar, D. Serjeantson and T. Waldron (Oxford, New York: Oxford University Press, 2006), 176–88; N. J. Sykes, 'The Impact of the Normans on Hunting Practices in England', in *Food in Medieval England: Diet and Nutrition*, eds C. M. Woolgar, D. Serjeantson and T. Waldron (Oxford, New York: Oxford University Press, 2006), 162–75.

[120] L. M. Cantor and J. Hatherly, 'The Medieval Parks of England', *Geography* 64, no. 2 (Apr. 1979): 71.

[121] S. A. Mileson, 'The Importance of Parks in Fifteenth-Century Society', in *The Fifteenth Century V: Of Mice and Men: Image, Belief and Regulation in Late Medieval England*, ed. Linda Clark (Woodbridge: Boydell Press, 2005), 23.

queen consort was crowned, she was endowed with lands and estates as part of the dower that was meant to provide for her maintenance. She was granted and owned a substantial number of holdings, and this placed her among the greatest landowners of the period. While this was an unusual arrangement in relation to the queen's marital status, it could be viewed simply as a formalisation, for practical reasons, of a common scenario among married elite and noblewomen. In this scenario, many married noblewomen operated in reality as autonomous landowners and administrators without necessarily being encumbered by the lack of legal technical title. Gender, therefore, was a negative factor in that queens, as married women, could not technically own lands. It was their status as royal consorts that served as the crucial feature elevating them in terms of landownership. Nonetheless, even though the role of landowner was a core part of being the queen in late fifteenth-century England, there were limitations.

Being a landowner was a transient role for queens. While their gender and marital status did not prevent them from owning lands, the evidence shows that most of the landholdings owned by the queens were only held for the term of their natural lives, both as consort and possibly later as queen dowager. These lands could not be sold and reverted to the Crown on the queen's death. In the case of this group of queens, the chaos that resulted in disrupted dynastic bloodlines meant that the lands of the queen consort did not remain in her family line. Therefore, except for Elizabeth of York, the marital family ownership of each queen's lands granted in dower ended with her lifetime. This transience, however, did not break or even significantly disrupt the overall continuity that can be observed in the holding of lands by queens throughout the late medieval period. The position of the queen was consistently bolstered by lands as economic resources even while the individual women and their marital families, beyond their lifetimes, were not. By the late fifteenth century there was an established practice of granting lands and estates to queens for their provision and maintenance. This practice, supported by the findings from a comparative analysis of queenly landholdings, reveals that there was a thread of continuity discernible in decisions about which lands were granted to queens. Despite the apparent shift in the locus and a reduction in the geographic spread of queenly lands, most evident when this group of fifteenth-century queens is compared with queens from previous centuries, there was a solid enough core of landholdings being allocated to one queen after another to suggest that precedent and tradition were adhered to in the making of such decisions.

This is an interesting point given what we know about the political and domestic unrest in the later fifteenth century. Each individual queen as landholder during this period can be considered a transient situation, one that looked as if it was an interruption and a break with the past. Yet, taken altogether, the queens' positions as landholders formed a continuous whole. By looking at three queens rather than one, I have established that the queen as landholder was an essential and accepted part of the economic landscape no matter who occupied the position at any one time. The fact that there appears to have been a core group of lands that passed from one queen to another, typically augmented by additional landed grants, indicates that lands earmarked for the queens' provision was a tradition that outweighed political exigencies, dynastic ruptures in the monarchy and even the change from foreign to native-born queens. In the period under consideration, a degree of continuity of queenship and landed sources of wealth can be observed. In this way, queenship itself was more robust than the bloodlines of the women who filled this position, rendering its resources temporary for the individuals involved but relatively permanent for the position itself. The individual was important but her stewardship was transient; hence, each individual landowner queen represented a step in the ownership of lands that belonged to her in theory but in reality were the preserve of the station in life which she had attained by virtue of her marriage to the king.

This continuity in queenly landownership is, nonetheless, offset by the changes that were engendered at least partly by the disruption to the monarchic system. Although this study has revealed many similarities in the landownership of these different queens, it has also established that major if subtle changes occurred in the methods used to provide for the queens consort during the transition from the Lancastrian to the Yorkist regime. For a variety of reasons, the queens after Margaret of Anjou were no longer granted a fixed and stated amount of revenue as part of their dower and the resources that this revenue was drawn from became overwhelmingly related to lands and landed property. These changes reveal another perspective on the impact of the dynastic disruptions that has not been extensively considered in the past and speaks to the constant evolution of medieval queenship. To some extent these changes may even be positioned as a major point of difference between medieval and early modern queenship in England.

Judgements about the quantity and significance of each queen's landholdings cannot be easily made. Each of the queens in this study owned lands and estates in various geographical regions with differing degrees of overlap. In terms of quantity, Elizabeth Woodville appears to have owned the largest number of different lands and holdings, while Elizabeth of York apparently possessed the smallest set. Economic and social changes do, however, provide useful additional backdrops and contextual information to our analysis. This means, for one thing, that Elizabeth of York was not necessarily the poorest or least well-off queen in relation to resources, both financial and otherwise. Neither does it follow that she was the least influential since she owned a good deal in the comparatively wealthy southern counties and regions of England. The wider socio-economic context also presents other possible factors in the apparent shift of queens' landholdings further south and consolidation towards more concentrated holdings in fewer counties.

The analysis so far has been less about drawing definitive conclusions about the economic wealth and resources of each individual queen than about illuminating the essential nature of the later fifteenth-century queen as a landowner. Comparative examination of the landholdings of the queens of this study has better illuminated the extent of the queens' positions as landholders, what benefits they might have gained because of their positions, and what this meant for their place in the economic landscape of the period. The queens in this study were considered to be part of the economic life of society in such a way as to demonstrate the continuity of queenship in economic terms. That the concept of the queen as landowner and landholder endured and even strengthened in the face of the peculiar challenges of this period is testament to its resilience.

3

MANAGING THE QUEEN'S LANDS

Here begin the rules, which Robert Grosseteste the good bishop of Lincoln made for the Countess of Lincoln, on how to guard and govern lands and household. He who will keep to the rules will live well and comfortably off his demesne and keep himself and his people.[1]

This inscription marks the beginning of a set of rules that was compiled by Robert Grosseteste, the thirteenth-century bishop of Lincoln.[2] The rules included advice for the management of estates and rules for the domestic arrangements of the household, and it was one of the best known contemporary treatises on estate and household management.[3] This treatise was specifically addressed to Margaret de Lacy, the widowed countess of Lincoln, who presided over a large magnate household and vast complex of landholdings.[4] The practical nature of the advice offered in this treatise demonstrates the bishop's concern for the countess' level of competence in administrative matters now that she had been widowed and had assumed sole control of the family's properties.[5] It also suggests that the bishop accepted the idea that a noble widow could assume direct ownership and governance of her own lands. The bishop was not alone in his beliefs, judging from descriptions by his contemporary Gerald of Wales, who said that Matilda de Saint Valery, wife of William de Braose, a Welsh Marcher lord, was 'well equipped to rule her household' and 'highly skilled in preserving her property'.[6] These viewpoints

---

[1] Dorothea Oschinsky, *Walter of Henley and Other Treatises on Estate Management and Accounting* (Oxford: Clarendon Press, 1971), 389.
[2] Oschinsky, *Walter of Henley*, 387–415.
[3] *Ibid.*, vii.
[4] For further discussion of this treatise, its contents and the nature of the relationship between the bishop and the countess of Lincoln, see Louise J. Wilkinson, 'The Rules of Robert Grosseteste Reconsidered: The Lady as Estate and Household Manager in Thirteenth-Century England', in *The Medieval Household in Christian Europe, c.850–1550*, eds Cordelia Beattie, Anna Maslakovic, and Sarah Rees Jones (Turnhout: Brepols, 2003), 293–306.
[5] Wilkinson, 'The Rules of Robert Grosseteste Reconsidered', 298, 300.
[6] Gerald of Wales, *The Journey Through Wales/The Description of Wales*, ed. and trans. Lewis Thorpe (London: Penguin, 1978), 83.

are indicative of a general acceptance of the idea that all women, not only those who had been widowed, could participate actively and effectively in household and estate administration.[7] In other words, medieval women were regarded as possessing the innate aptitude to acquire the expertise necessary to undertake household and estate administration.

By the fifteenth century, Grosseteste's rules and other such didactic treatises were no longer widely used.[8] However, the earlier acceptance of women as estate administrators appears to have survived. As Christine de Pisan famously advised fellow female landholders in the early fifteenth century, a married noblewoman would 'do well to be a very good manager of the estate and [should] know all about the work on the land and at what time and in what season one ought to perform what operations'.[9] Notwithstanding its French setting and the tangle of literary and real-life features contained in de Pisan's *The Treasure of the City of Ladies* (with a corresponding number of possible interpretations), its sentiments point to the reality of life for many a married noblewoman in the late medieval period, including in England. It was assuredly incumbent on such a lady to involve herself in the daily running of the estates of the family so that she could be aware of what was necessary for effective estate management. Many elite women in late medieval England were just such efficient landholders and administrators, often filling the role of estate administrator on their families' estates autonomously and with their husbands' recognition and trust.[10]

The queens in this study were more than high-born married women involving themselves as a matter of necessity in the administration of family estates. Since they were considered landowners in their own right, it might be expected that the queens would have involved themselves in administration just as other landowners did. The question is whether they did so. Did our queens participate in any way in estate management and if they did, how did they interact with their estate officials at the different levels? Did they exercise their power and authority to set policy and direction? How did they compare with each other as administrators? This chapter addresses these questions

---

[7] Wilkinson, 'The Rules of Robert Grosseteste Reconsidered', 294.

[8] Oschinsky, *Walter of Henley*, 199. For some discussion of similar works on household and estate management written earlier than the Rules of Robert Grosseteste, see Fiona Whelan, 'Administering the Household, 1180–1250: From Daniel of Beccles to Robert Grosseteste', in *The Elite Household in England, 1100–1550: Proceedings of the 2016 Harlaxton Symposium*, ed. C. M. Woolgar (Donington: Shaun Tyas, 2018), 185–203.

[9] Christine de Pisan, *The Treasure of the City of Ladies; or, The Book of the Three Virtues*, trans. S. Lawson (Harmondsworth: Penguin, 1985), 131.

[10] See Rowena E. Archer, '"How ladies … who live on their manors ought to manage their households and estates": Women as Landholders and Administrators in the Later Middle Ages', in *Woman is a Worthy Wight: Women in English Society c.1200–1500*, ed. P. J. P. Goldberg (Stroud: Sutton, 1992), 149–81.

by examining how the lands and estates of the queens were managed during the periods in which each individual occupied the position of consort.[11] It outlines the general organisation of the queens' administrative machineries and briefly discusses the people who served the queens in this capacity. In so doing, it assesses the level of involvement of each individual queen in her own administration and tests the assumption that every time a new queen was crowned change was bound to follow in her footsteps.

ORGANISATION AND STRUCTURE

Management of the queens' lands was organised to cater for two different aspects of estate administration – stewardship and financial accounting. Many officials who served the queens often had duties that encompassed both these facets, but each aspect had its own focus and should be considered separately. Stewardship, or operational management, was typically focused on the manor. The reasons for this lay behind the development of administrative structures of land from the pre-Conquest and Anglo-Norman periods. Land in medieval England was generally divided into shires, also known as counties.[12] Each shire was divided into smaller units called hundreds, also known as *wapentakes* in some counties.[13] The hundred was ostensibly a 'district assessed for the purposes of taxation at 100 hides' but the veracity of this origin story is unclear.[14] The hundred and the *wapentake* were functionally the same and operated as units of local government. Occasionally, as occurred in the northern counties, the ward replaced the hundred or *wapentake*. All of these were administratively comparable and typically composed of vills or villages. However, the vill was not the administrative unit in the eyes of the government or landholders. While vills were the physical manifestation of territorial organisation, the manor was the most basic unit of administration of any estate and the one that most conspicuously featured in Domesday

---

[11] Due to time constraints and the uneven survival rate for manorial records, the holdings selected for detailed examination are Hertingfordbury in Hertfordshire, Pleshey in Essex and the Honour of Tutbury manor in Staffordshire because they were all granted to Margaret of Anjou and later to Elizabeth Woodville, and Gillingham, Dorset, Feckenham in Worcestershire, Mashbury and Havering-atte-Bower in Essex, all of which were granted in turn to each of the queens of this study. See Appendix 3 for lists of the extant documents consulted for these estates.

[12] Pollock and Maitland, *The History of English Law*, 585.

[13] The term '*wapentake*' is of Scandinavian origin and was used in the counties of Derby, Leicester, Lincoln, Nottingham, and the North and West Ridings of York. H. C. Darby, 'Domesday England', in *A New Historical Geography of England*, ed. H. C. Darby (Cambridge: Cambridge University Press, 1973), 40–2.

[14] *Ibid.*, 42.

Book.¹⁵ The two were not identical and a confusing number of variations could occur. Occasionally, a manor would coincide with a vill but this combination was not commonly found. More typically, a vill could be composed of a few manors or, alternatively, it could be one of several components that made up a large manorial unit.¹⁶ In short, there was no typically standardised structure or appearance for either manors or vills.

As discussed in the previous chapter, the term 'manor' has had multiple meanings but, by the fifteenth century, the legal and administrative meanings had converged, with the legal aspect becoming paramount. A holding was now not deemed to constitute a manor unless a court, in which the lord's rights of jurisdiction over the tenants were exercised, was held on that land.¹⁷ This was true whether or not a holding had a physical building located on it. The manor court was, in essence, a key component of estate administration. It served two purposes where the lord was concerned, the first being a source of revenue and the second as the instrument through which the lord exercised power, authority and influence.¹⁸ The 'perquisites' of the courts referred to the revenues obtained from each sitting of a court and included various types of fines and fees. These were described in the accounts drawn up by the local estate officials and rendered the manor courts important throughout the medieval period as significant sources of revenue to the landowner. Manor courts also served as useful tools by which the lords of the estate could exert control and keep order among their tenants. The court dealt with general estate business and, by enforcing the rules and customs of the land, ensured that all were made aware of how lands were to be used and what services were owed to the lord. Tenant-lord obligations and relations, as well as relations among tenants themselves, were thus key focal points of court business.¹⁹

What I have discussed so far may give the impression that a relatively straightforward administrative structure was used widely during the fifteenth century. However, alongside the fixed system of shires, counties and hundreds lay a more fluid system of honours and baronies, generally divided into bailiwicks, which were groups of manors. Honours and baronies were imposed on the customary pre-Conquest system of shires and hundreds by the Normans, and, unlike the older fixed entities, these could alter in composition as a

---

[15] *Ibid.*, 43.
[16] Bailey, *The English Manor*, 6–7; Bruce M. S. Campbell, 'The Land', in *A Social History of England, 1200–1500*, eds Rosemary Horrox and W. Mark Ormrod (Cambridge: Cambridge University Press, 2006), 191.
[17] Harvey, *Manorial Records*, 2.
[18] Christopher Dyer, 'A Redistribution of Incomes in Fifteenth-Century England?', *Past and Present* 39 (Apr. 1968): 26.
[19] Denis Stuart, *Manorial Records: An Introduction to Their Transcription and Translation* (Chichester: Phillimore, 1992), 1.

result of grants, marriages or the whims of fate.[20] They were not always geographically fixed or of consistent composition; the holdings that made up the honour or barony could be scattered among different counties or shires, and its composition could change periodically. The Honour of Leicester in the fourteenth century neatly illustrates this point since it was quite different from the county of Leicester during this period. The Honour was made up of lands not only in Leicestershire but also in the counties of Kent, Dorset, Wiltshire, Suffolk and Norfolk.[21] In practice, even from the early days of the Conquest and certainly by the late thirteenth century, the honour and barony existed side by side. These two terms had by now become conflated and were used interchangeably in the legal and administrative sense.[22]

In summary, local management in terms of supervision and direction of work practices on the estates usually centred on the manor. However, the larger the complex of landholdings owned by any one lord or landholder, the more hierarchical a system of administration was needed. Essentially, then, the queens' landholdings were organised for estate management purposes as follows. All the manors were grouped into bailiwicks. Bailiwicks could be grouped under an honour or exist within a lordship, while honours and lordships could either operate under the aegis of separate receivers or be further grouped into larger receiverships whenever it was deemed necessary.

Organisation of the queens' landholdings for the purposes of financial accounting can be discerned from the accounts produced by the queen's officials, which were meant to record financial information with a view to working out the queen's due income. Generally, receiverships functioned as the financial nodes of estate management and information about revenues was organised in the household accounts according to the various receiverships. The queens' receivers collected revenue from local officials, made payments for various expenses and then handed over the queen's dues to her receiver-general or some other senior official. This model of financial accountability was similar to that employed by other landowners with very large holdings. Studies of the financial aspects of large noble landholdings have typically dealt with large administrative units, such as bailiwicks or receiverships. A case in point is Joel Rosenthal's research into the estates of Richard, duke of York, which delves into local administration by discussing his manors but considers

---

[20] Levi Fox, *The Administration of the Honor of Leicester in the Fourteenth Century* (Leicester: E. Backus, 1940), 295.
[21] *Ibid.*
[22] J. F. Baldwin's work on the household administration of Henry Lacy and Thomas of Lancaster and Levi Fox's economic study of the Honour of Leicester makes little or no distinction between the honour and the barony. J. F. Baldwin, 'The Household Administration of Henry Lacy and Thomas of Lancaster', *EHR* 42 (1927): 183; Fox, *The Administration of the Honor of Leicester*, 297.

the receivership to be the more appropriate unit for an examination of his lordship's income.[23] J. M. W. Bean, too, uses manorial accounts, primarily those composed by bailiffs, to examine the sources of the Percy family's landed income but concentrates on receivers' accounts to investigate overall revenues, an indication that he, too, considers financial management and accounting to be focused on the receivership.[24]

Interestingly, it is unclear how manors and other holdings were usually grouped into receiverships. Rosenthal, for one, does not specify exactly what constituted a receivership for the fifteenth-century estates of the duke of York but he proposes guidelines that he thinks the duke may have followed when setting up his receiverships. Rosenthal's work on the duke's manorial accounts shows that receiverships roughly corresponded to groups of manors within shires and honours.[25] Likewise, the Percy estates appear to have been arranged along geographical lines, with the family being served by separate receivers for their estates in the counties of Yorkshire, Northumberland, Cumberland and Sussex.[26] This arrangement appears entirely logical and might be expected to apply to the queens in this study.

Yet this does not quite look to be the case. Margaret of Anjou and Elizabeth Woodville were both served by almost a dozen receivers each, but their receiverships do not appear to have been organised strictly geographically. Instead, the extant evidence reveals slightly different sorts of groupings, complicated by confusing naming conventions for the groups of lands owned by the Crown and by the Duchy of Lancaster and which were granted in dower to the queens.[27] Additionally, both queens had receivers for single holdings. Margaret was served by separate receivers for the castle, manor and honour of Tutbury and for the castle, town, lordship and honour of Leicester. The castles and lordships of Kenilworth, Berkhamsted and Haverford also constituted separate receiverships, a situation that appeared unchanged in the case of Kenilworth, which was owned both by Margaret and Elizabeth Woodville. Evidently, these particular landholdings were considered important enough to warrant a separate receiver each. The same appears to be true of Middleton and Merden as well as Marlborough and Devizes for Margaret. However,

---

[23] Joel T. Rosenthal, 'The Estates and Finances of Richard Duke of York (1411–1460)', *Studies in Medieval and Renaissance History* 2 (1965): 122.
[24] J. M. W. Bean, *The Estates of the Percy Family 1416–1537* (London: Oxford University Press, 1958), 3.
[25] For example, the duke owned numerous manors in the Honour of Clare as well as in shires including Yorkshire, Hertfordshire and Herefordshire. Rosenthal, 'The Estates and Finances of Richard Duke of York', 122-3, 176-7.
[26] Bean, *The Estates of the Percy Family*, 88–93.
[27] See also Myers, 'The Household of Queen Margaret of Anjou', 156–61; Myers, 'The Household of Queen Elizabeth Woodville', 261–9 for the income from different receiverships.

Middleton and Merden were not regranted to Margaret's successors, and both Marlborough and Devizes were absorbed into a larger receivership when granted to Elizabeth Woodville. Other receivers administered groups of lands in different shires and these groups could be made up of lands that were granted together, as in the Essex/Hertford/Middlesex group, or were lands that had been traditionally known as 'Partes Australes' (South Parts) and owned either by the Crown or the Duchy of Lancaster.[28] In addition, those Duchy of Lancaster lands in Northamptonshire that were granted to Elizabeth Woodville were administered by a different receiver from other lands in the same shire owned by the queen, despite their geographical proximity. In fact, holdings in the 'South Parts' of the Duchy of Lancaster that were grouped under one receiver during the queenship of Margaret of Anjou were administered by a number of different receivers after being granted to Elizabeth Woodville, possibly because she owned a lot of other individual holdings there.[29]

Elizabeth of York's lands, too, were grouped in a similar manner to Margaret's and Elizabeth Woodville's in the early years of her time as queen. But these groupings began to be altered after 1497 when she received the lands of her late grandmother, Cecily Neville, the dowager duchess of York. By 1502, the last year of the queen's life, the receiverships of her lands were now of groups that were more geographically related. These were Hereford and Worcester; Somerset and Dorset; Wiltshire, Berkshire and Hampshire; Gloucester and Wiltshire; Hertford, and finally Essex. There was, however, a separate receiver for the lordship of Fotheringhay, which was granted to her by the king in 1495.[30] A separate receiver was also appointed for the manor and forest of Feckenham, a lordship that had previously been granted in dower to both Margaret of Anjou and Elizabeth Woodville.[31] In comparison with her predecessors, it appears that Elizabeth of York's lands were eventually rearranged into receiverships along geographical lines.

Closer examination shows that two major factors determining the organisation and structure of the queens' lands were the timing of the grants and

[28] The groups are clearly laid out in extant land valors and receivers accounts.
[29] William Osgodby served as receiver for the 'south parts' under Margaret of Anjou. Myers, 'The Household of Queen Margaret of Anjou', 158. During Elizabeth Woodville's time, her holdings in the 'south parts' were administered by at least three receivers simultaneously – Thomas Mauncell, Maurice Kidwelly and John Rotherham were listed as the receivers for the period 1466–67. Myers, 'The Household of Queen Elizabeth Woodville', 266–8.
[30] CPR 1494–1509, 14; Queen's Book, fol. 17.
[31] The manor and lordship of Feckenham is listed separately in the household account of Margaret of Anjou even though no individual is named as the receiver. The household account for Elizabeth Woodville is not completely legible in some parts. Therefore, it is possible that Feckenham was listed either singly or in another receivership but that the information is no longer legible. Myers, 'The Household of Queen Margaret of Anjou', 163.

the location of the holdings being granted. Consider the case of the manors of Odiham in Hampshire and Gillingham in Dorset, which were granted to Margaret as compensation for the loss of revenues from Pembroke. Both manors were administered by the same receiver even though they were not located in the same shire. They were not, however, placed in the same receivership as other lands in Northamptonshire that were also part of the same grant, possibly because Northamptonshire was too geographically distant from Hampshire or Dorset. Odiham and Gillingham were later granted to Elizabeth Woodville as part of her dower in 1465 but this time they were placed within the jurisdiction of a receiver who also administered other lands in Hampshire, Berkshire, Wiltshire, Dorset and Buckinghamshire, and were included in the same grant.[32] Undoubtedly, in this case, both location and the timing of the grants were important factors.

THE QUEEN'S ESTATE OFFICIALS

Where estate personnel were concerned, Johnstone likens the queen's administrative machinery to a wheel.[33] The queen's household lay at the centre of the wheel and a great many spokes led out to individual administrative units. To a certain extent it is helpful to also visualise different layers of officials superimposed on the wheel as concentric circles beginning in the middle and emanating outwards. Here I consider the queen's officials to be situated on three essential layers or circles. On the outermost circle at the end of the spokes were the personnel who served at the local level in a variety of positions and were generally recruited from among the tenantry. Moving inwards, there were stewards and receivers, whose authority could be relatively locally based or wider in jurisdiction. At this level, these posts were complemented by a range of other positions, such as park keepers, foresters, gamekeepers, and castle constables. Most of these posts tended to be appointments made at the landholders' pleasure and not typically drawn from local tenantry. Finally, at the heart of the wheel and within the queen's household were the centrally placed officials, the queen's auditors, receivers-general and council members. I categorise these officials as overseers within the queen's administrative machinery and discuss them later.

Like others who owned widespread landholdings, the queens were served at the local level by several different officials, including bailiffs, reeves, and collectors of receipts.[34] Medieval estate treatises, such as Walter of Henley's Husbandry and the anonymously written Seneschaucy from the thirteenth

---

[32] CPR 1461–67, 430, 445. See Table 6 for receiverships under the queens in this study.
[33] Johnstone II, 291.
[34] See Bailey, *The English Manor*, 98–9 for examples of the wide range of estate officers who might serve the lord.

century, contain much instructional information on the duties and hierarchy of bailiffs and reeves. The bailiff was the overall manager, while the reeve was his junior acting in the role of a foreman.[35] The major duties of both these officials related to supervising the work of the manor as carried out by the many different workers, and their respective duties complemented each other, requiring high levels of knowledge and capability on their parts.[36] As the senior official, it was the bailiff who theoretically bore primary responsibility for and whose name appeared on the financial account but the reeve and bailiff were meant to work together to account for all receipts, expenses and other financial items.[37] It would not be true to say, however, that all estates were always served by all these different officials. For example, the medieval manor of Havering-atte-Bower did not have a reeve, only a bailiff or farmer.[38] Furthermore, even in the thirteenth and fourteenth centuries bailiffs, reeves, farmers and the like often carried out duties that differed markedly from what is described in the medieval treatises.[39]

In any case, by the fifteenth century, the world of the estate as envisioned in the above-mentioned treatises had changed quite radically. The now generally high level of leasing arrangements resulted in changes in the roles of officials.[40] Properties that were leased out, an arrangement known as 'farming' in the case of demesne lands, did not require the same levels of supervision as before and local officials sometimes became chiefly responsible for the collection of rents more than anything else.[41] It is not surprising that there were large numbers of accounts prepared by collectors of receipts rather than bailiffs or reeves. Just as often, demesne lands that had been farmed were financially accounted for by the farmers themselves, hence the existence of many manorial accounts prepared by farmers.[42] What is more, the office of the feodary, also known

---

[35] Oschinsky, *Walter of Henley*, 94.
[36] Ibid., 269–81.
[37] Ibid., 291.
[38] The manorial accounts show no evidence of the presence of a reeve, a circumstance supported by Marjorie McIntosh's study of Havering from the thirteenth to the fifteenth century. Marjorie K. McIntosh, *Autonomy and Community: The Royal Manor of Havering, 1200-1500* (Cambridge; New York: Cambridge University Press, 1986), Appendix I.
[39] The farmer was not an agriculturalist in the present-day meaning but an individual who was responsible for the payment of a 'farm', or fee, to the landowner. See H. S. Bennett, 'The Reeve and the Manor in the Fourteenth Century', *EHR* 41, no. 163 (Jul. 1926): 358–65.
[40] Bailey, *The English Manor*, 108–11.
[41] This happened on many estates, such as the Honour of Tutbury. Jean Birrell, 'The Honour of Tutbury in the Fourteenth and Fifteenth Centuries' (unpublished MA thesis, University of Birmingham, 1962), 6.
[42] The manor of Mashbury is a case in point. Extant manorial accounts from the late 1430s until the 1480s include large numbers of farmers' accounts even though

as the bailiff of fees (*ballivus feodorum*), became an increasingly common one from the fourteenth century. A feodary was often responsible for a wide geographical area and the monies they collected formed a significant portion of the landowners' revenues.[43]

The duties and functions of the bailiff, reeve and even the farmer by this period perhaps also became blurred to the point where it was not always clear whether there was much, if any, difference between these posts.[44] The extant financial accounts for the manor of Hertingfordbury during the period 1456–96 were compiled by either the reeve or the bailiff but all of them are highly similar in form and content. This is not in itself unusual since manorial accounting in late medieval England had become quite standardised, resulting in a highly consistent format for financial accounts at the local estate level.[45] But the fact that the person named on several of the Hertingfordbury accounts is styled as the reeve suggests that this post was no longer always regarded as subordinate to a bailiff and that the reeve could and did on occasion assume financial responsibility for the estate. One such individual was John Draper, who served in both positions in Hertingfordbury. He was named as reeve for the accounting years 1460 and 1462 and as bailiff in the accounts for 1461, 1464 and 1466.[46] It is possible that Draper compiled the accounts when he was reeve simply because the post of bailiff was vacant. Moreover, the fact that the extant bailiff accounts record a payment of a stipend to a reeve shows that Hertingfordbury was typically served by both a reeve and a bailiff, though there is nothing to suggest that one individual could not fill both posts simultaneously. Nonetheless, Draper could have been known as the bailiff or the reeve at one time or another because his duties were the same and the titles had become interchangeable. The extant manorial accounts for the manor of Feckenham and the Honour of Tutbury manor lend further support to this idea of a blurring of duties and nomenclature. All of them were compiled by the reeve of the manor and, again, all are remarkably similar in structure not only to each other but to bailiff accounts on other estates, such as Hertingfordbury manor.[47]

---

there was also a reeve for Mashbury. The farmer may not have utilised the manor himself but was responsible for the payment of the fee-farm. Corresponding reeve accounts, if they existed, have not been located. See Appendix 3 for a list of extant farmers' accounts for Mashbury.

[43] Receivers' accounts for queens' lands, for example, in TNA DL29/711/11474, list receipts from bailiffs of fees.

[44] Noel Denholm-Young makes this observation for fourteenth-century English noble estates. Denholm-Young, *Seignorial Administration in England* (London: Cass, 1937), 32.

[45] Bailey, *The English Manor*, 105.

[46] TNA DL29/53/1008–1011; HALS DE/P/T638.

[47] See Appendix 3 for the extant accounts examined for this study for the manor of Feckenham and the Honour of Tutbury manor.

In the case of farmers, from the late 1460s in particular, accounts show that the farmer had begun to be held responsible for the receipts of the perquisites of the manor court as well as more regularly making allowances for customary repairs on the manor before delivering payment to the receiver.[48] Farmers' accounts, in effect, began to resemble those rendered by bailiffs on other estates owned by the queens, thereby pointing to a confluence in the roles of bailiffs, reeves and farmers, although perhaps mainly on smaller manors. Studies have shown that there were instances in which bailiffs and reeves aspired to and did move into the positions of farmers by leasing estates themselves.[49] In such situations it is entirely possible that the duties of all three positions converged on the one individual. All this suggests that changes in estate stewardship processes were not necessarily affected or influenced by the identity of the landowner. Rather, it was changes in land use and tenure that drove these adjustments in the administrative machinery of the queens' landholdings.

Another way to judge the relative importance of the local officials is to examine levels of remuneration. In theory, since the post of bailiff was filled by appointing an outsider, it came with a fixed and consistent annual salary. This payment was called a fee on some properties but known as a stipend on others. Conversely, reeves were drawn from the local tenantry and thus were meant to be acquitted of their villein duties in return for their service as reeves.[50] In practice, some also received regular payments in the form of stipends. Others, such as the reeves for the manor of the Honour of Tutbury, were paid an allowance for their financial duties.[51] Unsurprisingly, the amounts of stipends or fees paid to bailiffs, reeves and other local officials varied depending on the property. The bailiff of Gillingham received a stipend of 40*s* throughout the period 1474–1502, as did the bailiff of Havering-atte-Bower. However, Havering's bailiff began to receive a much higher stipend of 100*s* from 1478, an indication that this manor had become much more important to its owner.[52] Similarly, the bailiff for the liberty of Cookham and Bray received a fee of 53*s* 4*d* while Corsham's and Benham Lovell's bailiffs were paid only 13*s* 4*d*, amounts that undoubtedly reflected the size and importance of the estates. In comparison, Feckenham's reeve was paid 10*s* annually while Merston Meysy's

---

[48] For example, the farmers' accounts for Mashbury demonstrate this development. TNA DL29/43/840–851.

[49] For examples of individuals who did so, see Christopher Dyer, 'A Suffolk Farmer in the Fifteenth Century', *The Agricultural History Review* 55, no. 1 (2007):1–22; Barbara Harvey, 'The Leasing of the Abbot of Westminster's Demesnes in the Later Middle Ages', *EcHR* 22, no. 1 (1969): 17–27.

[50] Denholm-Young, *Seignorial Administration in England*, 34.

[51] The allowance was set at 1*d* per day and for the manor of the Honour of Tutbury, this allowance remained unchanged for the years between 1440 and 1485, for which there are extant reeve accounts.

[52] TNA DL29/724/11800–11803, SC6/HENVII/1135–1138; DL29/41/794–99; SC6/1094/6–7.

reeve collected 6s 8d for his duties.[53] These sums are on par with those paid to the *messor* and the accounts clerk, for instance, which demonstrates the clear seniority of the bailiff in comparison with reeves and the like. As the post of collector of receipts became more widespread in the latter half of the 1400s, the accounts began to show records of stipends paid to these individuals. There are examples of collectors of receipts being paid relatively large fees of 40s, as in the case of Marlborough, or 20s in Hamstead Marshall.[54] What this shows is that while bailiffs continued to be ranked highly at local levels, collectors of receipts and reeves could be and were given financial accounting responsibilities, meaning that they became just as important as bailiffs on at least some estates. The blurring of duties and in the naming of the posts is unremarkable in this context.

Who were the individuals who served at the local levels of estate administration? According to medieval estate treatises, the bailiff was meant to be an outsider appointed and paid by the lord, while the reeve typically was one of the manorial tenants and should have been elected as being the 'best husbandman and farmer and as the most suitable person for looking after the lord's interests'.[55] While there is little direct evidence for the queens' lands to show exactly how, in reality, either bailiff or reeve was selected for any estate, there are clues to suggest that treatise guidelines only occasionally still held true in the later fifteenth century. The extant accounts for Gillingham in Dorset, for instance, show a significant level of continuity in the individuals who served as bailiff. John Baron, John Mervyn and Gilbert Thomson each served as bailiff for four years between 1466 and 1482, often but not always in consecutive years, and there is little evidence showing that they were outsiders.[56] Another noted example is the manor of Hertingfordbury, where the previously mentioned John Draper served as reeve and/or bailiff for almost a decade from 1460. Accounts show that one William Southwode, named by Margaret of Anjou as her bailiff of Hertingfordbury in an undated letter, had previously served as reeve, at least for a year, in 1456.[57] He was appointed bailiff again in 1468 after Draper and occupied this post for approximately six years thereafter. Southwode evidently agreed to serve again in the post in 1477, going on to do so for another decade while surviving both the usurpation of Richard III and the violent birth of the Tudor monarchy in the 1480s.[58] That Southwode remained in the post through two changes in the monarchy may be a testament to his flexible loyalties. Alternatively, such

---

[53] TNA DL29/724/11800–11803, SC6/HENVII/1135–1138.
[54] TNA DL29/724/11800–11803, SC6/HENVII/1135–1138.
[55] Oschinsky, *Walter of Henley*, 275, 291.
[56] TNA DL29/724/11804–11817.
[57] HHLA Court roll 21/7; *The Letters of Margaret of Anjou*, 83 (no. 47).
[58] TNA DL29/53/1008–1021; HALS DE/P/T638; HHLA Court rolls 19/9, 21/11, 21/18.

continuity could also mean that the bailiffs of Hertingfordbury manor were not actually outsiders at all and that the post was filled by appointing the most important tenant of the area or the one with the closest ties to the manor. This argument is strengthened by the fact that the bailiff for 1489–90 and possibly some two years before and three years after was one William Draper.[59] By this time, the manor was no longer owned by the queen as it was not included in Elizabeth of York's dower. If William Draper was a relative, possibly the son, of John Draper, it would be more logical to presume that the Drapers were local tenants and that the post of bailiff was being filled by local residents.

Similar continuity in service can be observed in the case of other local officials, such as reeves. Reeve accounts for the Honour of Tutbury demonstrate a high level of stability with individuals such as Thomas Orchard fulfilling the duties of reeve for approximately two decades.[60] Others such as John Agard served as ward collector of receipts for a decade from 1476.[61] Reeves and collectors of receipts obviously could be local persons who were elected, ostensibly, on an annual basis.[62] These individuals were the most visible and physically present representatives of officialdom on the estate since they typically lived among the residents.[63] Yet the duties of the reeves, especially their financial responsibilities, could be quite onerous, rendering the post an unattractive one. Hence, the same person may have served as reeve for years on end because no one else could be found who was willing to undertake the duties or because the landholder, having gained a satisfactory incumbent, wished to obtain a consistent level of service and thus prevailed upon the individual to stay in the post.

This continuity in serving officials was not evident on all the queens' holdings. Most of the bailiff accounts for the lordship and manor of Pleshey from 1452 until 1482, during which first Margaret of Anjou and then Elizabeth Woodville was queen, named a different accounting official from one financial year to the next, albeit there are some individuals who were named more than once.[64] It is unclear why this occurred and the change from one queen to another as landowner may or may not have been a significant factor, but there is a clue to be found in two accounts for the accounting years 1477 and 1478. In the first account, Thomas Ardern is named as bailiff '*et aliorum*' ('and others'), that is to say, there was more than one bailiff for Pleshey at the time.[65] Ardern's name being on the account surely meant that he was the bailiff who held responsibility for that year's account. The second account is

---

[59] HHLA Court roll 19/12.
[60] TNA DL29/369/6186, 6189, DL29/371/6200, DL29/372/6202, 6204, 6206.
[61] TNA DL29/372/6208, 6209, DL29/373/6212.
[62] Bailey, *The English Manor*, 98.
[63] Bennett, 'The Reeve and the Manor', 360–1.
[64] TNA DL29/43/829–840, DL29/44/841–851, SC6/1093/15–16.
[65] TNA DL29/44/848.

even more explicit, naming William Ward as the *capitalis ballivus*, or head bailiff.[66] This meant that at least two bailiffs served Pleshey at least some of the time, a situation that is entirely possible given the importance of the lordship. It also suggests that the financial responsibilities incumbent on the bailiffs were undertaken by a different person each year, either intentionally to spread the workload around or because no single individual was willing to shoulder the responsibilities every year.

Moving on to the more senior level of estate administration, we find stewards and receivers. In relation to management and supervision, the local estate officials were theoretically answerable to the steward of lands.[67] The Husbandry stated that this senior official was normally responsible for a number of manors and was expected to visit each of them several times a year.[68] He was not, however, a financial officer and so was not liable for the drawing up of financial accounts for the landowner. This means that it is difficult to find evidence for the duties and functions of this official. Nevertheless, in the fifteenth century the steward remained an important person in the life of an estate, even with the changing agrarian landscape and increasing trend towards leasing. As Margaret of Anjou's letters reveal, issues to do with repairs on the estate or the appointment of a bailiff were among the many important matters brought to the attention of the steward of lands in the fifteenth century.[69]

The receiver's job, as laid out in a memorandum of 1484, was 'to ride, survey, receive and remember in every behalf that might be most for the king's profit and thereof yearly to make report'.[70] His responsibilities were primarily financial in nature. His job was to collect the revenues and this implies that he was not as intimately involved as the steward was with the management or the specifics of administration on each of the estates within his jurisdiction, even though it was more than likely that he was knowledgeable enough about such matters.[71] Additionally, the receiver could be responsible for the revenues of

---

[66] TNA DL29/44/849.
[67] There existed two different stewardship posts, one for lands and the other for households. Only the duties and responsibilities of the steward of lands were outlined in estate treatises such as the Seneschaucy. Oschinsky, *Walter of Henley*, 265–9.
[68] Ibid., 265.
[69] For example, *The Letters of Margaret of Anjou*, 52, 58 (nos 28, 31).
[70] The memorandum has been summarised in Wolffe, *The Royal Demesne in English History*, 187–8. There were different types of receivers, receivers of revenues from lands, queen's gold and other non-manorial sources. For example, Thomas Stidolf served as Elizabeth Woodville's receiver of queen's gold and fee-farms but not her revenues from lands. Johnstone II, 285.
[71] See Carole Rawcliffe, *The Staffords, Earls of Stafford and Dukes of Buckingham 1394–1521* (Cambridge: Cambridge University Press, 1978), 46, for a description of the duties of a receiver of the Stafford estates in the fifteenth century and the type of person who might have been employed in such a capacity.

Table 5: Annual Fees for Stewards of Lands.[1]

Lands[2]	Name	Landholder	Year(s)[3]	Yearly Fee
Essex/Hertford/Middlesex (includes properties in London & Surrey)	William Tyrell, esquire	Margaret of Anjou	1453, 1455–58, 1460	£20
	Thomas Mountgomery, knight	Crown	1461–63	£20
		Elizabeth Woodville	1464–77, 1479–80, 1482	£20
Essex/Suffolk[4]	John Risley, knight	Elizabeth of York	1487, 1489–95, 1497–98, 1500	£20
Duchy of Lancaster (DL) lands in Northamptonshire (South Parts)	William Lord Hastings	Elizabeth Woodville	1466	£10
Norfolk/Suffolk/Cambridgeshire	Anthony Woodville, Lord Scales	Elizabeth Woodville	1466, 1472	£10
DL lands in Oxford, Buckinghamshire and Hereford[5]	William de la Pole, earl of Suffolk	Margaret of Anjou	1445, 1446, 1448	£13 6s 8d
Pevensey and other lands in Sussex	Richard Ffenys, knight	Elizabeth Woodville	1466	£6 13s 4d

1 This table was compiled using the queens' household accounts, extant land valors, and receivers accounts listed in Appendix 3.
2 The names of the groups of lands are as labelled in the primary sources and refer to receiverships. Refer to Appendix 1 for the lists of lands owned by each of the queens in each of the counties.
3 The years are those for which manorial documents are extant or that are corroborated by other extant evidence.
4 This group comprises those properties in the Essex/Hertford/Middlesex group that were granted to Elizabeth of York.
5 Lands in Oxfordshire and Buckinghamshire that were granted to the queens after Margaret of Anjou were absorbed into the receivership for DL lands that were inherited from the earldom of Hereford.

Table 5 (continued).

Lands	Name	Landholder	Year(s)	Yearly Fee
Partes Australes (all DL lands in the South Parts)	Edmund Hungerford, knight	Margaret of Anjou	1443–60	100s (Kingston) £14 (Wiltshire lands)
DL lands in Dorset (South Parts)	John, Lord Audeley	Crown/DL	1461–64	100s
		Elizabeth Woodville	1465–80	100s
DL lands in Wiltshire (South Parts)	Robert Poyntz, knight	Crown/DL	1461–64	100s
		Elizabeth Woodville	1465–69	100s
	Robert Poyntz & Roger Toucotes (joint stewards)	Elizabeth Woodville	1470	100s
	Roger Toucotes, knight	Elizabeth Woodville	1471–80	100s
	Thomas Wenselow, esq	Crown	1461	100s
	Thomas Wenselow & Thomas Prudde, esq (joint stewards)	Crown	1462	100s
DL lands in Berkshire & Hampshire (South Parts)	Thomas Prudde	Crown	1463, 1464	100s
		Elizabeth Woodville	1465–70	100s
	John Duddley, esq	Elizabeth Woodville	1471–80	100s

DL lands in Dorset & Wiltshire (inherited from earldom of Hereford)	Robert Poyntz	Elizabeth Woodville	1466	40s
	Robert Poyntz & Roger Toucotes (joint stewards)	Elizabeth Woodville	1468	40s
	Roger Toucotes	Elizabeth Woodville	1473	40s
Geddington, Northamptonshire	Robert Iseham	Elizabeth Woodville	1466	100s
Haseley & Pyrton, Hereford (part of DL lands inherited from earldom of Hereford)	Humphrey Forster, esq	Elizabeth Woodville	1466	40s
Cookham & Bray, Berkshire (part of Crown lands in the South Parts)	William Norres, knight	Elizabeth Woodville	1466, 1468–80, 1488, 1489, 1496, 1503	£4
	John, Lord Audeley	Elizabeth Woodville	1466, 1468–70	53s 4d
	William, Lord Stourton	Elizabeth Woodville	1471–76	53s 4d
Gillingham, Dorset (part of Crown lands in the South Parts)	Thomas Grey, marquis of Dorset	Elizabeth Woodville	1477–80	53s 4d
	John Cheyne, knight	Elizabeth of York	1488, 1489, 1496	53s 4d
	Giles, Lord Daubeney	Elizabeth of York	1503	53s 4d
Borough of Marlborough, Wiltshire (part of Crown lands in the South Parts)	George Darell, knight	Elizabeth Woodville	1466	20s
Devizes, Wiltshire (part of Crown lands in the South Parts)	?? Beauchamp (first name missing in manuscript)	Elizabeth Woodville	1466	20s

Table 5 (continued).

Lands	Name	Landholder	Year(s)	Yearly Fee
Marlborough & Devizes, Wiltshire (part of Crown lands in the South Parts)	George Darell	Elizabeth Woodville	1468–72	40s
	Roger Toucotes	Elizabeth Woodville	1473–80	40s
	Richard Neville, earl of Warwick	Elizabeth Woodville	1466	40s
Feckenham, Worcester	Humphrey (or John?) Savage, knight	Elizabeth of York	1488, 1489, 1490	40s
	Gilbert Talbot, knight	Elizabeth of York	1494–1500	40s
Odiham, Hampshire (part of Crown lands in the South Parts)	Richard Nanfan, knight	Elizabeth of York	1496, 1503	40s
	Thomas Lymerik, knight	Elizabeth Woodville	1466	26s 8d
	Lord Sutherwike	Elizabeth Woodville	1468, 1469	26s 8d
Corsham, Wiltshire (part of Crown lands in the South Parts)	Richard Haute, esq	Elizabeth Woodville	1470–80	26s 8d
	Walter Hungerford, knight	Elizabeth of York	1488, 1489, 1501, 1502	26s 8d
Havering-atte-Bower, Essex (part of Crown lands in Essex, Surrey, Kent, London during Elizabeth Woodville's time, and the Essex/Suffolk group during Elizabeth of York's time)	Thomas Mountgomery	Elizabeth Woodville	1464–73, 1475, 1479, 1482	£6
		Elizabeth of York	1487–1493	£6
	Thomas Lovell, knight	Elizabeth of York	1494–1502	£6

	Lord Strange	Elizabeth Woodville	1468–78	40s
Langley Marish & Wraysbury, Buckinghamshire (part of Crown lands in the South Parts)	James Haute, esq	Elizabeth Woodville	1479, 1480	40s
	John Litton, esq	Elizabeth of York	1488, 1489	26s 8d
	Robert Litton (possibly a relative of John Litton)	Elizabeth of York	1496, 1503	26s 8d
Banstead & Walton, Surrey	Nicholas Gaynesford, esq	Elizabeth of York	1488, 1489, 1496	13s 4d
(part of Crown lands in the South Parts)	Richard Carewe, knight	Crown	1503	13s 4d

Table 6: Annual Fees for Receivers.[1]

Lands/Receivership[2]	Name	Landholder	Year(s)[3]	Yearly Fee
Essex/Hertford/Middlesex (includes properties in London & Surrey)	William Nanseglos	Margaret of Anjou	1453, 1455–58, 1460	£10
	Roger Ree, esq	Crown	1461–63	£10
		Elizabeth Woodville	1466, 1468, 1473	£10
	Nicholas Gaynesford, esq	Elizabeth Woodville	1475–77, 1479, 80	£10
	John Berdfield	Elizabeth Woodville	1482	£10
	John Berdfield	Elizabeth of York	1487–96	£10
Essex/Suffolk[4]	Thomas Baxster	Elizabeth of York	1497–99	£10
	William Poyntz	Elizabeth of York	1500–03	£10

1. This table was compiled using the queens' household accounts, extant land valors, and receivers accounts listed in Appendix 3.
2. The names of the groups of lands are as labelled in the primary sources and refer to receiverships. Refer to Appendix 1 for the lists of lands owned by each of the queens in each of the counties.
3. The years are those for which manorial documents are extant or that are corroborated by other extant evidence.
4. This group comprises those properties in the Essex/Hertford/Middlesex group that were granted to Elizabeth of York.

Duchy of Lancaster (DL) lands in Northamptonshire (South Parts)	William Stevens	Elizabeth Woodville	1466	£10
	John Holcote	Elizabeth Woodville	1472	£10
Norfolk/Suffolk/Cambridgeshire	Nicholas Sharp, esq & Christopher Sharp (joint receivers)	Elizabeth Woodville	1466	£6 13s 4d
	Christopher Sharp	Elizabeth Woodville	1472	£6 13s 4d
DL lands in Oxford, Buckinghamshire and Hereford[5]	William Osgodby	Margaret of Anjou	1445, 1446, 1448	£10
	Thomas Doge	Margaret of Anjou	1443–49	£6 13s 4d
Partes Australes (all DL lands in the South Parts; administratively split up after 1465)	Walter Gorfen	Margaret of Anjou	1450–60	£6 13s 4d
	Thomas Mauncell, esq	Crown	1461–64	£6 13s 4d
		Elizabeth Woodville	1465	£6 13s 4d

5 Lands in Oxfordshire and Buckinghamshire that were granted to the queens after Margaret of Anjou were absorbed into the receivership for DL lands that were inherited from the earldom of Hereford.

Table 6 (continued).

Lands/Receivership	Name	Landholder	Year(s)	Yearly Fee
DL lands in Wiltshire, Dorset, Oxford and others (South Parts)	Thomas Mauncell, esq	Elizabeth Woodville	1466	66s 8d
	Maurice Kidwelly	Elizabeth Woodville	1466	66s 8d
	Maurice Kidwelly (now the sole receiver for DL lands in South Parts, incorporating Mauncell's duties as in 1466)	Elizabeth Woodville	1468–80	£6 13s 4d
DL lands in Wiltshire, Dorset, Oxford and others (inherited from the earldom of Hereford)	Thomas Mauncell	Elizabeth Woodville	1466	36s 8d
	Maurice Kidwelly	Elizabeth Woodville	1466	36s 8d
DL lands in Hampshire, Oxford, Berkshire, Buckinghamshire, Wiltshire and Dorset (inherited from the earldom of Hereford)	Maurice Kidwelly (now the sole receiver for all DL lands inherited from the earldom of Hereford, incorporating Mauncell's duties as in 1466)	Elizabeth Woodville	1468, 1473, 1477	100s

	John Rotherham	Elizabeth Woodville	1466	£10
	Richard Bryan	Elizabeth Woodville	1468–79	£13 6s 4d
Partes Australes de Corona (Crown lands in the South Parts)	William Harle	Elizabeth Woodville	1480	£13 6s 4d
	George Chaderton	Elizabeth of York	1488, 1489, 1496	£13 6s 8d
	Jasper Fylongley	Crown	1503	£10
			1464, 1466, 1467	100s
Essex de Corona (Crown lands in Essex, Surrey, Kent, London)	Thomas Holbach	Elizabeth Woodville	1468–71, 1473, 1475, 1477	40s
			1479, 1482	100s
Northamptonshire lands	Martin Haute, esq	Elizabeth Woodville	1465, 1466, 1472	£4
Sutton, Lincoln	John Fogge, knight	Elizabeth Woodville	1468	£4
	Thomas Burgh, knight	Elizabeth Woodville	1473, 1477	£4
Pevensey & lands in Sussex	Nicholas Britte	Elizabeth Woodville	1466	66s 8d

Table 6 (continued).

Lands/Receivership	Name	Landholder	Year(s)	Yearly Fee
Feckenham, Worcester	Richard Harreys	Elizabeth of York	1488–90, 1494–1500, 1502	40s
Wiltshire lands	Edmund Tame	Elizabeth of York	1501	£13 6s 8d
		Crown	1503	£13 6s 8d
Berkhamsted & Kings Langley, Hertford	Owen William	Elizabeth of York	1500, 1501	100s
		Crown	1503	100s

more than one individual holding whilst also taking care of the disbursement of sums for various types of expenditure. As an example, accounts drawn up over the latter half of the fifteenth century by the receiver for the queens' lands in Essex, Hertford and Middlesex typically record a list of fees and wages paid to various officials. They also record annuities paid out as well as allowances such as reimbursements for travel expenses.[72]

The posts of steward and receiver were both salaried, the wages usually being recorded in the accounts as fees. As in the case of local officials, there were different rates of pay for these positions at different locations and stewards and receivers were not as a rule paid the same amounts. As Tables 5 and 6 show, stewards were generally, though not always, paid more than receivers. Anthony Woodville, Lord Scales, was paid £10 as steward for the queen's lands in Norfolk, Suffolk and Cambridgeshire in 1472, while the corresponding receiver, Christopher Sharp, was paid only £6 13s 4d. Likewise, Elizabeth Woodville paid the receivers for her lands in Essex, Hertford and Middlesex £10, which was half of what the steward, Thomas Mountgomery, was paid. Yet there were exceptions, such as the manor of Feckenham, where 40s was the fee for both steward and receiver. Higher fees might indicate that stewards were more valued officials than receivers. However, such stark comparisons are not necessarily feasible. After all, the duties of a steward and a receiver were not the same. Moreover, a steward was often appointed to oversee a single holding, but that same estate did not necessarily have its own receiver. Estates such as Gillingham, Corsham, Havering-atte-Bower, and many others were managed by an individual steward but incorporated into specific receiverships for financial purposes. As these posts are not strictly comparable, it is difficult to definitively conclude on the basis of fees paid that stewards were valued more than receivers.

Nonetheless, there are other salient observations to be made in relation to the fees for stewards and receivers. One obvious feature in the tables of fees is that there appear to have been standard rates of pay on the different groups of lands or estates and these rates hardly ever changed despite the frequent monarchic changes of the period. This is most clearly demonstrated in the case of estates for which we have extant documents spanning the years from Margaret of Anjou to Elizabeth of York. One instance is the receivership that included the Essex lands, where the steward was always paid £20 and the receiver £10; another is the manor of Havering-atte-Bower whose steward's fee remained unchanged through the years at £6. Naturally, the most highly paid stewards and receivers were those overseeing receiverships that comprised large groups of lands or included the most valuable and important estates. If we judge only by the officials' fees, among the most important receiverships to the queens were the Essex/Hertford/Middlesex group, the Essex/Surrey/Kent/London group and various groups with Duchy of Lancaster or Crown

---

[72] TNA DL29/58/1103–1108 and DL29/59/1109–1114.

lands. Certain single estates were also considered extremely important, such as Geddington in Northamptonshire and Havering-atte-Bower in Essex, and their stewards were paid commensurately higher fees.

Some important, though brief, points should be made about the background and social standing of the individuals who served as stewards and receivers.[73] Unlike reeves or even bailiffs, persons appointed as stewards and receivers were not local manorial tenants but were drawn from the ranks of the nobility and gentry. In fact, the social standing of those who are listed as stewards in the extant evidence appears to be generally higher than those who served as receivers. Most of the stewards were nobles and knights while many of the receivers were esquires or of gentry stock. It is tempting to claim there is a direct correlation between the high level of fees for stewards and the generally higher status and background of the incumbents. But such a conclusion is problematic in the face of clear exceptions. The manor of Feckenham is an obvious case. Nobles such as Richard Neville, earl of Warwick, and Sir Gilbert Talbot served as stewards for Feckenham in the latter half of the fifteenth century, while its receiver was Richard Harreys, who hailed from a gentry family. Yet they all earned the same fee of 40s. Other cases include the manors of Langley Marish and Wraysbury, Buckinghamshire, which shared a steward, and the manor of Corsham in Wiltshire. In each of these manors, the fees did not change even when a person of lower status replaced an incumbent as steward.

Judging by what we know of their lives and careers, the men who served in the queens' administrative machineries were highly capable individuals possessing considerable experience in administration and finance. Families such as the Kidwellys, Leventhorpes and Sapcotes specialised in estate management, with members sometimes taking on a variety of roles serving different lords.[74] Maurice Kidwelly was one such individual. He served not only as receiver for almost a decade of the Duchy of Lancaster lands in Hampshire, Oxfordshire, Berkshire, Buckinghamshire, Wiltshire and Dorset that were granted to Elizabeth Woodville in dower but also in various other capacities including king's surveyor and receiver of the lordship of Kidwelly in Wales.[75] Another member of the Kidwelly family, Morgan, served as king's attorney as well as steward in Dorset during Richard III's reign.[76]

Needless to say, competence had to be accompanied by loyalty to the monarch, at least outwardly. John Viscount Beaumont, a loyal Lancastrian

---

[73] An extended examination of the backgrounds of the estate officials of the queens is beyond the scope of this book but see Alexander R. Brondarbit, *Power-Brokers and the Yorkist State, 1461–1485* (Woodbridge: Boydell Press, 2020) for a study of influential figures and families of the period.

[74] B. P. Wolffe, 'The Management of the English Royal Estates under the Yorkist Kings', *EHR* 71 (1956): 3.

[75] Somerville, *The History of the Duchy of Lancaster*, 623.

[76] *Ibid.*, 628.

Managing the Queen's Lands

who died fighting for Henry VI, served as Margaret of Anjou's chief steward of lands.[77] Roger Ree, receiver for the queen's lands in Essex, Hertfordshire and Middlesex, was first appointed by Edward IV as reward for his loyalty to the Yorkist cause and continued to serve in that capacity when the lands were granted to Edward's queen in dower.[78] It was to be expected, of course, that there were some who adapted themselves to changes in the political landscape, as in the case of John Berdfield. He served Elizabeth Woodville from either 1481 or 1482 as receiver for her lands in Essex, Hertfordshire and Middlesex but disappears from the records during the political tumult surrounding the brief reigns of Edward V and Richard III. He re-emerged, however, in 1485 on the accession of Henry VII, having been appointed receiver of duchy lands in Essex, Hertford and Middlesex, and thereafter occupying the post until his death.[79] Clearly, posts such as receivers and stewards went to men able to demonstrate their loyalties to the current occupant of the throne.

OVERSEEING THE QUEEN'S ESTATES

In relation to overall supervision, a key question is who was responsible for the higher-level management of the queens' estates. We might expect that the queens themselves would have made periodic visits to at least some of their properties to conduct checks and carry out supervisory tasks. However, given the quantity and extent of the landholdings, they could not have supervised all their estates and properties unaided.

Among the most important senior officials who oversaw the administration of the queen's estates were the auditors, receivers-general and members of the queen's council. The general role of the queen's auditor was to oversee and check. Yet the lack of sources with specific information or formal instruction about their duties makes it unclear as to what precisely they were meant to concern themselves with. Evidence of their work lies primarily in the existence of two main types of accounts they compiled for the queens, land valors and accounts of arrears, but they also made their mark in checking the queens' household accounts. In the course of their duties, auditors are likely to have travelled frequently and for long distances. Even with the assistance of one or more clerks, the various payments recorded in the household accounts of Margaret and Elizabeth Woodville bear testament to the many journeys that auditors undertook to the various properties.[80] Their high standing in the

---

[77] Beaumont made the ultimate sacrifice, fighting and dying on the Lancastrian side at the battle of Northampton in 1460. Myers, 'The Household of Queen Margaret of Anjou', 153.
[78] Somerville, *The History of the Duchy of Lancaster*, 608.
[79] *Ibid.*, 608.
[80] Myers, 'The Household of Queen Elizabeth Woodville', 296–7; Myers, 'The Household of Queen Margaret of Anjou', 192–3.

Financing Queenship in Late Fifteenth Century England

royal administrations is not in doubt, not least because their fees were usually on par with the queens' most important stewards and receivers. Records show that all the queens valued their auditors enough to pay them £10 in fees as well as allowances for various work expenses.[81] In the case of Margaret of Anjou's auditors, they also occasionally received New Year's gifts from the queen, undoubtedly a sign of her appreciation for their services.[82] Moreover, the fact that no official in the queens' households or estate administrations appears to have been exempt from the audit process is also indicative of the high level of importance placed on the auditor's work.[83]

The individuals who served as the queens' auditors were vastly capable and experienced men. Most, if not all, of them also functioned in other capacities. Margaret's auditors in the early 1450s, John Walsh and Nicholas Sharp, also held a host of other positions throughout their careers. Walsh was, at different times, an auditor for both the Duchy of Lancaster and the Duchy of Cornwall as well as for the queen, and he also served for a period as deputy to the king's chamberlain.[84] Sharp served as auditor for Queen Margaret, Eton and King's College in Cambridge, and he also filled the posts of receiver-general and attorney-general for the Duchy of Lancaster and receiver and feodary for various duchy lands.[85] Elizabeth Woodville's two auditors were just as talented, with John Stanford not only serving the queen but also gaining life appointments as auditor for Crown lands and for lands belonging to the late duke of Norfolk and the late duchess of Somerset.[86] Her other auditor, Robert Browne, served both the queen and the Duchy of Lancaster as auditor, though the queen appears to have dispensed with his services after 1472.[87] There are, unfortunately, few surviving records related to Elizabeth of York's auditors apart from her expense account recording one payment of £10 in fees to Richard Bedell for acting as the queen's auditor in 1502. It is, however, possible that he came from a gentry family used to royal service since there are records of other Bedells, such as William Bedell serving as king's sergeant-at-arms

---

[81] Myers, 'The Household of Queen Elizabeth Woodville', 295–6 (p. 23); Myers, 'The Household of Queen Margaret of Anjou', 192–3 (fol. 15b); Queen's book, fol. 92.

[82] TNA E101/410/2. There is, unfortunately, no extant evidence for Elizabeth Woodville's and Elizabeth of York's New Year's gifts.

[83] For instance, Elizabeth Woodville's household account contains notations by auditors, some of which disallow or reduce the fees recorded in the account. Myers, 'The Household of Queen Elizabeth Woodville', 294–9, 303–4.

[84] Somerville, *The History of the Duchy of Lancaster*, 439–40.

[85] Somerville, *The History of the Duchy of Lancaster*, 399–400.

[86] *Ibid.*, 440.

[87] The land valor for 1473 (TNA DL29/735/12057) was drawn up by John Stanford, now the queen's sole auditor. Somerville, *The History of the Duchy of Lancaster*, 441.

up until 1491 and later being called to serve on several royal commissions of peace between the years 1500 and 1509.[88]

Unlike the auditor, the post of receiver-general does not seem to have been crucial for the smooth administration of noble estates. There is evidence of their existence only on the very largest complexes of landholdings and then not even consistently. The powerful Percy family, earls of Northumberland, were holders of a very large landed inheritance that rivalled even the Duchy of Lancaster in territorial dimensions.[89] Yet there is no trace in the records before 1489 of an official described as the receiver-general of all the estates. After that date, administrative changes resulted in the creation of a post of receiver-general for the south parts and a keeper of the coffers who appears to have fulfilled the duties of receiver-general for the rest of the earl's landholdings.[90] Correspondingly, the head of the administration of the estates of Richard, duke of York, was by no means always a receiver-general. Only a few extant receivers' accounts for these estates reference such an official and Rosenthal suggests it was likely that each of the receivers was, therefore, usually directly responsible to the lord's auditors. Some receivers might even have reported directly to the lord himself or his auditors even when there was a receiver-general.[91]

For the queens in this study, the evidence confirms the existence of receivers-general serving each of them, at least for some of the time. In Margaret's case, William Cotton, the receiver-general for the Duchy of Lancaster, also served as her receiver-general and treasurer, at least from 1452. On his death in 1455, his post in the queen's administration passed to Robert Tanfield, who was previously Margaret's attorney-general.[92] Elizabeth Woodville also utilised the services of a receiver-general, John Forster, at least in the 1460s. In terms of remuneration, Cotton and Forster, at least, received £50 in fees for their services from their royal mistresses and the occasional gift as well.[93] In Elizabeth of York's case, her receiver-general of almost a decade from the early years, Edmund Chaderton, had previously served Richard III as his treasurer of the chamber and clerk of the hanaper. Chaderton received a general pardon from the new Tudor king in 1485 and rose high in royal

---

[88] CPR 1485–1494, 430; CPR 1494–1509, 646–9, 652, 655.
[89] Bean, *The Estates of the Percy Family*, 3.
[90] *Ibid.*, 161. The keeper of the coffers received the revenues from the receivers for all the lands except the south parts.
[91] Rosenthal, 'The Estates and Finances of Richard Duke of York', 169.
[92] Somerville, *The History of the Duchy of Lancaster*, 209; Josiah Wedgwood, *History of Parliament: Biographies of the Members of the Commons House, 1439–1509* (London: His Majesty's Stationery Office, 1936), 840–1.
[93] Cotton is recorded as being the recipient of a New Year's gift from Margaret of Anjou in 1448. TNA E101/410/2.

service, attaining the post of receiver-general to the queen by 1487 or possibly earlier.[94] From 1495, however, Chaderton was no longer taking receipt of the queen's revenue as her receiver-general. Instead, various accounts record payments of revenue from her receivers to one Richard Decons. Curiously, Decons was not styled as receiver-general in any of the records. He was paid a fee of £10 in 1502 for holding the office of the signet and £16 13s 4d for receiving the queen's revenue and to reimburse his travel costs, but he does not seem to have been actually appointed as receiver-general.[95] When compared with the likes of Cotton and Forster, the Tudors may well have saved a lot of money by replacing Chaderton with Decons, even though there is no evidence as yet showing how much Chaderton himself was paid as receiver-general. Clearly, at least some of the functions of a receiver-general could be performed by an individual who was not appointed as such.

Obvious comparisons in relation to receivers-general can be made with other elite women of the period. Studies of women such as Margaret Beaufort, mother to Henry VII, and Cecily Neville, dowager duchess of York and grandmother of Elizabeth of York, have included brief forays into the management of their estates. In neither case has any evidence been found of a receiver-general among their officials. Instead, the impression we get is of two elite women who were such active and involved estate managers that they had no need of receivers-general.[96] In light of this information, it is worth considering whether each queen's administration always included a receiver-general and just how important such an official really was. I have already shown that this post could technically be dispensed with in Elizabeth of York's case. In Elizabeth Woodville's case, there are some receivers' accounts for the queens' lands that refer to payments being made to the receiver-general of the time. But there are also others that make no such specific references, recording only that payments were delivered to the queen's household, sometimes to her chamber or to her coffer. This is amply demonstrated as follows. Accounts rendered for 1464 to 1467 by Roger Ree, receiver for Elizabeth Woodville's dower lands in Essex, Hertford and Middlesex, refer to delivery of receipts to John Forster, the queen's receiver-general.[97] In contrast, Ree's accounts from 1470 onwards record only that payments were delivered to the queen's chamber.[98] Similarly, the receiver for lands granted to her from the traditional 'South Parts' of the Duchy of Lancaster lands recorded in his accounts for the 1470s that revenues were delivered to the queen's coffer.[99] We can, therefore, infer that there were

---

[94] CPR 1485–1494, 41; TNA DL29/736/12067.
[95] TNA DL29/736/12067, 12068; WAM 12172, 12173; Queen's Book, fol. 92.
[96] J. L. Laynesmith, *Cecily Duchess of York* (London; New York: Bloomsbury Academic, 2017), 107–9.
[97] TNA SC6/1093/17.
[98] TNA SC6/1094/5.
[99] TNA DL29/711/11464–11476.

Managing the Queen's Lands

periods of time during which there was no receiver-general serving Elizabeth Woodville or, alternatively, that the receiver-general was not always the hub through which the queens' revenues passed.

Nonetheless, the presence or absence of a receiver-general in the queen's administration does not facilitate firm conclusions about the queen's personal level of involvement in estate administration. The reason for queens being served by a receiver-general could simply have been because their administrations, at least in the fifteenth century, were modelled on the Duchy of Lancaster, which always had a receiver-general from 1399, when the duke at that time also became the new king, Henry IV. But a receiver-general could have provided an additional level of continuity and stability for an administration that had to deal with numerous geographically scattered estates. Moreover, an appointment to such a post represented a royal opportunity to exercise patronage and present rewards for service.[100] Still, just because one queen or another was served by a receiver-general does not mean that the queens themselves were passive landowners or administrators. Instead, the evidence suggests that the receiver-general's role in the queen's administration was not so all-encompassing and powerful that they pushed the queens wholly into the background.

The last, but by no means least, part of the queen's administrative machinery that I now turn to discuss relates to policy-making. This role was performed by the queen's council, which existed as far back as the thirteenth century.[101] Unfortunately, the paucity of evidence for records of meetings or of policies for estate management for the period means that it is difficult to know the exact workings of the queens' councils in the later fifteenth century. That these councils kept records of their meetings appears to be true at least from the fifteenth century onwards.[102] However, without those records, it is almost impossible to ascertain how the meetings were conducted, what, if any, protocols or rituals existed for council business, and how decisions were made in council. Neither is it known who convened the meetings, whether they were led by any particular members, or how frequently the queen herself attended these meetings. What we do know is little indeed. Both Margaret of Anjou's and Elizabeth Woodville's councils met in chambers in the palace of

---

[100] R. H. Hilton, trans. and ed. *Ministers' Accounts of the Warwickshire Estates of the Duke of Clarence 1479–80* (Oxford: Oxford University Press, 1952), xxix. This method of payment was also recognised in the household ordinances of Edward IV. A. R. Myers, *The Household of Edward IV: The Black Book and the Ordinance of 1478* (Manchester: Manchester University Press, 1959), 98.

[101] For queens' councils in the thirteenth to fifteenth centuries in England, see Anne Crawford, 'The Queen's Council in the Middle Ages', *EHR* 116, no. 469 (Nov. 2001): 1193–1211.

[102] Crawford, 'The Queen's Council', 1193.

Westminster that had been assigned for that purpose as well as for storage of the queens' financial records. The council chambers had a keeper, ushers were paid to attend council members and messengers were assigned to the council.[103] Payments for relevant council expenses pepper the queens' household accounts. Examples include £10 to Thomas Lord Scales for daily attendance at Queen Margaret's council meetings, payments to Elizabeth Woodville's receiver-general and chancellor for journeys involving council business, payments to auditors to accompany council members, and payments of fees to various council members.[104] Such expenses suggest that the councils conducted frequent and regular meetings to deal with the queens' affairs, although it is impossible to say whether all council members were always present at the meetings. It also points to the councils' important roles in the queens' household and estate administrations.

The fact that the councils were composed of some or even all the most important household and estate officials and included those well-versed in the law is another indication of their standing. In addition to select outsiders, such as Edmund, duke of Somerset, who sat on Margaret of Anjou's council, the councils were composed of officials who managed the queens' landholdings and served in their households. Margaret's council included her chief steward of lands, secretary, chancellor, chamberlain, receiver-general, and attorney-general. Other less senior officials, such as the knight carvers or stewards, treasurer of the chamber, and the attorneys and apprentices-at-law, also appear to have served on her council. The council for Elizabeth Woodville was also composed of her most senior officials, including the receiver-general, chamberlain, chancellor, attorney-general, secretary and stewards. While there is no evidence that these councils were fixed in composition or number, the most senior officials probably made up the core of the council. They may have served as permanent members, while the minor officials attended council meetings only intermittently or as needed.

The backgrounds of some of the men who served on the queens' councils, like those of the other estate officials, were not necessarily of the noblest origins. A. L. Brown's survey of those who served as king's councillors concludes that the kings of the fifteenth century moved away from past heavy reliance on clerics and instead became increasingly dependent on the gentry for advice and service.[105] J. R. Lander further suggests that, while the

---

[103] CPR 1452–61, 114, 487; Crawford, 'The Queen's Council', 1206–07; Myers, 'The Household of Queen Elizabeth Woodville', 293–5, 297; Myers, 'The Household of Queen Margaret of Anjou', 151, 193–5.

[104] Crawford, 'The Queen's Council', 1206; Myers, 'The Household of Queen Elizabeth Woodville', 293–5, 297; Myers, 'The Household of Queen Margaret of Anjou', 190–6.

[105] A. L. Brown, 'The King's Councillors in Fifteenth-Century England', *TRHS* 19 (1969): 117.

loyalties of the individual were not discounted as a factor, Edward IV, for one, was content to accept service from whomsoever would offer it.[106] Edward evidently valued competence and a willingness to give service even when the individual's affiliations to the Yorkist cause were looser than strictly desired. Likewise, those who served the queens in the fifteenth century in their households and on their councils were those of gentle, sometimes noble, birth. Men such as William Cotton and Robert Tanfield, who served Margaret of Anjou, as well as John Forster and the Haute family, the latter of whom were prominent in Yorkist service, were all either of gentry stock or minor nobles who had made careers out of providing administrative and conciliar service to their monarchs and to the greater nobility in the land.[107] Tellingly, the frequent occurrence of duchy or king's men serving the queens resulted in a high level of interconnectivity between the administrations of the queens, the kings and the Duchy of Lancaster, thereby almost certainly ensuring that the queens' councils reflected similar attitudes as the other kingly and noble councils.[108]

Concerning council work, Johnstone's research on the households of the queens in fourteenth-century England affirms the council's primary role in acting as the driving force turning the wheel that was the queen's estate administration.[109] Johnstone categorises the types of issues handled by the queens' councils as being administrative, judicial and advisory but does not attempt to define any one of them as more important than the others.[110] For the first category, it is true that there are few indications in the queens' household accounts of the involvement of their councils in daily or even semi-regular administration.[111] However, other existing evidence does point to the queens' councils being concerned with a range of estate management issues, including appointments of officials, repairs to property, and dealing with supervisory difficulties. A memorandum written by Richard Croke, one of Margaret's clerks to the council, made note of investigations and enquiries into such matters as illegal fishing, an inquest into a drowning and customary payments for the right to pasture.[112] During Elizabeth Woodville's time as queen, one of her clerks to the council wrote of repairs being required for the mill and the pale of the park at Maresfield and the actions needed to effect these repairs.[113] There is, notwithstanding these examples, no suggestion that

---

[106] J. R. Lander, 'Council, Administration and Councillors, 1461–85', *BIHR* 32 (1959): 156.
[107] The Hautes were prominent in Duchy of Lancaster service. Wedgwood, *History of Parliament*, 227–8, 840–1.
[108] Crawford, 'The Queen's Council', 1205.
[109] Johnstone II, 291.
[110] *Ibid.*, 292.
[111] Myers, 'The Household of Queen Margaret of Anjou', 152.
[112] TNA E163/28/2; Crawford, 'The Queen's Council', 1207.
[113] TNA E298/45; Crawford, 'The Queen's Council', 1207.

councils were consistently and regularly involved on a local level with estate supervision since such affairs were more typically the concern of the bailiffs, reeves and stewards. What is evident, however, is that the councils were not averse to becoming involved with whatever business needed their or the queen's attention. This is true even though it is far from clear that there was a strict demarcation between matters that should have been dealt with at council level and those that should have remained the preserve of the estate officials.

There is much more evidence to show that the queens' councils frequently concerned themselves with judicial matters. This is unremarkable since, in common with baronial councils in general, many of the council members were themselves lawyers and all three queens were served not only by an attorney-general but also by sizeable teams of lawyers and legal apprentices. William Cotton and John Forster, receivers-general for Margaret and Elizabeth Woodville, were both lawyers. Margaret also had an attorney-general and ten attorneys and apprentices-at-law on her payroll. Elizabeth Woodville was served by an attorney-general, solicitor-general and six other sergeants-at-law, attorneys and legal apprentices. There are only two attorneys and two sergeants-at-law listed in Elizabeth of York's household but there may have been more whose wages were recorded on some source other than the queen's Privy Purse expense account. It is, regrettably, impossible to say whether lawyers were included on the queens' councils because of the amount of judicial work they were engaged in or whether councils involved themselves in judicial matters because there were lawyers at hand to handle the work.[114] In her discussion of several specific cases, Anne Crawford's illustration of the breadth of judicial activities undertaken by the queens' councils highlights the importance of this aspect of council work.[115] As she points out, some of the most routine legal matters to come before the council were disputes between tenants, either within the queens' estates or involving outside parties, disputes between tenants and officials, and complaints against officials.[116] A noted example of a case that the queen's council became involved in was the dispute between the Abbot of Ramsey and the tenants of Elizabeth Woodville at Godmanchester. The matter was referred to in the queen's household account because payments were dispensed for the reimbursement of expenses incurred by council members while dealing with this dispute.[117]

---

[114] Carole Rawcliffe asserts that most, if not all, baronial councils included lawyers retained for their professional services. Rawcliffe, 'Baronial Councils in the Later Middle Ages', in *Patronage, Pedigree and Power in Later Medieval England*, ed. Charles Ross (Gloucester: Sutton, 1979), 90.

[115] Among the most important records that clearly formed the basis for Crawford's discussion were TNA E298/1–4 and E298/45. Crawford, 'The Queen's Council', 1209–11.

[116] *Ibid.*, 1209.

[117] Myers, 'The Household of Queen Elizabeth Woodville', 259, 308–9.

That the council could act as arbitrator is clear; what it also represented was a higher body to whom tenants and officials could bring matters, short of the queen herself. The case involving Sir Philip Coke and the collector of rents at the manor of Havering-atte-Bower in 1497 illustrated how the council could, in effect, act as a court of appeal. Violent disagreement between Coke and the rent collector resulted in Coke physically assaulting the latter. This forced the council to intervene, although it is questionable how willingly the judgement of the council was accepted by Coke.[118] In a different situation, Elizabeth of York's council instigated action by the manorial court regarding regulations for a market at Romford.[119] These cases represent some of the milestones in the gradual progression by which councils, not just those of the queens but also of the Duchy of Lancaster, evolved into courts.[120] On this basis it is evident that while the queen's council began life as an advisory body, the advisory and administrative functions gradually receded in importance relative to the judicial functions. Despite the lack of direct supporting evidence, this development could mean that the level of interaction between the queen and her council may have reduced to a point where the council acted autonomously and merely kept the queen informed of developments in relation to the business at hand.

THE QUEEN AS ADMINISTRATOR

The preceding discussion has brought to the fore the question of the level of participation by the queens themselves in the business of managing their estates. The examples of noblewomen such as Margaret Beaufort and Cecily Neville undeniably show that women could be efficient, involved landowners and administrators even if they were assisted by an army of officials and a council.[121] This point is further attested to in a 1472 letter by John Paston III to his brother, John Paston II. The Pastons were attempting to regain ownership and control of Caister Castle from the duke of Norfolk; this letter outlined a secret meeting and attempt at negotiation with the duchess of Norfolk.[122] The letter makes it clear that the duchess was an interested party and was prepared to refer the matter for further consideration to the duchy council, a scenario

---

[118] McIntosh, *Autonomy and Community*, 65.
[119] *Ibid.*, 251.
[120] Crawford, 'The Queen's Council', 1211.
[121] Michael K. Jones and Malcolm Underwood, *The King's Mother: Lady Margaret Beaufort, Countess of Richmond and Derby* (Cambridge; New York: Cambridge University Press, 1992), 93–136; Laynesmith, *Cecily Duchess of York*, 107–10.
[122] *Paston Letters and Papers of the Fifteenth Century*, 3 parts, ed. Norman Davis (Oxford; New York: Oxford University Press for The Early English Text Society S. S. 20–2, 2004), *Part I*, 578–9; Rawcliffe, 'Baronial Councils', 89.

indicative of the duchess' interest in estate affairs as well as the council's level of authority in the matter.

Not all great landowners, male or female, were involved administrators. The council of John of Gaunt, duke of Lancaster, appears to have been an independent unit that drove the everyday administration of the duchy because the duke himself was too busy to do so.[123] Council members provided the close continuing supervision that the duke could not, and in this capacity the advisory aspects of a council's work are illuminated. Records for the duke's lands in the Honour of Leicester and from his register containing estate letters, writs and warrants show that the duke often acted on the advice of his council on myriad estate matters, many of which were administrative issues. As Somerville would have it, the council's original function was to advise, and it would be surprising if the council did not fulfil this fundamental duty to its lord.[124]

Not having such relevant and direct records as estate letters, more peripheral evidence has been examined to ascertain how involved the queens were as administrators. There is no question that queens could participate in estate administration; the issue is whether the queens in this study were likely to have exercised frequent and active involvement or the converse. There is little evidence to show, for example, that any of the queens were personally involved in the regular selection of estate officials, probably not even at the level of stewards and receivers, much less local estate officials. It is probable, though, that their approval at least was sought in the appointment of new officials in their household at the level of receiver-general, auditor or council member.

Myers, at least, is convinced that Margaret of Anjou, for one, was very likely to have been a forceful enough personality to be in command of her council, the implication being that her council would be led by her wishes.[125] The queen's own correspondence supports this view of her as an assertive person who was not content to leave all matters of estate to her council. Her letter to one Edmund Pyrcan, squire, reprimanded him for threatening William Southwode, her bailiff at Hertingfordbury, and gave him the option of complaining either to her council or directly to her.[126] In like manner, she wrote to another squire, Thomas Bawlde, the prosecutor in a suit against one of her tenants at Walden, Essex, telling him that he might bring the suit to be examined by her and her council.[127] These specific cases could be regarded as trivial matters, more appropriately dealt with by the council or other officials such as the stewards. Yet there were clearly occasions when intervention by the queen was justified and necessary. Her letter to Henry Viscount

---

[123] Somerville, *The History of the Duchy of Lancaster*, 121.
[124] *Ibid.*, 121.
[125] Myers, 'The Household of Queen Margaret of Anjou', 152.
[126] *The Letters of Margaret of Anjou*, 83 (no. 47).
[127] *The Letters of Margaret of Anjou*, 87–8 (no. 50).

Bourchier urged him to set a date to meet with her council in the matter of a dispute involving her tenants at Walden. The tone of the letter suggested that Bourchier had been backward in dealing with the matter. Hence, the queen may have taken it upon herself to write such a letter or did so on advisement by her council.[128] At face value, these letters certainly convey the impression of a queen who was an interested and involved landholder, making herself available to be consulted and ensuring that she was kept informed of estate affairs.[129]

Regrettably, there is less such useful evidence related to Elizabeth Woodville. Myers notes several disallowances of payments to council and other members in the queen's household account, acknowledging that these could not have been approved by any except the queen herself. At the same time, he disavows any suggestion that this queen would have participated in regular operational household or estate management.[130] All the same, this impression of the queen is contradicted by other evidence such as correspondence that demonstrated her active concern as a landholder.[131] One such letter was written by Elizabeth to her steward in Norfolk, William Harleton, concerning a tenant who had asked to be exempted from a fine. From the wording of the letter, we can infer that the queen's decision to grant the tenant his request was taken with advice from her council.[132] A further example was another letter by the queen, this time written to Sir William Stonor, censuring him in brusque language for his alleged usurpation of her hunting rights in her forest of Barnwood and Exhill. Her request that he show any commission that he might have received from the king to either herself personally or to her council makes two distinct points.[133] The first is that she was cognisant of matters concerning her landholdings, having been informed either by her council or by her officials. The second is that she was not always minded to leave issues to be dealt with by her officials. In yet another letter, this time to John de Vere, earl of Oxford, she requested that the earl facilitate the handing over of a manor to Simon Bliaunt, who was possibly a retainer of John Howard, a member of the Norfolk and Howard families and later duke of Norfolk.[134] Crawford's suggestion that John Howard

---

[128] *The Letters of Margaret of Anjou*, 111 (no. 62).

[129] Crawford cautions against assuming that the queen's letters were personally written by her. However, the tone and language of the letters point towards the queen having at least dictated them even if she did not scribe them personally.

[130] Myers, 'The Household of Queen Elizabeth Woodville', 259.

[131] *Letters of the Queens of England*, 134.

[132] TNA DL30/105/1490; J. L. Laynesmith, 'Elizabeth Woodville: The Knight's Widow', in *Later Plantagenet and the Wars of the Roses Consorts: Power, Influence and Dynasty*, eds Aidan Norrie, Carolyn Harris, J. L. Laynesmith, Danna R. Messer and Elena Woodacre (Cham: Palgrave Macmillan, 2023), 224.

[133] *Letters of the Queens of England*, 135.

[134] This letter was originally published in Fenn's edition of the Paston letters as being written by Elizabeth of York. Crawford has subsequently asserted that the dating is

may have prompted the queen's action in writing the letter serves to support the notion that the queen could be relied upon to take an interest in estate affairs and was perceived as possessing the influence necessary to bring about the desired result. While these letters do not conclusively prove that Elizabeth Woodville was a fully active and involved landholder and administrator, they do at least suggest that she is likely to have received regular updates on estate matters and acted as an administratively energetic landowner on at least some occasions. It is also worth remembering that frequent council meetings were held at Windsor in the queen's presence, another indication that the queen probably was actively and regularly involved in administration.[135]

In the case of Elizabeth of York, there is little evidence from which to gauge her level of interest and participation in estate management. Notwithstanding, there exists an example from which we might tentatively draw some conclusions. In her study of the royal manor of Havering-atte-Bower, Marjorie McIntosh discusses an event that occurred in 1487 in which, according to the records, the queen and her council decided to send a rent collector, Thomas Elrington, to live at Havering, armed with a range of instructions and wider duties than had traditionally been undertaken by previous holders of this post. In the interests of demonstrating in part the history of Havering's autonomy as a community, McIntosh outlines the responses of the tenants and other subsequent events that resulted from the original action of sending the rent collector.[136] For my purposes, a significant point in this narrative is that the queen showed an active interest in the matter of Havering's recalcitrant tenants and worked with her council in an attempt to deal with the situation. While the council became more extensively involved in later legal disputes directly resulting from the arrival of the rent collector, the records show that the queen was directly involved at the start. Such slim pickings are by no means sufficient to conclude that Elizabeth of York was active in the administration of her estate, even at policy level. One could even observe that Havering was an atypical example given the Havering community was used to 'scant seigneurial domination and minimal interference by external authorities', meaning that unrest on Havering did not necessarily occur on other royal holdings that were accustomed to closer owner supervision.[137] However, even this one event supports the view that this queen was not entirely uninterested in estate management, that her council did not act totally autonomously with no input from her at all, and that policies were not wholly set without any say by the queen.

---

incorrect and includes it among Elizabeth Woodville's letters based on the events described in the letter. *Letters of the Queens of England*, 135–6.
[135] Myers, 'The Household of Queen Elizabeth Woodville', 292–3; Rawcliffe, 'Baronial Councils', 99–100.
[136] McIntosh, *Autonomy and Community*, 64–6.
[137] *Ibid.*, 1.

Managing the Queen's Lands

Clues as to how active these queens were in estate administration may also be gleaned from what we know of their relationships with their tenants. Peasant discontent and bad relations between lords and peasants were not uncommon features throughout the centuries preceding the fifteenth in England. What we see in fifteenth-century England is more outward and public manifestations of the discontent that had always simmered below the surface.[138] Such manifestations occurred in different forms in various locations, including unrest on the estates of the bishopric of Worcester, landlord–tenant struggles in Halesowen in Warwickshire, the Fauconberg uprising that originated in Kent, and the attack on officials by the men of Brentwood in Essex.[139] Noble lords in the later fifteenth century, such as Edward, duke of Buckingham, experienced many incidents of resistance by their tenants across their lands, resistance that typically played out in the manorial courts.[140] Any perception of unfair dealings by landowners could be enough to provoke violent and hostile responses on the part of the peasantry and tenants. The Great Revolt of 1381 appears to have been a wake-up call of sorts to lords and peasants alike but, for some scholars, it is not unique and serves merely as a larger and more geographically inclusive event than many others have done.[141]

Given this general state of affairs, we might expect to find similar cases of passive or even outright resistance as well as evidence of general discontent on the queens' lands. To this end, the previously mentioned case of Elrington, the rent collector who attempted to collect debts owed to the queen by tenants in Havering-atte-Bower, can yet again serve as a signal example. Violent actions by Havering's tenants in response to Elrington's efforts are no doubt one reason why Crawford has specifically cited this manor as an example that 'all was not well on the queens' lands.'[142] There are other indications of the existence of recalcitrant peasant tenantry on other queens' lands, such as on the manor of Pleasaunce in Greenwich. I highlighted previously that neither Margaret of Anjou nor Elizabeth Woodville was always able to collect what

---

[138] E. B. Fryde, *Peasants and Landlords in Later Medieval England* (London: Sutton, 1996), 3–4.

[139] Christopher Dyer, *Lords and Peasants in a Changing Society: The Estates of the Bishopric of Worcester, 680–1540* (Cambridge: Cambridge University Press, 1980), 264–82; L. R. Poos, *A Rural Society after the Black Death: Essex 1350–1525* (Cambridge: Cambridge University Press, 1991), 231–63; C. F. Richmond, 'Fauconberg's Kentish Rising of May 1471', *EHR* 85, no. 337 (Oct. 1970): 673–92.

[140] Barbara J. Harris, 'Landlords and Tenants in England in the Later Middle Ages: The Buckingham Estates', *Past and Present* 43 (May 1969): 146–50.

[141] R. H. Hilton, 'Peasant Movements in England before 1381', *EcHR*, New Series 2, no. 2 (1949): 117; Zvi Razi, 'The Struggles between the Abbots of Halesowen and their Tenants in the Thirteenth and Fourteenth Centuries', in *Social Relations and Ideas: Essays in Honour of R. H. Hilton*, eds T. H. Aston et al. (Cambridge: Cambridge University Press, 1983), 151.

[142] Crawford, 'The Queen's Council', 1208.

was due to them in revenue from the tenants of this manor. There is more than one possible reason for this failure of the manor tenants to render their dues to the queen and I previously suggested that residual loyalty to the disgraced owner, the late duke of Gloucester, could have been a possible factor. But it is also worth considering whether the locality of the manor and the type of people who lived there played a part. The manor of Pleasaunce was located in the southern parts of England, close to London and not too far from counties such as Essex. Londoners were known for their independent-mindedness and at least one scholar regards rural society in Essex as being 'near the epicentre of many of the period's most spectacular social and agrarian revolts and uprisings'.[143] Additional research is needed for any more conclusive assertions but, on the face of it, this self-governing spirit could have played some part in the reluctance exhibited by the tenants of the manor of Pleasaunce to pay their dues to the landowner queen.

What, then, might we venture to say about the queens' relationships with their tenants? It is entirely possible that our queens enjoyed no better a relationship with their tenants than any other landholding lord of the time did. The records show every sign that the uneasy relations endured by other lords and landholders with their tenants was also the lot of the queens. In Margaret of Anjou's case, the discussions have shown that she was as conscious of her rights and demanding of her dues as any other noble lord. Much the same may be said for Elizabeth Woodville, even if only at the executive level. Whatever the reasons and on whosoever's orders, her auditors appear to have been even more zealous in their duties than Margaret's. It is likely that this zeal was exhibited at the local level as well since a queen who exhibited tendencies towards restrictively prudent household economy would surely have been anxious to collect whatever she was owed in rents and fees. It is difficult to surmise that Elizabeth Woodville could have had any better a relationship with her tenants than Margaret did.

In comparison, Elizabeth of York tends to be represented without much connection with politics or the mundane subjects of landholdings, finance and administration. Unlike Margaret of Anjou, this Elizabeth was not forced to take up a major role in the political arena and she did not have to navigate her way around a sea of political operators to fight to maintain her rights and those of her son. Unlike her mother, the younger Elizabeth was not perceived as being so obviously surrounded by a coterie of family members who were wholly interested in their own worldly gains. Instead, the image held by contemporaries and modern historians alike are of a queen who was 'beautiful, fertile, pious and good, with apparently no thoughts beyond her God, her husband and her children'.[144] Still, Elizabeth of York may have been

---

[143] Poos, *A Rural Society after the Black Death*, 231.

[144] Anne Crawford, 'The King's Burden? The Consequences of Royal Marriage in

astute enough to have operated more discreetly behind the scenes and with a degree of power that is not openly discernible in the records. What is more, the lack of evidence does not mean that the queen was not interested in her lands and resources. She was apparently frequently in debt, given that her dower appeared not to be sufficient to cover her expenses, and, since Henry VII's household was known to have paid some of her bills, she was seemingly not fully financially independent.[145] It would have made sense for her to instruct her administrative machinery to be vigilant in pursuing her dues and for her to have taken active part when it suited her interests. The incidents at Havering fit this scenario. The lack of records demonstrating direct participation by Elizabeth of York in the management of her estates do not preclude either interest on her part or relevant direction provided by her to her council and officials. As a matter of fact, her itinerary during the last year of her life shows that she was crossing through many of her lands and it is more than possible that the queen met with at least some of her officials during these trips, conducting business that we do not now possess any records for.[146]

To sum up, troubling events on their estates and revenue losses are unlikely to have escaped the notice of the queens. There is every possibility that fervent attention to duty was exhibited by their officials at all levels of estate administration, especially in those regions that posed problems for them as landowners. The analysis and evidence clearly point to the queens being as active in the myriad levels of estate management as any other noble landowner might have needed to be in the face of various difficulties. In other words, when things were going well, the queens might have left daily or regular operational issues to their councils and their officials; when faced with trouble, they exerted themselves in whatever way necessary to resolve the problems that occurred.

CONCLUSIONS

This examination has demonstrated how much tradition and continuity influenced the organisation and management of the queens' lands and estates, whether or not the lands were continuously owned by queens. These lands were generally structured along very similar lines to other large landholdings of the period. The traditional systems of land organisation dating from the pre-Conquest period with post-Conquest Norman features superimposed

---

Fifteenth-Century England', in *Patronage, the Crown and the Provinces in Later Medieval England*, ed. Ralph A. Griffiths (Gloucester: Sutton, 1981), 53; Harvey, *Elizabeth of York*, 148; Laynesmith, *The Last Medieval Queens*, 21.

[145] Okerlund, *Elizabeth of York*, 136.
[146] *Ibid.*, 187–8.

upon them still existed in the late fifteenth century and formed the basis for administration by landholders in general, including the queens in this study.

In a similar manner, the evidence on the administrative machinery for each of the queens shows that there was sometimes little change in local officials from one queen to another, even when an estate was returned to the Crown before being granted in dower to the next queen. Tradition, best practice, and expediency typically drove decisions in such matters as how local posts were filled, and it is possible that the identity of the landholder was relatively unimportant in this respect. The fact that the landholder was the queen was significant only insofar as the queen was a highly ranked noble. Status transcended gender in the holding and administration of lands in this case and, therefore, the queen's gender mattered little, if at all. The evolution of the roles of the receivers and stewards illustrates how changes in land tenure and use were the primary factors that forced the queen's administrative machinery to change its processes in response. Such developments point to the fact that the administration of queens' landholdings shared the same economic and social concerns and faced the same issues as other large complexes of estates.

Moreover, the political and military unrest of the period appears not to have significantly influenced how the queens' lands and estates were organised and managed. The many changes in monarchy that occurred as a result of the Lancaster–York feud might have foreshadowed major changes in the administrative machinery of the queens' lands. Yet this did not happen. General changes that occurred in the administration of queenly landholdings seem to have been driven by economic and social imperatives stemming from changes in demography or land tenure, among other things. Dynastic upheaval was not after all a primary factor in administrative alterations. This is noteworthy because it points to a thread of continuity fostered by tradition that kept the system in place despite the major successional ruptures. Obviously, it cannot be concluded that the same dynastic changes had no impact at all, particularly in the upper levels of the estate administrations. Yet, in point of fact, there is little evidence to suggest that the administrative system at any level was wholly overturned or changed when the particular queen consort changed rapidly, as it did during Henry VI's Readeption in 1470–71. This was almost certainly because there was not enough time for the system to adjust to a new queen. To a certain extent, therefore, the system in place may have rendered the specific identity of the landowner queen comparatively irrelevant.

In terms of actual involvement, each of the queens was a relatively active participant in the administration of her landholdings. There is no certainty that a receiver-general functioned at all times for all of the queens nor is it clear that all the queens' receivers were accountable at all times to such an official. There are indications that the queens' councils could but did not operate fully autonomously without interaction from the queens in estate matters. Furthermore, there is enough evidence to show that each of the queens was far from a passive landowner who took no part in estate administration at any level. They appear to have been kept informed of estate matters, notably in cases of high urgency or if violence escalated. When they needed to, they stepped in, writing letters or taking action via their officials. In effect, they acted as administrators of their own lands and estates in the same way that other landowners would expect and be expected to do.

The queens relied on their economic wealth so it was only logical that they look after their vested economic interests. I do not presume that all the queens were energetic and interested administrators as well as formal landholders and it is possible that a queen such as Margaret of Anjou was a more active and direct administrator than the other queens were. But that does not mean that the less overtly active queens on the economic scene, or those perceived to be so, were less able or willing to exercise agency in economic terms. The discussion on the state of relations between the queens and their tenants shows that it was entirely in step with the general state of tenant–lord relations in fifteenth-century England. As with developments and changes in estate organisation and administration, it is likely that it mattered little to the queens' tenants what her gender was; her status as the highest-ranked woman in the land was what mattered, even if it was her officials who carried out the actual everyday business of estate management. The continuity in estate administration on the queens' lands was carried through by tradition and precedent and the queens' periods of ownership were transient ones in the life of an estate. Nonetheless, each individual queen's ownership and administration of lands meant that they possessed the material means to exercise their queenship and were able to reap the benefits of having those economic resources during the course of their lives.

PART II

USING THE QUEEN'S RESOURCES:
THE 'SERVICE' ECONOMY

4

THE QUEEN'S HOUSEHOLD

The house I call here the man, the woman, their children, their servauntes bonde and free, their cattell, their housholde stuffe, and all other things, which are reckoned in their possession, so long as all these remaine togeather in one…[1]

Sir Thomas Smith, in this late sixteenth-century quotation, revealed what he considered the household to be based on. The central figures were a husband, his wife, and their children; they were joined by several others, including animals, possessions and servants, all of them under a single roof. Smith's definition provides a helpful portrait of the premodern household, although there was a great deal of variety as might be expected. While elite households were also focused on similar figures, they were often much larger than the average household. Royal households in particular could be quite fluid and typically included a wide variety of persons who were related to or served the head of the household. For this study's purposes, I regard the queen's household as having encompassed all who served the queen in relation to her domestic needs whether they physically resided under the same roof as she did or permanently lived elsewhere.[2] It also included those of the queen's immediate family and relations who lived at least semi-permanently in her household and were supported financially by her. The heir to the throne typically had his own household, as in the cases of Margaret and Henry's son, Edward, Edward IV and Elizabeth Woodville's heir, the future Edward

[1] Thomas Smith, *De Republica Anglorum: the maner of governement or policie of the realme of Englande* (London: Henrie Midleton for Gregorie Seton, 1583), 13, https://quod.lib.umich.edu/e/eebo/A12533.0001.001/1:3.11?rgn=div2;view=fulltext.

[2] This definition is an adaptation of the one used by Kate Mertes. In her study of the late medieval English noble household, she defines the household as 'a collection of servants, friends and other retainers, around a noble and possibly his immediate family, all of whom lived together under the same roof(s) as a single community, for the purpose of creating the mode of life desired by the noble master and providing suitably for needs'. However, this definition would necessarily exclude most of the senior individuals who served the queen in her household, many of whom would not have permanently resided there. Mertes, *The English Noble Household, 1250–1600: Good Governance and Politic Rule* (Oxford; New York: Blackwell, 1988), 5.

V, and Arthur, the son of Henry VII and Elizabeth of York. Royal children other than the heir could reside in the queen's household, as did Edward IV and Elizabeth Woodville's daughters, Elizabeth and Mary, for whose upkeep the queen received an additional grant of £400 a year.[3] Conversely, the royal children could be maintained in a household of their own, such as was established at Eltham, Kent, for Henry VII and Elizabeth of York's other children, Henry, Margaret and Mary.[4]

The structures for queens' households that have been outlined by Johnstone and St John for the fourteenth-century English queens remain foundational for understanding late medieval English queens' households.[5] Yet these households did not remain unchanged into the late fifteenth century and one important objective of this chapter is to assess how much continuity can be observed in the fifteenth-century queens' households in comparison with each other's, with the kings', and with those of English queens from earlier periods. It uses a range of sources, including extant household accounts and royal or noble household ordinances, to outline the structural organisation of the queens' households and to examine household administration and the people who served the queens. Despite the differences in the structural layout and the periods in which they were compiled, the household accounts for these queens serve as crucial starting points. There is, however, a complication in that these accounts appear to have categorised household personnel and servants into *infra* and *extra hospicium*, meaning within and outside the household. In her brief discussion of queenly households, J. L. Laynesmith suggests that those serving the queens *extra hospicium* were involved with their finances and lands rather than actual household operations.[6] This may be true, yet it implies that there was a strict demarcation between the two groups. I contend that such firm boundaries between those serving the queens in relation to their finances, lands and households did not exist and no such distinction will be applied here.

Before beginning this exploration of the queen's household, I must briefly discuss an important feature of premodern English royal households, which is that separate establishments were often set up for the king and the queen in the late medieval period. The idea of the queen's household operating independently of the king's is not so fanciful when English consorts are compared with their counterparts on the European continent. Caroline zum Kolk, writing on the household of the queen of France, asserts that an independent and autonomous establishment for the queen existed from as early on as the

[3] CPR 1467-77, 110.
[4] Thomas Penn, *Winter King: The Dawn of Tudor England* (London: Allen Lane, 2011), 101.
[5] Johnstone I, 231-64, 284-9; St John, *Three Medieval Queens*, 65-72.
[6] Laynesmith, *The Last Medieval Queens*, 225.

Merovingian and Carolingian periods.[7] Likewise, medieval Portuguese queens consort also appear to have been in charge of households that were entirely separate from the kings'.[8] Nevertheless, in England, at least, the idea of an autonomous queenly household was unusual because elite and noble married couples did not typically establish separate formal households for the lord and his lady.[9] This idea of autonomy and separation naturally implies that the king and queen each possessed distinct households with their own staff and organisational structure. Yet the question of how separate the households of the king and queen really were hinges on what we understand the term 'separation' to mean. Studies of early medieval English queens such as Matilda of Scotland (c.1080–1118; r. 1100–1118) have proposed that, to a certain extent, queens of post-Conquest England had always maintained their own households.[10] They had their own servants and personal attendants even though their expenses were predominantly borne by their husbands. Then again, St John refers to the queen's household as 'an independent unit …[that] was also integrated into the king's household', a possible indication that fourteenth-century royal households were not considered to be strictly separate entities.[11]

The establishment by Henry III in 1236 of a separately accountable wardrobe for his new queen, the twelve-year-old Eleanor of Provence, marks a watershed moment in the development of English queens' households as discrete units.[12] The significance of this event lies in the fact that the 'wardrobe' of the new queen was not just a physical space for storage but a financial office with its own staff and accounting requirements.[13] This additional feature was

---

[7] Caroline zum Kolk, 'The Household of the Queen of France in the Sixteenth Century', *The Court Historian* 14, no. 1 (2009): 4–5.

[8] Ana Maria S. A. Rodrigues and Manuela Santos Silva, 'Private Properties, Seigniorial Tributes, and Jurisdictional Rents: The Income of the Queens of Portugal in the Late Middle Ages', in *Women and Wealth in Late Medieval Europe*, ed. Theresa Earenfight (New York: Palgrave Macmillan, 2010), 210.

[9] There could be exceptions, however. Louise Wilkinson asserts that the thirteenth-century household of Eleanor de Montfort, Countess of Leicester and Pembroke was administered at times as a separate financial entity from that of her husband's. The countess and her husband could, therefore, be considered to have had separate households to some extent. Louise J. Wilkinson, ed. and trans. *The Household Roll of Eleanor de Montfort, Countess of Leicester and Pembroke, 1265: British Library, Additional MS 8877* (Woodbridge: Boydell Press for the Pipe Roll Society, 2020), xvii.

[10] Lois L. Huneycutt, *Matilda of Scotland: A Study in Medieval Queenship* (Woodbridge: Boydell Press, 2003), 99–102.

[11] St John, *Three Medieval Queens*, 65.

[12] Johnstone I, 231; St John, *Three Medieval Queens*, 66.

[13] T. F. Tout, *Chapters in the Administrative History of Mediaeval England: The Wardrobe, the Chamber and the Small Seals*, Vol. I (Manchester: Manchester University Press, 1930), 253.

what now differentiated the queen's household from the king's. This separation could, of course, be discarded again, as demonstrated by the absorption of the household of Philippa of Hainault into that of her husband, Edward III, in 1360.[14] This 'merger of the royal households' remained in place until 1369 when the queen died, and appears in part to have been a necessary measure to put her finances in order.[15] Nonetheless, this was an atypical situation applicable to this specific queen and it arguably had no lasting negative impact on the concept of separate households for the king and his consort.[16] The households of our fifteenth-century queens were set up as wholly separate from those of their royal husbands'.

This conceptual separation was frequently matched by physical separation. Kings and queens did not always live together in the same residence at the same time. They went their own way on occasions, travelling with separate household servants and officials, and making individual journeys on their own for different reasons. Naturally there would have been many times when they resided under the same roof and on those occasions conceptual separation of the royal households could then collide with the issue of close physical proximity. I will return to this matter when considering household management but suffice it to say for now that the households of the queens in this study operated independently of those of the kings.

ORGANISATION AND STRUCTURE

That the queen's household was likely to be among the largest and most hierarchical in the land is not in doubt. But how were they organised and where were they located? Some of the most useful sources for this exploration of royal household structure are the 1452–53 extant household account for Margaret of Anjou, the Black Book of the household of Edward IV and the royal ordinances drawn up in 1445 and 1478.[17] The Black Book and the royal ordinances provide valuable information about how the royal households were meant to have been set up but they are admittedly mostly concerned with the king's household. Still, combined with Johnstone's and St John's work on earlier queens, these sources provide a firm basis for a theoretical outline

---

[14] Chris Given-Wilson demonstrates that 1360 was the correct date for the instigation by Edward III to merge the royal households. Chris Given-Wilson, 'The Merger of Edward III's and Queen Philippa's Households', *BIHR* 51 (1978): 183.

[15] Tingle suggests that Queen Philippa's financial troubles was only one of a range of possible reasons the merger took place. Tingle, *Chaucer's Queens*, 102–8.

[16] Given-Wilson discusses the extent to which the two royal households were merged and suggests that after 1360 there still existed some separation between the royal households for administration and accounting. Given-Wilson, 'The Merger', 185–6.

[17] Myers, *The Black Book*; Myers, 'The Household of Queen Margaret of Anjou'. See Table 7 for a list of relevant household ordinances.

of the households of the queens in this study.[18] Fortunately, the material available in Margaret's household account allows us to compare theory with practice. Alone among the extant relevant records, Margaret's account includes lists of names and wages of the general household staff, that is, the clerks, esquires, yeomen, grooms and pages.[19] Occasionally, the receiver-general, William Cotton, also listed the particular household department to which the individual was attached or his special occupation.[20] While the sources provide us with the most details for Margaret of Anjou's household, there is no reason to believe from the available evidence that this structure differed significantly for the households of the two queens Elizabeth.

The centre of the queen's household was the chamber. The chamber was the queen's personal space and catered to her most intimate necessities, including clothing, toileting and bedding. It was staffed by a variety of persons of high and low ranks, some of whom occupied posts connected to specific duties within the chamber, such as the page of the robes or the groom of the beds. In administrative and financial terms, the chamber functioned autonomously within the queens' households, a situation attested to by the lump sum payments directed to it in the receiver-general's and various receiver accounts for both Margaret and Elizabeth Woodville.[21] These lump sum payments also support a conclusion that, unlike the fourteenth-century queens Isabella of France and Philippa of Hainault, these fifteenth-century queens did not receive separate endowments for their chamber expenses.[22]

The wardrobe was the financial and secretarial hub of the queen's household, the office to which other departments in the household accounted for purchases and expenditure. But there was also a different meaning for the term 'wardrobe', that is, as a physical location that typically served as storage for the queen's personal items. In the fourteenth century, this was referred to as the privy wardrobe (*parva garderoba*) but by the fifteenth century it was more commonly known as the queen's closet or the robes. Another division was the great wardrobe (*magna garderoba*), not to be confused with the privy wardrobe. Traditionally, the great wardrobe was concerned with the purchase and provisioning of household items such as clothing and livery, and bulk purchases of high value materials including spices, wax and general household consumables. The expenses for this department could be substantial. Margaret

---

[18] Johnstone I, 231–64, 284–9; St John, *Three Medieval Queens*, 65–72.
[19] Myers, 'The Household of Queen Margaret of Anjou', 181–90 (fols 12a–14a).
[20] According to Cotton in the account, this information was assembled from chequerolls which recorded the names of all who served the queen in the household and the number of days of their attendance. Myers, 'The Household of Queen Margaret of Anjou', 145, 184.
[21] Myers, 'The Household of Queen Elizabeth Woodville', 317–18; Myers, 'The Household of Queen Margaret of Anjou', 206–7.
[22] Johnstone II, 277.

of Anjou's keeper of the great wardrobe, John Norrys, was allowed approximately £2000 for expenses in 1451–52 while the corresponding expenses in Elizabeth Woodville's household in 1466–67 totalled nearly £1200.[23] Presumably, the keeper of the great wardrobe accounted for his expenses in subsidiary accounts that probably resembled the extant wardrobe accounts of the fifteenth-century kings but that, unfortunately, remain lost to us for now.

For the provision of services, there were several departments organised along the lines of labour division. As per the royal household ordinances, there were household sections that saw to the procurement, preparation and delivery of food and drink to the household: the pantry, buttery and kitchen.[24] The kitchen was subdivided into smaller units responsible for a variety of items and the associated tasks necessary for provisioning, preparation and delivery: the saucery, spicery, scullery, larder, cellar, chandlery, scaldinghouse, acattery and stores.[25] Each of these household divisions was headed by a yeoman or esquire who was directly responsible to the steward of the house. There was also sometimes a clerk or other individual attached to that division who accounted financially to the treasurer of the household. One division that we know existed in the queens' households but that is seldom mentioned in the household accounts was the marshalsea or the stables. This department took care of all the household's needs related to transport, including the maintenance of equipment such as carriages, carts and coaches. It also looked after the stabling of horses and was usually responsible for the care of the hunting hounds and birds of prey. Other departments that lack visibility in the sources and about which very little is known include the queen's household chapel.[26] There are clear references to the queen's chaplains and musicians in other sources, such as the account for the expenses of the funeral of Elizabeth of York.[27] Yet the household accounts make little mention

---

[23] Myers, 'The Household of Queen Elizabeth Woodville', 316; Myers, 'The Household of Queen Margaret of Anjou', 205.

[24] The 1445 and 1478 household ordinances outlined the divisions allowed for the king's household, listing the numbers of staff for each division and their allowances. Myers, *The Black Book*, 69–75, 223–8.

[25] The work of many of these household sections roughly corresponds to present-day meanings. However, the scaldinghouse oversaw the boiling of poultry, the acattery bought meat and fish for the household and the chandlery was responsible for candles.

[26] Fiona Kisby's work on the royal household chapel, or more precisely, the household chapel of Henry VII, in the early Tudor period is particularly useful. An aspect of Kisby's work compares this department with the household chapel of the king's mother, Lady Margaret Beaufort, acknowledged as a noblewoman of great stature during the period and whose household might have rivalled that of the queen. Fiona Louise Kisby, 'The Royal Household Chapel in Early-Tudor London, 1485–1547' (unpublished PhD thesis, Royal Holloway and Bedford New College, University of London, 1996).

[27] TNA LC2/1, fol. 63.

of wages or allowances for such individuals, a circumstance that implies the existence of separate accounts for autonomous departments that would have recorded those wages or fees.

The elaborate division of the queens' households largely mirrored those of the kings'.[28] Indeed, the Black Book of the household of Edward IV expressly stated that the queen's service 'must be nygh like unto the king, and for her ladyes and other worshipfull men and jentylwomen, theire services and lyverez … as hit is to the kings household [men]'.[29] Queenly household structure was theoretically modelled after the king's but the divisions were smaller in size and scale. Additionally, there are many similar features when we compare the households of queens in the fifteenth century with those of the fourteenth century. St John outlines the main sections of the queens' households and they essentially match those of the fifteenth-century queens', with the queen's chamber, wardrobe and great wardrobe being the most important ones.[30] The main points of difference relate to which officials were considered the most senior and important in the fifteenth-century households and the fact that some posts in the households of the fourteenth-century queens appeared to be no longer present in those of the later fifteenth-century queens. Specifically, there is no sign of a cofferer or controller in any of the sources for the queens in this study, posts that were clearly included in the households of fourteenth-century queens such as Philippa of Hainault.[31]

Table 7: Fifteenth-Century Household Ordinances.

Known Name	Year	Description
The Ordinance of 1445	1445	Provisions for regulating the household of Henry VI. Published as A. R. Myers, 'Some Household Ordinances of Henry VI', *BJRL*, 36, no. 2 (1954), 449–67 and *BJRL*, 37, no. 1 (1954), 11–13, repr. in *Crown, Household and Parliament*, 231–50.
The Ordinance of 1454	1454	Provisions for regulating the household of Henry VI. Published in *Proceedings and Ordinances of the Privy Council, vol. VI, 22 Henry VI 1443 to 39 Henry VI 1461*, ed. N. H. Nicolas (London: Record Commission, 1837), 220–33.

---

[28] Harris, *English Aristocratic Women*, 215.
[29] Myers, *The Black Book*, 92.
[30] St John, *Three Medieval Queens*, 65–72.
[31] The cofferer traditionally looked after the treasures of the household that were placed in a coffer, that is, a chest or strongbox for holding valuables.

The Black Book of the Household of Edward IV	unclear	Provisions for regulating the household of Edward IV. Published in A. R. Myers, *The Household of Edward IV: The Black Book and the Ordinance of 1478* (Manchester: Manchester University Press, 1959), 76–197.
The Provisions of 1471	1471	Provisions for regulating the household of Edward IV. Published in A. R. Myers, *The Household of Edward IV: The Black Book and the Ordinance of 1478* (Manchester: Manchester University Press, 1959), 198–202.
The Ordinance of 1478	1478	Provisions for regulating the household of Edward IV. Published in A. R. Myers, ed. *The Household of Edward IV: The Black Book and the Ordinance of 1478* (Manchester: Manchester University Press, 1959), 203–28.
Orders and Rules of the House of the Princess Cecill, Mother of King Edward IV	unclear	Published in *A Collection of Ordinances and Regulations for the Government of the Royal Household* (London: John Nichols for the Society of Antiquaries, 1790), 37–9, 109–35.
Articles Ordained by King Henry VII for the Regulation of His Household	1494	Provisions for regulating the household of Henry VII. Published in *A Collection of Ordinances and Regulations for the Government of the Royal Household* (London: John Nichols for the Society of Antiquaries, 1790), 109–35.
Ordinances by Margaret Countess of Richmond and Derby	unclear	Ordinances for royal childbirth and christenings. Published in John Leland, *De Rebus Britannicis Collectanea*, vol. IV, ed. T. Hearne (London: Benjamin White, 1774), 179–84.

The question of size, or the number of personnel, is problematic due to uncertainty over who should be counted as being part of the queen's household. Nonetheless, the working definition established earlier helps us assess how large each queen's household might have been, even if only estimates can be made. Margaret of Anjou's household account recorded wages and fees paid to 148 persons in her household ranging from the pages to the most senior officials.[32] In Elizabeth Woodville's case, we can confidently identify only fifty-

---

[32] Myers states that 151 servants were paid wages by the queen, thereby implying that this was the size of Margaret's household. However, there were two individuals who were probably counted twice because they were each listed as serving in two

The Queen's Household

five persons from the extant 1466–67 account as serving in her household. Finally, in the account recording the expenses for the funeral of Elizabeth of York in 1503, the queen's household numbered 209 persons.[33] These are significantly disparate figures and there is no guarantee that they are either accurate or complete.

Several issues arise when comparing these figures. Firstly, it is difficult to make clear comparisons of the numbers of general household staff for each of these queens. Margaret's recorded wage lists show that there were twenty-three esquires, fifty-five yeomen and grooms, and sixteen pages. For Elizabeth Woodville, the main issue is that there are no extant sources to testify to the numbers of general staff within her household. Certain yeomen and grooms are listed in transactions involving payments by warrant for specific allowances, thus giving us their names. In addition, some posts such as clerks of the signet and chancery register are recorded in her household account with the amounts in fees paid. However, there are no general lists of wages paid to this queen's esquires, yeomen, grooms or pages. The absence of such categorised wage information as found in Margaret of Anjou's household account makes it impossible to ascertain exactly how many such individuals served in Elizabeth Woodville's household. The situation for Elizabeth of York is much better since the account for her funeral expenses lists her household staff not only by their assigned department but typically also by rank. It appears that this queen had at least fifty yeomen and grooms in her household and six pages.[34] At face value, therefore, both Margaret and Elizabeth of York had similar numbers of yeomen, grooms and pages in their households, a situation that supports a contention that the older Elizabeth's household staff was of comparable size.

These figures are complicated by another issue regarding household divisions. Neither Margaret's nor Elizabeth Woodville's household accounts mention important departments such as the marshalsea (or stables) and the chapel. Yet we know from other evidence that these departments existed. This suggests that only those individuals whose wages were disbursed by the queens' receivers-general were included in the extant household accounts. Many of the staff serving within each of the divisions, notably in Elizabeth Woodville's household, cannot be found in the household account, almost certainly because their wages were accounted for by an assigned household department clerk. Happily, references in the account for Elizabeth of York's funeral expenses make it possible to observe that this queen had eight

---

different household posts and one individual whose post precluded him from being numbered among the queen's servants but who appears to have been included in the count. Myers, *The Black Book*, 9.

[33] TNA LC2/1, fols 36–81.

[34] In the lists of queen's household staff, there are at least eight other persons listed who served in the kitchen and as footmen and messengers but whose rank was unspecified. They are not included in these numbers. TNA LC2/1, fol. 64r.

chaplains in her household and forty-one staff in her stables.[35] How these numbers compare with the corresponding divisions in the households of the other queens is much more difficult to say.

A useful exercise to undertake is to compare the estimated sizes of the queens' households with information from various household ordinances issued in the fifteenth century. The royal ordinance of 1445 was aimed at setting down regulations for improved economic efficiency in the royal households, an issue of prime concern during the reign of Henry VI. While it focused mainly on the king's household, certain provisions were made with the queen's household in mind; a list of authorised household staff for the queen was included. The total number of personnel allowed to the queen was sixty-six and, generally, all these persons occupied posts that involved close personal attendance upon the royal consort.[36] Yet, in comparison, another ordinance issued just nine years later in 1454 stipulated that the queen's household was to be limited to 120 people but did not list the individual posts allowed for.[37] It appears that the queen's allowable household staff had doubled in 1454 from the figure in 1445, while the king's household had been reduced, a somewhat contradictory situation.[38] These specified household sizes were not drastically changed in the regulations and ordinances issued in the 1470s, with the queen's household numbers being restricted to one hundred servants in the Black Book, a figure not very much reduced from that of the 1454 ordinance.[39]

On reflection, not all these figures are necessarily inconsistent, but neither are they much help in trying to determine the exact sizes of the queens' households. For a start, none of the household ordinances specifies allowable numbers for general household staff, aside from the queen's chamber whose servants were listed in the 1445 ordinance. The ordinance of 1454 and the Black Book regulations did nothing more except affirm how many household staff the queen was allowed, with no other prescribed details about personnel or household management. Since only the maximum number of staff is stated, we cannot know exactly what the writers of these ordinances meant to limit with regards to specific posts. Myers' assertion that Margaret of Anjou's household had numbered 151 persons in 1452 as well as the calculations from the extant account undertaken in this study includes personal attendants and any number

---

[35] Elizabeth of York's marshalsea was referred to as the queen's stables in the funeral account. TNA LC2/1, fols 63r, 75r.
[36] Myers, *The Black Book*, 8, 71–2.
[37] *Proceedings and Ordinances of the Privy Council of England, vol. VI, 22 Henry VI 1443 to 39 Henry VI 1461*, ed. N. H. Nicolas (London: Spottiswoode, 1837), 233; Myers, *The Black Book*, 9, note 3.
[38] Crawford, 'The King's Burden?', 49.
[39] Myers, *The Black Book*, 93. The Ordinance of 1478 did not specify what the size of the queen's household should be.

The Queen's Household

of other officials and general household staff. Without knowing who the ordinance makers were including as part of the queen's household, it is impossible to make precise comparisons between theoretical and actual numbers.

It is also difficult to compare the sizes of the queens' households in this study with those of the kings', noble households or other queens' households from previous centuries. Compared with the kings', the queens' households were clearly much smaller. Even so, it might be expected that they would be akin in size to other noble households. Kate Mertes estimates the sizes of a variety of households over the period of her study, that is, from 1250 until 1600. She found that the average size of an earl's household in the fifteenth century could be more than 200 persons, although there was, naturally, a wide variety.[40] James Ross, however, notes that two payrolls of the first duke of Buckingham showed a total of 107 servants in 1450 and 129 in 1457. The twelfth earl of Oxford, in contrast, paid wages to fifty-one servants in 1430–31 while his son employed 124 household servants in 1507–8.[41] Allowing for the possibility that the sizes of the queens' households have been vastly underestimated for lack of relevant evidence, I would suggest that they were generally on par with the households of higher-ranked nobles.

The households of the queens of the later fifteenth century appear to have been smaller than those of the queens of the fourteenth century. Even though C. M. Woolgar asserts that royal households increased in size from the fourteenth to the fifteenth century, the numbers for the queens' households belie this proposition.[42] According to St John, Isabella of France's household numbered approximately 183 in 1311–12 while Philippa of Hainault's was more than 135 in size in the year 1340–41.[43] Judging by the apparent numbers for the households of the fifteenth-century queens, it appears that queenly households had decreased in size from the fourteenth to the late-fifteenth century. In any case, no matter what the exact sizes of the queens' households were in the later fifteenth century, it is important to note that the inclusion of maximum numbers of allowable staff in the fifteenth-century ordinances was primarily driven by the necessity to achieve, or at least be seen to be working to achieve, greater overall levels of financial frugality. Image may well have been the primary consideration rather than exact detail in relation to the size of the queen's household and, in that light, clarification of the ambiguous figures becomes somewhat redundant.

---

[40] Mertes, *The English Noble Household*, 187.
[41] James Ross, 'The Noble Household as a Political Centre in the Early Tudor Period', in *The Elite Household in England, 1100–1550: Proceedings of the 2016 Harlaxton Symposium*, ed. C. M. Woolgar (Donington: Shaun Tyas, 2018), 79.
[42] C. M. Woolgar, *The Great Household in Late Medieval England* (New Haven, CT: Yale University Press, 1999), 10.
[43] St John, *Three Medieval Queens*, 68.

Another important fact is that, like other elite and large landowners, medieval kings and queens moved around quite a lot. In Thurley's words, medieval royal households were peripatetic units, 'almost constantly on the move'.[44] This meant that the queens' households were not usually permanently located in any one place since the royal consorts understandably travelled between their residences. Margaret of Anjou's extant letters provide evidence that she was living in different residences at different times. Two of her favourites, if her letters are any indication, were the manor of Pleshey in Essex and the palace at Windsor. Elizabeth of York's itinerary for the year between March 1502 and February 1503 also presents a compelling picture of her itinerant lifestyle, evident from the number of moves she made between several different royal residences. Disregarding the queen's progress to Wales during the year, it appears that she favoured, in this year at least, royal dwellings situated relatively closely to each other in the south, including the palaces at Westminster, Richmond, and Windsor.[45] In point of fact, queens of the later fifteenth century were probably travelling much less frequently than their predecessors in the thirteenth and fourteenth centuries. By the end of the fifteenth century, the households of the kings appear to have been moving less and less often. Edward IV, for one, moved between about ten different royal residences compared with his fourteenth-century namesake, Edward I, who made ten times as many moves.[46] Their queens' movements surely followed the same trend. There is the added probability that the queens in this study, particularly the two Elizabeths, did not need to travel the distances their predecessors did. Thurley's work demonstrates an increased concentration of royal residences around London and the south of England. This, together with my earlier survey of the lands owned by Margaret and the two Elizabeths, points to a smaller geographical area of queens' and royal residences. This does not, of course, discount the likelihood that the queens also travelled to locations other than their own or the kings' properties.

The queens' lifestyles, therefore, suggest that the size and composition of their households mattered a great deal. My earlier proposition that the sizes of queenly households had decreased by the late fifteenth century makes sense not just against the background of the financial difficulties of Henry VI and his Yorkist and Tudor successor kings but also in light of the consistent increase in costs for travel, food and general household maintenance. As the expenditure of the travelling household of the sixteenth-century duke of Buckingham Edward Stafford shows, it could be extremely expensive for a nobleman to travel, in part given the need to showcase magnificence in keeping with his

---

[44] Thurley, *The Royal Palaces of Tudor England*, 1.
[45] Okerlund, *Elizabeth of York*, 188.
[46] Woolgar, *The Great Household*, 46.

high status.[47] Such factors would similarly have been important for the queens. They, too, were not immune from the financial exigencies of the period and smaller households would obviously incur fewer costs when travelling.

A related question is whether the queens always travelled with their entire household and all their necessaries. Woolgar shows that great noble households were sometimes divided into separate parts: the permanent household, a riding or travelling household and a secret household, that is, a small group accompanying the lord when a full household was not needed.[48] This idea is supported by Audrey Thorstad's work on the duke of Buckingham's travelling arrangements, which implies the existence of a permanent base for the duke and his household.[49] While there is no direct evidence that similar compositional separation in the queens' household personnel occurred, especially for Margaret of Anjou and Elizabeth Woodville, Elizabeth of York's extant expense account shows that preparations for the queen's residential moves seem to have been undertaken by a core group of household staff, typically consisting of two or three yeomen of the queen's chamber, two or three grooms, and one to three pages.[50] In addition, household members, usually grooms, would accompany the queen's possessions (most frequently her jewels but also plate and wardrobe items) as they were taken from one residence to another in advance of the queen herself for yet another residential move.[51] These scenarios suggest that it is entirely likely that Elizabeth of York at least travelled with many if not all of her possessions and probably the bulk of her household personnel.

HOUSEHOLD MANAGEMENT

The management of a large noble household, let alone a royal one, encompasses many different aspects, including provisioning food for the household, managing finances and expenditure on the necessities of life, and catering for the lord's lifestyle. Even a brief glance at existing literature on the household and its functions and management reveals just how wide-ranging the topic

---

[47] Audrey M. Thorstad, 'There and Back Again: The Hospitality and Consumption of a Sixteenth-Century English Travelling Household', in *Royal and Elite Households in Medieval and Early Modern Europe: More Than Just a Castle*, ed. Theresa Earenfight (Leiden: Brill, 2018), 357–77.
[48] Woolgar, *The Great Household*, 15.
[49] See Thorstad, 'There and Back Again', 357–77.
[50] For the year 1503, the names that most frequently appear in this group are William Hamerton, Edmond Burton, Edmond Levesey, George Hamerton, John Browne, John Bright, William Pole, Edmond Calverd and Henry Roper. For example, see Queen's Book, fols 48, 51, 55 and 61.
[51] See Queen's Book, fols 44, 50, 52, 57, 58, 62, 63, 73 and 82.

can be.[52] Hence, this chapter focuses on those aspects that inform our perception and extend our understanding of the queens' needs for economic and financial resources and their competence as heads of their households.

On operational management, there are few salient sources that shed light on how the queens' households were actually administered. All the ordinances issued in relation to royal households in the latter half of the fifteenth century appear to be predominantly concerned with limiting the numbers of personnel. Moreover, there is a vagueness about the wording that suggests there was less concern for how the queens' households were explicitly managed than for the kings'. For example, the Black Book of Edward IV limited the queen's household to one hundred persons but when the entire passage is read in context, it can be interpreted to mean that the limit applied to periods when the king and queen were residing under the same roof.[53] The ordinance of 1454, in comparison, allowed the queen a household of 120 but does not list how the numbers were to be apportioned among the different household departments, something that is done for the king's household.[54]

Nonetheless, the above-mentioned ordinances and articles issued for royal households, as well as other related sources, provide some useful guidance as to what was theoretically allowed, if not what was carried out. Scholarship on the households of nobles, kings and queens from other chronological periods also provide pointers as to how our queens' households might have been run on a daily basis.[55] Woolgar demonstrates that elite households were set up to be run according to a schedule that outlined such things as times for the serving of meals.[56] It is reasonable to surmise that the queens' households operated on similar schedules. Also, the daily schedules of households, even royal households, could not be separated from the religious aspects of life. The liturgical calendar played an important role in determining household rhythms.[57] Daily prayers and masses could be the predominant force governing the

---

[52] The following is a small selection of publications covering different types of research into medieval households: Beattie, Maslakovic and Jones, eds., *The Medieval Household in Christian Europe*; Glenn D. Burger and Rory G. Critten, eds., *Household Knowledges in Late-Medieval England and France* (Manchester: Manchester University Press, 2019); Earenfight, ed., *Royal and Elite Households in Medieval and Early Modern Europe*; Mertes, *The English Noble Household*; Woolgar, ed., *The Elite Household in England*; Woolgar, *The Great Household*.

[53] Myers, *The Black Book*, 92–3.

[54] *Proceedings and Ordinances of the Privy Council*, 233.

[55] Such works include Chris Given-Wilson, *The Royal Household and the King's Affinity: Service, Politics and Finance in England, 1360–1413* (New Haven, CT: Yale University Press, 1986); Johnstone I, 231–88; Mertes, *The English Noble Household*; Woolgar, *The Great Household*.

[56] Woolgar, *The Great Household*, 85.

[57] Ibid., 84.

regular life of the household.[58] Festivals, feast days and holy days were less frequent but household tasks during these events would have been dictated by the queen's level of participation in such proceedings. Then, there would have been domestic or outside events that might have disrupted household schedules, such as when each of the royal Yorkist children were born or when Arthur, Prince of Wales, married Catherine of Aragon in November 1501.

The households of high-ranking noblewomen provide further guidance on the running of a queenly establishment. A particular example was the domestic schedule of Cecily Neville, duchess of York, mother of Edward IV and Richard III and grandmother of Elizabeth of York. The orders and rules of Cecily Neville's household outlined a typical day in the life of this widowed noblewoman and delineated specific periods in the day for religious worship, meals, recreation and business.[59] Tasks undertaken by Cecily Neville's officials and servants would have been prioritised according to the lady's schedule. This information is not, of course, strictly transferable to any queen's household since this duchess' schedule typifies that of an older widow, with no children and of a pious nature. But they afford us a glimpse into how a noble or even a royal household (given Cecily Neville's status) might have conducted itself operationally.

An additional source that aids our understanding of household business is the set of ordinances said to have been issued by Margaret Beaufort, Henry VII's mother.[60] These ordinances addressed the events of childbirth and christening, laying out precise instructions for the benefit of the queen and the deliverance of her child as well as for the christening of said royal child. They are quite detailed in terms of the tasks that were to be undertaken, and they also touch on such matters as how to decorate the church used for the christening. All these ordinances provide rules and regulations, which are vital insights into the ideals that households were meant to strive for and follow. Whether the queens' households did so is a much more difficult question to answer given the dearth of evidence.

In the case of financial management, there are some significant details in the sources on how household finances for the queens were managed. In the later fifteenth century, the queen's receiver-general, who was also her household treasurer, was responsible for the finances and was assisted by many different individuals. Typically, if the structure outlined in the fifteenth-century ordinances was followed, each of the major household divisions would have had a clerk who would prepare the different types of records that

---

[58] Laynesmith, *Cecily Duchess of York*, 102–10.
[59] *A Collection of Ordinances and Regulations for the Government of the Royal Household: Made in Divers Reigns, From King Edward III to King William and Queen Mary, Also Receipts in Ancient Cookery* (London: John Nichols for the Society of Antiquaries, 1790), 37–9, 109–35.
[60] John Leland, *De Rebus Britannicis Collectanea*, vol. IV, ed. T. Hearne (London; Benjamin White, 1774), 179–84.

went towards making up complete sets of household accounts. The queens employed a variety of different clerks, including a clerk of the receipts, clerk of the queen's closet, clerk of the chancery register and clerk of the avenary.[61] It is not certain that all the queens' households included all these different posts but it is possible that the tasks undertaken were similar even if the designated titles were different. For instance, a clerk of receipts is recorded among the household staff for Margaret of Anjou and Elizabeth Woodville but not for Elizabeth of York. Perhaps the clerk of the queen's closet fulfilled the duties of the clerk of receipts in the younger Elizabeth's household, a parallel scenario to that of her most senior financial officer, Richard Decons, who was noted as the receiver of the queen's revenues and monies and keeper of the queen's Privy Purse rather than as her receiver-general. Interestingly, this would have made the clerk of the queen's closet a more important post in Elizabeth of York's time than it had been in the past.

How then was money received and disbursed in the queens' households? By the fifteenth century, even in a smaller noble household, efficient financial management called for meticulous recording of receipts and expenditures using such documentary forms as day and weekly books, books of purchases, provisions and supplies, and wages bills.[62] It is highly probable that the queens' households employed similar processes, presumably motivated by the same desire for efficient management and fraud prevention.[63] The receiver-general's accounts for Margaret of Anjou and Elizabeth Woodville recorded various payments made to household divisions but, alas, no records for any of the individual divisions appear to have survived. Hence, we can only speculate on the likely procedures followed by distinct departments. In both of these accounts, there are lump sum payments made to the clerk of the avenary, the keeper of the great wardrobe and the queen's Privy Purse or chamber.[64] Margaret's account, alone among the queens of this study, also records several payments to Edward Ellesmere, the keeper of the queen's jewels.[65] These large payments indicate that some of the household divisions received funds, which were then disbursed by the department clerk or other official and accounted for in separate departmental records. Elizabeth of York's Privy Purse expense account likewise offers tantalising indications that her stables, at least, were

---

[61] The avenary was the part of the marshalsea or stables that ensured the provision of oats for the horses.

[62] E. M. Myatt-Price, 'Cromwell Household Accounts, 1417–1476', in *Studies in the History of Accounting*, ed. A. C. Littleton (London: Sweet & Maxwell, 1956), 99, 111.

[63] Mertes, *The English Noble Household*, Chapter 3, discusses methods of household accounting as employed in many noble households.

[64] Myers, 'The Household of Queen Elizabeth Woodville', 316–18; Myers, 'The Household of Queen Margaret of Anjou', 202, 204–5, 208.

[65] Myers, 'The Household of Queen Margaret of Anjou', 205–6.

The Queen's Household

funded using a similar process; her clerks of the avenary or stables were given significantly large sums of money for expenses several times in a year.[66]

There are, unfortunately, no transactions relating to payments made to departments involved in the provision of victuals, that is, the kitchen, pantry or buttery. On this aspect of household management, the available records are silent. The officials ostensibly in charge of managing the queens' households, the chancellor and chamberlain, leave little trace in our sources. It is not even clear whether lump sums were paid to these officials for separate funding and accounting of household provisioning departments. The reasons for this are inconclusive but one possibility is that these positions may have been no more than sinecures, with actual administration being undertaken by others. If we examine various types of accounts from the kings' households, we find that records relating to the provision of food and drink are sometimes found in the accounts prepared by the treasurer or controller of the household.[67] This suggests that those divisions in the queens' households concerned with such matters could have been funded from the wardrobe or directly from the chamber. Were they available to us, records of other household officials, such as the keeper of the wardrobe, might reveal transactions relating to the 'lower-stairs' departments such as the kitchens.[68] Such speculation remains moot for now precisely because we lack any such records.

Household departments could also have been funded in other ways. As with most noble households, the queen's income came from various sources. The household accounts show that the receivers-general of Margaret and Elizabeth Woodville acted as intermediaries in the sense that they received income on the one hand and disbursed funds on the other. But what if the intermediaries were deleted from the equation? For instance, several payments in Elizabeth Woodville's household account were made directly to the intended recipients rather than via the hand of John Forster, the receiver-general.[69] For Elizabeth of York, there are payments missing from her account; for example, there are no references to wardrobe charges. This may point to the keeper of the queen's wardrobe receiving funds directly from specific income sources rather than such funds being allocated by her senior financial officer. It is entirely possible that for all our queens those household divisions not recorded as receiving funds from the receivers-general obtained them directly from receivers or bailiffs themselves, these transactions presumably being recorded in the

---

[66] See Queen's Book, fols 38, 45, 53, 65.
[67] For example, TNA E101/409/16, E101/412/2, E101/412/11. These are the sections labelled 'Diet' in accounts of a keeper of the household wardrobe, a treasurer of the household and a controller.
[68] Woolgar states that the royal household had always used a system of cash accounting, one that does not lend itself to convoluted record keeping. Woolgar, *Household Accounts from Medieval England, Part 1*, 64.
[69] Myers, 'The Household of Queen Elizabeth Woodville', 265.

accounts of the individual household divisions or in relevant estate records.[70] It is also probable that provisions were obtained in kind by the kitchens and other sections of the households, either in the form of purveyance, rent paid with non-cash items or demesne produce.[71] Regrettably again, the extant documents have not produced supporting evidence for any of these tantalising options, which must remain speculative for now.

Another important issue is how the royal households functioned when the kings and their queens happened to be residing in one property at the same time. The queens' households could and did exist as separate units from the kings' households; they functioned autonomously, with myriad officials to ensure the smooth running of the household in both operational and financial terms. It is no stretch of the imagination, therefore, to picture friction occurring when the king's and the queen's households were situated in the same residence at the same time. In the case of fourteenth-century queens, Woolgar asserts that the queen's household ceased 'to function as a separate administrative entity' in such a scenario.[72] Unfortunately, for the queens in this study, there is little evidence to shed light on how the two households might have operated in those situations. One solitary crumb of information can be gleaned, although it does not appear to be related to functional matters. The Black Book of Edward IV mandated a rate of £7 per day that the queen was meant to pay to the king 'whan she cumith to [the king's] court'.[73] As it happens, this is exactly the rate that Margaret of Anjou paid in 1452 for the periods during which she resided with the king.[74] Clearly, queens of the later fifteenth century were expected to contribute towards the cost of keeping their households under the same roof as the kings' when the royal couples resided together and the amount set down in the Black Book may have been decided upon in adherence with the rate that Queen Margaret paid.[75] The question remains as to whether the queen paid the king's household only when they were both living under the roof of one of the king's residences or also for properties that were owned by the queen herself.

---

[70] Accounts of receivers or even manorial documents would presumably be able to verify that such procedures were carried out. While no supporting evidence has been found in the extant documents consulted for this study, this does not negate the possibility of such procedures being followed.

[71] Mertes, *The English Noble Household*, 95. See also Chris Given-Wilson, 'Purveyance for the Royal Household 1362–1413', *BIHR* 56 (1983): 145–63, for more information on the issue of purveyance for medieval royal households in England.

[72] C. M. Woolgar, *The Senses in Late Medieval England* (New Haven, CT; London: Yale University Press, 2006), 229.

[73] Myers, *The Black Book*, 92–3.

[74] Myers, 'The Household of Queen Margaret of Anjou', 207 (fol. 21a).

[75] Whether or not Elizabeth Woodville or Elizabeth of York made any such payments is unclear since there is no extant evidence to show that they did so.

The Queen's Household

The fact that the queen made part payment for the costs of her household does not, however, tell us how the two households functioned together. In this regard, the physical layout of a royal residence may tell us a little more. The king's manor at Eltham, for one, was renovated in 1445 with the queen's needs in mind. Specifically, a new hall with a scullery, saucery and serving-place was built, as was a new great chamber and kitchen, presumably because the current ones were deemed inadequate for the royal couple's needs.[76] Such extensive renovations for Eltham as well as other evidence for the physical layout of royal residences point towards separate quarters existing for the king and queen, no matter whether one or the other owned the specific property.[77] This implies that when the king and queen were living together, they still required the exclusive services of at least a portion of their household staff, most probably those who served them in their chambers. As for those personnel who served in the kitchens and stables, among other departments, we remain in the dark as to how they functioned while under the same roof together. What is likely is that their royal masters left it to the stewards of the respective households to organise the staff and construct a coherent and effective working relationship during those periods of living together.

At this juncture, it is worth revisiting past conclusions about the financial competence of these three queens. If previous scholarly research is any guide, the seemingly ample revenues enjoyed by each queen did not always result in household financial efficiency. Briefly, the prevailing scholarly opinion is that Margaret of Anjou's household was a profligate one, Elizabeth Woodville was the more financially responsible queen, and Elizabeth of York's financial situation was constantly precarious because she regularly spent more than she received in funds.[78] At first glance, it does not seem possible to conclusively challenge these assumptions about either the state of each queen's finances or their individual financial competence. However, both issues are worth re-considering if only to explore the reasons for these judgements.

Perceptions of Margaret's and Elizabeth Woodville's financial situations stem primarily from analysis of their extant household accounts. Yet differences in content between these accounts preclude straightforward comparisons of overall expenditure and lump-sum payments made by each queen. The wages of personnel in the ranks of esquires, yeomen, grooms and pages for Margaret's household accounted for an impost of nearly £370 on her finances. The omission in Elizabeth Woodville's account suggests that those types of wages were accounted for in a different manner. In addition,

---

[76] Colvin, ed., *The History of the King's Works, Vol. II*, 936.
[77] Delman, 'The Queen's House before Queen's House', 15–18.
[78] See, for example, Dunn, 'Margaret of Anjou: Queen Consort of Henry VI', 129; Myers, 'The Household of Queen Elizabeth Woodville', 256; Myers, 'The Household of Queen Margaret of Anjou', 142; Okerlund, *Elizabeth of York*, 198–9.

her account did not record any payments made to the king's treasurer of the household as Margaret's account did. Given that Margaret's payments to the king's treasurer amounted to nearly £1800, this means that disregarding these payments and the wages of £370 leaves Margaret's expenses at approximately £5400. This amount is much closer to the total household expenditure for Elizabeth Woodville, which was approximately £4600. It is not clear how those comparable wages were paid in Elizabeth's household; neither is it evident why no payments to the king's treasurer were recorded even though it is highly unlikely that the couple did not spend any time at all under the same roof in that accounting year. Without evidence to show otherwise, it is just as probable that such payments were made directly by Elizabeth's chamber or Privy Purse, in which case Elizabeth does look to be a more economically prudent queen after all.[79] Nevertheless, taking into account the adjustments made, the household of Margaret of Anjou does not appear quite as extravagant as that of Elizabeth Woodville as has previously been concluded. What lends this statement more weight is the fact that Margaret's account was drawn up in her seventh or eighth year as queen, while Elizabeth had only been crowned queen for two to three years in the year of her extant account. A queen in her seventh or eighth year may well have had to incur greater expenditure than someone who had only been queen for a quarter of that time and had perhaps not yet grown accustomed to her status and required mode of living.

In Elizabeth of York's case, there appear to be compelling reasons to question her financial competence. The queen made several different payments to settle bills to merchants such as tailors, mercers and goldsmiths, but many of them were recorded as part payments rather than settlements of the entire debt.[80] These frequent partial payments are strong signs of Elizabeth of York's pecuniary troubles, as are the large number of transactions in the Privy Purse expense account recording the queen's debts to various gentlemen and ladies in her court. Additionally, there are many different transactions recorded in the expense and receipt books of the king's chamber for the period 1485–1521 relating to the queen. Some of these are recorded as being debts owed by the queen which were settled by the king. William Hungate was given about £1300 to pay the queen's debts in November 1493.[81] Another vast sum of £2000 was delivered directly to the queen for the payment of further debts in February 1497.[82] Other transactions recorded sums that were lent to the

[79] There is a record of a payment of 500 marks (£333 6s 8d) made to the king's treasurer of the household by Elizabeth of York's keeper of the Privy Purse, Richard Decons. Queen's Book, fol. 75.
[80] For example, Queen's Book, fols 43, 50, 59, 63, 66, 68.
[81] *The Chamber Books*, BL Add MS 7099, fol. 13, https://www.tudorchamberbooks.org/edition/folio/7099_fo_013.xml.
[82] *The Chamber Books*, TNA E101/414/6, fol. 60v, https://www.tudorchamberbooks.org/edition/folio/E101_414_6_fo_060v.xml.

The Queen's Household

queen but involved far lower amounts. These included £100 in April 1494, £6 13s 4d in April 1498, and £10 in 1500.[83] While there is no clear indication of the exact nature of the queen's debts nor the reasons why the king would have lent money to the queen, the fact that the king did so presents a vivid picture of a queen who was chronically in debt. Such a picture naturally does not further the idea of a financially competent queen.

Yet there are additional relevant issues to bear in mind. For one, the evidence of her Privy Purse expense account alone is not definitive evidence of financial insecurity or a financially incompetent queen. There are, after all, no other Privy Purse expense accounts to compare with, either belonging to this queen or for the other queens in this study. By their very nature, Privy Purse expense accounts record very personal and detailed information about queenly expenditure, and the level of minutiae of the recorded transactions in the queen's account matches that of the king's own Privy Purse expense account. It is also worth noting that Arlene Okerlund observes that the personal finances of Henry VII and his queen appeared to be somewhat tangled. While allowing that Elizabeth of York's dower possibly never was enough to ensure her financial independence, she asserts that 'Henry and she [the queen] shared a somewhat muddled system where Henry paid some of her bills and they lent each other money'.[84] It may be that the demarcation between financial matters within the purview of the king's and queen's households became a little opaque during the reign of Henry VII. Perhaps in practice it became habitual for the queen's debtors to receive payment from either the king's or the queen's household officials. The queen's sudden death in 1503 would have thrown her household into chaos and it is possible that her officials had become accustomed to not always having to pay the queen's bills. This procedural fluidity, rather than impecunity on the queen's part, might help explain why the king's household settled debts and paid wages for the queen's servants after her death.[85] In short, the answer to the question of Elizabeth of York's financial competence remains inconclusive.

A final observation relates to the queens' levels of participation in the management of their own households. Myers asserts that Margaret's treasurer's persistent pursuit of her claims to queen's gold was in keeping with 'what is already known of the Queen' and presumably was a reference to the queen's

---

[83] *The Chamber Books*, BL Add MS 7099, fol. 16, https://www.tudorchamberbooks.org/edition/folio/7099_fo_016.xml, TNA E101/414/16, fol. 24r, https://www.tudorchamberbooks.org/edition/folio/LL_E101_414_16_fo024r.xml, TNA E101/415/3, fol. 28r, https://www.tudorchamberbooks.org/edition/folio/E101_415_3_fo_028r.xml.

[84] Okerlund, *Elizabeth of York*, 136.

[85] For example, *The Chamber Books*, BL Add MS 59899, fols 53r, 56v, 57v, 60r, https://www.tudorchamberbooks.org/edition/manuscript/BL_Add_MS_59899/folio.

personal tenacity and insistence on her rights.[86] Notwithstanding, there is little else to suggest that Margaret was actively engaged in the management of her household, particularly the operational aspects. In Elizabeth Woodville's case, there are several instances in her account of auditor corrections or cancellations of fees, recorded with the note 'disallowed by mandate of the lady queen' or 'disallowed by mandate of the same'.[87] These notations point to this queen being actively engaged with her household finances, at least at the highest level.[88] There also appears to be slight evidence supporting a high level of active involvement by Elizabeth of York. Even so, the fact that her signature appears at the bottom of many of the pages in her Privy Purse expense account means that, as with Elizabeth Woodville, we can infer that this queen was involved at least in the overall supervision of her household finances.[89] Despite the lack of evidence, since I have already shown that the queens could be active in estate administration, we can presume that household administration was similarly handled. Other high-ranking landowners knew when to leave the running of operations both of their estates and their households to their officials and when to intercede and make their presence felt. Surely the queens also trusted their own household officials to see to daily matters and routines while they themselves kept a watchful eye overall.

HOUSEHOLD PERSONNEL

Earenfight, in her study of Catherine of Aragon's household in the period 1501–04, states that people are 'the fabric, the essence of the royal household'.[90] The people who served the queens in our study did so in many different positions and, at least at the lower levels, were organised into various departments.[91]

At the most senior level in the queen's household were posts such as the chamberlain, chancellor, receiver-general, treasurer and stewards. The official head of the household was the chamberlain or the chancellor and the head of finances was the treasurer. These posts in the queens' households were often given to important noblemen who may or may not have been involved in daily

---

[86] Myers, 'The Household of Queen Margaret of Anjou', 142.
[87] 'Disallocatur mandato domine regine' or 'Disallocatur mandato predicto'. Myers, 'The Household of Queen Elizabeth Woodville', 290, 291, 294–7, 299, 305, 307.
[88] Laynesmith, *The Last Medieval Queens*, 223.
[89] Nicolas, ed., *The Privy Purse Expenses of Elizabeth of York*, xcvi. The queen's signature appears at the bottom of twenty-seven out of sixty-eight folios of payments. Queen's Book, fols 29–55.
[90] Theresa Earenfight, 'A Precarious Household: Catherine of Aragon in England, 1501–1504', in *Royal and Elite Households in Medieval and Early Modern Europe*, ed. Theresa Earenfight (Leiden: Brill, 2018), 340.
[91] See Table 8 for household posts and personnel in the households of the queens in this study.

Table 8: The Queens' Household Officials and Personnel.[1]

Position/Role	Margaret of Anjou (1452–53)	Elizabeth Woodville (1466–67)	Elizabeth of York (1501–03)
Chief Steward	John, Viscount Beaumont		
Chancellor	Laurence Booth (Bothe)	Roger Radcliff	Edmund Chaderton
Chamberlain	John Wenlock	John Bourchier, Lord Berners	Thomas Butler, earl of Ormond
Vice-Chamberlain			Robert Poynyt
Treasurer of the Chamber	Edward Ellesmere		
Keeper of the Queen's Jewels	Edward Ellesmere		
Keeper of the Great Wardrobe	John Norrys	William Kerver	
Steward	Edward Hull	Humphrey Bourchier	
	Andrew Ogard	James Haute	
Master of the Queen's Horse		John Woodville	Roger Cotton[2]
Receiver-General	William Cotton	John Forster	Richard Decons[3]
Queen's Solicitor		Robert Iseham	
Auditor	John Walsh	John Stanford	Richard Bedell
	Nicholas Sharp	Robert Browne	

[1] TNA DL28/5/8, E36/207, E36/210, LC2/1; SJC, SJLM/9/2/1, https://www.sjcarchives.org.uk/institutional/index.php/list-of-officers-servants-elizabeth-of-york. The information in this table is derived from these extant sources for the households of the queens in this study. The lists of personnel are only for the stated years and are not necessarily complete.

[2] Roger Cotton was also styled as Head of the Queen's Stable.

[3] Richard Decons was not styled in the sources as Receiver-General but he performed the tasks of one. He was called the Keeper of the Queen's Purse and received wages for receiving the queen's revenues and for holding the office of the signet.

Table 8 (continued).

Position/Role	Margaret of Anjou (1452–53)	Elizabeth Woodville (1466–67)	Elizabeth of York (1501–03)
Attorney-general/Queen's Attorney	Robert Tanfield	John Dyve	Richard Elyot
Queen's Attorney in Chancery	John Vailard		
Queen's Attorney on Court of King's Bench	Thomas Lloyd	Thomas Luyt	
Queen's Attorney on Court of Common Pleas	Simon Elleryngton	Thomas Thoralde	William Mordant
Queen's Attorney in Royal Exchequer	William Essex John Croke		
Miscellaneous officials			Richard Empson Morgan Kidwelly[4] Richard Cutlerd William Denton – carver Ralph Verney – carver James Haute – sewer ? Bekynsall – sewer ? Fowler – sewer

[4] The extant sources do not state what positions Kidwelly and Cutlerd served in and thus received wages for.

Apprentice-at-law	Ralph Poole			
	Robert Danby	Henry Suthill		
	Walter Moile	Thomas Urswick		
	Thomas Billyng			
	John Nedeham			
Serjeant-at-law		Thomas Yonge		John Mordant
		John Catesby		Humphrey Conysby
Clerk of the Register of the Chancery	Richard Croke	Alexander Rowton		
Clerk of the Receipt	William Nanseglos	Thomas Holbache		
Clerk of the Closet	William Crosseley			? Harding
Clerk of the Signet	George Ashby	John Aleyn		Griffith Richards
Clerk of the Jewels	Jacob/James Fynaunce			
Clerk of the Queen's Council				John Pagenam
Clerk of the Avenary	John Hattecliff			Thomas Acworth
Clerk of the Stable				Richard Cotton
Keeper of the Council Chamber	William (John?) Randolf	John Wode		John Holand
Messenger of the Council	Roger Morecroft	David Gough		
Queen's Messenger	John Sergeant			Owen Whitstones
Queen's Harbinger	William Fawkner			
Keeper of the New Tower at Westminster	Roger Morecroft	David Gough		

Table 8 (continued).

Position/Role	Margaret of Anjou (1452–53)	Elizabeth Woodville (1466–67)	Elizabeth of York (1501–03)
			Gentlemen Ushers
			Henry Pole
			William Crowmer
			William Bulstrode
			Nicholas Hyde
			Gentlemen Waiters
			Thomas Twisday
			Anthony Cotton
			Richard Brampton – gentleman of the pantry[6]
			John Ricroft – gentleman of the kitchen
Household Esquires[5]	23 esquires listed in household account	John Hulcote	

[5] Names for esquires, yeomen, grooms and pages were listed only in Queen Margaret's household account. Only a very few names for these household personnel can be gleaned from the sources for Elizabeth Woodville.

[6] It is unclear whether Brampton was an esquire or a yeoman.

		Sewers of the Chamber[7]
		Hamlet Clegg
		John Shirley
		Thomas Lacy
		Yeoman Ushers
	Ralph Dale	Robert Alyn
	James Redemayn – yeoman of the horses	John Hamerton
		John Awordon
	John Apole – yeoman of the carriage store	Arnold Chollerton
		John Abell
Household Yeomen	30 yeomen listed in household account	*17 persons listed as yeomen of the chamber*
		2 persons listed as yeomen of the kitchen
		11 persons listed as yeomen in the queen's stables

---

7   The rank of the sewers is unclear.

Table 8 (continued).

Position/Role	Margaret of Anjou (1452–53)	Elizabeth Woodville (1466–67)	Elizabeth of York (1501–03)
Household Grooms	25 grooms listed in household account	Richard Griffith Thomas Bowen – footman[8] John Parker – footman	Thomas Barton – footman[9] Richard Chollerton – footman 12 grooms listed in the household account 6 grooms listed for the Queen's stables
Household Pages	17 pages listed in household account		7 pages listed in the household account
Miscellaneous	Marion – laundress	Agnes Moryson – laundress John Faux – minstrel Richard Montak – minstrel William Holden – minstrel	Richard Payn – almoner Nicholas Maior – saddler Agnes Dean – laundress Beatrix Bradowe – rocker Emma Bragges – rocker Alice Williams – rocker

8   The footmen were probably grooms or pages.
9   The rank of the footmen is unclear.

Miscellaneous (continued)

Laurence Travers – attendant
Marques Loryden – minstrel
Janin Marcazin – minstrel
Richard Devouse – minstrel
Oliver Auferton – keeper of queen's goshawk

Queen's Stables

6 sumptermen listed

15 palfreymen listed

administration. Sir John Wenlock and Laurence Bothe, cleric, for instance, served Queen Margaret as her chamberlain and chancellor, but it is unclear how extensive or involved their daily duties were. Myers speculates that the chamberlain's primary financial responsibility was to authorise payments from the queen's Privy Purse but such a task need not have involved everyday ministrations on the official's part.[92] The fees of £40 paid to each of them were the same as those paid to Elizabeth Woodville's chamberlain and chancellor, Lord Berners and Dr Roger Radcliff.[93] In Dr Radcliff's case, incidentally, his fees were reduced by the auditor. There is no recorded reason for this action, but one possibility is that the queen did not believe that Radcliff had earnt such a substantial amount.

While the chamberlain's and chancellor's annual fees were considerable, these amounts did not make them the highest paid officials in any of the queens' households. If we take into account only wages, the most important officials were the chief steward of lands and receiver-general who served Margaret of Anjou, the receiver-general in Elizabeth Woodville's household, and the keeper of the Privy Purse for Elizabeth of York. Margaret's chief steward of lands, John Viscount Beaumont, received 100 marks (£66 13s 4d) for serving the queen in this capacity. This was the same amount that Philippa of Hainault's steward of lands was paid, an indication of the level of importance accorded to this post.[94] The receivers-general were paid £50 each for their efforts, significantly less than the chief steward's fee.[95] These were the highest fees paid to any official in either of their households. In contrast, Elizabeth of York's keeper of the Privy Purse, who was Richard Decons in 1502, was paid only £20 in fees for holding the office of the signet and for receiving the queen's monies, and there is no evidence to show whether he was paid separately for serving as keeper of the Queen's Privy Purse. Still, he appears to have been the highest-paid of Elizabeth of York's household officials.

There were two different steward posts in elite establishments, one for lands and one for the household. The previous chapter discussed the position of steward of lands, and we know much about his responsibilities from didactic sources. As might be expected, the queens were served by several stewards of lands. The steward of the household, as the name suggests, was meant to be in charge of the household.[96] His role was that of a modern-day supervisor, the person who enforced overall household policy and maintained order

[92] Myers, 'The Household of Queen Margaret of Anjou', 150.
[93] Myers, 'The Household of Queen Elizabeth Woodville', 287, 290; Myers, 'The Household of Queen Margaret of Anjou', 181, 190.
[94] Johnstone I, 254.
[95] Myers, 'The Household of Queen Elizabeth Woodville', 287; Myers, 'The Household of Queen Margaret of Anjou', 190.
[96] Mertes, *The English Noble Household*, 22; Woolgar, *The Great Household*, 17.

and discipline among its staff.[97] Where this steward was concerned, Myers states that there is no mention of any such post in either of the accounts for Margaret and Elizabeth Woodville.[98] This is not strictly accurate as there are individuals recorded as being stewards in these household accounts, that is, Edward Hull and Andrew Ogard for Margaret and Humphrey Bourchier and James Haute for Elizabeth Woodville. It is not entirely certain that they held the posts as stewards of the household but it is more likely than not that they did so and reported to the chamberlain or chancellor.[99] It is true, however, that this specific post is absent from any records we have for Elizabeth of York. This points to different arrangements being adopted in her household. The responsibilities of the household steward may have been divided among several senior figures, such as the keeper of the great wardrobe, the treasurer or the chamberlain, thus negating the need for a household steward. In terms of fees, the stewards of the household were paid more than stewards of lands, which probably means that they were considered the more important of the two posts. Margaret's stewards were each paid 40 marks (£26 13s 4d) in fees, as were Elizabeth Woodville's two stewards. These fees were lower than those of the receiver-general, chamberlain and chancellor but still higher than the highest paid of any of the queens' stewards of lands.[100]

Where financial responsibilities were concerned, the treasurer and the receiver-general were very likely the most important posts. They kept watch over and recorded expenses of all sorts, presumably taking accounts from the different household divisions, although the exact areas of responsibility for each in the households of our queens is unclear. The convenience of embodying the responsibilities of both these positions in a single individual is probably why such an arrangement began to be adopted in the middle of the fourteenth century, when Philippa of Hainault was queen. The practice was fully entrenched by the later fifteenth century. Each of the queens in this study was served by a single person acting as both treasurer and receiver-general. William Cotton served Margaret of Anjou in both capacities; so did John Forster during Elizabeth Woodville's time as queen. In Elizabeth of York's case, Richard Decons was her most senior financial officer. No record has been found showing that Elizabeth of York had a treasurer of the household, but the keeper of the queen's Privy Purse possibly undertook the duties of the former. Closer examination shows that several of Elizabeth of York's expenses involved far from trivial amounts, perhaps an indication that Decons' post

---

[97] Mertes, *The English Noble Household*, 22.
[98] Myers, 'The Household of Queen Margaret of Anjou', 152, n. 1.
[99] This conclusion is based on the fact that information about specific stewards of queens' lands and properties can be gleaned from the extant manorial accounts consulted for this study and none of the aforementioned individuals appear anywhere other than in the household accounts.
[100] See Table 5.

as keeper of the Privy Purse had become more important during her time compared with her predecessors.[101]

Other officials found in some but not all the queens' households were the keeper or master of the queen's jewels, the treasurer of the queen's chamber, and the master of horse, this last official overseeing the marshalsea, or stables.[102] Again, we encounter individuals who simultaneously served the queen in multiple capacities. A case in point was Margaret's treasurer of the chamber, John Norrys, who also served as her master of jewels. This arrangement was continued by Edward Ellesmere when Norrys surrendered these posts to become her keeper of the great wardrobe. Norrys and Ellesmere are but two examples of one individual holding more than one post simultaneously in the queen's household.

At the more junior levels, we find 'middle management' staff, individuals to whom we can ascribe duties of overseeing the performance of household tasks as well as actually performing some of the tasks themselves. The cook in the kitchen would have been one of these, together with the marshal of the hall and the marshal of the stables. Gentlemen ushers, carvers and sewers were probably overseers rather than general servants, or perhaps they performed ceremonial rather than actual roles in the household, which would have meant more junior staff taking on overseer duties in practice.[103] A host of other clerks had specific duties in finances and accounting. Most of our queens' households included a clerk of the receipt, a clerk of the register of the chancellery, a clerk of the signet, and a clerk of the queen's closet. The household accounts are littered with references to these posts since they received individual fees, allowances for necessary expenditure, and financial compensation for journeys made while going about their duties. A specific post found in Margaret's household but not in the households of her successors was the clerk of jewels. Jacob/James Fynaunce, who filled this post in 1452–53, worked under the direction of Edward Ellesmere, the keeper of the queen's jewels, and kept records of the queen's gifts and purchases.[104]

The clerks of the stables and clerks of the avenary, who, as previously discussed, tended to the finances of the marshalsea, were also considered

---

[101] Significantly large payments from the Privy Purse included payments for bills to goldsmiths, mercers, and a skinner. Queen's Book, fols 31, 44, 63, 66, 67. For examples of payments to the queen's stables, see Queen's Book, fols 38, 45, 53, 65, 90, 95.

[102] An individual named Thomas Lovell is recorded as having filled the post of treasurer of the queen's chamber, one who may have assisted the keeper of the queen's Privy Purse.

[103] Carvers and sewers were household servants whose duties included service at mealtimes. Neal, 'The Queen's Grace', 128.

[104] Fynaunce earned £6 13s 4d a year in this post. Myers, 'The Household of Queen Margaret of Anjou', 186.

The Queen's Household

'middle management' personnel. They, too, could oversee the administration and everyday operations either in place of or as deputy to the master of horse. In Margaret's household, the clerk of the avenary, John Hatcliffe, received back payments not only for buying fodder for horses but also for sundry expenses in the stables.[105] It is evident that Hatcliffe bore the responsibilities financially and possibly administratively as well for the stables. Such transactions also support the idea that Margaret did not have a master of horse serving her, with those duties falling to the clerk of the avenary. Interestingly, the clerk of the avenary was recorded before the clerk of the stables in the list of personnel from the queen's stables who were given a clothing allowance for their attendance at the funeral of Elizabeth of York. Since many of the lists of other categories of household staff were ordered from most to least important, it is highly probable the clerk of the avenary ranked as more essential than the clerk of the stables.[106]

Our knowledge of different household posts and the people who filled them is complicated by the fact that distinctions of rank were based on status or social rank as well as work specialty. This hierarchy consisted of, from highest to lowest ranked, *armigerus, valettus, garcio* and *pagettus*, that is, esquires, yeomen, grooms and pages. Mertes has extensively discussed these different ranks and I will not reiterate her work here; suffice it to note that this household hierarchy was unquestionably applied in the later fifteenth century queens' households.[107] Some of the yeomen are listed as being attached to particular household divisions, such as William Barnet, a yeoman of poultry, and John Browe, a yeoman of the acattery.[108] Most of them, however, as well as the esquires, do not appear to have had specific designations, and this surely indicates that members of these two ranks were not typically assigned tasks according to a strict demarcation.[109] Grooms and pages were assigned duties in specific areas and, although they may have performed tasks requiring some skill, they were almost certainly expected to also carry out menial tasks such as sweeping out the chambers, general tidying, and putting away clothing and other items.

Many other household members who appear in the sources for our queens do not fit neatly into the household divisions thus far encountered. These include minstrels, harpers, midwives, chaplains, footmen, messengers and laundresses, who were regularly employed in the royal households.[110] The

---

[105] Myers, 'The Household of Queen Margaret of Anjou', 204–5.
[106] TNA LC2/1, fol. 75.
[107] Mertes, *The English Noble Household*, 26–31.
[108] Myers, 'The Household of Queen Margaret of Anjou', 187.
[109] Mertes, *The English Noble Household*, 26–9.
[110] For example, CPR 1446–52, 512; CPR 1467–77, 154; CPR 1476–85, 157, 241; CPR 1485–94, 424–5, 452; Myers, 'The Household of Queen Elizabeth Woodville', 311; Myers, 'The Household of Queen Margaret of Anjou', 197.

queens' households sometimes included rockers for babies or attendants for children.[111] In Elizabeth Woodville's household, Cecily Pesemersh was employed as an attendant to the ten-year-old Katherine Woodville, the queen's sister, who was the Duchess of Buckingham but was being looked after in the queen's household.[112] Elizabeth of York's household staff included three women, Beatrix Bradowe, Emma Bragges and Alice Williams, who were rockers for Henry, Margaret and Edward Courtenay, the three children of Lady Katherine Courtenay, the queen's sister, who resided in the queen's household.[113] All of these individuals were essential household members, as were large numbers of what Mertes refers to as 'below stairs' servants.[114] Menial servants in every corner of the household have tended to leave little or no mark in the account books, making it next to impossible to trace them even though they were vital to daily domestic operations. They were almost certainly the ones who would have spread rushes on the floors, carried water to the rooms for washing and replenished the candleholders with fresh candles, to name but a few of the hundreds of menial jobs in any household. Neal's research is testament to the amount of information about the careers of the higher-ranked household members that can be gleaned by cross-referencing with sources such as the Patent and Close Rolls.[115] It is practically impossible to do the same for the lower ranks.

With some significant exceptions, all the queens' officials and servants were men. Single men were generally preferred as servants, particularly at the lower status levels.[116] Married men did, however, serve in the queen's household, many as officials and in senior household posts, while their wives often served in the same household. Among them were Thomas Sharnborne and Giles Saintlowe, esquires, who both served in Margaret of Anjou's household and were married to two of the queen's ladies.[117] A relatively small number of women among the household personnel was by no means an unusual arrangement. The household of one noblewoman, Joan de Valence, in 1297 contained only one woman among the eighty-five identifiable servants. The Duchess of Clarence's household in 1468 was made up of mostly male servants, with only twelve out of 144 persons being female.[118] So was the mid-fifteenth

---

[111] Rockers were individuals employed to rock the cradles of infants.
[112] Myers, 'The Household of Queen Elizabeth Woodville', 312.
[113] Queen's Book, fol. 91.
[114] Mertes, *The English Noble Household*, 32.
[115] Neal, 'The Queen's Grace', Appendix VI. His notes demonstrate that a substantial amount of cross-referencing has been done.
[116] Mertes, *The English Noble Household*, 57–8.
[117] Myers, 'The Household of Queen Margaret of Anjou', 183.
[118] Woolgar, *The Great Household*, 34.

century household of Lady Margaret Beaufort, the king's mother, where only two out of thirty servants were female.[119]

Notwithstanding this general preponderance of men among the household personnel, one distinctive group in the queens' households comprised the queens' ladies.[120] Like all other queens consort, Margaret of Anjou, Elizabeth Woodville and Elizabeth of York were attended by a number of noble and gentlewomen, many of whom were on par with or even outranked the majority of the men in the same households.[121] These ladies were among those in closest attendance upon the queen. In effect, the presence of the queen's ladies was, in St John's opinion, the 'only visible difference between the composition of the queen's household and the king's'.[122] The most senior of these women would have been the most highly ranked and highest paid for their services, as in the case of Anne, Lady Bourchier. The lady was Elizabeth Woodville's sister and her most senior personal attendant, and she was paid an annual wage of £40.[123] Regrettably, there is little didactic information about the duties of the queens' female attendants.[124] This is not surprising, however, since their primary function was to be the queen's companions and to tend to her personal needs. This would have encompassed a wide range of different duties and jobs. For example, they would have helped their royal mistresses to dress and assisted them with toileting and other intimate tasks. They would have run errands for them, participated in leisure activities and travelled with them on visits to family and friends.[125] In the case of Elizabeth of York, at least, it seems they also lent the queen money on occasions.[126]

---

[119] Jones and Underwood, *The King's Mother*, 138.

[120] The queens' ladies, both in the English royal households and those in continental Europe, including Castile, France, Sweden and the Hapsburg courts, have been the subject of a number of important studies. For example, see the range of essays in *The Politics of Female Households: Ladies-in-Waiting Across Early Modern Europe*, eds. Nadine Akkerman and Birgit Houben (Leiden: Brill, 2013); Caroline Dunn, 'Serving Isabella of France: From Queen Consort to Dowager', in *Royal and Elite Households in Medieval and Early Modern Europe: More Than Just a Castle*, ed. Theresa Earenfight (Leiden: Brill, 2018), 169–201; Maria Narbona-Cárceles, 'Woman at Court: A Prosopographic Study of the Court of Carlos III of Navarre (1387–1485)', *Medieval Prosopography* 22 (2001): 31–64; zum Kolk, 'The Household of the Queen of France in the Sixteenth Century'.

[121] See Table 9 for lists of the queens' ladies. Woolgar, *The Senses*, 231.

[122] St John, *Three Medieval Queens*, 66–7.

[123] Myers, 'The Household of Queen Elizabeth Woodville', 288.

[124] The Eltham Ordinances of 1526 lists in some detail the duties of the gentlemen, ushers and grooms of the king's privy chamber but not of the female counterparts in the queen's household. Harris, *English Aristocratic Women*, 227.

[125] Harris, *English Aristocratic Women*, 228.

[126] For example, see Queen's Book, fols 32, 35, 36, 39, 60.

Table 9: The Queens' Ladies.[127]

Role	Margaret of Anjou (1452–53)	Elizabeth Woodville (1466–67)	Elizabeth of York (1501–03)
Personal Attendant/ Lady-in-Waiting	Ismanie, Lady Scales Isabel, Lady Grey Lady Margaret Roos Lady Isabelle Dacre	Anne, Lady Bourchier Elizabeth, Lady Scales Lady Alice Fogge Lady Johanne Norris Lady Elizabeth Uvedale	Lady Elizabeth Stafford Lady Eleanor Verney Dame Jane Guildford Dame Elisabeth Peche
'Damsel'/ Gentlewoman	Barbaline Herberquyne Osanna Herman Rose Merston Margaret Stanlowe Katherine Penyson Katherine Whittingham Agnes Parr Matilda Lowes Jamona Sharnborne Edith Burgh Eleanor Roos	Anne Hastings Elizabeth Donne Eleanor Prudde Alice Hulcote Margaret Stanley Katherine Faversham Mary Genyngham	Elisabeth Denton Mary Radcliff Anne Crowmer Eleanor Jones Mary Denys Elisabeth Catesby Margaret Bourne Margaret Belknap Elisabeth Lee Anne Weston Elyn Brent Anne Browne Margaret Wotton Elisabeth Fitzherbert
Chamberer	Johanna Prynce Johanna Bateresby	Johanna Martyn Beatrice Notsount	Alice Skeling Elisabeth Baptiste Frances Baptiste
Totals	**17**	**14**	**21**

[127] TNA DL28/5/8, E36/207, E36/210. The information in this table is derived from these extant sources for the households of the queens in this study. The ladies listed are those receiving wages in the queens' households but it is not always clear what positions the ladies occupied, especially for Elizabeth of York's household. The lists are only for the stated years and may not be complete.

The Queen's Household

The queen's ladies formed an important group in the households but the queens themselves did not have complete freedom of choice in selecting the women who would serve them.[128] Their husbands, the kings, would have wielded much influence in the matter. Henry VII's mother, Lady Margaret Beaufort, also appears to have had some say in appointments to Elizabeth of York's household, as seen from one occasion when the countess dismissed a man seeking to enter the queen's service.[129] Only the 1445 household ordinance attempted to prescribe exactly how many ladies of different ranks were to attend the queen consort. According to this ordinance, the number of ladies allowed to attend the queen numbered twenty-two at the most, including a countess, a baroness, two gentlewomen and an assortment of other women servants.[130] As outlined in Table 9, seventeen women were listed as receiving salaries in Margaret of Anjou's household and fourteen in Elizabeth Woodville's household.[131] Forty-seven women were recorded in the expense account for Elizabeth of York's funeral as being part of the late queen's household, compared with only twenty-one listed in the Privy Purse expense account as receiving wages.[132] This discrepancy can be explained by noting that there would certainly have been female family members and noblewomen who accompanied and served the queens on myriad occasions but were not actually paid wages as household members. Of Elizabeth Woodville's many sisters and female relatives, only Anne, Lady Bourchier, and Elizabeth, Lady Scales, are listed in the extant account as being paid wages.[133] Likewise, none of Elizabeth of York's sisters were paid wages as members of her household.

As might be expected, a post in the queen's household was much sought after and there were various ways whereby one could gain such a prestigious appointment. One method that applied specifically in Margaret of Anjou's case was as follows. Foreign-born queens were often accompanied by female companions when they came to their new country-by-marriage, and some stayed behind with their mistress. Among Margaret's attendants were Barbaline Herberquyne, Osanna Herman and Jamona Cherneys, who came over to England with her and stayed to serve in her household after her marriage. One or more of these foreign-born attendants eventually became naturalised and went on to marry men in royal service, thus binding themselves even more firmly to the queen's service and her adopted country.

---

[128] Laynesmith, *The Last Medieval Queens*, 228.
[129] Jones and Underwood, *The King's Mother*, 161.
[130] Myers, 'Some Household Ordinances of Henry VI', 245.
[131] Myers, 'The Household of Queen Elizabeth Woodville', 288–9; Myers, 'The Household of Queen Margaret of Anjou', 182–4.
[132] TNA LC2/1, fol. 78r.
[133] Myers, 'The Household of Queen Elizabeth Woodville', 288.

No matter what the background of the queen herself was, however, there were other established methods of gaining royal appointments. An individual's family background and connections counted for much in their efforts to attain a position in the queen's service. Where the queen's ladies were concerned, female family members such as sisters and cousins understandably tended to become the queen's principal attendants. Elizabeth Woodville's sister, Anne Lady Bourchier, and her sister-in-law, Elizabeth Lady Scales, were her most senior personal attendants. Similarly, Elizabeth of York's sisters Katherine and Cecily served as her ladies.[134] The queen's close male family members could also be given official positions within her household, as in the cases of Anthony and John Woodville, two of Elizabeth Woodville's brothers.[135]

Many families often possessed a tradition of royal service.[136] Such traditions no doubt played a large part in enabling aspiring young men to gain positions in the royal households. The Haute family of Kent epitomised an English gentry family whose members served in the upper ranks of the royal households. They were active in the regional community in the late medieval period, but their influence began to extend beyond the regions into the wider sphere, including that of the court following the marriage of Elizabeth Woodville to Edward IV in 1464.[137] As it transpired, the Hautes were related to the Woodvilles by marriage since one of Queen Elizabeth's paternal aunts was married to one of the sons of Sir Nicholas Haute, a knight of the shire.[138] Several members of the Haute family provided royal service at different periods. Among them was Sir Richard Haute, who served Princess Elizabeth, the king's eldest daughter, as carver during Edward IV's reign and was later appointed to the household of the young Edward V.[139] He survived the reign

---

[134] Queen's Book, fol. 91; Laynesmith, *The Last Medieval Queens*, 228–9; Myers, 'The Household of Queen Elizabeth Woodville', 288. Note that neither Katherine nor Cecily is listed as receiving wages in Elizabeth of York's extant Privy Purse expense account.

[135] Anthony Lord Scales served his sister, the queen, as a steward of lands, while John was her master of horse.

[136] An extensive examination of the backgrounds of all the individuals and families who served in the English queens' households utilising methods such as social network theory is a monumental project beyond the scope of this study. For comparable work undertaken on the households of Iberian queens, see, for example, Diana Pelaz Flores, *La Casa de la Reina en la Corona de Castilla (1418-1496)* (Valladolid: Universidad de Valladolid, 2017) and the range of articles in the following special issue, *The Iberian Queens' Households: Dynamics, Social Strategies and Royal Power*, published in *Royal Studies Journal*, 10, no. 1 (2023).

[137] P. W. Fleming, 'The Hautes and Their "Circle": Culture and the English Gentry', in *England in the Fifteenth Century: Proceedings of the 1986 Harlaxton Symposium*, ed. Daniel Williams (Woodbridge: Boydell Press, 1987), 86.

[138] Elizabeth Woodville's aunt, Jane Woodville, married William Haute, a son of Sir Nicholas.

[139] TNA E404/74/1; CPR 1467–77, 366.

The Queen's Household

of Richard III and went on to offer valued service to Henry VII as, among other things, king's carver and knight of the king's body.[140] Royal service was further provided by three generations of Hautes in the form of Martin, his son James, and James' son Henry. Martin was a yeoman of the king's household and Elizabeth Woodville's receiver for her holdings in Rockingham in the 1460s.[141] Later he served the queen as an usher in her chamber.[142] James was a king's esquire who also served as steward to Elizabeth Woodville.[143] He, too, survived the tumultuous years after Edward IV died and later prospered in Henry VII's service in various capacities, including as bailiff of Donyngton, Berkshire, and steward in Hanslap, Northamptonshire.[144] He may well have been the same individual as one 'Jaques Hawte' who was noted as under-keeper of Kenilworth and a member of the household of Elizabeth of York.[145] James' son Henry continued the family tradition by serving as a royal chaplain during the first Tudor king's reign.[146] The many instances of continued royal service by different generations shows just how prominent the Haute family became at court.

There are other examples that demonstrate a multiplicity of the same last names in royal service. The Cottons are another case in point. Elizabeth of York, throughout her time as queen, was served by no less than three members of the extended Cotton family: Roger, who was her master of horse, Anthony, who was a gentleman waiter, and Richard as clerk of the stables.[147] Even in the more junior ranks of yeomen and below, there were examples where more than one member of an extended family was engaged in royal service. John, William and George Hamerton were all employed as staff in the household of the queen in 1503, John and William as yeomen and George as a groom porter.[148] A recommendation from a relative who was already in royal service was obviously often enough to gain similar employment.

Where the lower-ranked posts and most menial servants were concerned, recruitment was influenced by two interrelated factors – affinity and geography. The lowest ranked of the queen's household servants were probably drawn from the geographical areas surrounding the principal places of residence and there would have existed ties of affinity between the queen and the locals. Such was the case for servants in many noble houses and it was an obviously

---

[140] CPR 1485–94, 199, 365; Fleming, 'The Hautes and Their "Circle"', 88.
[141] Myers, 'The Household of Queen Elizabeth Woodville', 261.
[142] CPR 1476–85, 18.
[143] Myers, 'The Household of Queen Elizabeth Woodville', 287.
[144] CPR 1485–94, 14; CPR 1494–1509, 57.
[145] Nicolas, ed., *The Privy Purse Expenses of Elizabeth of York*, 200.
[146] Fleming, 'The Hautes and Their "Circle"', 91–2; Neal, 'The Queen's Grace', 176.
[147] TNA LC2/1, fols 63, 75r; *Materials for a History*, vol. II, 134.
[148] Nicolas, ed., *The Privy Purse Expenses of Elizabeth of York*, 200.

convenient arrangement.[149] There is no reason to believe that the queens' various residences operated any differently. The servants would come from the nearby areas and regions and were likely drawn from yeomen or peasant families. They presented as obvious choices for household service, service that served to facilitate connections between local families and tenantry with the queen while functioning as a source of income to the locals concerned.

Unsurprisingly, individuals sometimes changed jobs within the household rather than remain in the same position indefinitely. William Cotton initially served Margaret of Anjou as keeper of the great wardrobe and kept this post for several years, even after becoming her receiver-general in 1446.[150] In 1453, he relinquished the post to John Norrys, who had been serving as treasurer of the chamber and master of the queen's jewels up until then. When Norrys became keeper of the great wardrobe, Edward Ellesmere took over Norrys' former posts. Richard Decons was another case; he served as Elizabeth of York's keeper of the Privy Purse and receiver of monies but began his career in her service as clerk of the signet.

Service to the queen did not preclude these men from occupying positions outside her household. Indeed, being able to acquire other posts in royal service was a clear sign of favour and the high value placed on their capabilities. Many of the queen's officials and servants also held posts in the king's household at one time or another, sometimes simultaneously. It was natural not only for a queen's household members to be drawn from families who had records of accomplishment in royal service but for the queen's and king's households to share the available administrative talent. Examples of the interlaced threads connecting queens' households with many other great households abound for all the queens in this study. Thomas Parker not only served as Margaret's receiver for Haverford in 1452–53 but also held the posts of usher of the king's chamber and king's esquire at the same time.[151] Nicholas Sharp and John Walsh, auditors in Margaret's household, also served as auditors for the Duchy of Lancaster and in the king's household.[152] John Stanford was another individual who worked in multiple great establishments; he was an auditor for Elizabeth Woodville and for the South Parts of the Duchy of Lancaster. In addition, he acquired in 1484 a life appointment as auditor for Crown lands and the lands lately held by John, duke of Norfolk, and Margaret, duchess of Somerset.[153] Elizabeth Woodville's keeper of the great wardrobe, William Kerver, served at the same time as receiver-general for the Duchy of Lancaster. Elizabeth of York's household was no different. Many of her officials and

---

[149] Mertes, *The English Noble Household*, 61.
[150] Somerville, *The History of the Duchy of Lancaster*, 399.
[151] Myers, 'The Household of Queen Margaret of Anjou', 160.
[152] *Ibid.*, 192–3.
[153] Somerville, *The History of the Duchy of Lancaster*, 440.

servants also held posts, either simultaneously or at different times, in the king's household. They include Thomas Lovell, her first treasurer, William Denton, a household carver, and William Crowmer, one of her ushers.[154]

One might suppose that the domestic upheaval that resulted in so many monarchic changes would have upended the typical practice of family connections and traditions providing entry to royal service. Yet loyalty to one or other political cause does not seem to have been a definitive bar to service in other royal households. It was, of course, possible to survive and thrive in those circumstances for individuals and families who could and chose to adapt to changing political realities. Whilst Margaret's receiver-general, William Cotton, remained loyal to the Lancastrian queen and died fighting on her side in 1455, her chamberlain, John Wenlock, came to terms with Edward IV and served him as lieutenant of Calais.[155] Her clerk of the signet, George Ashby, also remained a loyal Lancastrian but the family evidently managed to accommodate themselves to later changes in the political climate as a grandson of Ashby served as a clerk of the signet to Henry VII. Edmund Chaderton and the earl of Ormonde, Thomas Butler, served Elizabeth of York at one time as chancellor and chamberlain, respectively. Both these noblemen had obtained their posts in the queen's household based on their loyalties. However, Chaderton, at least, was originally a Yorkist who was a prominent member of Richard III's court, serving him as clerk of the hanaper and treasurer of the chamber. He was pardoned by Henry VII, became chancellor to the queen consort and found enough favour with his royal mistress for her to later nominate him to the post of justice in eyre of her forests.[156]

In practice, good and faithful service to one regime often resulted in continuity in service with future kings and queens, even in the face of dynastic changes. Many of the men serving in the estates within the Duchy of Lancaster and Elizabeth Woodville's household were, in Myers' words, 'found to have been serving Henry VI and then to have continued without a break to serve Edward IV'.[157] This continuity of service persisted in later years and, as discussed earlier, the Hautes present as a prime example in this regard. In similar fashion, several members of Elizabeth of York's household, both men and women, went on to serve Catherine of Aragon, queen to Elizabeth's son, Henry VIII. Richard Decons was Elizabeth's keeper of the Privy Purse in the later years, was confirmed by Henry VII as receiver-general of the late queen's lands after 1503 and later served Catherine as secretary of the chamber.[158]

---

[154] CPR 1485–94, 95; CPR 1494–1509, 269; TNA LC2/1, fol. 63.
[155] Dunn, 'Margaret of Anjou: Queen Consort of Henry VI', 135; Myers, 'The Household of Queen Margaret of Anjou', 153.
[156] CPR 1485–94, 41, 318; Neal, 'The Queen's Grace', 126.
[157] Myers, 'The Household of Queen Elizabeth Woodville', 259.
[158] LP, I: 82. Decons is listed as secretary of Catherine of Aragon's chamber in the list of royal household personnel for the queen's coronation.

Several of Elizabeth of York's ladies, including Eleanor Verney and Anne Weston, joined Catherine of Aragon's household some years after Elizabeth's death.[159] Evidently, even though royal households of all periods valued loyal service, it was deemed only logical to recruit from among the ranks of those who had experience in providing such service. This held true even during periods when political allegiances of the past might have cast a shadow of doubt on the loyalties of potential household personnel.

CONCLUSIONS

In physical and structural terms, the queens' households shared many similarities with those of the consorts from previous centuries and with other noble households. Yet, at the same time, the queens' households were closely modelled on those of the kings. This ideal was manifested in the regulations of the ordinances issued in the later fifteenth century in which the restrictions and expectations, particularly in size and economic efficiency, are shown to have been applied to the queens' households as well. Moreover, changes that occurred in the queens' households appear to have mirrored changes that occurred in the kings' households or were driven by the wishes of the kings and their officials. The queens' households were more like the kings' than not. Yet, notwithstanding these similarities and the structural alterations in the queens' households, they still resembled those of the queens of the fourteenth century enough to conclude that continuity existed and prevailed despite political unrest, instability in government, and dynastic interruption to the monarchy.

Some significant observations can be made with regard to the queens' household personnel. Firstly, each of the queens' households had similar posts in their household administration. What changed from Margaret's household to Elizabeth of York's household was that the importance of the most senior officials shifted in response to changes in household process and procedural methods. The queen's chamber gained a much higher level of importance in Elizabeth of York's time as queen than in Margaret's. This is unsurprising given the change in regime from the Yorkists to the Tudors, which eventuated in, among other things, changes in the organisation of the king's household. Since the queen's household resembled the king's in many ways, it is logical to presume that such changes percolated into the queen's household as well. Secondly, the various factors affecting how the queens' households recruited staff were relatively consistent among all three queens. Family background and traditions of service and loyalty were the most influential factors, meaning that members of families with strong ties and customs of royal service could be found in all the queens' households. Given that members of

---

[159] Michelle Beer, *Queenship at the Renaissance Courts of Britain: Catherine of Aragon and Margaret Tudor, 1503–1533* (Woodbridge: Boydell Press, 2018), 41–2.

The Queen's Household

the same families could be found serving kings, queens and the nobility either simultaneously or at different times in their careers, it typically also meant that many connections could be found between the households of the queens, kings and nobles. These connections were relatively robust considering how loyalties and political allegiances of noble and gentry families were tested by the political unrest during this period. This level of consistency is noteworthy in the face of the key shift in queenship during this period: the transition from the norm of foreign brides for the king to domestic-born queens. All the queens in the latter half of the fifteenth century, except for Margaret of Anjou, were English-born and bred, including Anne Neville, the consort of Richard III, who has not been included in this study. Yet the different backgrounds of Margaret of Anjou and the two queens Elizabeth did not appear to have largely affected the drivers for recruitment to the queens' households.

These observations indicate that tradition and precedent were key forces behind household organisation and management, as they were with estate organisation and management. It is also significant that the regime changes from Lancastrian to Yorkist and eventually to Tudor governments, with the attendant domestic unrest, military conflict and instability, were not primary causes of permanent change in how queenly households were organised and managed. What ended up causing major changes in household organisation and administration was the need for greater household economy and efficiency and the personal preferences of the kings. In other words, the political problems of the period that resulted in violent changes in government and monarchy did not of themselves result in alterations in methods of household management.

The household was a fluid establishment that not only served to provide the queen with the necessities of life but also helped her function in a variety of modes within the society of the day. The discussion on financial management has demonstrated that it is far from clear cut as to whether we should continue to accept the conventional reputation of the financial competence of each of our queens. It is, however, clearer that the queens as a group were likely to be as involved as might be expected in the operational management of the household. Daily functional management by any of the queens was improbable but an overseer role was much more likely. Ultimately, the households of the queens were the focus of expenditure in part because they served to facilitate the queens' efforts in the cultivation of relationships and contacts and operated as conduits through which they connected with their networks. The availability of economic resources provided the crucial foundations for such expenditure and queens would have struggled to independently maintain their households without them.

5

THE QUEEN'S AFFINITY

And of Ladys followyng the Queene in the said p[ro]cession The Duches of Buk thelder bering up the trayne the Duches of Suff my Lady Mgrete her sister & the Duches of Bedford ... in all xiii Duchesses and Countesses, ... xiiii Baronesses and in Scarlet xii ladys Banarettes.[1]

Queens were typically accompanied by many persons at public and private events. As this brief description from the coronation of Elizabeth Woodville shows, the queen's entourage often included her ladies and gentlewomen as well as various officials, well-wishers and probably hangers-on. The question here is who, of the many individuals who surrounded a queen, could reliably be counted as being members of her affinity.

The term 'affinity' has often been used for this body of people by late medievalists, but it defies easy description.[2] Scholars have characterised this group slightly differently, sometimes even contradictorily, with the result being that what we call the affinity lacks concrete definition.[3] Affinity has been used interchangeably with retinue[4] and at least one scholar believes that it possesses the same basic features as a clientele.[5] Then again, one may regard the affinity as being on the same footing as a network, whether kinship, social, cultural or even political. However, an affinity was not necessarily the same as a network, although there could be significant overlaps. It was, in fact, more formal than

---

[1] *The Coronation of Elizabeth Wydeville, Queen Consort of Edward IV, on May 26th 1465: A Contemporary Account Set Forth from a XV Century Manuscript*, ed. George Smith (Cliftonville: Gloucester Reprints, 1975), 16.

[2] Simon Adams, 'Baronial Contexts? Continuity and Change in the Noble Affinity, 1400–1600', in *The End of the Middle Ages? England in the Fifteenth and Sixteenth Centuries*, ed. J. L. Watts (Stroud: Sutton, 1998), 158.

[3] Key studies of affinities include the following: Christine Carpenter, 'The Beauchamp Affinity: A Study in the Working of Bastard Feudalism', *EHR* 95, no. 376 (1980): 514–32; M. Cherry, 'The Courtenay Earls of Devon: The Formation and Disintegration of a Late Medieval Aristocratic Affinity', *Southern History* 1 (1979): 71–97; Given-Wilson, *The Royal Household and the King's Affinity*; Simon Walker, *The Lancastrian Affinity, 1361–1399* (Oxford: Clarendon Press, 1990).

[4] St John, *Three Medieval Queens*, 72.

[5] Adams, 'Baronial Contexts?', 158.

a network and, more importantly, it appears to have been recognised as such, with its members being connected in some way and headed by a specific individual.[6] Those within the late medieval affinity of the Courtenay earls of Devon were said to have understood themselves to be part of this entity and to have been aware of close connections between each other and between themselves and the earl.[7] For Simon Walker, the essential characteristic of an affinity was that its members were 'possessed of some material incentive for their loyalty, in the form of an office or annuity from the duke'.[8] In contrast, Rosemary Horrox's study of Richard III's affinity asserts that ties of service were the determinant of the degree of closeness an individual had to the king. Horrox implies that there could be no membership of Richard's affinity without the individual providing some form of service to him, whether it was grounded and buttressed financially or by more tenuous means.[9] In the case of queenly affinities, I follow Horrox's determinant and consider reciprocal service, above and beyond what was expected in return for regular wages and fees, to be the tie that bound the queens and the people in their affinities.

I should at this point further clarify the idea of 'service' within the context of examining the queens' affinities. Anne Curry and Elizabeth Matthew state that service 'was the word commonly used for the work, whether paid or unpaid, performed by a servant, attendant or official for his or her lord or lady, master or mistress'.[10] This meaning is indeed applicable to how I have so far used the word 'service' in this book, primarily in the chapters on management of the queens' lands and households. However, the term 'service' can encompass much more than the understanding set out by Curry and Matthew. For this chapter's purposes, medieval service was more than a task or series of tasks. It was a mindset, an attitude, a way of life, and, as such, was open-ended in a way that defies easy categorisation or even comprehension.[11] Service was manifested as tasks but prompted by obligation, duty and more besides. As Horrox emphasises, 'service was defined not by the nature of the tasks being

---

[6] Material manifestations of recognition in an affinity are not within the scope of this book but for a book-length study of the livery collar, which is arguably an important method of such recognition, see the following: Matthew J. Ward, *The Livery Collar in Late Medieval England and Wales: Politics, Identity and Affinity* (Woodbridge: Boydell Press, 2016).

[7] Cherry, 'The Courtenay Earls of Devon', 79.

[8] Walker, *The Lancastrian Affinity*, 8–10.

[9] Horrox, *Richard III*, 27.

[10] Anne Curry and Elizabeth Matthew, 'Introduction', in *Concepts and Patterns of Service in the Later Middle Ages*, eds Anne Curry and Elizabeth Matthew (Woodbridge: Boydell Press, 2000), xiv.

[11] Horrox's essay on medieval service is particularly illuminating on this concept. Rosemary Horrox, 'Service', in *Fifteenth-Century Attitudes: Perceptions of Society in Late Medieval England*, ed. Rosemary Horrox (Cambridge; New York: Cambridge University Press, 1994), 61–78.

The Queen's Affinity

performed, but by the relationship involved: that of master and man'.[12] Not all duties and tasks were prescribed in a fixed manner and one accepted that one could be called upon to do whatever the lord needed to be done at that point in time so long as it was service that was essentially commensurate with one's rank. In other words, for the individuals who were included in the queens' affinities, service was whatever was asked of them by the queens in keeping with their respective statuses.

In light of the previous two chapters, it is tempting to equate the queens' affinities with the people who served them in their household and estate administrations. Admittedly, this chapter will show that significant overlaps existed between the queens' households and their affinities. I contend, however, that the affinity was peopled from a much wider pool than just the queen's household and that there was a greater expectation of reciprocity in the relationship a queen had with her affinity than in the one between a queen and her servants. These additional elements are what differentiated the queenly affinity from the queenly household. Just as scholars have sought to illuminate how kingly and noble affinities were bound together, this chapter aims to explore the ties that bound the queen consort with the members of her affinity.[13] Essentially, these ties were an understanding of the kind of bond that was recognisable through membership of a queen's affinity, and this was, in part, what formalised the arrangement. To this end, the chapter uses the household and estate records that survive for these queens as well as letters, chronicles and other peripheral evidence to draw out information on their affinities. It sets out the structure, explores how queenly affinities were established and maintained, how the affinities served their queens and what benefits accrued to them in return. Just as the queen's household was a primary beneficiary of her economic resources, so, too, did the queen's affinity rely on her having the financial means to establish and maintain it.

STRUCTURE AND ESTABLISHMENT

The purpose of an affinity was martial in its origins and for late medieval kings and nobles, military obligations no doubt continued to figure heavily in the service provided.[14] The affinity of a queen typically lacked the military aspect in its framework and did not serve her in this manner, although this chapter will discuss this aspect for Margaret of Anjou. Instead, as for fourteenth-century English queens, the retinues of the queens in this study, which would have

---

[12] Horrox, 'Service', 63.
[13] For kingly affinities, see, for example, Given-Wilson, *The Royal Household and the King's Affinity*; Horrox, *Richard III;* D. A. L. Morgan, 'The King's Affinity in the Polity of Yorkist England', *TRHS* 23 (1973): 1–25.
[14] St John, *Three Medieval Queens*, 73.

been peopled by their affinities, fulfilled social, administrative and security purposes.[15] The queen's affinity may be visualised as a series of concentric circles similar to Chris Given-Wilson's model for late medieval kings, with placings being determined by status and personal relationship with the head of the affinity.[16] The innermost circle comprised those individuals who were the most senior in hierarchy and status and who stood closest to the queen, such as her family, closest ladies and most important household and estate officials. The next circle included those lower on the status ladder, such as the next-in-rank waged household officials and female companions or attendants as well as annuitants of the queens. The outermost circles comprised those members with the loosest ties to the queens, whether through blood, material connections or general goodwill manifested in such ways as signal service performed by one party on behalf of the other. Just as the Lancastrian household formed the core of John of Gaunt's affinity, so, too, did the queens' households lie at the heart of their affinities.[17] The elite or royal household was, in Earenfight's words, 'the center of complex networks of power'.[18]

Ordinarily, close and even some extended members of the king's and queen's families might be expected to figure prominently in the closest circles of their affinities. However, that did not hold true for all the queens in this study. Since Margaret of Anjou was foreign-born, her natal family did not factor very much in her life as queen of England. Although her kinswoman, Marie, daughter of Count Charles of Maine, came to England to marry Thomas Courtenay, heir of the earl of Devon, she does not appear to have served in Margaret's household nor spent much time in Margaret's entourage. Henry VI, too, by the time of his marriage to Margaret in 1445, did not have very many close family members still living. Two of his three uncles, Thomas, duke of Clarence, and John, duke of Bedford, had died by this time and had had no legitimate children. Both queens dowager, his step-grandmother, Joan of Navarre, and his mother, Katherine of Valois, had died in 1437, and his closest living relatives were his half-brothers, Jasper and Edmund Tudor.[19]

In fact, Margaret's closest friends and acquaintances grew to include some of those with whom she formed early bonds on her first voyage to England in 1444. William de la Pole, earl of Suffolk, and his wife, Alice Chaucer, were among the highest-ranking nobles who travelled to France to accompany the

---

[15] Ibid., 79.

[16] Given-Wilson, *The Royal Household and the King's Affinity*, 203–4.

[17] Walker, *The Lancastrian Affinity*, 10.

[18] Theresa Earenfight, 'Introduction: Personal Relations, Political Agency, and Economic Clout in Medieval and Early Modern Royal and Elite Households', in *Royal and Elite Households in Medieval and Early Modern Europe: More Than Just a Castle*, ed. Theresa Earenfight (Leiden: Brill, 2018), 10.

[19] Jasper and Edmund Tudor were Katherine of Valois' sons from her second marriage to Owen Tudor, a gentleman of her household.

The Queen's Affinity

young queen-to-be to England. Margaret developed close friendships with both Suffolk and his wife, an unsurprising circumstance given the large part he played in the arrangements and negotiations for her marriage. In addition, given the ages of the couple, the young Margaret may have regarded them as surrogate elders and looked to them for guidance and advice in the early years of her life in England.[20] Her continued close association with the widowed Lady Suffolk is perhaps attested to by the fact that in 1471 the victorious-at-battle Edward IV placed the widowed and now childless former queen into Lady Suffolk's care, where she remained until her return to France in 1475.[21]

Other high-ranking individuals who formed part of the closest circles of Margaret's affinity included women such as Margaret, countess of Shrewsbury, Ismanie Lady Scales, Lady Talbot, Jacquetta, dowager duchess of Bedford, and the countess of Salisbury. Some of these women very likely first got to know Margaret on that first journey she undertook to England and remained close to the queen for many years. Lady Scales, for example, appears to have been among her closest and most trusted friends, serving the queen as a personal attendant in her household and receiving New Year's gifts on several occasions.[22] Moreover, she was included in a delegation sent in 1461 by the city of London to negotiate with the king and queen, an inclusion that suggested the city elders believed she would have been favourably received by the royal couple.[23] Another lady-in-waiting who may have had a particularly close relationship with Margaret was Katherine Vaux, who married Sir William Vaux but is named as Katherine Penyson in the queen's extant household account. Katherine loyally served her mistress, continuing to do so even when Margaret was placed under house arrest after the Lancastrians lost to the Yorkists. In effect, these women and other wives of lower-ranked knights and esquires as well as a dozen or so ladies-in-waiting would have formed her female retinue and comprised at least part of the core of her affinity.

The cases of Elizabeth Woodville and Elizabeth of York contrast quite sharply with that of Margaret due to their background. These queens consort were English-born and thus represented a highly significant shift in this aspect of queenship in late medieval England. Unlike the foreign-born Margaret, the family members of the two Elizabeths stood high at court and prospered at least partly because they were related to these queens. It stands to reason that many of their family members would be counted as part of their affinities. Both queens included one or more of their sisters among their ladies. Elizabeth

---

[20] Dunn, 'Margaret of Anjou: Queen Consort of Henry VI', 134; Laynesmith, *The Last Medieval Queens*, 210.

[21] Dunn, 'Margaret of Anjou: Queen Consort of Henry VI', 134; Maurer, *Margaret of Anjou*, 208.

[22] For example, see TNA E101/409/14; E101/410/8; Myers, 'The Jewels of Queen Margaret of Anjou', 223.

[23] Maurer, *Margaret of Anjou*, 197.

Woodville's sister Anne Lady Bourchier served as one of her principal ladies as did her sister-in-law, Elizabeth Lady Scales, and her first cousin, Alice Fogge. Likewise, Elizabeth of York's sisters Katherine and Cecily and her cousin Elizabeth Stafford served in her household at various times after she became queen.[24] Several other female relatives of the younger Elizabeth, including her sister Anne, her cousin Margaret of Clarence, and her aunt, the countess of Rivers, all formed part of her entourage during her years as queen.

The queen's closest affinity did not only include female family members and friends. While women served the queens as ladies-in-waiting and personal attendants, the most important household and estate posts were filled by men, some of whom were seconded from the king's service. If the household and jewel accounts are any indication, Margaret held her most senior household officials in high regard and they in turn greatly benefitted materially from her goodwill towards them. Among the most frequently encountered names in these records are John Wenlock, Edward Ellesmere, John Norrys, William and Laurence Bothe, and William Cotton, all of whom were king's men as well as being in the queen's service.[25] Margaret also grew close to Edmund Beaufort, duke of Somerset, and John Viscount Beaumont, each of whom served in succession as her chief steward of lands and were among the most powerful magnates in the land in 1453.[26] Elizabeth Woodville and Elizabeth of York were also served by men from noble families such as the Bourchiers and Hollands and by capable administrators such as Roger Radcliff, John Forster and Edmund Chaderton. All these men may reliably be counted among the queens' affinities, even though they often served both the queen and the king and could also be associated with one or other of the most highly ranked noble families in the land.[27]

It is in the outer-most circles that it is most difficult to identify who might have been counted as part of the queens' affinities since the ties in these circles were the loosest. Service as the defining feature of membership in queenly affinities means that we can include all those who served the queens in their households, but those with the lowest statuses and ranks were the least likely to have close and resilient ties with the queens beyond financially remunerated service or other financial ties.[28] It is precisely that looseness in relationship that might preclude them from being formally counted as part of

---

[24] Harris, *English Aristocratic Women*, 218.
[25] Each of these men occupied various posts within the king's service and in the administration of the Duchy of Lancaster. See the index for their biographies in Somerville, *The History of the Duchy of Lancaster*, vol. I.
[26] Griffiths, *The Reign of King Henry VI*, 257.
[27] For example, John Norrys was an associate of Suffolk's but prospered in royal service, particularly the queen's.
[28] In these outer circles, we can include the lowest-ranked household members such as pages and menial servants, most of whom were unnamed in the household accounts.

the queens' affinities, and the problems with identifying individuals make the process even more difficult.

How did the queens establish their affinities? The previous chapter discussed several factors that influenced how the queens' household personnel were recruited or appointed, including family connections and traditions of service. These factors are similar to those that influenced the setting up and maintenance of affinities. One of the most important methods was marriage. In Martin Cherry's opinion, marriage 'was the single most important cohesive element in attaching families' to the circles of the Courtenay earls of Devon.[29] As he sees it, those who formed the liveries of the earl of Devon in the late fourteenth century, that is, the knights, esquires and lawyers, may have formed the core of the earl's affinity but many more members of Devonshire political society were bound to the earl by marriage ties and, therefore, extended his affinity far beyond its core. The same can be said of queens' affinities. Scholars researching European royal consorts, such as Una McIlvenna, Pauline Matarasso and Rubén González Cuerva, have long recognised that the likes of Catherine de Medici, Anne of Brittany and Maria of Austria, to name but a few, were well aware of the benefits of using marriage to extend their influence and build alliances.[30] Arranging marriages for household members was clearly a key way to help establish and strengthen the bond tying many members of the queens' affinities to their mistresses.

Of Margaret of Anjou's ladies, many were eventually married to king's men who were either already serving the queen or now gained the opportunity to serve her in some capacity. Jamona Cherneys married Thomas Sharnborne, a royal courtier who provided service to both king and queen by serving as an esquire in Margaret's household and as the king's escheator in Norfolk and Suffolk.[31] Two other queen's ladies, Katherine Whittingham and Edith Burgh, were respectively married to Robert Whittingham, keeper of the queen's great wardrobe (from at least 1458), and Giles Saintlowe, queen's esquire. These marriages probably brought these gentlemen within the ambit of the queen's circle, thus adding them to her affinity. Alternatively, it is just as plausible that being part of the king's household had already brought them within the queen's affinity to some extent

---

[29] Cherry, 'The Courtenay Earls of Devon', 76.
[30] Rubén González Cuerva, *Maria of Austria, Holy Roman Empress (1528-1603): Dynastic Networker* (Abingdon; New York: Routledge, 2022), 79-81; Pauline Matarasso, *Queen's Mate: Three Women of Power in France on the Eve of the Renaissance* (Aldershot: Ashgate, 2001), 175-6; Una McIlvenna, '"A Stable of Whores?" The "Flying Squadron" of Catherine De Medici', in *The Politics of Female Households: Ladies-in-Waiting across Early Modern Europe*, eds Nadine Akkerman and Birgit Houben (Leiden: Brill, 2013), 197-8.
[31] CPR 1446-52, 454; Wedgwood, *History of Parliament*, 764.

and that marriage to one of the queen's ladies and employment in the queen's household served instead as reinforcements of that bond.

For Elizabeth Woodville, marriage was a definite feature in the glue that held her affinity together. Each of the marriages made by the children of Elizabeth's parents, Richard Woodville and Jacquetta St Pol, widowed duchess of Bedford, was greatly advantageous to the family as a whole. More than that, both Elizabeth Woodville and, later, Elizabeth of York were able to use their own families to build their affinities through marriage, a method that was much more difficult for a foreign-born queen consort such as Margaret of Anjou. Marriages created bonds of kinship and ties between the queens' families and illustrious old noble families such as the Ferrers of Groby, the Greys of Ruthin, the Bourchiers and the Arundels, several members of whom served Elizabeth Woodville in official capacities.[32] It brought these noble families within the ambit of the queens' circles and, in so doing, enlarged the queens' affinities. Among them was John Bourchier, Lord Berners, who was not only the queen's chamberlain but was distantly related to her by virtue of being a brother of William Bourchier, the husband of Anne, the queen's sister. His son Humphrey also served the queen as a steward and carver. Another example of this convoluted web of relations can be seen with James Haute, who was another of Queen Elizabeth's stewards and carvers. He, too, was a kinsman of the queen's, being related to William Haute, the queen's uncle by marriage to her aunt, Jane Woodville. The Hautes were but one of many families who provided steadfast service to the Crown and who were connected by blood and marital ties, although it is not always clear whether service to the king and queen engendered loyalty that was cemented by marriage or vice versa. In the final analysis, it is clear that both men and women of English aristocratic and gentry families from the mid-fifteenth to mid-sixteenth centuries obtained service to the Crown and entry into royal affinities at least partly by making use of familial connections.[33]

For many others, traditions of loyalty and service were the factors that brought them into the queens' affinities. Margaret Bryan was a lady-in-waiting to Elizabeth of York's daughter-in-law, Catherine of Aragon, and came from a family with strong connections to the Yorkists and later the Tudors. Her grandfather was John Bourchier and her father was Sir Humphrey Bourchier, both of whom were queen's men. Lady Bryan's daughters as well as a ward were later able to benefit from these connections as they were brought to court by her while she was in service to Catherine of Aragon. Similarly, Lady Jane Guildford, one of Elizabeth of York's own ladies, originally came from the Vauxs. They were a family who had supported both the Lancastrians and the

---

[32] Michael Hicks, 'The Changing Role of the Wydevilles in Yorkist Politics to 1483', in *Patronage, Pedigree and Power in Later Medieval England*, ed. C. D. Ross (Gloucester: Sutton, 1979), 63.

[33] Harris, *English Aristocratic Women*, chapter 9, especially 218–19.

The Queen's Affinity

Tudors, their steadfast loyalty being demonstrated particularly by Lady Jane's mother, Katherine Vaux, who served Margaret of Anjou and remained with her in exile.[34] These two cases illustrate how such records of service could tie a family with the queen and her affinity and how such connections could stand that family in good stead.

Others came within the circles of the queens' affinities because they initially served people who were connected to the queens. The previous chapter on the queens' household administrations contains many examples of individuals who served the queens but also served the kings either simultaneously or at different times. The likes of Thomas Parker, Nicholas Sharp, William Kerver, Thomas Lovell and William Crowmer served others besides the queen. Thomas Shelford, a servant of the chamber in Queen Margaret's household, was another example. Shelford entered her service after serving in the company of the duke of Suffolk. It was probably this service that recommended him to the queen in the first place and the primary reason for his move into the queen's household.[35] Likewise, Robert Iseham, Elizabeth Woodville's steward of her manor of Geddington, was a trusted servant of the queen's first father-in-law, Edward Grey, and had been entrusted with the task of helping the lady obtain her marriage portion on the death of her first husband, Sir John Grey.[36] He continued on in her affinity when she became queen. More family connections can be seen to operate in the case of Thomas Twyday, a gentleman waiter in Elizabeth of York's household. His affinity with the queen's family began with his earlier service as a page of the chamber to the queen's father, Edward IV.[37]

Lands and economic resources, too, played their part in forming the queen's affinities. Horrox contends that service to a lord was primarily, though not only, determined by land, saying that the lord 'normally drew the core of his following from the area where his estates lay'.[38] She demonstrates comprehensively how Richard as duke of Gloucester built an affinity with its roots in his lands and properties, showing that the lord's maintenance of his local interests encompassing his servants, tenants and followers was a crucial foundation without which the affinity could founder.[39] To a certain

---

[34] Harris, *English Aristocratic Women*, 218–19.
[35] Margaret of Anjou wrote on Shelford's behalf when he sought marriage with the daughter of 'oon Hall of Larkfeld' and specifically mentioned that Thomas had first served the duke, implying that she had agreed to him serving in her chamber because of his good service to the duke. *The Letters of Margaret of Anjou*, 12 (no. 3).
[36] Myers, 'The Household of Queen Elizabeth Woodville', 295.
[37] Neal, 'The Queen's Grace', 130.
[38] Horrox, *Richard III*, 27.
[39] In relation to bastard feudalism, Horrox repudiates the idea that lands or cash fees created feudal ties, asserting that such items only formalised the tie. Horrox, 'Service', 74.

extent, their economic resources served similar functions for the queens. We have seen how marital ties and traditions of service could form and bind those of the queens' affinities who were closest to her. But in the outer circles economic resources played a much more significant role. The queens' lands functioned as recruitment grounds for the general household and estate staff and their lowest-ranked servants. Just as for any other landholder, estate officials such as farmers, bailiffs and reeves were drawn from the local following on queens' lands.[40] The men who occupied these posts formed the affinities at this level, though their allegiances probably shifted from one landowner to another relatively easily. An example may be gleaned from the case of the manor of Mashbury, Essex. During the period between the late 1450s and the mid-1470s, the owner of the manor changed from Margaret of Anjou to the Crown (when ownership reverted on the accession of Edward IV) and, eventually, to Elizabeth Woodville when she was granted the manor as part of her dower lands. John Altheworthe occupied the post of farmer of the manor during this entire period.[41] Clearly, at this level, the landowner's identity caused no major shift in the manor's administration and the political allegiances of manor officials could obviously be relatively flexible.

As a final point, it would not be wholly true to say that all those employed by the queens and counted among their affinities always adhered exclusively to their loyalties to the queen. Contemporaries did not consider the idea or practice of belonging to more than one affinity to be unacceptable.[42] Far from it. Among other things, connections and ties could operate as mechanisms for social mobility and, logically, the greater the number of connections one had, the more opportunities one could possibly take advantage of.[43] Except where military service was concerned, therefore, multiple connections and ties of service were not regarded as being out of place in the context of fifteenth-century feudalism and were both accepted and sought after. In any case, there were hierarchical considerations at play that kept in check any possible competing priorities among the different forms of service owed by any one individual.[44] Theoretically, to be counted as a member of a queen's affinity should have meant that, excepting only the king, the queen had first call on that individual's priorities over all other connections.

---

[40] Closer examination of receiver and bailiff accounts demonstrate a continuity of names and repetition across related accounts as well as court rolls where available.
[41] John Altheworthe's name appears as farmer on all the extant accounts for Mashbury spanning the above-mentioned period. TNA DL29/43/830–43.
[42] Horrox, 'Service', 71.
[43] Ward, *English Noblewomen*, 139.
[44] Horrox, 'Service', 71–2.

BENEFITS TO THE AFFINITY

A vital point to make in relation to the benefits that could accrue to members of the queens' affinities is that service provided to the queen and generally reciprocated in the form of benefits was founded on the concepts of 'good lordship' and 'good ladyship'. In other words, medieval expectations of these concepts may be summed up in the idea of service. In her assessment of Richard III's affinity, Horrox stresses the *mutuality* of service, which she deemed to be the most important characteristic of the relationship between a lord and his man.[45] Service to his lord, in its myriad forms, was required of a man and this had its benefits, both as straightforward financial rewards as well as the less tangible and visible ones. The lord was, in his turn, expected to exert himself on behalf of his man when and if required. Good lordship and good ladyship were intrinsically bound up with these expectations and the reciprocity they entailed. In relation to queens, these ideas recall the writings of de Pisan. Her advice to 'all great queens, ladies and princesses' included ideas on how such upper-ranked women should conduct themselves and treat those around them.[46] She believed that the queen should act as a mediator and should take an interest in and pursue actions on behalf of those who served her, a role that was a central tenet of good ladyship.[47] Yet the exercise of good ladyship did not necessarily operate along set terms. There were no intrinsically explicit boundaries on who should benefit from the largesse dispensed by the queen. Still, those who counted themselves and were counted among the queens' affinities, in particular the nobles and gentry, certainly expected to benefit from this association over and above the general level of munificence extended as part of good ladyship. As might be expected, these benefits could take many forms, including but not limited to festive and occasional gifts, grants, annuities, patronage and intercession.

Margaret of Anjou's jewel accounts, among other evidence, bear witness to some of the material benefits that could accrue to those who served the queen or were counted within her affinity. In the lists of gifts recorded in the accounts, there are traditional New Year's gifts to many different persons, from the king to the lowest-ranked individuals who served the queen.[48] The accounts also occasionally list rewards to various servants and officials that

---

[45] Horrox, *Richard III*, 1, 5.
[46] de Pisan, *The Treasure of the City of Ladies*, 35.
[47] Ibid., 50–2.
[48] For more detailed discussion of Margaret of Anjou's New Year's gifts, see Maurer, *Margaret of Anjou*, 85–90; Myers, 'The Jewels of Queen Margaret of Anjou'; Michele Seah, 'Gifts and Rewards: Exploring the Expenditure of Late Medieval English Queens', *Journal of Medieval History* 50, no. 5 (2024): 581–97, https://doi.org/10.10 80/03044181.2024.2415637; Nicola Tallis, *All the Queen's Jewels 1445–1548: Power, Majesty and Display* (London; New York: Routledge, 2023), 196–8.

appear to be over and above what they might have expected to receive. For example, two of the jewel accounts record special gifts to Edward Ellesmere, John Norrys and Nicholas Sharp.[49] These gifts are listed separately from the New Year's gifts and no reasons are recorded. One can only speculate that they might have been given for important tasks performed or for generally valued service to the queen.

Occasionally, those who served the queens were granted specific holdings 'for good service', not only to the queen but also to the king. Margaret's chamberlain, John Wenlock, was granted four messuages in April 1448 for just such a stated reason.[50] Geoffrey William, a page of the queen's kitchen, was granted for life two mills in Cardigan, South Wales, at Margaret's request. A marriage or the birth of a child could be other occasions for the queens to show favour and good ladyship by giving gifts. The queen gave very generous wedding gifts to Richard Birchley and Thomas Mouseherst, a groom and a yeoman in her household.[51] Little direct evidence exists for Elizabeth Woodville's gift-giving but there are many examples of individuals in royal service during Edward IV's reign who received grants for life. There can be no doubt that members of Elizabeth's household and affinity benefitted in this way as well. Neither was Elizabeth of York behind in showing her appreciation in the form of gifts or rewards, as demonstrated by the number of such transactions in her Privy Purse expense account. In 1502, for instance, sundry rewards were distributed at Easter to officers of the kitchen, gate porters, and staff in the squillery and saucery.[52]

Annuities were another way that the queens could demonstrate their appreciation for service and show that they valued the people who served them. As the name suggests, an annuity was a sum of money paid to a person, typically on a yearly basis. Lists of annuitants, that is, individuals being paid such regular amounts, are contained in the extant household accounts for all three queens, an indication that some annuities were paid out by the receiver-general from the queen's overall revenues.[53] However, annuities could also be paid from the receipts of monies from specific landholdings and those were recorded in receivers' accounts.[54] Some of the listed individuals had served the queens themselves, as in the case of all the annuitants listed in Margaret's household account. Another example is Elizabeth of York's midwife, Alice

---

[49] TNA E101/409/14, E101/410/11.
[50] CPR 1446–52, 152.
[51] TNA E101/410/11.
[52] Queen's Book, fol. 29.
[53] Myers, 'The Household of Queen Elizabeth Woodville', 300–4 (pp. 26–9); Myers, 'The Household of Queen Margaret of Anjou', 196–8 (fols 17a–17b); Queen's Book, fol. 93.
[54] For examples for Margaret of Anjou, see TNA DL29/58/1103–1107 (receivers' accounts for Essex, Hertford and Middlesex). For examples for Elizabeth Woodville, see TNA DL29/41/800, 801, 802; SC6/1094/5 (receivers' accounts for Essex, Surrey and Kent).

Massy, who received an annuity of £10, which was paid from the queen's Privy Purse. Others, such as some of the annuitants listed in Elizabeth Woodville's household account, were styled more generally as having had positions in the service of the Crown, which could have meant that they served in the king's household rather than the queen's. Still others were not waged servants or officials at all but had obviously rendered service of some kind or were singularly favoured by the queen. Specific reasons why people were receiving annuities were recorded from time to time. Thomas Sandeland, yeoman of the king's chamber, was granted an annuity for life of 10 marks 'for his good service to the king's father in England and Ireland', the king being Edward IV.[55] The payment came from the fee farm of the manor of Wrokewarden, Salop, which was a royal manor and not endowed on the queen. Other grants were couched in more general terms. Margaret of Anjou paid Edmund, duke of Somerset, an annuity of 100 marks for 'good counsel and praiseworthy service'.[56] Elizabeth Woodville's annuitants included Richard Roos, a king's knight who had provided the queen with his 'good and gracious service' on diverse occasions.[57] More often than not, however, there were few specific reasons listed as part of the record of payment of an annuity nor were reasons included in the original grant.

Gifts, grants of money or landholdings, and annuities are examples of the concrete material benefits that could come the way of individuals in the queens' affinities. Nonetheless, the queens also demonstrated their willingness to reciprocate good service with other concrete actions. These included but were probably not limited to arranging or facilitating suitable marriages, issuing grants of offices within their power, lending their support to those who were seeking appointment to benefices or estate offices, and interceding on behalf of their servants and affiliates in property disputes and oppressive actions from other parties. The facilitation of marriages, as noted, was a key method of establishing and maintaining bonds of affinity. For the parties involved, the marriages could be most beneficial for them and their families. At least two of Margaret of Anjou's ladies married esquires who had successful careers in elite service. One such lady was Rose Merston, whose husband, John Merston, not only served in the queen's household as an esquire but was also treasurer of the king's chamber and keeper of the king's jewels.[58] Sir John Paston entered the ambit of the queen's affinity by marrying Anne Haute, who was related to Elizabeth Woodville. The Hautes were a family with strong traditions of service to the Crown and this marriage enabled Paston

---

[55] CPR 1467–77, 159.
[56] 'pro bono consilio sui et laudabili servicio'; Myers, 'The Household of Queen Margaret of Anjou', 196.
[57] 'boni et gratuity servicii sui ... regine'; Myers, 'The Household of Queen Elizabeth Woodville', 303.
[58] Somerville, *The History of the Duchy of Lancaster*, 611.

to elicit help from the queen in his efforts to claim some possessions of Sir John Fastolf.[59] The queen's siblings could be especially attractive matches for the nobility because marriage could draw them much more closely into royal circles, as in the case of Lord Thomas Howard. Lord Howard married Anne, sister of Elizabeth of York, and this marriage helped to rehabilitate his family for their previous support of Richard III.[60]

In Margaret of Anjou's case, extant letters show that she clearly attempted to live up to her side of the bargain where her relationship to her affinity was concerned. Maurer regards these letters as a 'window upon her efforts to act as good lady', having analysed a total of eighty-two letters against the prism of good ladyship. She establishes that the queen generally conformed to expectations in terms of intercession, patronage and general good ladyship.[61] There are other points that can be elucidated from Margaret's extant correspondence. Maurer concludes that sixty-eight of the eighty-two letters she analysed were written by the queen in the interests of another person besides herself and further categorises these according to whether an appeal was being made to the queen and who was making the appeal.[62]

Closer examination reveals that at least twenty-four letters out of the total number are related to individuals who can undoubtedly be categorised as being part of Margaret's affinity. Examples include Thomas Shelford, a chamber servant, Michael Tregory, her chaplain, Nicholas Carent, a clerk in the secretary's department, and Edmund Clere, a household esquire.[63] Eight of these letters are related to persons named as royal servants serving either the king alone or both the king and queen. Another five letters concern individuals who cannot clearly be identified as being associated with the queen but on whose behalf the queen had written at the request of someone who was known to her. A case in point was the letter Margaret wrote to the duke of Exeter in the matter of the dispossession suffered by Rauf Josselyn, which she did because his cousin, Thomas Sharnborne, queen's esquire, had asked her to do so.[64] It is clear that Thomas had brought the issue to the queen's attention and was seeking to turn to his cousin's advantage the fact that the queen and the duchess of Exeter were particularly close.[65] In addition, no less than fifteen other letters are concerned with persons whose association with the queen is unclear. These fifteen letters present an enticing possibility

---

[59] Davis, ed., *Paston Letters and Papers of the Fifteenth Century Part II*, 400; Laynesmith, 'Elizabeth Woodville: The Knight's Widow', 225.
[60] Warnicke, *Elizabeth of York and Her Six Daughters-in-Law*, 120.
[61] Maurer, *Margaret of Anjou*, Chapter 4.
[62] Maurer, *Margaret of Anjou*, 55.
[63] *The Letters of Margaret of Anjou*, 12, 32, 34, 44 (nos 3, 17, 18, 22).
[64] *The Letters of Margaret of Anjou*, 92 (no. 54).
[65] The duchess was listed in most of the extant jewel accounts as a recipient of costly gifts at New Year's from the queen. TNA E101/409/17; E101/410/2; E101/410/8.

The Queen's Affinity

that even more correspondence, besides the above-mentioned twenty-four, can be categorised as having been written on behalf of members of or others associated with her affinity. In one case, the queen wrote to Sir John Steward concerning a suit by John Lovell relating to the manor of Hardington in Middlesex.[66] The letter was dated by Cecil Monro in his nineteenth-century publication of Margaret's surviving letters to the period between 1445 and 1457, during which the queen's household included one Geoffrey Lovell.[67] It is entirely possible that John Lovell was related in some way to Geoffrey Lovell and, since the queen was a landholder in Middlesex, she was surely seen as a suitable person to appeal to for help.

While it is not always known whether the appeals made by Margaret were successful, it is obvious that those who asked for the queen's help in various situations held a certain level of expectation. Hope of success was implied in the very asking of the queen's help. What is just as clear is that the queen was evidently willing to be importuned in this way. Her servants and affinity provided her with service in many different forms; such service entailed and anticipated reciprocity on the queen's part and she was honour-bound to fulfil such expectations. The letters are a clear demonstration of the reciprocal service that formed the framework under which a queen's, and indeed any lord's or king's, affinity operated. Where the queens' affinities were concerned, this reciprocity of service went over and above what one would expect of good ladyship.

The lack of surviving correspondence for Elizabeth Woodville comparable to what survives for Margaret of Anjou can only be lamented. One of the few letters extant for this queen was written to John de Vere, earl of Oxford in the late 1460s. The queen wrote on behalf of Simon Bliaunt in his attempts to gain possession of the manor of Hemnals, Bliaunt being a supporter of the group of Yorkists headed by Sir John Howard, later duke of Norfolk. She urged de Vere to support Bliaunt's claim, a position that he was unlikely to adopt since the Paston family who controlled the disputed manor at the time were members of his own affinity. Crawford suggests that Howard himself may have been the instigator of the queen's efforts, given his connection with the Bliaunts.[68] If this is correct, it seems fanciful considering de Vere's relationship with the Pastons that Howard could realistically have expected the queen to succeed in her intervention. It is just as possible that Howard wanted to be able to show that he had made the effort on Bliaunt's behalf. Then again, it may indicate that there was hopeful anticipation on the parts of Bliaunt and Howard that the queen's high rank and connections would be able to surmount local loyalties and bonds of affinity in so important a matter. There is no record that

---

[66] *The Letters of Margaret of Anjou*, 98–9 (no. 58).
[67] *Letters of Queen Margaret of Anjou and Bishop Beckington and others*, ed. Cecil Monro (New York: Johnson Reprint Corp., 1968, reprint of 1863 edition), 157.
[68] *Letters of the Queens of England*, 135.

Elizabeth Woodville was able to successfully influence the earl of Oxford, but the case illustrates the efforts that the queen was willing to expend on behalf of the general Yorkist affinity. This attitude is further borne out by another letter recorded by the city of Coventry, to which the queen wrote vouching for the future good behaviour of one Reynold Bulkley, a servant of the king, and assuring the city's officials that appropriate action would be taken in relation to his past quarrels within the city boundaries.[69]

There is also evidence for Elizabeth Woodville's efforts in relation to grants to benefices and other positions. In 1472, the queen was granted the right to bestow and dispose of the post of canon and prebend in the king's free chapel of St Stephen within the palace of Westminster.[70] It is highly plausible to say that she would have been inclined to fill the vacant post by granting the living to a member of her own affinity, perhaps one of her household chaplains. Likewise, in 1477, Elizabeth nominated a number of persons of her affinity, including Richard Haute, a distant kinsman, to posts as justices in eyre in her forests.[71] These examples are demonstrations of the queen's attempts to fulfil her obligations, although doubtless balanced with the need to maintain good relations in other quarters.

As with Elizabeth Woodville, almost none of Elizabeth of York's letters have survived.[72] One letter, however, written in 1499, allows us a glimpse of what must have been a typical act of intercession or patronage by the queen, in this regard related to the grant of a parish living. Elizabeth wrote to the Prior of Christ Church, Canterbury, reminding him that she had been promised the grant of the living of the parish church of All Saints in Lombard Street, London, when it next fell vacant.[73] She had now been informed that the said benefice had become vacant and awaited the appointment of a new incumbent. She went on to state that she intended to 'enter the name of whichever of our chaplains we shall think able and suitable to have charge of the curacy there'.[74] So, either one of Elizabeth's household chaplains had specifically applied to be granted the said living or the queen had been informed of the vacancy at All Saints parish church, perhaps by a senior household official. The vacancy now gave her the chance to exercise some good ladyship and bestow a significant

---

[69] *The Coventry Leet Book or Mayor's Register*, ed. M. D. Harris, EETS, Original Series, no. 134 (London: Kegan Paul, 1907–13), 407.
[70] CPR 1467–77, 360.
[71] CPR 1476–85, 51–2.
[72] *Letters of the Queens of England*, 157–8.
[73] Neal states that Elizabeth asked for a *carte blanche* right to grant the living of All Hallows in Gracechurch Street. These details are different from the letter printed by Crawford. However, after comparing the different sources cited by Neal and Crawford, I have concluded that the two letters are the same. *Letters of the Queens of England*, 158; Neal, 'The Queen's Grace', 139–40.
[74] *Letters of the Queens of England*, 158.

The Queen's Affinity

benefit upon a member of her affinity. It is highly probable that she had obtained the said promise in connection with a different matter in the past and, moreover, was used to being on the lookout for such opportunities.

That Elizabeth of York was able to offer solid prospects for advancement to her affinity was illustrated by other evidence as well. There are records of grants to the queen outlining her rights to dispose where she desired, for example, the right (together with the bishop of Ely) to present the next canon or prebend of the chapel of St Stephen in Westminster palace.[75] The queen also probably recommended Thomas Burton, a yeoman of her household, to the post of keeper of the park at Wedale, Yorkshire that he was granted in 1486.[76] In 1489, she again recommended a member of her affinity, Edmund Chaderton, as justice in eyre in forests that she owned.[77] That she possessed influence with the king in no small measure is clear from the case of the vacant see of Worcester in 1498. The bishop of Worcester, Giovanni Gigli, died in August that year in Rome and there were several candidates for the position, one of whom was Adriano Castellesi, clerk of the papal camera. Castellesi was close to Henry VII and acted as his informant in Rome. He was also a favourite of Pope Alexander VI, who wrote to Margaret Beaufort, the king's mother, urging her to promote Castellesi even more in the eyes of the king (who was already well disposed towards him).[78] Unfortunately for Castellesi, the letter reveals that Henry had already promised the bishopric of Worcester to his queen's confessor.[79] As it transpires, it is uncertain whether the queen's confessor was eventually appointed to the see of Worcester since the individual is not named in the related correspondence. Nevertheless, the fact that Henry was willing to consider and even defer to his wife's wishes in this important matter speaks volumes for the amount of influence the queen possessed.

Even if the queens did not make specific recommendations, members of their affinity could benefit indirectly from the queen's patronage by gaining important posts in other royal or noble households. Laurence Bothe and Giles Saintlowe were but two members of Queen Margaret's household and affinity who did so. Bothe, who was the queen's chancellor, was appointed as the new keeper of the privy seal when it was vacated by Thomas Liseux in August 1456, while Saintlowe became the keeper of the great wardrobe in the household of Edward, prince of Wales.[80] This overlapping of service is, in

---

[75] CPR 1485–94, 65.
[76] CPR 1485–94, 109.
[77] CPR 1485–94, 318.
[78] SJC, SJLM/6/8, https://www.sjcarchives.org.uk/institutional/index.php/d56-165.
[79] Malcolm Underwood, 'The Pope, the Queen and the King's Mother: or, the Rise and Fall of Adriano Castellesi', in *The Reign of Henry VII: Proceedings of the 1993 Harlaxton Symposium*, ed. Benjamin Thompson (Stamford: Paul Watkins, 1995), 72–3.
[80] Griffiths, *The Reign of King Henry VI*, 773; J. L. Laynesmith, 'Constructing Queenship at Coventry: Pageantry and Politics at Margaret of Anjou's "Secret Harbour"', in *The*

effect, a primary reason why the lines between the king's and queen's affinities tended to become quite blurred.

Thus far we have seen many examples of individuals who were part of multiple affinities, not just the queen's but also the king's and occasionally other nobles. The domestic unrest of the later fifteenth century proved not to be an absolute bar to continued membership in the royal affinities, even as monarchic dynasties changed and political leanings with them. It could even be suggested that past royal service or being part of other royal affinities was of benefit to individuals if they could convince the new regime that such service demonstrated competence enough that they should be re-engaged. An examination of the lists of those who served in the queens' households or were counted as part of their affinities reveals many family names that appear more than once, sometimes multiple times. While it is not always possible to ascertain that individuals sharing family names were related to each other, many were. The Vaux family, again, was a noted example. Not only did Lady Jane Guildford, who was born a Vaux, serve Elizabeth of York but her mother served Margaret of Anjou, and Lady Jane's son Henry later became Henry VIII's Master of the Revels and a member of the king's Privy Chamber.[81] This was clearly a two-way street in terms of benefits to the family. The Vauxs benefitted from their service as part of the royal households and affinities by being able to place later generations of Vauxs at court and in royal service. In doing so, they built up that tradition of service that helped them become prominent, with their members continuing to be deemed worthwhile candidates for successive royal service.

SERVICE TO THE QUEEN

The benefits that accrued to members of the queens' affinities obviously did not come free. Previous chapters in this study have explored the work performed by the queens' household and estate personnel in return for the wages and fees paid to them. But more than that was often required and provided as part of the underlying expectation of being a member of the queens' affinities. The service referred to here was not necessarily spoken of or summarily demanded; it was part of the fabric of life and one's place in society during this period. In the case of kings and nobles, the military aspect was a paramount feature underpinning the affinity relationship. That was not usually the case with the queens' affinities. Instead, open-ended service to the queens in social and administrative terms lay at the core of being a member of their affinities.

Fifteenth Century III: Authority and Subversion, ed. Linda Clark (Woodbridge: Boydell Press, 2003), 139.

[81] Harris, *English Aristocratic Women*, 218.

The Queen's Affinity

The military aspect should, however, be considered in Margaret of Anjou's case. Isabella of France was the only queen in the fourteenth century to be involved in military activity and her affinity was a key reason for her successful deposition of her husband, Edward II. She cultivated the connections made with members of her affinity by rewarding her followers and using her relationships with them to gather support for her cause.[82] Her case demonstrated how a queen might use her affinity for different purposes than expected. Like Isabella before her, Margaret of Anjou was unlike the other queens in the fifteenth century in that she called on her affinity to render service in military terms. Their circumstances were not the same, of course. Margaret was not rebelling against Henry VI as Isabella did against Edward II. For this reason, it is more difficult to establish just how effective Margaret's ties of affinity were, both militarily and politically. Isabella's affinity was greatly enhanced while she was in France in 1325-26, principally because of the alliances she formed with the Mortimers and the count of Hainault. This means that a large portion of her affinity was comprised of retainers brought over from France and, thus, the overlapping of affinities that men typically had with respect to a king and his queen were probably not largely present where Isabella and Edward II were concerned. Conversely, many who served Margaret of Anjou and were counted as part of her affinity also had roles to play in the king's household and the administration of the Duchy of Lancaster.[83] One consequence of this is that it is difficult to separate the queen's affinity distinctly and wholly from that of the king's in the case of the last Lancastrian monarchy. Many people during the late 1450s believed that it was the queen and her affinity who ruled the realm as the Lancastrians battled the duke of York and his adherents.[84] However, the queen was not at odds with the king and, therefore, those who counted themselves as being part of the royal affinities did not face any conundrum in choosing loyalties.

Notwithstanding the potential for military mobilisation, the queens' affinities more typically engaged in service of the non-military kind, and they did so in a range of circumstances and scenarios. They provided service during the routines of everyday life, for instance. Where leisure activities were concerned, there were pastimes which the queens undertook with their ladies and gentlewomen, perhaps also with the gentlemen within their networks. The members of the queens' affinities, who may also have had waged roles in the queens' households, served as companions at work and at play. They kept company with the queens and shared their activities. In common with other noble ladies of the period and indeed queens in general, Elizabeth of York had her amusements.

---

[82] St John, *Three Medieval Queens*, 80.
[83] The many examples include Sir John Wenlock, Giles Saintlowe, and Robert Whittingham. Griffiths, *The Reign of King Henry VI*, 782.
[84] See, for example, 'No. 159 "Margaret prepares for war: the battle of Blore Heath, 1459"', reproduced in *English Historical Documents, Vol. IV, 1327-1485*, 282.

She played at dice, hunted with hounds and hawks, and indulged in card games during the Christmas festivities. Her mother, the elder Queen Elizabeth, also enjoyed the hunt and was recorded by the Bluemantle Pursuivant as playing games of bowls and ninepins as well as dancing when the king and his companions came to her chamber.[85] There is little available evidence of Margaret's participation in such activities as card games but much more that shows she hunted often enough, both at her own residences and those of her friends and supporters.[86] The hunt, together with many other leisurely pursuits, facilitated opportunities for interaction, thus enabling the queens to maintain and extend the good health of their connections with their affinities.

The queens' affinities also performed a range of minor services, and there are few better examples than those recorded in Elizabeth of York's Privy Purse expense account. This account shows that the queen's staff and members of her affinity took receipt of funds for the royal purse and disbursed rewards to servants who brought gifts from their lords or ladies to the queen. They transported the queen's alms to her chosen destinations or recipients and even lent money to their royal mistress.[87] Such tasks figured as part of the common services afforded by the queen's affinity and were valued by the queens. Many an annuity or grant was awarded on the basis of the recipient having provided 'good and faithful service' with little reference to specifics, though the recipient's past role in royal service could be a good indicator.[88] It is not unreasonable to assume that small tasks were deemed to be just as essential as larger ones and all of them contributed to an overall assessment of good service provided by the individual.

There were occasional private events at which several members of the queens' affinities would have been expected to carry out specific tasks. If Margaret Beaufort's ordinances or Henry VII's articles for the regulation of his household are any guide, the queen's delivery in childbed was one such event. Rules and regulations for the birth of royal children were set out in these ordinances and some members of the queens' affinities would have parts

---

[85] 'Appendix XV: The Record of Bluemantle Pursuivant, 1471–1472', as printed in Charles Lethbridge Kingsford, *English Historical Literature in the Fifteenth Century* (New York: Burt Franklin, 1962, reprint of 1913 edition), 386.
[86] For example, see *The Letters of Margaret of Anjou*, 162, 164 (nos 87 and 88).
[87] Queen's Book, fols 32, 34, 35, 36, 39, 41, 45, 46, 54, 68, 76.
[88] Cases include Richard Birchley, who held posts as king's sergeant and groom of the queen's chamber, and was granted other offices for life in 1451 'for good service to the king and queen Margaret'. Similarly, Giles Saintlowe and his wife Edith who was one of the queen's ladies were granted 20 marks yearly in 1455 for their services to the king and queen. On the other hand, Elizabeth Darcy, who was in charge of the king's nursery, was granted for life 'a tun of wine yearly in the port of London' in 1481 for her good service to the king and queen (Edward IV and Elizabeth Woodville). It can be assumed that her good service related specifically to the royal nursery. CPR 1446–52, 510; CPR 1452–61, 243; CPR 1476–85, 241.

The Queen's Affinity

to play in them. The queen expected to be attended upon when she entered her confinement, but all men were excluded on these occasions. Since only women could enter the confinement chamber, women assumed all the roles usually performed by the men and undertook all the 'masculine' activities as well as the 'feminine' ones.[89] Some of the women attending the queens in confinement and childbed would have been their salaried ladies-in-waiting and personal attendants but other women, including close female family members, would have attended the queens as well. Elizabeth Woodville's mother, Jacquetta, took on a principal role in the queen's churching ceremony and was probably involved in the confinement as well. Elizabeth of York's mother, Elizabeth Woodville, as well as her mother-in-law, Margaret Beaufort, both attended the queen during her confinement.[90]

Other events at which the queens' affinities provided service were public occasions of various kinds. An example was the christening of a royal child, an event at which members of the king's and queen's affinities played key roles since royal parents did not typically attend the christenings of their own children. A lady of ducal or comparable rank carried the royal infant and another carried the chrism cloth. An earl or his equivalent would bear the train if the child was a prince, and a countess would do so for a princess. High-ranking nobles of both royal affinities would serve as the child's godparents.[91] Such was the case at the christening of Princess Bridget, the youngest child of Edward IV and Elizabeth Woodville, which took place in November 1480 at the chapel of the royal palace of Eltham. A short account of this event notes that many family members took on the principal roles, including the king's mother, Cecily Neville, the infant princess' eldest sister, Elizabeth of York, and Lord and Lady Maltravers, who were the princesses' aunt (the former Margaret Woodville) and her husband (Thomas Fitzalan). Cecily Neville and Princess Elizabeth of York served as the infant's godmothers, Lord Maltravers carried the basin and Lady Maltravers carried the chrism cloth.[92] Similarly, when Arthur, first-born son of Henry VII and Elizabeth of York, was christened, many of the queen's closest affinity played the leading roles at this

---

[89] See Rachel Delman's work on female constructions of power and space that explores, among other things, the gender implications of female-only events in elite households from 1444 to 1541. Rachel M. Delman, 'Gendered Viewing, Childbirth and Female Authority in the Residence of Alice Chaucer, Duchess of Suffolk, at Ewelme, Oxfordshire', *Journal of Medieval History* 45, no. 2 (2019): 181–203.

[90] See Laynesmith, *The Last Medieval Queens*, 112–15, for more discussion of the ceremony surrounding the queen's confinement and churching in the later fifteenth ceremony.

[91] Regulations for a royal christening are laid out in the ordinances by Margaret Beaufort, countess of Richmond and Derby, which are printed in Leland, *De Rebus Britannicis Collectanea*, vol. IV, 181–2.

[92] Pauline E. Routh, 'Princess Bridget', *The Ricardian* 3 (1975): 13–14.

important occasion. They included the queen's mother, the dowager queen, Elizabeth Woodville, who served as the prince's godmother, and the queen's sisters, Cecily and Anne, who respectively carried the young prince and the chrism cloth.[93]

The queen's churching was another event at which her affinity provided crucial service.[94] Churching was a religious purification rite that women needed to undergo approximately a month after childbirth before they could resume their normal place in the church and society at large. The procession following the queen to the church would have consisted of large numbers of men and women of the court; there were approximately sixty maidens and ladies as well as more than one hundred men (counts, dukes, choir members, musicians, priests and scholars) in the procession for Elizabeth Woodville's churching. Notwithstanding such a large entourage, the queen's churching ceremony was not a public affair. The account written by Gabriel Tetzel, who witnessed Elizabeth Woodville's first churching in 1465 while travelling with his lord, Baron Leo of Rozmital, serves as a valuable record of this ritual. Yet it does not appear that Tetzel or his lord were present in the church itself. As Tetzel tells it, the queen, after rising from her child-bed in the morning, went to church, where she was escorted by two dukes and was followed by 'her mother and maidens and ladies to the number of sixty'.[95] The ceremony at the church was followed by a banquet signalling the queen's re-entry into court life, an event that Carolyn Donohue in her study of the construction of Yorkist monarchy describes as a 'grand spectacle of chivalric cordiality'.[96] It is clear from Tetzel's description of the event as well as from what we know about churching as a ceremony that the queen's female affinity members were important participants.

One rather sad duty that members of the queens' affinities may have had to perform for their royal mistress was attendance at the funerals of royal children. Extant documents for the funeral of Princess Mary, one of the daughters of Edward IV and Elizabeth Woodville, show that ladies were conspicuous at this particular event, although the queen herself was not

---

[93] See Leland, *De Rebus Britannicis Collectanea*, vol. IV, 204–7, for a contemporary narrative of the prince's christening.

[94] See Laynesmith, *The Last Medieval Queens*, 115–19, for in-depth discussion of the queen's churching as a queenship ritual. For additional information on churching as spectacle and theatre, see Gail McMurray Gibson, 'Blessing from Sun and Moon: Churching as Women's Theater', in *Bodies and Disciplines: Intersections of Literature and History in Fifteenth-Century England*, eds Barbara Hanawalt and David Wallace (Minneapolis: University of Minnesota Press, 1996), 139–54.

[95] *The Travels of Leo of Rozmital: through Germany, Flanders, England, France, Spain, Portugal and Italy 1465–1467*, ed. and trans. Malcolm Letts (Cambridge: Cambridge University Press for the Hakluyt Society, 1957), 46.

[96] Carolyn Donohue, 'Public Display and the Construction of Monarchy in Yorkist England, 1461–85' (unpublished PhD thesis, University of York, 2013), 181.

present as per protocol.[97] Instead, close relatives of the queen were present to honour and mourn the deceased princess. They included ladies such as Jane Woodville, the queen's sister (the widowed Lady Grey of Ruthin), Joan, Lady Strange, and Lady Katherine Grey, the latter two being the queen's nieces. Joan, Lady Dacre, the wife of the queen's chamberlain, Lord Dacre, was also in attendance. The fact that Lady Dacre did not herself serve in the queen's household is a clear indication that members of the queen's affinity stepped up to serve the queen on such occasions.

As part of their duties as the royal consort, the queens would have attended many other public events. Tournaments, court festivities, royal progresses, banquets and disguisings, civic entries and the hosting of foreign visitors were some of the rituals, revels and entertainments that provided opportunities for the queens' affinities to lend their presence and more in service. For Margaret of Anjou, little evidence in relation to her role at public events seems to have survived. However, there do exist records in the Coventry Leet book that are related to visits by Henry VI and Margaret to the city of Coventry. These visits included events such as a Whitsunday procession and various pageants and plays held in their honour.[98] Likewise, there are records of visits and royal progresses undertaken by Elizabeth Woodville, such as her 1469 visit to Norwich. The queen was accompanied by many lords and ladies, who were doubtless all members of her affinity (and possibly the king's as well) and bound to offer her service. While their presence at these many public events was certainly crucial, there is little indication that queens and their entourages were typically much more than spectators as opposed to being active participants. This would be true chiefly in the case of tournaments, royal progresses, civic entries and the hosting of foreign visitors. The overall picture at most public events seems to be one of attendance and observance by the queens, lending their queenly presence in company with their entourage and affinity.

Nevertheless, there are several cases pointing to the queens' more active part in the organisation of revelries and significant events. Warnicke paints a general picture of Elizabeth of York as an inactive and passive queen, but this viewpoint is not wholly supported by other scholars.[99] Michelle Beer, for one, whose work explores the queenship of Catherine of Aragon and her sister-in-law, Margaret Tudor, queen to James IV of Scotland, argues that Elizabeth of York was an integral force behind much of the early Tudor pageantry and often was personally involved in organising court revels. The queen is known to have paid for clothing needed by the minstrels performing in disguisings in June and December 1502, expenditure that was surely warranted only if

---

[97] These are examined in Anne F. Sutton and Livia Visser-Fuchs, 'The Royal Burials of the House of York at Windsor: II. Princess Mary, May 1482 and Queen Elizabeth Woodville, June 1492', *The Ricardian* 11 (1999): 446–51.
[98] *The Coventry Leet Book*, 299, 300.
[99] Warnicke, *Elizabeth of York and Her Six Daughters-in-Law*, Chapter 6.

she had a hand in organising these performances.[100] She also furnished funds for yuletide entertainment and the setting of Christmas carols.[101] In the case of the wedding reception for Catherine of Aragon in 1501, Elizabeth of York was far from a passive bystander. She was actively involved in the selection of ladies who would greet the Spanish princess on her arrival, keep her company and facilitate her acclimation to her new home.[102] The queen was also responsible for a number of important matters related to the reception, including the provisioning of transport and the outfitting of harnesses and saddles for Catherine and her entourage.[103]

In addition, the queens would occasionally organise banquets in their own chambers for various reasons. The Bluemantle Pursuivant recorded the visit in 1472 of Louis of Bruges, Lord Gruthuse, to the court of Edward IV, noting in detail the splendidly lavish hospitality bestowed by the English king on his guests.[104] For the most part, Edward's queen, Elizabeth Woodville, played hostess beside her king during the tours and amusements staged in honour of Lord Gruthuse. At one stage, however, she hosted a great banquet in her chamber, with seating arrangements that displayed a similar degree of formality as that detected in Tetzel's description of the same queen's churching ceremony.[105] As at previous receptions, there was music, dancing and participation in games, with the king and queen being attended at this banquet by family members including the king's sister, the duchess of Exeter, the queen's sister-in-law, Lady Rivers, and the royal princess, the future queen Elizabeth of York. There is little doubt that the queens' active participation in and organisation of such events was aided by crucial service from her affinity.

On the whole, the queens' affinities served them in two distinct ways. Individuals performed specific tasks, service that the queens no doubt expected, but, just as importantly, their very presence added gravitas to the queenly image and role. As shown in the case of Prince Arthur, for example, royal christenings were occasions where the closest members of the queen's affinity demonstrated their roles in the hierarchy by performing specific and important duties. But on other public occasions where the queens were more passive observers than active participants, the presence of members of their affinities, especially those of the highest ranks, added impact to the queen's contribution to the public image and representation of monarchy. No queen could be unattended, and her affinity enhanced her persona in the same way

---

[100] Queen's Book, fols 40, 76.
[101] Beer, *Queenship at the Renaissance Courts of Britain*, 36–7.
[102] *The Receyt of the Ladie Kateryne*, ed. Gordon Kipling, EETS, Original Series, no. 296 (Oxford: Oxford University Press for the Early English Text Society, 1990), 5; Warnicke, *Elizabeth of York and Her Six Daughters-in-Law*, 174–5.
[103] Beer, *Queenship at the Renaissance Courts of Britain*, 35.
[104] 'Appendix XV: The Record of Bluemantle Pursuivant, 1471–1472', 379–88.
[105] *The Travels of Leo of Rozmital*, 45–8.

The Queen's Affinity

the king's affinity enhanced his. The attendance of the queen and her affinity at tournaments, revelries and entertainments, as much as the king's, encouraged the staging of music, pageantry and disguises.[106] They were a full half of the overall picture and could not be omitted without something being lost. To illustrate this point, I need only refer to the sombreness of the court when Elizabeth of York died. On her death, the king retreated into solitude, both to mourn and because he succumbed to illness, while the late queen's household found itself without its central focus. The court was left bereft of its royal principals.[107] Then also, when Elizabeth's son, Henry VIII, sent his queen, Catherine of Aragon, away to the country in 1531 in obvious displeasure, the courtier Edward Hall lamented the absence of joy and mirth without the presence of the queen and her ladies.[108]

Service to the queen did not end precisely on her death as might be expected. In fact, the rituals associated with death, like other rituals, 'required participants and an audience'.[109] Scholars of premodern royal funerals and burials have, among other things, drawn attention to the many rituals that took place and acknowledge that many members of the deceased's household and affinity played crucial roles in those rituals.[110] Admittedly, past research has tended to focus on kings rather than queens. Nonetheless, the death rituals of premodern English queens are just as deserving of examination for their 'cultural, biological and political significance'.[111] In the *Liber regie capelle*, a late 1440s book of ritual in the English royal chapel, the elaborate instructions concerning the preparation of a king's body for burial and the ceremonial of

---

[106] Warnicke, *Elizabeth of York and Her Six Daughters-in-Law*, 182.

[107] Penn, *Winter King*, 112.

[108] Edward Hall's lament is quoted in Warnicke, *Elizabeth of York and Her Six Daughters-in-Law*, 196.

[109] Lucinda H. S. Dean, *Death and the Royal Succession in Scotland, c.1214-c.1543: Ritual, Ceremony and Power* (Woodbridge: Boydell Press, 2024), 7.

[110] Relevant research on royal burials and funerals includes the following works: Hélène Bloem, 'The Processions and Decorations at the Royal Funeral of Anne of Brittany', *Bibliothèque d'Humanisme et Renaissance* 54, no. 1 (1992): 131–60; Elizabeth A. R. Brown, 'The Ceremonial of Royal Succession in Capetian France: The Double Funeral of Louis X', *Traditio* 34 (1978), 227–71; Elizabeth A. R. Brown, 'The Ceremonial of Royal Succession in Capetian France: The Funeral of Philip V', *Speculum* 55, no. 2 (1980): 266–93; Dean, *Death and the Royal Succession*; Ralph E. Giesey, *The Royal Funeral Ceremony in Renaissance France* (Geneva: Librairie E. Droz, 1960); John Carmi Parsons, '"Never was a body buried in England with such solemnity and honour": The Burials and Posthumous Commemorations of English Queens to 1500', in *Queens and Queenship in Medieval Europe: Proceedings of a Conference held at King's College London, April 1995*, ed. Anne J. Duggan (Woodbridge: Boydell Press, 1997), 317–37; Sutton and Visser-Fuchs, 'The Royal Burials of the House of York at Windsor'.

[111] Warnicke, *Elizabeth of York and Her Six Daughters-in-Law*, 207.

the funeral are not repeated for that of a queen. Instead, there is a passage that brusquely informs the reader of the futility of describing specific details for a queen because 'the exequies of a queen who leaves this world are entirely carried out in the form noted above'.[112] In other words, a queen's funeral was meant to include the same details and rituals as that of a king's, although presumably only in the case where she predeceased her husband the king.[113] Whether or not this theoretical equality in death of a king and a queen translated into reality is less important for our purposes. What is more relevant is what the evidence for actual funerals shows in terms of involvement on the part of the deceased's household and affinity.

Of the queens in this study, only Elizabeth of York died while she was still queen consort. Margaret of Anjou and Elizabeth Woodville were technically dowager queens, widows who outlived their husbands. Yet Margaret was attainted by the ruling Yorkist regime and died in poverty in France in August 1482 while Elizabeth Woodville died in June 1492, having surrendered her property as dowager queen and retired to Bermondsey Abbey. We can, therefore, rely only on evidence for Elizabeth of York's funeral to discuss the significance of the funeral in the ending of service to the queen consort. Moreover, there is little extant evidence for Margaret's funeral and Elizabeth Woodville's funeral was by all accounts a very low-key affair. Happily, this task is made easier by the existence of a narrative and financial accounts for the younger Elizabeth's funeral, which can be used to highlight the roles of the household members and members of the queenly affinity.[114]

The evidence for Elizabeth of York's funeral reveals that members of her household and affinity did indeed actively participate in the queen's final journey.[115] One of the primary roles at royal funerals was that of chief mourner, and it would have been assumed by someone who ranked among those closest to the deceased. Hence, at Elizabeth of York's funeral Lady Elizabeth Stafford (on the first day), one of the queen's principal ladies, and Lady Katherine Courtenay (on subsequent days) served as chief mourner, the latter having not been able to attend on the first day. It should be noted that Lady Courtenay was Elizabeth of York's sister and while it is uncertain whether she was a formally waged member of the queen's household, she clearly formed part of the queen's entourage and affinity. In addition, the procession following the bier was peopled by knights and esquires as well as

---

[112] As quoted in Parsons, '"Never was a body buried in England"', 317–18.

[113] This view is expressed by the authors in Sutton and Visser-Fuchs, 'The Royal Burials of the House of York at Windsor', 452–3.

[114] *The Antiquarian Repertory*, vol. 4, eds. F. Grose and T. Astle (London: Edward Jeffrey, 1807–8), 654–63; TNA LC2/1 fols 36–79.

[115] See Laynesmith, *The Last Medieval Queens*, 122–27 and Warnicke, *Elizabeth of York and Her Six Daughters-in-Law*, 208–11 for extended descriptions and analysis of Elizabeth of York's funeral based on the account in *The Antiquarian Repertory*.

ladies and gentlewomen who served in the queen's household. As an aside, all who took part in the procession were supplied by the great wardrobe with black fabric for mourning clothes, no matter whether they served in the king's or queen's households or whether they were obliged to attend the funeral for some other reason.[116] Lady Courtenay, as chief mourner, led other ladies of the queen's household and affinity as well as other men of the royal households in watching over the coffin during the nights spent in vigil. She also led the women in first presenting the palls, which were laid in the coffin.[117] Laynesmith points out that women were prominent participants at this funeral not only because this was the funeral of a woman but also because women tended to be particularly associated with mourning.[118] Nevertheless, the ladies departed once the final requiem mass was completed, leaving the men to carry out the physical tasks of burying the queen.

A most significant ritual was performed once Elizabeth of York's coffin had been lowered into the grave, which was the temporary one that her body lay in until it was moved in 1509 to a magnificent double tomb in Westminster Abbey. As stated in the narrative, the queen's chamberlain and her gentlemen ushers broke the staffs of their offices and threw them into the grave.[119] This appears to have been the traditional protocol; the ceremonial breaking of the staffs signalled that the bonds of service and affinity to the queen were formally ended and they were no longer bound to their royal mistress.[120] This particular ritual is not mentioned in the account of the funeral of Elizabeth Woodville nor is there much evidence that it formed part of the ritual contexts for other past English queens consort, notwithstanding that there are few such sources to be examined in the first place.[121] It was, however, carried out during the funeral of King Edward IV of England and clearly formed part of the funeral rituals for French royals from the fourteenth century at least.[122] The funeral of Anne of Brittany, queen of France, who died in 1514, forms an interesting point of comparison with Elizabeth of York's. Members of Anne's household and affinity were active participants at her funeral. Her king of

---

[116] TNA LC2/1 fols 59–78.

[117] Laynesmith and Warnicke both point out that there was a discrepancy between the numbers of palls in the narrative and the lists of ladies and palls in the accounts. Laynesmith, *The Last Medieval Queens*, 125 n. 260; Warnicke, *Elizabeth of York and Her Six Daughters-in-Law*, 235 n. 16.

[118] Laynesmith, *The Last Medieval Queens*, 125.

[119] *The Antiquarian Repertory*, vol. 4, 663. The queen's chamberlain was Thomas Butler, the earl of Ormond and her gentlemen ushers were Henry Pole, William Crowmer and William Bulstrode.

[120] Note that the household of Isabella of France, who died in 1358 as dowager queen, was considered to cease to exist from her funeral. CCR 1354–60, 549.

[121] Parsons, "'Never was a body buried in England'", 323.

[122] Giesey, *The Royal Funeral Ceremony*, 74–5; Ross, *Edward IV*, 417.

arms deposited several devices of office on the coffin and her stewards broke their staffs of office, throwing them into the grave with the queen's coffin.[123] Similarly, the same ritual was performed at the sixteenth-century funeral of Anne of Cleves, Henry VIII's discarded fourth queen, who had, nonetheless, managed to maintain good relations with the king.[124] Obviously, participation in the funeral and burial rituals for a deceased queen was one of the last obligations owed by those who served her. The burial of the queen marked the effective dissolution of her household and affinities, and the individuals within them were no longer formally bound to her.

CONCLUSIONS

The experiences of the queens in this study demonstrate that ties of affinity are not just concentric circles but also resemble web- or mesh-like networks. Marriage, traditions of loyalty and service, social connections, and lands and economic resources all interacted to bind the members of the affinities not only to the queens at the centre but also to each other. In other words, the bonds extended in many different directions, not just inwards and outwards in the fashion of a circular model but also sideways. The more ties created by these mechanisms, the stronger would be the affinities. These bonds would be further strengthened by other mechanisms such as gift exchange, which functioned not only to maintain ties but also as crucial aspects of the reward and service framework of an affinity.

No matter the shape of the affinity, the queens remained the central focus but with links that radiate outward. They lay at the centre of their affinities while people occupied places on these circles surrounding them in a hierarchy based upon rank and seniority on the one hand and degrees of intimacy on the other. All the affinities of the queens in this study may be viewed in this way; the differences lay in the individuals placed on those circles. Those among the affinities who were nearest to each queen tended to be those with the closest blood-ties and/or those who had the most intimate relationships with the queens, such as their siblings and friends of long standing and shared experiences. In common among the queens, the next closest circles were typically populated by the men who served in their households, on their councils and in their estate administrations. In studying these structures, we become aware of the overlaps that could exist between the queens' affinities and those of the kings and even some of the highest-ranking nobles. Overlaps between the affinities of the kings and queens, for the most part, should not be unexpected as scholars have recently asserted that kingship and queenship should be considered complementary to each other; kings and queens worked in tandem

---

[123] Matarasso, *Queen's Mate*, 278.
[124] Warnicke, *Elizabeth of York and Her Six Daughters-in-Law*, 230.

towards similar goals, no doubt assisted by their servants and entourages.[125] Fluidity and overlap in personnel with those of the kings could and did exist for the fourteenth-century queens.[126] This trend evidently continued into the fifteenth century. Similar strands of continuity existed for these queens' affinities, and, in comparison with other medieval affinities, we also see the strong pull of tradition in spite of political and dynastic disruption as well as shifts in backgrounds and political allegiances of the queens consort themselves.

Good ladyship as a lived concept encompassed ideas of reciprocity and service. However, since the ethos of service in the context of fifteenth-century life posits that it was wide-ranging, reciprocal and all-encompassing, the affinities of the queens had every right to expect a level over and above that of good ladyship. They almost certainly did hold such expectations as well. While it was incumbent on the queen to act as a good lady in the same sense that a lord, king or even a typical noblewoman might do towards the general population, the individual assembling an affinity held out the additional but unspoken promise of extra efforts in this area for prospective members. This added potential provided impetus for a secure belief on the part of those who counted themselves as members of the queens' affinities. They understood themselves to be included in a whole and solid community, framed by definite boundaries as opposed to an imagined one. What is more, the queen's proximity to the king gave her affinity a concrete link to the highest echelons of the kingdom with attendant additional possibilities in the form of rewards and connections. This additional feature, thus, acted as a supplementary inducement to continued membership in the queens' affinities.

The reward and service framework underpinned the queens' affinities, but it was in turn made possible only by the existence of financial and economic resources at the queens' disposal. The lands and resources of the queens provided the material foundations upon which their affinities were constructed. That the queens depended on their resources to maintain their affinities is unarguable, a point emphatically demonstrated by the case of the sixteenth-century queen Catherine of Aragon, consort to Henry VIII and Elizabeth of York's daughter-in-law. In the aftermath of the king's estrangement from his wife, Catherine's estates were taken by Henry in his attempts to be rid of her. The king's actions resulted in the queen's utter inability to adequately support herself financially or to maintain her affinity and support networks.[127] Assuming the queens possessed adequate resources,

---

[125] Theresa Earenfight, 'Without the Persona of the Prince: Kings, Queens and the Idea of Monarchy in Late Medieval Europe', *Gender & History* 19, no. 1 (Apr. 2007): 14; Zita Rohr, *Yolande of Aragon (1381–1442) Family and Power: The Reverse of the Tapestry* (Basingstoke: Palgrave Macmillan, 2016), 4.

[126] St John, *Three Medieval Queens*, 72.

[127] Michelle Beer, 'A Queenly Affinity? Catherine of Aragon's Estates and Henry VIII's Great Matter', *Historical Research* 91, no. 253 (Aug. 2018): 444.

however, the ties between them and their affinities were buttressed by the belief and expectation of reciprocal service. The queens expected their affinities to provide them with extensive services, some of which they were materially compensated for while others were probably, though perhaps unconsciously, added to a pool of expectation for future possible benefit or reward in financial and non-financial terms. Like the queen's household, the queen's affinity is a categorical example of how the queens made use of their financial and economic resources. Our exploration of the queenly affinity attests to its embodiment of the intrinsic value of such resources to the queens. There is no better way to situate the queens' resources and link them to the queen's place in the social context of their world.

CONCLUSION

These three queens – Margaret of Anjou, Elizabeth Woodville and Elizabeth of York – operated as economic players in a world where their gender and marital status would ordinarily render them legally invisible. They were able to benefit from the possession and availability of economic resources, and they used them to assert their power, authority and influence in the economic arena of queenship. Moreover, they did so against a backdrop of conflict and political upheaval that effected changes in the dynastic bloodlines of the monarchy. The circumstances of the periods during which each individual became queen were not the same and neither were their backgrounds and loyalties. All these factors form a part of the framework for this study and, in the process of completing it, several themes encapsulating the discussions have emerged: change, continuity, gender and power/agency.

Changes related to the queens' economic resources can be perceived in various ways. As in the fourteenth century, later fifteenth-century queens could be given a wide variety of different grants and their dower grants still formed the basis of their economic resources. The main types available to them remained, as for the queens of the previous century, the traditional entitlement of queen's gold, non-landed grants and landed resources. What changed was the monetary importance and measurable benefits of these different types to each queen in this study. One of the major alterations was in the importance of landed versus non-landed resources, an obvious modification that occurred in the transition from Margaret of Anjou to her successors, the two queens Elizabeth. Like the fourteenth-century queens Eleanor of Provence and Eleanor of Castile, Margaret's most financially important resources were her non-landed grants, which were meant to contribute more than two-thirds of her dower revenues. As it happened, they turned out to be rather unreliable sources for Margaret. Conversely, the dowers of both queens Elizabeth contained almost no resources that were not landed ones. This does not mean that they did not subsequently benefit from such grants as wardships and cash allowances, but the initial provisions made for the queens dramatically changed after Margaret of Anjou's time. For Elizabeth Woodville and Elizabeth of York, lands and estates in dower grants became the primary means of providing for their needs. Those were their key sources, both in monetary terms and other benefits. This is not to say that Margaret of Anjou did not value her lands granted in dower even though they were lower in value in proportion to her overall expected revenues. In fact, although she theoretically drew more income from non-landed sources, her landed sources of revenue proved to be more reliable overall than her non-landed ones. In contrast to lands, queen's gold, which was a crucial resource for many of the fourteenth-century queens, became much less monetarily important to the queens in this study. Even though it was clear that they still considered queen's gold to be their rightful prerogative, this particular resource yielded them far fewer quantifiable benefits in proportion to their total revenues. Thus, it could no longer be considered either a large or dependable source of queenly income in the later fifteenth century.

Change was also evident in the legal and practical status of these queens as landowners and holders of their dower lands, especially for the period moving from the fourteenth to the late fifteenth century. Each queen in this study was practically, if not strictly legally, the owner of a significant complex of lands and estates, the bulk of which were granted as part of her dower. The legal ambiguity surrounding the status of the later fifteenth-century queens in relation to their lands should have had implications for their roles as landholders and administrators as well as for how they could use these resources to exercise queenship. Nonetheless, it appears that, in reality, they were viewed by and they viewed themselves as legal owners who were entitled to all the rights yet were also bound by their administrative responsibilities.

Notwithstanding these observable variations, there is much that supports the existence of continuity in the face of the challenges posed to queenship and the monarchy during this period. Comparative examination of the queens' landed resources demonstrates a commonality in the grants of lands and fee-farms, with many similarities in the groups of landed resources granted to each queen. Likewise, each of the queen's households and affinities exhibited far more similarities in composition and management than might be expected in light of the significant differences between the backgrounds and allegiances of the queens. These are strong indications that tradition and precedent operated as consistent drivers for decisions made about issues such as which lands should be granted in dower. These same drivers also factored heavily in the administrations of those lands and estates. As well as the queens' estates being organised and administered along very similar lines to those of other great landowners in the period, there appears to have been very little substantive change in estate administrative methods from Margaret of Anjou to Elizabeth of York. Tradition and best practice were key considerations for administrative decision-making, most notably at the local manorial level. To a certain degree, it may have mattered little to the local tenantry and estate officials who the specific landowner was, especially if the estate was but one in a large complex of holdings. Even more significant is the fact that tradition and precedent were not inevitably deterred or deflected by the exigencies of war or political instability that had resulted in disrupted royal bloodlines and consequent changes in government. It could even be said that continuity in administrative machineries helped keep them afloat and functioning in the face of said disruption, particularly during the early 1470s, which saw such frequent and rapid changes in the position of king and queen consort.

Yet, hand in hand with continuity in relation to landed resources, we can discern transience in the individual tenures of the queens. Each of the queens was granted lands in dower that were meant for her use and benefit during her lifetime, after which they reverted to the Crown. During the time that the queens owned these lands, they received the revenues, used the lands for their own benefit and exercised the rights and responsibilities of a landowner. However, each consort's period as the landowner takes on an air of impermanence when viewed in the longer term. This was because, at least for the lands granted in dower, the queens were not themselves allowed to pass these lands and estates directly to their heirs, and because there was sometimes a chronological gap between the ownership of those lands by individual queens. The queens thus appear more as stewards of these lands, albeit perhaps in the same manner as any lord or nobleman is a 'steward' of familial lands for future generations.

The transient nature of this distinct group of queens owning their lands was compounded by the period during which these individuals lived. In peaceable times, the reversion of a queen's lands to the Crown meant that they would then become available for the next queen consort who typically would be her daughter-in-law, thus keeping the lands within her marital family. In those situations, the transience of a queen's landownership becomes obscured in the longer-term continuity of the royal family's landownership. Unfortunately, the chaotic events of the latter half of the fifteenth century meant that the family hold of each queen on the lands was strikingly tenuous. This fragile dynastic hold made the ownership of each of these queens appear even briefer and more temporary than usual. The interesting point is that the dynastic ruptures of this time did not in fact totally unsettle the continuity in landownership for queenship itself. There were certain lands that continued to be passed on from one individual to another in spite of the fact that they were from different bloodlines and even different backgrounds altogether. Hence, we see that while the individual landowning roles of Margaret of Anjou and Elizabeth Woodville as queen consort were transitory, the landed resources of the position of queen remained relatively constant. Each of the queens in this study project transience in their roles as landholders and estate administrators, even while, taken as a whole, they connect to form a thread of continuity in queenly landownership.

The reasons underlying the transient ownership of queens' lands were also bound up with the gendered economic landscape of the period. The queens in this study were women who occupied the position by virtue of being married to the king. Yet their gender and marital status did not present as overwhelming obstacles to landownership as one might assume, even though they were theoretically subject to the frameworks governing the lives of married women of the period in relation to owning lands and property. The legal and social framework within which medieval English noblewomen lived essentially prevented married women from lawfully owning and administering their own lands and property, and queens were first and foremost married women. The idea of the queen as landholder, therefore, sits uneasily within this societal context. In addition, ownership of the lands granted in dower was constrained for these queens in different ways from ownership of lands bought and sold during their lifetimes, principally in relation to their ability to dispose of or alienate them as they wished. They might in principle have been landowners, but in relation to dower lands they could not theoretically exercise each and every right of a typical landholder.

Despite these constraints, the evidence suggests that the idea of a queen as landholder and administrator in the later fifteenth century was not regarded as anything other than right and proper in the scheme of things. The queens appear to have acted as any other great magnate would do in questions pertaining to lands and property, and they were treated as such without undue consideration of their gender or marital status. It was, in fact, their social status that proved to be the overriding consideration. The fact that the owner of a particular estate was the queen was important primarily because she was the highest-ranked individual after the king. It is admittedly difficult to conclusively determine exactly how involved each of the queens in this study was in the administration of their estates. However, I argue that the queens were important players in the economic landscape and, just as crucially, their economic roles were contemporarily accepted as being part of the fabric of society. In order to understand why and how such a paradoxical scenario could have existed, it is useful to refer to Allyson Poska's concept of 'agentic gender norms', which extends what might have been regarded as acceptable behaviour and offers us a way to comprehend conflicting contemporary expectations about the queens as women versus their queenly economic roles.[1] Poska suggests that there existed in the premodern period gender expectations for women that allowed for independent action and the exertion of power and authority on their parts in spite of the restrictions placed upon them. As Wiesner-Hanks put it, these expectations viewed women as 'capable, economically productive, rational, qualified, skilled and competent' but operated in tandem with 'standard patriarchal norms in which women were judged mentally, physically, and morally inferior'.[2] Seen through this lens, it becomes much easier to accept that gender, both as biological and social construct, was less of an issue where the queen as a landowner was concerned. The queens as landowners appear to have been much less viewed

---

[1] Allyson M. Poska, 'The Case for Agentic Gender Norms for Women in Early Modern Europe', *Gender & History* 30, no. 2 (2018): 360–1.

[2] *Ibid.*, 354–5; Wiesner-Hanks, 'Women's Agency', 12–14.

Conclusion

as exceptional individuals than we might anticipate precisely because they were expected to fulfil those roles. It follows that a viewpoint of them as interested and informed participants in the management of their landholdings is not at all out of the ordinary.[3]

Unsurprisingly, it is in the exercise of their rights and responsibilities as landowners and administrators that we see manifestations of queenly power and agency in economic terms. Economic agency, even power, is evident in the exertions undertaken by the queens, through writing letters on behalf of their tenants, making grants and so on. We also see displays of agency in other actions, such as the queens' assertions of their rights whenever they wished to bring any issues to the attention of recalcitrant associates, their attempts to collect what they were owed in financial obligations, and in evidence that they regarded queen's gold and court perquisites as their dues and accordingly took action to collect their entitlements. Where their lands and estates were concerned, the queens in this study acted as administrators in the same way that other landowners would be expected to do. While they naturally reaped the benefits and exercised the rights bestowed upon them as landholders, they were also cognisant of their responsibilities and sought to carry them out as best they could. They could be and often were active and engaged economic managers and there is little reason to argue otherwise. In a similar manner, queenly agency can also be detected from the queens' participation in household management. Indications of the state of the queens' finances may be gleaned from household records as much as from estate records, and the hand of the queens in exercising economic agency was as much present in their interest and participation in household management as it was in matters concerning their landholdings. In effect, this study has shown that queens consort were part of the economic landscape in a way that was similar to but transcended the active participation of many other medieval married women as landholders and as estate and household administrators. These roles were much more formalised for the queens and clearly were essential parts of and embedded in the nature of fifteenth-century queenship in England.

There also existed distinct overall connections between the queens' economic resources and their other roles and positions in the world they lived in. The examination of the queens' households and affinities illustrates that the queens' economic capital was transformed into a variety of other forms, including social, symbolic and even political, through the utilisation of mechanisms for the establishment and maintenance of these entities. The queens used the material resources at their disposal to fund their households and their lifestyles. The households and affinities in turn facilitated and helped

---

[3] The idea that capable royal and noblewomen were not necessarily exceptional in medieval society is strongly endorsed in the following collection of essays: Heather J. Tanner, ed., *Medieval Elite Women and the Exercise of Power, 1100–1400: Moving Beyond the Exceptionalist Debate* (Cham: Palgrave Macmillan, 2019).

the queens fulfil the roles incumbent in their status. There is no question, therefore, that economic resources provided the material foundations for the queens and for queenship more broadly. Without their material resources it is unlikely that these individuals would have been successful queens. They could not have maintained their households or conducted themselves as queens on the public stage without financial resources. The building and maintenance of affinities and social networks, as well as the exercise of good ladyship and patronage, was not possible without the material means underpinning them. In any event, a vein of economic insecurity could yet be a constant in the life of a queen. This was evident in the sustained battles undertaken by Margaret of Anjou and her officials to obtain the revenues she was owed. It was also apparent in the slow but sure decline in the quantity of revenue obtainable from queen's gold, ostensibly an ancient and undeniable right belonging to queens consort but one that was constantly regarded as an irksome burden on those who incurred the obligation.

While the primary focus of this book has remained firmly on the specific individuals who were consorts in the later fifteenth century, its findings are also significant for queenship itself. By the end of this period, the established practice of granting mainly lands and estates to queens for their provision and maintenance had helped to further embed these individuals in the economic landscape. More than that, this book has shown that there was a great deal of continuity in providing for the position itself, even while there were limits on what an individual queen could regard as hers, for herself or her heirs. Despite the tumult of this period, the queenly position kept a straight course amidst change, at least in economic terms. Queenship, in essence, emerges as one of the great survivors of the political unrest in the later fifteenth century.

APPENDIX 1: THE QUEENS' LANDS AND HOLDINGS – A COMPOSITE LIST

Holdings owned by all the queens are underlined.
Spellings used in this appendix are as in the sources, modern spelling in brackets here:
Benestede (Banstead), Charlewode (Charlwood), Cokeham (Cookham), Cosseham (Corsham), Devyse (Devizes), Esyndon (Essendon), Fekenham (Feckenham), Gedyngton (Geddington), Grenewiche (Greenwich), Gyllngham (Gillingham), Hadley (Hadleigh), Hamstede Marshall (Hamstead Marshall), Hedyngham (Hedingham), Hertfordyngbury (Hertingfordbury), Kenelworth (Kenilworth), Langley Marreys (Langley Marish), Marleburgh (Marlborough), Masshebury (Mashbury), Melkesham (Melksham), Mindipp (Mendip), Petirsham (Petersham), Pevesham (Pewsham), Plecy (Pleshey), Rach (Rache), Rockyngham (Rockingham), Shene (Sheen), Swaloufeld (Swallowfield), Wyrardesbury(Wraysbury), Yerkhull (Yarkhill).

Note:
A legend for the documents consulted is listed at the conclusion of this appendix.

County	Margaret of Anjou	Elizabeth Woodville	Elizabeth of York
Bedfordshire		**m**	
		(*manor*) Stotfold	

County	Margaret of Anjou	Elizabeth Woodville	Elizabeth of York
Berkshire	**B**	**a, d, k**	**2**
	(*manor*) Hamstede Marshall	(*manors*) Cokeham	Cokeham
		Bray	Bray
		d, k	Swaloufeld
		Swaloufeld (2 parts)	Hamstede Marshall
		Hamstede Marshall	Benham (Benham Lovell)
		Benham (Benham Lovell)	Holbenham, Westbroke
		c, d	
		(2 messuages, 2 carucates of land, 40 acres meadow, 20 acres wood)	**5**
		Holbenham, Westbroke	(*manor/lordship*) Newbury
		j, k	Wokefield
		Swaloufeld (remaining 3rd part)	Stratfield Mortimer
		l	
		(*manors/lordships*)	
		East Garston	
		Lambourn (Chipping Lambourne)	
		Hungerford	
		Wood Speen	
		Hinton	
		Up Lambourn (Upper Lamborne)	

Buckinghamshire	A		**a, d, k**
	(*manor*) Crondon	(*manor*) Wyrardesbury	
			c, d, k
	D	(*manor/lordship*) Langley Marreys	
	(*castle/lordship/manor/town*) Haverford		**1**
		(*manor*) Crendon (Crondon?)	
			m
		(*manor*) Medmenham	
			1
			(*manor*) Great Lynforde (given when a princess)
			2
			Wyrardesbury
			Langley Marreys
Cambridgeshire			**m**
		(*manor*) Hynton	
Derbyshire	A		**m**
	(*manors*) Duffield, Beaurepare, Holbrook, Allerwassle, Southwode, Heighege, Edrichay, Holand, Byggyng, Irtonwode, Bouteshale, Brassington, Matloke, Hertington, Spondon, Scropton	(4 *messuages*, 300 *acres land*) Melton, Wylyngton, Assheborne and Howys	
	(*hundred*) Gresley, Appultre		
	Bailiwick of supplementary portion of new liberties in co. Derby		
	(*wards*) Duffield, Holand, Colbrook, Beaurepare		
	(*castle/manor*) Melbourne		
	(*farm*) Querrere de Rouclys		
	(*castle/lordship*) High Peak		

County	Margaret of Anjou	Elizabeth Woodville	Elizabeth of York
Derbyshire (continued)	(*issue of the land*) Wynnelondes New liberties in Peak		
Dorset	E	**a, d, k**	**2**
	(*manor/town/barton/forest*) Gyllyngham	(*manor/town/barton*) Gyllyngham	Gyllyngham
		1	**5**
		(*manors/lordships*) Kingston Lacy Wimborne Shepwick Blandford Gussage	(*manor/lordship & hundred*) Pymperne (*manors/lordships*) Gussage Bohun Tarrant Gunville
Essex	A	**a, d, k**	**3**
	(*castle/township/manor*) Plecy	(*manors/lordships*) Bradwell, Havering-atte-Bower	(*manor*) Brettes
	(*manors*) High Ester, Waltham, Masshebury, Badowe, Dunmowe, Leighes, Wykes, Walden, Depeden (Debden), Quendon, Northampstead, Farnham, Shenfield (*bailiwicks*)	**c, d, k**	**2, 4**
		(*castle/manor/lordship*) Hadley	(*manors/lordships*) Great Waltham Badowe Masshebury Dunmowe
		i	
		(*castle/lordship/manor*) Hedyngham	

Essex (continued)	Honour of Tutbury, Lancaster and Leicester in co. Essex, Hertford, Middlesex, London, Surrey (*manor*)	(*lordship/manor*) Earls Colne, Benteley, Canfeld, Stanstede Monfichet	Leighes Farnham
	Wathersfield (Wethersfield?)	**l**	**2**
	B	(*castle/township/manor*) Plecy	(*manors/lordships*) Bradwell
	(*castle/lordship*) Colchester (*hundred*) Tendryng	(*manors*) High Ester, Wykes, Walden, Depeden, Quendon, Shenfield, Wethersfield (Wathersfield)	Havering-atte-Bower Hadley (*& castle*)
	D	**k, l**	
	(*lordship/manor*) Hadley (2 parts of manor) Bradwell, Havering-atte-Bower	(*manors*) Waltham, Masshebury, Badowe, Dunmowe, Leighes, Farnham	
		n	
		(*manors*) West Thorndon, Feldhous and Gyngraff (bought from Richard, duke of Gloucester but sold to Thomas, archbishop of Canterbury before 1482)	
		p	
		(*manor*) Woodham Ferrers	

County	Margaret of Anjou	Elizabeth Woodville	Elizabeth of York
Gloucestershire			**5**
			(*manors/lordships*) Lychelade
			Bardesley
			Brymmesfeld
			Mussarder (Misenden?)
			(*manors/lordships*) Charleton & Doughton
			Wynston
			Bisley
Hampshire (Southampton in the primary records)	**E**	**a, d**	**2**
	(*castle/lordship/manor/hundred*) Odiham	(*manors/lordships*) Lokerley Tuderley	(*castle/lordship/manor/hundred*) Odiham
		a, d, k	**5**
		(*castle/lordship/manor/hundred*) Odiham	(*manors/lordships*) Hooke Mortimer Worthy Mortimer
		l	
		Somborne Weston Hartley Longstock	

Herefordshire	A		5
	(*manor*) Yerkhull		(*manor/lordship*) Mawardyne Marcle
Hertfordshire	A	1	5
	(*castle/town*) Hertford	(*manors*)	(*manor/lordship*) Berkhamsted
	(*manors*)	Hertford (*& castle*)	Langley
	Hertfordyngbury	Hertfordyngbury	Kyngeslane
	Esyndon	Esyndon	
	Bayford	Bayford	
	D	Nuthamstead near Barkway	
	(*castles/lordships/manors*)	m	
	Berkhamsted	Weston by Baldok	
Huntingdonshire		c, d, e	
		Huntingdon (*castle and honour*)	
		m	
		(*manor*) Fennystanton, Hylton	
Kent	B	b, g	
	(*manor*) Myddelton	(*manor*) Plesaunce at Grenewiche	
	(*hundred*) Myddelton & Merden		
	F		
	(*manor*) Plesaunce at Grenewiche		

County	Margaret of Anjou	Elizabeth Woodville	Elizabeth of York
Leicestershire	A (*castle/town/lordship/honour*) Leicester (*manor/bailiwick*) Desseford, Shulton (*manor/borough/foreign bailiwick*) Hynkeley (*bailiwicks*) Glenfeld, Belgrave & Syleby, Carleton (*manor*) Stapulford agistment of park of Frith (*bailiwick*) Stapulford Hethelye, Honour of Leicester (*manors*) Foxston, Smeton, Langron, Swannyngton (*farms/mills*) town of Leicester	m (*manor*) Dysworth, Segrave	
Lincolnshire		i (*manors/lordships*) Sutton, Tydde	

London	A	g
	(*hospitality*) Blaunch Appelton	(*messuages/inn/tenement*) Ormonds Inn in London
	(*tenements*) Stywardesynne, parish of St Olav	
Middlesex	A	i
	(*manor*) Enfield	(*manors/lordships*) Busshy, Edgeware
	(*tenements*) Hakeneys (Hackney)	l
		(*manors*) Enfield, Hackney
		m
		(*manor*) Tyburn
Norfolk		l
		(listed as being in Suffolk/Cambridge)
		(*manors/lordships*) Wighton, Fakenham, Aylsham, Snettisham, Smithdon, Soham, Gimingham, Tunstead, Thetford, Rodmere, Methwold, Gallow, Brothercross, Beeston next the sea (Beeston Regis), Fulmodeston
		(*bailiwicks/hundreds*) North & South Erpingham, Elmsett, Somersham, Offton

County	Margaret of Anjou	Elizabeth Woodville	Elizabeth of York
Northamptonshire	D	a, d	7
	(*castle/lordship/manor*) Morend	(*castle/lordship/forest/bailiwick*) Rockyngham	(*town/manor/lordship*) Foderyngey
		(*herbages/pannages*) Benefeld (Binfeld)	(Fotheringhay – formerly held by queen's grandfather, Richard, duke of York)
	E	(*king's parks*) Brigstoke (Bryxstoke) & Cliffe	
	(*castle/lordship/manor/forest*) Rockyngham	c, d	
	(*town/manor*)	(*hundred/bailiff office*) Falwesley	
	Brigstoke (Bryxstoke)	(*manor*) Kyngesclyffe	
	(*woods/bailiwicks*) Cliffe & Brigstoke	(*town/manor/lordship*) Bryxstoke (Bryggestoke)	
		(*manor/lordship*) Gedyngton	
		l	
		(*castle/lordship/manor/hundred*) Higham Ferrers	
		(*manor*) Raunds	
		(*park*) Irchester	
		(*manors/lordships*) Rushden, Desborough, Weldon, Wardington, Passenham, Daventry, Rumbelow's in Daventry, Glatton, Holme	
		p	
		(*manor*) Brington	

Northamptonshire (continued)	**o** (*from Neal: shares in the Tresham lands – manors/lordships*) Rushton, Houghton Magna, Siwell, Liveden with lands/tenements Northampton, Rothwell, Kintresthorpe, Abindon, Ekton, Wendlingborough, Harrowdon Parva, Willougby, Asby Mars, Donnington, Barton Comitis, Churchbrampton, Hanging Houghton, Aldwincle, Stanwick, Ringstead, Rounds, Cotes, Denford, Knoston, Archestreet, Haslebeck (& *advowson*), Hannington, Binfield, Braddon (& *advowson*)
Oxfordshire	**A** (*manors*) Haseley, Kirtelyngton, Dadington, Piryton (Pyrton), Ascote **i (for 7 yrs)** (*lordship/manor*) Woodstock Hamborugh (Hamborough), Stonefeld, Bladon, Wotton (*hundred*) Wotton **l** (*manors*) Haseley, Kirtelyngton, Dadington, Piryton (Pyrton), Ascote
Salop (Shropshire)	**m** (*castle/town/manor*) Dynesbrau, Leon, Hewlyngton, Bromfeld, Yale, Wrexham, Almore and Stodysdene

County	Margaret of Anjou	Elizabeth Woodville	Elizabeth of York
Somerset			5
			(*forests*) Exmoor, Rach, Mindipp
			(*manor/lordship*) Odcombe
			(*manor/lordship & borough*) Milverton
			(*manor/lordship*) Heygrove (Hygrove)
			(*castle/borough*) Brugewater (Bridgwater)
			(*borough*) Warham
			(*manor/lordship*) Knolle
			Stuple and Criche
			Wyke
			Weymouth
			Portland
			Helwell
			Marshwood
			(*hundreds*) Roughborow, Russheme (?Bussheme), Hasellore

Staffordshire	**A**	**1**	
	(*castle/manor/honour*) Tutbury	(*bailiwick*) Honour of Tutbury	
	(*manors*)		
	Rolleston, Barton, Marchington Uttoxeter, Adgarseley		
	(*bailiwicks*) Acard (Rodman), New liberties		
	(*wards*)		
	Tutbury, Barton, Yoxhale Marchington, Uttoxeter		
Suffolk		**d**	**2**
		Great Wrattyng (Talworth Wrattyng)	Great Wrattyng (Talworth Wrattyng)
		i	
		Lavenham	
Surrey	**A**	**a, d, k**	**2**
	(*manor*) Walton	Benestede	Benestede
		Walton	Walton
		d, k	Charlewode
		Charlewode	
		f, g	
		(*manor/lordship/park/warren*)	
		Shene	
		(*king's lordships*)	

County	Margaret of Anjou	Elizabeth Woodville	Elizabeth of York
Surrey (continued)		Petirsham	
		Hamme	
		m	
		(*castle/domain/town/manor*) Reygate, Dorking	
		(*tolneth*) Guldeford, Suthwerk	
Sussex		**l**	
		(*manors/lordships*) Willingdon, Maresfield, East Grinstead, Seaford, Endlewick	
		(*messuage/virgate of land*) Bourn	
		(*bailiwick of port-reeve*) Pevensey, Southward, Westward, Cotlesward	
		(*bailiwick of court of castle-port*) Pevensey	
		m	
		(*demesnes/manors*)	
		Boseham, Funtyngdon, Stowghton, Stoke, Thorney, Wassyngton, Mechyng	
		(*castle/domain/town/borough/manor*) Lewes, Brembre, Shorham, Horsham, Seford, Pydynghoo	
		(*manor*)	

Sussex (continued)		Clayton, Alyngton, Worth, Middelton, Brighthelmestone, Pycombe, Iforde, Northeys, Kyngesbernes, Knappe, Westgrenestede, Bedyng and Cokefeld
	(*chase*) Cleres	
	(*park*) St Leonards, Worthe	
	(*hundreds*) Buttynghilstrete, Bercombe, Swanibergh, Holmestrowe, Yonesmere, Whalysbone, Ponynges, Fyssheresgate, Wyndham, Bretforde, Stenynge, Grenestede, Burbeche and Esewrith	
	(*sheriff's leet*) Nomanneslonde	
Warwickshire	**A**	**m**
	(*castle/lordship*) Kenelworth	(*manor*) Weston by Cheriton
Wiltshire	**B**	**a, d, k**
	(*castle/town/lordship*) Marleburgh	Cosseham
	(*forest*) Savernake	Marleburgh
	(*castle/town/park*) Devyse	Merston Meysy
	(*forests*) Melkesham, Pevesham	Devyse
		Roude
		(*forests*) Melkesham, Pevesham, Chippenham
		2
		Cosseham
		Marleburgh
		Selkesey (hundred)
		Merston Meysy
		Devyse
		Roude
		(*forests*) Melkesham, Pevesham, Chippenham

County	Margaret of Anjou	Elizabeth Woodville	Elizabeth of York
Wiltshire (continued)	C (apparently granted in bb – but not mentioned there) (*town/manor*) <u>Roude</u> (*forest*) <u>Chippenham</u>	c (*200 acres wood*) Hurst **d, k** Barton by Marleburgh (*forest*) <u>Savernake</u> (assarts) **k** Selkesey (hundred) **l** (*manor/lordship*) Easterton, Standen, Everleigh, Collingbourne, Aldbourne, Braden, Berwick, Trowbridge Oaksey, Poole, Manningford, Upavon	Barton by Marleburgh (*forest*) <u>Savernake</u> 5 (*manors/lordships*) Sevenhampton Highworth Cricklade Chelworth & Old Wootton Tockenham Winterbourne (Steepleton) Compton Somerford Keynes (*borough*) Wootton (*park/pasture*) Fasterne
Worcestershire	D (*manor/lordship/forest*) <u>Fekenham</u>	**c, d, k** (*manor/lordship/forest*) <u>Fekenham</u> **h** Cradeley Hagley	2 (*manor/lordship/forest*) <u>Fekenham</u> 5 (*manor/lordship*) Brymmesgrove Norton Odyngley Clyfton

Yorkshire	m	
	(*manors*) Donyngton, Thwayt	
Wales	G	e
	(*county, castle, lordship, with various properties as members*) Pembroke	Brekenok Haye (*king's lordships for the maintenance of Henry, duke of Buckingham & his brother Humphrey*)

Legend:

Margaret of Anjou:
A. RP v. 118–20 (19 Mar 1446)
B. Foedera XI; CPR 1446–52, 56 (24 Feb 1447)
C. CPR 1446–52, 559 (28 Feb 1452)
D. CPR 1452–61, 339–40 (3 Mar 1457). This is a ratification but they were all granted by parliament 19 Feb 1446/47. However, this grant does not appear in CPR 1446–52 even though it should have been recorded there. Berkhamsted is recorded in this patent roll as being in Buckinghamshire. It is located in Hertfordshire and is therefore listed as such in the appendix.
E. 'Henry VI: March 1453', in PROME, v-261. These properties were granted as compensation for the loss of Pembroke in 1453.
F. The grant relating to this property has not as yet been located. It was formerly owned by Humphrey, duke of Gloucester, and probably reverted back to the Crown as an attainted estate.
G. Originally granted in 1451 and valued in total as £400 2s 8d, this was revoked by the king and re-granted to Jasper Tudor in 1453.

Elizabeth Woodville:
a. CPR 1461–67, 430 (16 Mar 1465)
b. CPR 1461–67, 433 (22 Apr 1465)
c. CPR 1461–67, 445 (5 Jul 1465)
d. CPR 1461–67, 480-2 (31 Jan 1466). This grant invalidated previous grants of holdings to the queen.
e. CPR 1461–67, 464 (3 Sept 1465)
f. CPR 1461–67, 525 (21 Jul 1466)
g. CPR 1467–77, 64
h. CPR 1467–77, 419
i. CPR 1467–77, 543. These were shared lands.
j. CPR 1476–85, 169
k. CPR 1485–94, 75–7. These holdings were restored by Henry VII to Elizabeth Woodville as queen dowager.
l. 'Edward IV: June 1467', in PROME, v-628, no. 33 (7 Jul 1467). These were the lands known as the 'south parts'.
m. CCR 1476–85, 30. These were shares in the Huse quitclaim granted in 1476.
n. CCR 1476–85, 295. These lands were purchased outright in her own standing. The exact date they were sold is unclear but before 1482.
o. CPR 1467–77, 562. These were shares in the Tresham lands.
p. These holdings were the dower from her first marriage to Sir John Grey, Lancastrian supporter. As per CPR 1461–67, 533, these were held by the king in title and possession of his queen.

Elizabeth of York:
1. CPR 1467–77, 44
2. CPR 1485–94, 75–6 (Mar 1486); *Materials for a History of the Reign of Henry VII*, vol. II, 148–9. These lands were transferred from Elizabeth Woodville as restored by Henry VII. The transfer date is uncertain but, in this source, it does not read as if ownership by the new queen consort is confirmed by the king, only that monies and profits are to be paid to the queen. Note that, as per **4** and **6** below, letters patent dated 26 Nov 1487 granted Elizabeth of York these lands.
3. CPR 1485–94, 293. These holdings were granted during the minority of Edward, son and heir of George, duke of Clarence, and Isabel Neville, his wife.

4. CPR 1485–94, 369–70. These holdings are mentioned as having been granted on 26 Nov, 3 Henry VII (26 Nov 1487).
5. CPR 1485–94, 369–70; 'Henry VII: October 1495'; in PROME, vi-462. These holdings were granted to the queen as part of the reversion of lands on the death of Cecily, duchess of York, in May 1495.
6. CPR 1485–94, 378
7. CPR 1494–1509, 14 (27 Mar 1495)

APPENDIX 2: THE QUEENS' FEE-FARMS – A COMPOSITE LIST

Spellings used in this appendix are as in the sources, modern spelling in brackets here: Bolyngdene (Bullingdon), Cokeham (Cookham), Gedyngton (Geddington), Godyngton (Goddington), Hamstede Marshall (Hamstead Marshall), Hedyngton (Hedington), Kyngesthorpe (Kingsthorpe), Kyngesclyff (Kingscliff), Kyngton (Kington), Radewell (Radwell), Scardeburgh (Scarborough).

Place-name	Margaret of Anjou	Elizabeth Woodville[1]	Elizabeth of York[2]	Expected amount (for all queens unless otherwise indicated)		
				£	s	d
Bristol (town)	✓[3]		✓	102	15	6
Bedford (town)		✓	✓	20		

[1] Most of the listed fee-farms were included in the following grants: CPR 1461–67, 480–2 (31 January 1466); RP v. 628 (7 July 1467) – Huntingdon & Godmanchester. Note that several farms (as indicated) were originally granted in 1465 but retracted in 1466.

[2] CPR 1485–94, 75–7. Many of Elizabeth Woodville's fee-farms were restored in dower to her as queen dowager by Henry VII in 1486. *Materials for a History of the Reign of Henry VII*, vol. II, 148–9. All the queen dowager's lands and fee-farms were transferred to Elizabeth of York as her part of her dower when the queen dowager retired to Bermondsey Abbey in 1487. Those fee-farms restored to Elizabeth Woodville are present in both columns for Elizabeth Woodville and Elizabeth of York.

[3] CCR 1447–54, 222–5 (14 July 1451).

Place-name	Margaret of Anjou	Elizabeth Woodville	Elizabeth of York	Expected amount
Norwich (town)	✓ (£66 13s 4d)*	✓	✓[4] (£22 19s 3¾d)	20
Cambridge University – assize of ale and beer		✓		10
Abbey of St Albans		✓	✓	33 6 8
Radewell	✓[5]	✓	✓***	15
Barton of Bristol (manor and hundred)		✓	✓	60
Falwesley (manor)		✓		15
Ipswich (town)	✓ (£33 6s 8d)*	✓	✓	40
Abbey of Bury St Edmunds		✓	✓	40
Lowestoft (manor) & Luddynglond (hundred)		✓	✓***	9 16 9

4 Increased to £22 19s 3¾d in 1486 when the estate was re-granted to Elizabeth Woodville as queen dowager and remained the same on transfer to Elizabeth of York.
5 CPR 1452–61, 339–40. The specific value of this fee-farm was not stated in the grant nor was it recorded as received in Margaret's extant household account.

Nottingham (town)	✓ (£40)*	✓	54	12
Kyngsthorpe (town)	✓ (£10)** (£30)*	✓	40	
Derby (town)	✓ (£26 13s 4d)*	✓	40	
Hedyngton (manor) & Bolyngdene/Bullingdon (hundred)		✓	40	
Dorchester (town)		✓	20	
Powestock (manor)		✓***	12	
Calne (hundred and a water-mill)		✓***	15	
Oxford (town)		✓	35	
Southampton (town)	✓ (£100)*	✓	46	

6 Reduced to £34 12s in 1486 when the estate was re-granted to Elizabeth Woodville as queen dowager and remained the same on transfer to Elizabeth of York.

7 Reduced to £30 in 1486 when the estate was re-granted to Elizabeth Woodville as queen dowager and remained the same on transfer to Elizabeth of York.

Place-name	Margaret of Anjou	Elizabeth Woodville	Elizabeth of York	Expected amount
Godyngton (2 parts farm, 1 part manor)		✓	✓***	10
Shaftesbury (town)		✓	✓***	12[8]
Kyngton (farm)		✓	✓	12
Goscote (wapentake)		✓	✓***	5
Tamworth (moiety of town with increment)		✓	✓***	5 16
Framlond (hundred)		✓	✓***	12 18 5½
Peverell, Boulogne, Hagenet (honour)		✓	✓	5 8 4
Cambridge (town with increment)		✓	✓	70
Malmesbury (town with three hundreds)		✓	✓***	20
Forde (manor)		✓	✓	12
Shrewsbury (town)		✓	✓	20 17 6

[8] The original amount granted to Elizabeth Woodville on 5 July 1465 of £13 was soon after reduced to £12.

Rowley (manor)	✓***	10	6	8
Kynefare & Storton (manors and forest)	✓	9		
Huntingdon (town)	✓	63		
Godmanchester, co. Huntingdon	✓	120		
Andover, co. Hampshire (town)	✓[9]	unknown		
Wick, co. Hertford (town)	✓	unknown		
Gunthorp (town)	✓[10]	26	13	4
Queenhithe, London	✓	40		
(£10)^ (£30)*				
Colchester (town)	✓^	25		
Northampton (town)	✓^	10		

9 SR, vol. II, 595–7. The fee-farms for the towns of Andover and Wick were transferred to Elizabeth of York on the reversion of the estates of the late Cecily Neville, duchess of York in 1492. The values are not stated in the grant nor are revenues recorded in the extant account for the queen. The receivers' accounts for the regions that these towns are located in remains to be found.

10 RP v. 118–20 (19 Mar 1446). This is the only fee-farm listed in Margaret of Anjou's original dower grant of 1446.

Place-name	Margaret of Anjou	Elizabeth Woodville	Elizabeth of York	Expected amount
Scardeburgh (town) & Walgrave (manor)	✓ ^			27
Abbey of Oseney	✓ ^			10
Benham Lovell		✓ ^^		13
Kyngesclyff	✓ **	✓ (£20) ^^		40
Briggestoke	✓ **	✓ ^^		20
Gedyngton		✓ ^^		24
Wrattyng (Talworth Wrattyng)		✓ ^^		7
Seven hundreds of Cokeham & Bray		✓ ^^		8
Two parts of Swallowfield		✓ ^^		13 6 8
Hamstede Marshall		✓ ^^		10
Corby	✓ **			5
Halesowen			✓[11]	

[11] Halesowen is recorded in Elizabeth of York's Privy Purse expense account of 1502–3 as having paid a fee-farm of 103s 4d. However, since no trace of the grant in the records has been found, it is unclear how the queen acquired this fee-farm or whether the amount expected was paid in full.

Expected composite total of fee-farms *per annum*:

Margaret of Anjou – £628 2s 2d.
Elizabeth Woodville as queen consort – £1056 17s 10½d (*excludes farms retracted in 1466 grant*).
Elizabeth of York – £761 17s 2¼d (*excludes the fee-farm of Halesowen and the fee-farms from the lands and holdings of Cecily Neville, duchess of York as the amounts are unknown*).

Legend:

^ Fee-farms granted to Margaret of Anjou in 1447, totalling £82.
^^ Fee-farms granted to Elizabeth Woodville in 1465 but retracted in the 1466 grant since the manors/lordships were granted instead.
* Fee-farms granted to Margaret of Anjou in 1453 in recompense for the loss of the Pembroke estates, totalling £326 13s 4d.
** Group of fee-farms originally granted to Margaret of Anjou in 1447, but which she sued for livery only in 1453, totalling £75. CPR 1452–61, 339–40.
*** Group of fee-farms not recorded as paid either in full or partially in Elizabeth of York's Privy Purse expense account.

APPENDIX 3: EXTANT MANORIAL DOCUMENTS CONSULTED

The following tables list local official accounts consulted for each manor.

Manor of Hertingfordbury, Hertford

Reference	Description	Year	Location	Additional Information
Court Roll 21/7	Reeve account	1456–57	HHLA	NRA 32925 Gascoyne-Cecil
DL29/53/1007	Reeve account	1458–59	TNA	
DL29/53/1008	Reeve account	1460–61	TNA	
DL29/53/1009	Bailiff account	1461–62	TNA	
DE/P/T638	Reeve account	1462–63	HALS	NRA 26283 Cowper
DL29/53/1010	Bailiff account	1464–65	TNA	
DL29/53/1011	Bailiff account	1466–67	TNA	
DL29/53/1012-1017	Bailiff accounts	1468–74	TNA	
DL29/53/1018	Bailiff account	unclear	TNA	Header is torn so year is unclear, possibly 1475–76
DL29/53/1019	Bailiff account	1475–76	TNA	
DL29/53/1020-1021	Bailiff account	1477–79	TNA	
Accts 1/1	Rental	1477	HHLA	NRA 32925 Gascoyne-Cecil

Manor of Hertingfordbury, Hertford (continued)

Reference	Description	Year	Location	Additional Information
Court Roll 21/11	Bailiff account	1480–81	HHLA	NRA 32925 Gascoyne-Cecil
Court Roll 19/9	Bailiff account	1484–85	HHLA	NRA 32925 Gascoyne-Cecil
Court Roll 21/18	Bailiff account	1485–86	HHLA	NRA 32925 Gascoyne-Cecil
DE/P/T646	Court roll	1485–1508	HALS	
Court Roll 19/12	Bailiff account	1489–90	HHLA	NRA 32925 Gascoyne-Cecil
Court Roll 22/5	Bailiff account	1493–94	HHLA	NRA 32925 Gascoyne-Cecil
Court Roll 21/10	Bailiff account	1495–96	HHLA	NRA 32925 Gascoyne-Cecil

Manor of Pleshey, Essex

Reference	Description	Year	Location	Additional Information
SC6/1093/15	Bailiff account	1452–53	TNA	
DL29/43/829	Bailiff account	1454–55	TNA	
DL29/43/830	Bailiff account	Sep 1460–Mar 1461	TNA	
DL29/43/831-833	Bailiff account	1461–64	TNA	
DL29/43/835-837	Bailiff account	1464–67	TNA	
SC6/1093/16	Bailiff account	1467–68	TNA	
DL29/43/838-840	Bailiff account	1468–71	TNA	

DL29/44/841-846	Bailiff account	1471-77	TNA
DL29/44/848-851	Bailiff account	1477-81	TNA
DL30/71/882	Court roll	1461-84	TNA
DL30/72/891	Court roll	1483-85	TNA

Honour of Tutbury manor, Staffordshire

Reference	Description	Year	Location	Additional Information
DL29/369/6179	Reeve account	1440-41	TNA	
DL29/369/6181	Reeve account	1441-42	TNA	
DL29/370/6184	Reeve account	1444-45	TNA	
DL29/370/6186	Reeve account	1445-46	TNA	
DL29/370/6189	Reeve account	1448-49	TNA	
SC6/988/21	Reeve account	1461-62	TNA	
DL29/371/6200	Reeve account	1475-76	TNA	
DL29/372/6202	Reeve account	1476-77	TNA	
DL29/372/6204	Reeve account	1478-79	TNA	
DL29/372/6206	Reeve account	1480-81	TNA	
DL29/372/6208	Reeve account	1481-82	TNA	

Honour of Tutbury manor, Staffordshire (continued)

Reference	Description	Year	Location	Additional Information
DL29/372/6209	Reeve account	1482–83	TNA	
DL29/373/6212	Reeve account	1483–84	TNA	
DL29/373/6213	Reeve account	1484–85	TNA	

Manor of Gillingham, Dorset

Reference	Description	Year	Location	Additional Information
DL29/724/11800	Bailiff account	1474–75	TNA	
DL29/724/11801	Bailiff account	1477–78	TNA	Not labelled in TNA catalogue as including Gillingham account but manuscript evidence proves otherwise
DL29/724/11802	Bailiff account	1478–79	TNA	Not labelled in TNA catalogue as including Gillingham account but manuscript evidence proves otherwise
DL29/724/11803	Bailiff account	1483–84	TNA	
SC 6/HENVII/1135	Bailiff account	1492–93	TNA	
SC 6/HENVII/1136	Bailiff account	1494–95	TNA	Not labelled in TNA catalogue as including Gillingham account but manuscript evidence proves otherwise

| SC 6/HENVII/1137 | Bailiff account | 1496–97 | TNA | Not labelled in TNA catalogue as including Gillingham account but manuscript evidence proves otherwise |
| SC 6/HENVII/1138 | Bailiff account | 1502–03 | TNA | |

Manor of Feckenham, Worcestershire

Reference	Description	Year	Location	Additional Information
SC6/1068/6	Receiver account Reeve account (separate)	1461–66	TNA	
SC6/HENVII/982	Receiver account Reeve account (separate)	1490–92	TNA	
SC6/HENVII/1056	Reeve account	1493–95	TNA	
SC6/HENVII/983	Receiver account Reeve account (separate)	1494–96	TNA	
SC6/HENVII/984	Receiver account Reeve account (separate)	1495–97	TNA	
SC6/HENVII/985	Receiver account Reeve account (separate)	1496–98	TNA	
SC6/HENVII/986	Receiver account Reeve account (separate)	1498–1500	TNA	

Manor of Feckenham, Worcestershire (continued)

Reference	Description	Year	Location	Additional Information
SC6/HENVII/987	Receiver account Reeve account (separate)	1499–1501	TNA	
SC6/HENVII/988	Receiver account Reeve account (separate)	1500–02	TNA	
SC6/HENVII/1375	Reeve account	1502–04	TNA	
SC6/HENVII/1213	Reeve account	1504–06	TNA	

Manor of Mashbury, Essex

Reference	Description	Year	Location	Additional Information
DL29/42/825	Farmer account	1438–39	TNA	
DL29/43/826-828	Farmer account	1439–43	TNA	
SC6/1093/15	Farmer account	1452–53	TNA	
DL29/43/829	Reeve account	1454–55	TNA	
DL29/43/830-831	Farmer account	1460–62	TNA	
DL29/43/833	Farmer account	1462–63	TNA	
DL29/43/835-837	Farmer account	1464–67	TNA	
SC6/1093/16	Farmer account	1467–68	TNA	
DL29/43/838-840	Farmer account	1468–71	TNA	

| DL29/44/841–846 | Farmer account | 1471–77 | TNA |
| DL29/44/848–851 | Farmer account | 1477–83 | TNA |

Manor of Havering-atte-Bower, Essex[1]

Reference	Description	Year	Location	Additional Information
DL29/41/794	Bailiff account	1474–75	TNA	
DL29/41/796	Bailiff account	1477–78	TNA	
DL29/41/797	Bailiff account	1478–79	TNA	
DL29/41/798	Bailiff account	1479–80	TNA	
SC6/1094/6	Bailiff account	1480–81	TNA	
SC6/1094/7	Bailiff account	1481–82	TNA	
DL29/41/799	Bailiff account	1483–84	TNA	Includes two separate accounts
D/DU 102/44-46	Court roll	1453–56	Essex Record Office	
D/DU 102/47-50	Court roll	1464–68	Essex Record Office	
D/DU 102/134	Court roll	1468–69	Essex Record Office	

1 See McIntosh, *Autonomy and Community*, Appendix III, for a list of surviving rolls of the Havering Manor Court to 1500.

The following tables list the central official accounts consulted for this study. All listed documents are stored at The National Archives, London (TNA), except 12172 and 12173, which are located at the Westminster Abbey Library, Muniment Collection (WAM).

Receiver Accounts (ordered by region)

Reference	Region	Year	Landowner	Additional Information
DL29/41/800	Essex, Surrey, Kent, London	1464–73	Elizabeth Woodville	Includes several receivers accounts from years 1464-66
DL29/41/801	Essex, Surrey, Kent, London	1475–77	Elizabeth Woodville	Not labelled in TNA as queen's receiver account but manuscript evidence proves otherwise
SC6/1094/5	Essex, Surrey, Kent, London	1479–81	Elizabeth Woodville	Not labelled in TNA as queen's receiver account but manuscript evidence proves otherwise
DL29/41/802	Essex, Surrey, Kent, London	Mar 1482–Jun 1484	Elizabeth Woodville/ Crown	Covers the last two years of Edward IV's reign, Edward V's three months' reign and Richard III's first year as king Not labelled in TNA as queen's receiver account but manuscript evidence proves otherwise
DL29/58/1103	Essex, Hertford, Middlesex	1453–54	Margaret of Anjou	Not labelled in TNA as queen's receiver account but manuscript evidence proves otherwise
DL29/58/1104-1107	Essex, Hertford, Middlesex	1455–59	Margaret of Anjou	Not labelled in TNA as queen's receiver account but manuscript evidence proves otherwise

Reference	Counties	Date	Queen	Notes
DL29/58/1108	Essex, Hertford, Middlesex	Sep 1460–Feb 1461	Crown	
DL29/59/1109-1111	Essex, Hertford, Middlesex	1461–64	Crown	
DL29/59/1112-1114	Essex, Hertford, Middlesex	Mar 1464–Feb 1467	Elizabeth Woodville	Not labelled in TNA as queen's receiver account but manuscript evidence proves otherwise
SC6/1093/17	Essex, Hertford, Middlesex	1467–68	Elizabeth Woodville	
DL29/59/1115-1123	Essex, Hertford, Middlesex	1469–77	Elizabeth Woodville	Not labelled in TNA catalogue as queen's receiver account but manuscript evidence proves otherwise
DL29/44/847	Essex	1476–77	Elizabeth Woodville	Manuscript indicates this is the account of Thomas Cranford, receiver for Essex
DL29/59/1124	Essex, Hertford, Middlesex	1479–80	Elizabeth Woodville	Not labelled in TNA catalogue as queen's receiver account but manuscript evidence proves otherwise
DL29/59/1125	Essex, Hertford, Middlesex	1480–81	Elizabeth Woodville	Not labelled in TNA catalogue as queen's receiver account but manuscript evidence proves otherwise
DL29/59/1126	Essex, Hertford, Middlesex	Mar 1482–Jun 1484	Elizabeth Woodville	Not labelled in TNA catalogue as queen's receiver account but manuscript evidence proves otherwise
SC6/HENVII/141	Essex, Suffolk	1487–88	Elizabeth of York	
SC6/HENVII/1189-95	Essex, Suffolk	1489–95	Elizabeth of York	
SC6/HENVII/1196-97	Essex, Suffolk	1497–98	Elizabeth of York	

Receiver Accounts (continued)

Reference	Region	Year	Landowner	Additional Information
SC6/HENVII/1198-1200	Essex, Suffolk	1500–03	Elizabeth of York	
SC6/HENVII/252-54	Hertford	1500–03	Elizabeth of York	
SC6/1093/11	South Parts	1445–46	Margaret of Anjou	
SC6/1093/12	South Parts	1446–47	Margaret of Anjou	
SC6/1093/13	South Parts	1448–49	Margaret of Anjou	
DL29/710/11454-11459	South Parts	Sep 1459–Feb 1465	Crown	
DL29/711/11460	South Parts	1465–66	Elizabeth Woodville	Only includes Wiltshire, Dorset and Somerset lands
DL29/711/11461	South Parts	1465–66	Elizabeth Woodville	Not labelled in TNA catalogue as queen's receiver account but manuscript evidence proves otherwise
				Only includes Kingston Lacy in Dorset
				Not labelled in TNA catalogue as queen's receiver account but manuscript evidence proves otherwise
DL29/711/11462-11463	South Parts	1465–67	Elizabeth Woodville	Not labelled in TNA catalogue as queen's receiver account but manuscript evidence proves otherwise

DL29/711/11464-11476	South Parts	1468–82	Elizabeth Woodville	Not labelled in TNA catalogue as queen's receiver account but manuscript evidence proves otherwise
DL29/724/11804	South parts of Crown	1466–67	Elizabeth Woodville	Not labelled in TNA catalogue as queen's receiver account but manuscript evidence proves otherwise
DL29/724/11805-11817	South parts of Crown	1468–82	Elizabeth Woodville	Not labelled in TNA catalogue as queen's receiver account but manuscript evidence proves otherwise
SC6/HENVII/1140	South parts of Crown	1496–97	Elizabeth of York	
SC6/HENVII/1141	South parts of Crown	1503–04	Crown	
SC6/HENVII/982	Worcester	1490–91	Elizabeth of York	
SC6/HENVII/983-985	Worcester	1494–97	Elizabeth of York	
SC6/HENVII/986-988	Worcester	1498–1501	Elizabeth of York	

Miscellaneous Receiver Accounts

Reference	Year	Landowner	Additional Information
DL28/27/11	1473–74	Elizabeth Woodville	Compiled by Thomas Stidolf to record fee-farm receipts and receipts of queen's gold
DL28/27/11A	1481–82	Elizabeth Woodville	Compiled by Thomas Stidolf to record fee-farm receipts and receipts of queen's gold

Accounts of Arrears

Reference	Year	Landowner	Additional Information
SC6/1093/14	1449–50	Margaret of Anjou	
SC6/1094/8	1469–70	Elizabeth Woodville	
SC6/1094/9	1470–71	Elizabeth Woodville	
SC6/1094/10	1471–72	Elizabeth Woodville	

Land Valors

Reference	Year	Landowner	Additional Information
DL29/735/12052	1464–65	Elizabeth Woodville	
DL29/735/12053	Unknown	Elizabeth Woodville	Labelled in TNA catalogue as 1462–63, unclear because manuscript header is damaged; Myers asserted that this is the matching land valor for the extant household account dated 1466–67.
DL29/735/12054	Unknown	Possibly Elizabeth Woodville	Officials listed in this manuscript are similar to officials listed in other land valors for this queen
DL29/735/12056	1472–73	Elizabeth Woodville	Not labelled in TNA catalogue as queen's land valor but manuscript evidence proves otherwise
DL29/735/12057	1472–73	Elizabeth Woodville	
DL29/736/12059	Unknown	Elizabeth Woodville	Missing header; could be 1471–72
DL29/736/12064	Unknown	Possibly Elizabeth Woodville	Missing header; Officials listed in this manuscript are similar to officials listed in other land valors for this queen

DL29/736/12067	1488–89	Elizabeth of York	
DL29/736/12068	1489–90	Elizabeth of York	
12172	1496–97	Elizabeth of York	This valor is for all the lands owned by Elizabeth of York that were previously owned by Cecily Neville, duchess of York
12173	1496–97	Elizabeth of York	This valor is for all the lands owned by Elizabeth of York except for the York lands previously owned by Cecily Neville, duchess of York

SELECT BIBLIOGRAPHY

MANUSCRIPTS

Cambridge: St John's College Archives
SJLM/6/8
SJLM/9/2/1

Chelmsford, Essex: Essex Record Office
D/DU 102/44-50
D/DU 102/134

Hatfield, Hertfordshire: Hatfield House Library and Archives
Court Rolls 19/9, 19/12, 21/7, 21/10, 21/11, 21/18, 22/5

Hertford, Hertfordshire: Hertfordshire Archives and Local Studies
DE/P/T638, 646

London: British Library
Cotton MS Vespasian C XIV, folio 272b

London: The National Archives
C66
DL28
DL29
DL30
E5
E19
E36
E101
E163
E298
E404
LC2
SC6

London: Westminster Abbey Library, Muniment Collection
12172, 12173

Select Bibliography

CALENDARS

Calendar of the Charter Rolls preserved in the Public Record Office. AD 1427–1516, with an appendix, *AD 1215–1288*. London: His Majesty's Stationery Office, 1927.

Calendar of the Close Rolls, Edward III: Volume 10: 1354–1360. Edited by H. C. Maxwell Lyte. London: His Majesty's Stationery Office, 1908.

Calendar of the Close Rolls, Henry VI: Volume 5: 1447–1454. Edited by C. T. Flower. London: His Majesty's Stationery Office, 1947.

Calendar of the Close Rolls, Edward IV: Volume 1: 1461–1468. Edited by W. H. B. Bird and K. H. Ledward. London: His Majesty's Stationery Office, 1949.

Calendar of the Close Rolls, Edward IV: Volume 2: 1468–1476. Edited by W. H. B. Bird and K. H. Ledward. London: Her Majesty's Stationery Office, 1953.

Calendar of the Close Rolls, Edward IV, Edward V, Richard III 1476–1485. Edited by K. H. Ledward. London: Her Majesty's Stationery Office, 1954.

Calendar of Inquisitions Post Mortem: Henry VII, Volume 3: 21-24 Henry VII 1506–1509 with appendix covering additions 1485–1509. London: Her Majesty's Stationery Office 1955.

Calendar of the Patent Rolls, Edward III, Volume 2: 1330–1334. London: His Majesty's Stationery Office, 1893.

Calendar of the Patent Rolls, Edward III, Volume 3: 1334–1338. London: His Majesty's Stationery Office, 1895.

Calendar of the Patent Rolls, Edward III, Volume 8: 1348–1350. London: His Majesty's Stationery Office, 1905.

Calendar of the Patent Rolls, Henry IV, Volume 2: 1401–1405. London: His Majesty's Stationery Office, 1905.

Calendar of the Patent Rolls, Henry IV, Volume 3: 1405–1408. London: His Majesty's Stationery Office, 1907.

Calendar of the Patent Rolls, Henry IV, Volume 4: 1408–1413. London: His Majesty's Stationery Office, 1909.

Calendar of the Patent Rolls, Henry VI, Volume 4: 1441–1446. London: His Majesty's Stationery Office, 1908.

Calendar of the Patent Rolls, Henry VI, Volume 5: 1446–1452. London: His Majesty's Stationery Office, 1909.

Calendar of the Patent Rolls, Henry VI, Volume 6: 1452–1461. London: His Majesty's Stationery Office, 1910.

Calendar of the Patent Rolls, Edward IV, Volume 1: 1461–1467. London: His Majesty's Stationery Office, 1897.

Calendar of the Patent Rolls, Edward IV/Henry VI, Volume 1: 1467–1477. London: His Majesty's Stationery Office, 1900.

Calendar of the Patent Rolls, Edward IV, Henry VI, Richard III: 1467–1477. London: His Majesty's Stationery Office, 1901.

Calendar of the Patent Rolls, Henry VII, Volume 1: 1485–1494. London: His Majesty's Stationery Office, 1914.

Select Bibliography

Calendar of the Patent Rolls, Henry VII, Volume 2: 1494–1509. London: His Majesty's Stationery Office, 1916.

PRINTED PRIMARY SOURCES

The Antiquarian Repertory, Vol. 4. Edited by F. Grose and T. Astle. London, Edward Jeffery, 1807–8.

'Appendix XV: The Record of Bluemantle Pursuivant, 1471–1472'. In Charles Lethbridge Kingsford, *English Historical Literature in the Fifteenth Century: with an Appendix of Chronicles and Historical Pieces Hitherto for the Most Part Unpublished*, 379–88. New York: Burt Franklin, 1962, reprint of 1913 edition.

The Chamber Books of Henry VII and Henry VIII, 1485–1521. Edited by M. M. Condon, S. P. Harper, L. Liddy, S. Cunningham and J. Ross, https://www.tudorchamberbooks.org

A Collection of Ordinances and Regulations for the Government of the Royal Household: Made in Divers Reigns, From King Edward III to King William and Queen Mary, Also Receipts in Ancient Cookery. London: John Nichols for the Society of Antiquaries, 1790.

The Coronation of Elizabeth Wydeville, Queen Consort of Edward IV, on May 26th 1465: A Contemporary Account Set Forth from a XV Century Manuscript. Edited by George Smith. Cliftonville: Gloucester Reprints, 1975, first printed 1935.

The Coventry Leet Book or Mayor's Register. Edited by M. D. Harris. EETS. Original Series, no. 134. London: Kegan Paul, 1907–13.

de Pisan, Christine. *The Treasure of the City of Ladies; or, The Book of the Three Virtues*. Translated by S. Lawson. Harmondsworth: Penguin, 1985.

English Historical Documents, Volume IV, 1327–1485. Edited by A. R. Myers. London: Eyre & Spottiswoode, 1969.
  'No. 159 "Margaret prepares for war: the battle of Blore Heath, 1459"', 281–2.
  'No. 576 "Anonymous advice to investors in land in the fifteenth century"', 1012–13.

FitzNigel, Richard. *De Necessariis Observantiis Scaccarii Dialogus commonly called Dialogus de Scaccario*. Edited by Arthur Hughes, C. G. Crump and C. Johnson. Oxford: Clarendon Press, 1902.

———. *Dialogus de Scaccario: The Dialogue of the Exchequer; Constitutio Domus Regis: Disposition of the King's Household*. Edited and translated by Emilie Amt and S. D. Church. Oxford: Oxford University Press, 2007.

Gerald of Wales. *The Journey through Wales/The Description of Wales*. Edited and translated by Lewis Thorpe. London: Penguin, 1978.

The Great Chronicle of London. Edited by A. H. Thomas and I. D. Thornley. Gloucester: Alan Sutton, 1983.

Leland, John. *De Rebus Britannicis Collectanea*, Vol. IV. Edited by T. Hearne. London: Benjamin White, 1774.

Select Bibliography

Letters and Papers, Foreign and Domestic, Henry VIII, Volume 1, 1509–1514. Edited by J. S. Brewer. London: His Majesty's Stationery Office, 1920. British History Online, http://www.british-history.ac.uk/letters-papers-hen8/vol1.

The Letters of Margaret of Anjou. Edited by Helen Maurer and B. M. Cron. Woodbridge: Boydell Press, 2019.

Letters of Queen Margaret of Anjou and Bishop Beckington and others. Edited by Cecil Monro. New York: Johnson Reprint Corp., 1968, reprint of 1863 edition.

Letters of the Queens of England, 1100–1547. Edited by Anne Crawford. Stroud: Sutton, 1994.

Materials for a History of the Reign of Henry VII, 2 volumes. Edited by William Campbell. London: Longman, 1877.

Oschinsky, Dorothea. *Walter of Henley and Other Treatises on Estate Management and Accounting.* Oxford: Clarendon Press, 1971.

Parliament Rolls of Medieval England. Edited by Chris Given-Wilson, Paul Brand, Seymour Phillips, Mark Ormrod, Geoffrey Martin, Anne Curry and Rosemary Horrox. Woodbridge: Boydell Press, 2005. British History Online, http://www.british-history.ac.uk/no-series/parliament-rolls-medieval.

Paston Letters and Papers of the Fifteenth Century, 3 parts. Edited by Norman Davis. Oxford; New York: Oxford University Press for the Early English Text Society, Supplementary Series 20–2, 2004.

The Privy Purse Expenses of Elizabeth of York. Edited by Nicholas Harris Nicolas. London: Pickering, 1830.

Proceedings and Ordinances of the Privy Council of England, vol. VI, 22 Henry VI 1443 to 39 Henry VI 1461. Edited by N. H. Nicolas. London: Spottiswoode, 1837.

Prynne, William. *Aurum Reginae; or A Compendious Tractate, and Chronological Collection of Records in the Tower, and Court of Exchequer Concerning Queen-gold.* London: Ratcliffe, 1668.

The Receyt of the Ladie Kateryne. Edited by Gordon Kipling. EETS. Original Series, no. 296. Oxford: Oxford University Press for the Early English Text Society, 1990.

Rotuli Parliamentorum, ut et petitiones, et placita in Parliamento tempore Edwardi R.I. [ad finem Henrici R.VII.], 6 vols. London, House of Lords Record Office, 1767–77.

Rymer's Foedera, 5 vols, (volumes 8–12). Edited by Thomas Rymer. London: Apud Joannem Neulme, 1739–1745. British History Online, http://www.british-history.ac.uk/rymer-foedera/.

Smith, Thomas. *De Republica Anglorum: the maner of governement or policie of the realme of Englande.* London: Henrie Midleton for Gregorie Seton, 1583. https://quod.lib.umich.edu/e/eebo/A12533.0001.001/1:3.11?rgn=div2;view=fulltext.

Statutes of the Realm, 11 volumes. London: Great Britain Record Commission, 1810–28.

Select Bibliography

The Travels of Leo of Rozmital: through Germany, Flanders, England, France, Spain, Portugal and Italy 1465–1467. Edited and translated by Malcolm Letts. Cambridge: Cambridge University Press for the Hakluyt Society, 1957.

SECONDARY WORKS

Adams, Simon. 'Baronial Contexts? Continuity and Change in the Noble Affinity, 1400–1600'. In *The End of the Middle Ages? England in the Fifteenth and Sixteenth Centuries*, edited by J. L. Watts, 155–97. Stroud: Sutton, 1998.

Akkerman, Nadine, and Birgit Houben, eds. *The Politics of Female Households: Ladies-in-Waiting Across Early Modern Europe*. Leiden: Brill, 2013.

Archer, Rowena E. '"How ladies ... who live on their manors ought to manage their households and estates": Women as Landholders and Administrators in the Later Middle Ages'. In *Woman Is a Worthy Wight: Women in English Society c. 1200–1500*, edited by P. J. P. Goldberg, 149–81. Stroud: Sutton, 1992.

Bailey, Mark. *The English Manor, c.1200–c.1500*. Manchester: Manchester University Press, 2002.

Baker, Alan. 'Changes in the Later Middle Ages'. In *A New Historical Geography of England*, edited by H. C. Darby, 186–247. Cambridge: Cambridge University Press, 1973.

Baldwin, David. *Elizabeth Woodville: Mother of the Princes in the Tower*. Stroud: Sutton, 2002.

Baldwin, J. F. 'The Household Administration of Henry Lacy and Thomas of Lancaster'. *EHR* 42 (1927): 180–200.

Bárány, Attila. 'Medieval Queens and Queenship: A Retrospective on Income and Power'. In *Annual of Medieval Studies at the CEU*, 149–99. CEU, Budapest, 2013.

Bean, J. M. W. *The Estates of the Percy Family 1416–1537*. London: Oxford University Press, 1958.

Beattie, Cordelia, and Matthew Frank Stevens, eds. *Married Women and the Law in Premodern Northwest Europe*. Woodbridge: Boydell Press, 2013.

Beer, Michelle. 'A Queenly Affinity? Catherine of Aragon's Estates and Henry VIII's Great Matter'. *Historical Research* 91, no. 253 (Aug. 2018): 426–45.

———. *Queenship at the Renaissance Courts of Britain: Catherine of Aragon and Margaret Tudor, 1503–1533*. Woodbridge: Boydell Press, 2018.

Bell, Henry E. *An Introduction to the History and Records of the Court of Wards and Liveries*. London: Cambridge University Press, 1953.

Bennett, H. S. 'The Reeve and the Manor in the Fourteenth Century'. *EHR* 41, no. 163 (Jul. 1926): 358–65.

Birrell, Jean R. 'Deer and Deer Farming in Medieval England'. *The Agricultural History Review* 40, no. 2 (1992): 112–26.

———. 'The Forest Economy of the Honour of Tutbury in the Fourteenth and Fifteenth Centuries'. *University of Birmingham Historical Journal* 8 (1962): 114–34.

Select Bibliography

———. 'The Honour of Tutbury in the Fourteenth and Fifteenth Centuries'. Unpublished MA thesis, University of Birmingham, 1962.

———. 'Procuring, Preparing and Serving Venison in Late Medieval England'. In *Food in Medieval England: Diet and Nutrition*, edited by C. M. Woolgar, D. Serjeantson and T. Waldron, 176–88. Oxford, New York: Oxford University Press, 2006.

Blanchard, I. S. W. 'Economic Change in Derbyshire in the Late Middle Ages, 1272–1540'. Unpublished PhD thesis, University of London, 1967.

Bloem, Hélène. 'The Processions and Decorations at the Royal Funeral of Anne of Brittany'. *Bibliothèque d'Humanisme et Renaissance* 54, no. 1 (1992): 131–60.

Bourdieu, Pierre. 'The Forms of Capital'. In *Handbook of Theory and Research for the Sociology of Education*, edited by J. G. Richardson, 241–58. New York: Greenwood Press, 1986.

Brayson, Alex. 'Deficit Finance During the Early Majority of Henry VI of England, 1436–1444: The "Crisis" of the Medieval English "Tax State"'. *The Journal of European Economic History* 49, no. 1 (2020): 9–73.

Britnell, R. H. 'The Economic Context'. In *The Wars of the Roses*, edited by A. J. Pollard, 41–64. London: Macmillan, 1995.

Brondarbit, Alexander R. *Power-Brokers and the Yorkist State, 1461–1485*. Woodbridge: Boydell Press, 2020.

Brown, A. L. 'The King's Councillors in Fifteenth-Century England'. *TRHS* 19 (1969): 95–118.

Brown, Elizabeth A. R. 'The Ceremonial of Royal Succession in Capetian France: The Double Funeral of Louis X'. *Traditio* 34 (1978), 227–71.

———. 'The Ceremonial of Royal Succession in Capetian France: The Funeral of Philip V'. *Speculum* 55, no. 2 (1980): 266–93.

Buckatzsch, E. J. 'The Geographical Distribution of Wealth in England, 1086–1843'. *EcHR* 3 (1950): 180–202.

Burger, Glenn D., and Rory G. Critten, eds. *Household Knowledges in Late-Medieval England and France*. Manchester: Manchester University Press, 2019.

Campbell, Bruce M. S. 'The Land'. In *A Social History of England, 1200–1500*, edited by Rosemary Horrox and W. Mark Ormrod, 179–237. Cambridge: Cambridge University Press, 2006.

Cantor, L. M., and J. Hatherly. 'The Medieval Parks of England'. *Geography* 64, no. 2 (Apr. 1979): 71–85.

Carpenter, Christine. 'The Beauchamp Affinity: A Study in the Working of Bastard Feudalism'. *EHR* 95, no. 376 (1980): 514–32.

Cherry, M. 'The Courtenay Earls of Devon: The Formation and Disintegration of a Late Medieval Aristocratic Affinity'. *Southern History* 1 (1979): 71–97.

Colvin, H. M. ed. *The History of the King's Works, Volume II: The Middle Ages*. London: H. M. Stationery Office, 1963.

Crawford, Anne. 'The King's Burden? The Consequences of Royal Marriage in Fifteenth-Century England'. In *Patronage, the Crown and the Provinces in Later Medieval England*, edited by Ralph A. Griffiths, 33–56. Gloucester: Sutton, 1981.

Select Bibliography

———. 'The Queen's Council in the Middle Ages'. *EHR* 116, no. 469 (Nov. 2001): 1193–211.

Cron, Bonita. 'Margaret of Anjou: Tradition and Revision'. Unpublished MA thesis, Massey University, 1999.

Cuerva, Rubén González. *Maria of Austria, Holy Roman Empress (1528-1603): Dynastic Networker*. Abingdon; New York: Routledge, 2022.

Curry, Anne, and Elizabeth Matthew. 'Introduction'. In *Concepts and Patterns of Service in the Later Middle Ages*, edited by Anne Curry and Elizabeth Matthew, xi–xxxiii. Woodbridge: Boydell Press, 2000.

Darby, H. C. 'Domesday England'. In *A New Historical Geography of England*, edited by H. C. Darby, 39–74. Cambridge: Cambridge University Press, 1973.

Darby, H. C., R. E. Glasscock, J. Sheail, and G. R. Versey. 'The Changing Geographical Distribution of Wealth in England: 1086–1334–1525'. *Journal of Historical Geography* 5, no. 3 (1979): 247–62.

Davies, R. R. 'Baronial Accounts, Incomes, and Arrears in the Later Middle Ages'. *EcHR* 21, no. 2 (Aug. 1968): 211–29.

———. *Lords and Lordship in the British Isles in the Late Middle Ages*. Oxford: Oxford University Press, 2009.

Dean, Lucinda H. S. *Death and the Royal Succession in Scotland, c.1214–c.1543: Ritual, Ceremony and Power*. Woodbridge: Boydell Press, 2024.

Delman, Rachel M. 'Gendered Viewing, Childbirth and Female Authority in the Residence of Alice Chaucer, Duchess of Suffolk, at Ewelme, Oxfordshire'. *Journal of Medieval History* 45, no. 2 (2019): 181–203.

———. 'The Queen's House before Queen's House: Margaret of Anjou and Greenwich Palace, 1447–1453'. *Royal Studies Journal* 8, no. 2 (2021): 6–25.

Denholm-Young, Noel. *Seignorial Administration in England*. London: Cass, 1937.

Donohue, Carolyn. 'Public Display and the Construction of Monarchy in Yorkist England, 1461–85'. Unpublished PhD thesis, University of York, 2013.

Dunn, Caroline. 'Serving Isabella of France: From Queen Consort to Dowager Queen'. In *Royal and Elite Households in Medieval and Early Modern Europe: More Than Just a Castle*, edited by Theresa Earenfight, 169–201. Leiden: Brill, 2018.

Dunn, Diana. 'Margaret [Margaret of Anjou]'. In *Oxford Dictionary of National Biography*, https://www.oxforddnb.com, (2004).

———. 'Margaret of Anjou: Queen Consort of Henry VI: A Reassessment of Her Role, 1445–53'. In *Crown, Government and People in the Fifteenth Century*, edited by Rowena Archer, 107–43. Stroud: Sutton, 1995.

Dyer, Christopher. *Lords and Peasants in a Changing Society: The Estates of the Bishopric of Worcester, 680–1540*. Cambridge: Cambridge University Press, 1980.

———. 'A Redistribution of Incomes in Fifteenth-Century England?'. *Past and Present* 39 (Apr. 1968): 11–33.

———. 'A Suffolk Farmer in the Fifteenth Century'. *The Agricultural History Review* 55, no. 1 (2007): 1–22.

Select Bibliography

Earenfight, Theresa. 'Introduction: Personal Relations, Political Agency, and Economic Clout in Medieval and Early Modern Royal and Elite Households'. In *Royal and Elite Households in Medieval and Early Modern Europe: More Than Just a Castle*, edited by Theresa Earenfight, 1–14. Leiden: Brill, 2018.

———. 'A Lifetime of Power: Beyond Binaries of Gender'. In *Medieval Elite Women and the Exercise of Power, 1100–1400: Moving Beyond the Exceptionalist Debate*, edited by Heather J. Tanner, 271–93. Cham: Palgrave Macmillan, 2019.

———. 'A Precarious Household: Catherine of Aragon in England, 1501–1504'. In *Royal and Elite Households in Medieval and Early Modern Europe: More Than Just a Castle*, edited by Theresa Earenfight, 338–56. Leiden: Brill, 2018.

———. *Queenship in Medieval Europe*. Basingstoke: Palgrave Macmillan, 2013.

———. 'Without the Persona of the Prince: Kings, Queens and the Idea of Monarchy in Late Medieval Europe'. *Gender & History* 19, no. 1 (Apr. 2007): 1–21.

Ellis, Mary. *Using Manorial Records*. London: PRO Publications, 1997.

Erickson, Amy Louise. *Women and Property in Early Modern England*. London; New York: Routledge, 1993.

Fleming, P. W. 'The Hautes and Their "Circle": Culture and the English Gentry'. In *England in the Fifteenth Century: Proceedings of the 1986 Harlaxton Symposium*, edited by Daniel Williams, 85–102. Woodbridge: Boydell Press, 1987.

Flores, Diana Pelaz, ed. 'The Iberian Queen's Households: Dynamics, Social Strategies and Royal Power'. Special Issue. *Royal Studies Journal*, 10, no. 1 (2023).

———. *La Casa de la Reina en la Corona de Castilla (1418–1496)*. Valladolid: Universidad de Valladolid, 2017.

Fößel, Amalie. 'The Queen's Wealth in the Middle Ages'. *Majestas* 13 (2005): 23–45.

Foucault, Michel. *The History of Sexuality, Volume 1: An Introduction*, translated by Robert Hurley. London: Allen Lane, 1979.

Fox, Levi. *The Administration of the Honor of Leicester in the Fourteenth Century*. Leicester: E. Backus, 1940.

Froide, Amy. 'Marital Status as a Category of Difference: Singlewomen and Widows in Early Modern England'. In *Singlewomen in the European Past, 1250–1800*, edited by Judith M. Bennett and Amy Froide, 236–69. Philadelphia: University of Pennsylvania Press, 1999.

Fryde, E. B. *Peasants and Landlords in Later Medieval England*. London: Sutton, 1996.

Geaman, Kristen L. *Anne of Bohemia*. Abingdon; New York: Routledge, 2022.

———. 'Queen's Gold and Intercession: The Case of Eleanor of Aquitaine'. *Medieval Feminist Forum: A Journal of Gender and Sexuality* 46, no. 2 (2010): 10–33.

Gibson, Gail McMurray. 'Blessing from Sun and Moon: Churching as Women's Theater'. In *Bodies and Disciplines: Intersections of Literature and History in Fifteenth-Century England*, edited by Barbara Hanawalt and David Wallace, 139–54. Minneapolis: University of Minnesota Press, 1996.

Select Bibliography

Giesey, Ralph E. *The Royal Funeral Ceremony in Renaissance France*. Geneva: Librairie E. Droz, 1960.

Given-Wilson, Chris. 'The Merger of Edward III's and Queen Philippa's Households'. *BIHR* 51 (1978): 183–7.

——. 'Purveyance for the Royal Household 1362–1413'. *BIHR* 56 (1983): 145–63.

——. *The Royal Household and the King's Affinity: Service, Politics and Finance in England, 1360–1413*. New Haven, CT: Yale University Press, 1986.

Griffiths, Ralph A. *The Reign of King Henry VI: The Exercise of Royal Authority, 1422–1461*. London: Benn, 1981.

Harris, Barbara J. *English Aristocratic Women, 1450–1550: Marriage and Family, Property and Careers*. Oxford: Oxford University Press, 2002.

——. 'Landlords and Tenants in England in the Later Middle Ages: The Buckingham Estates'. *Past and Present* 43 (May 1969): 146–50.

Harvey, Barbara. 'The Leasing of the Abbot of Westminster's Demesnes in the Later Middle Ages'. *EcHR* 22, no. 1 (1969): 17–27.

Harvey, Nancy Lenz. *Elizabeth of York: Tudor Queen*. London: A. Barker, 1973.

Harvey, P. D. A. *Manorial Records*. London: British Records Association, 1999.

Hatcher, John. 'The Great Slump of the Mid-Fifteenth Century'. In *Progress and Problems in Medieval England: Essays in Honour of Edward Miller*, edited by Richard Britnell and John Hatcher, 237–72. New York: Cambridge University Press, 1996.

Hicks, Michael. 'Anne [née Anne Neville]'. In *Oxford Dictionary of National Biography*, https://www.oxforddnb.com, (2004).

——. *Anne Neville: Queen to Richard III*. Stroud: Tempus, 2006.

——. 'The Changing Role of the Wydevilles in Yorkist Politics to 1483'. In *Patronage, Pedigree and Power in Later Medieval England*, edited by C. D. Ross, 60–86. Gloucester: Sutton, 1979.

——. 'Elizabeth [née Elizabeth Woodville]'. In *Oxford Dictionary of National Biography*, https://www.oxforddnb.com, (2004).

Hilton, Lisa. *Queens Consort: England's Medieval Queens*. London: Weidenfeld & Nicolson, 2008.

Hilton, R. H. 'The Content and Sources of English Agrarian History before 1500'. *The Agricultural History Review* 3, no. 1 (1955): 3–19.

——, trans. and ed. *Ministers' Accounts of the Warwickshire Estates of the Duke of Clarence 1479–80*. Oxford: Oxford University Press, 1952.

——. 'Peasant Movements in England before 1381'. *EcHR*, New Series 2, no. 2 (1949): 117–36.

A History of the County of Wiltshire: Volume 4. Edited by Elizabeth Crittall. London: Victoria County History, 1959. British History Online, http://www.british-history.ac.uk/vch/wilts/vol4.

A History of the County of Worcester: Volume 3. London: Victoria County History, 1913. 111–20. British History Online, http://www.british-history.ac.uk/vch/worcs/vol3.

Select Bibliography

Horrox, Rosemary. 'Elizabeth [Elizabeth of York]'. In *Oxford Dictionary of National Biography*, https://www.oxforddnb.com, (2004).

——. *Richard III: A Study of Service*. Cambridge: Cambridge University Press, 1991.

——. 'Service'. In *Fifteenth-Century Attitudes: Perceptions of Society in Late Medieval England*, edited by Rosemary Horrox, 61–78. Cambridge; New York: Cambridge University Press, 1994.

Howell, Margaret. *Eleanor of Provence: Queenship in Thirteenth-Century England*. Oxford: Blackwell, 1998.

——. 'The Resources of Eleanor of Provence as Queen Consort'. *EHR* 102, no. 403 (1987): 372–93.

Huneycutt, Lois L. *Matilda of Scotland: A Study in Medieval Queenship*. Woodbridge: Boydell Press, 2003.

——. 'Power: Medieval Women's Power through Authority, Autonomy, and Influence'. In *A Cultural History of Women in the Middle Ages*, edited by Kim M. Phillips, 153–78. London: Bloomsbury Publishing PLC, 2013.

——. 'Queenship Studies Comes of Age'. *Medieval Feminist Forum: A Journal of Gender and Sexuality* 51, no. 2 (2016): 9–16.

Hurstfield, Joel. *The Queen's Wards: Wardship and Marriage under Elizabeth I*. Cambridge, Mass.: Harvard University Press, 1958.

Hutton, Shennan. *Women and Economic Activities in Late Medieval Ghent*. New York: Palgrave Macmillan, 2011.

Jenkinson, Hilary. 'Exchequer Tallies'. *Archaeologia* 62, no. 2 (1911): 367–80.

Johnstone, Hilda. 'The Queen's Household'. In *Chapters in the Administrative History of Mediaeval England: The Wardrobe, the Chamber and the Small Seals*, vol. V, edited by T. F. Tout, 231–89. Manchester: Manchester University Press, 1930.

——. 'The Queen's Household'. In *The English Government at Work, 1327–1336*, vol. I, edited by James F. Willard, William A. Morris, et al., 250–99. Cambridge, Mass.: The Mediaeval Academy of America, 1940.

Jones, Michael K., and Malcolm Underwood. *The King's Mother: Lady Margaret Beaufort, Countess of Richmond and Derby*. Cambridge; New York: Cambridge University Press, 1992.

Kelleher, Marie A. 'What Do We Mean by "Women and Power"?' *Medieval Feminist Forum: A Journal of Gender and Sexuality* 51, no. 2 (2016): 104–15.

Kisby, Fiona Louise. 'The Royal Household Chapel in Early-Tudor London, 1485–1547'. Unpublished PhD thesis, Royal Holloway and Bedford New College, University of London, 1996.

Lamphere, Louise. 'Strategies, Cooperation and Conflict among Women in Domestic Groups'. In *Woman, Culture and Society*, edited by Michelle Zimbalist Rosaldo and Louise Lamphere, 97–112. Stanford: Stanford University Press, 1974.

Lander, J. R. 'Council, Administration and Councillors, 1461–85'. *BIHR* 32 (1959): 138–80.

Select Bibliography

Laynesmith, J. L. *Cecily Duchess of York*. London; New York: Bloomsbury Academic, 2017.

———. 'Constructing Queenship at Coventry: Pageantry and Politics at Margaret of Anjou's "Secret Harbour"'. In *The Fifteenth Century III: Authority and Subversion*, edited by Linda Clark, 137–48. Woodbridge: Boydell Press, 2003.

———. 'Elizabeth Woodville: The Knight's Widow'. In *Later Plantagenet and the Wars of the Roses Consorts: Power, Influence and Dynasty*, edited by Aidan Norrie, Carolyn Harris, J. L. Laynesmith, Danna R. Messer and Elena Woodacre, 215–36. Cham: Palgrave Macmillan, 2023.

———. *The Last Medieval Queens: English Queenship 1445–1503*. Oxford; New York: Oxford University Press, 2004.

Levin, Carole. 'Margaret of Anjou: Passionate Mother'. In *Later Plantagenet and the Wars of the Roses Consorts: Power, Influence and Dynasty*, edited by Aidan Norrie, Carolyn Harris, J. L. Laynesmith, Danna R. Messer and Elena Woodacre, 195–213. Cham: Palgrave Macmillan, 2023.

Liddiard, Robert. 'Introduction'. In *Late Medieval Castles*, edited by Robert Liddiard, 1–17. Woodbridge: Boydell Press, 2016.

Loades, David. *The Tudor Queens of England*. London; New York: Continuum, 2009.

Loengard, Janet Senderowitz. '"Of the Gift of Her Husband": English Dower and Its Consequences in the Year 1200'. In *Women of the Medieval World: Essays in Honor of John H. Mundy*, edited by Julius Kirshner and Suzanne Wemple, 215–55. Oxford; New York: Blackwell, 1985.

Matarasso, Pauline. *Queen's Mate: Three Women of Power in France on the Eve of the Renaissance*. Aldershot: Ashgate, 2001.

Maurer, Helen E. *Margaret of Anjou: Queenship and Power in Late Medieval England*. Woodbridge: Boydell Press, 2003.

McFarlane, K. B. 'The Investment of Sir John Fastolf's Profits of War'. *TRHS* 7 (1957): 91–116.

McIlvenna, Una. '"A Stable of Whores?" The "Flying Squadron" of Catherine De Medici'. In *The Politics of Female Households: Ladies-in-Waiting across Early Modern Europe*, edited by Nadine Akkerman and Birgit Houben, 181–208. Leiden: Brill, 2013.

McIntosh, Marjorie K. *Autonomy and Community: The Royal Manor of Havering, 1200–1500*. Cambridge; New York: Cambridge University Press, 1986.

Mertes, Kate. 'Aristocracy'. In *Fifteenth-Century Attitudes: Perceptions of Society in Late Medieval England*, edited by Rosemary Horrox, 42–60. Cambridge; New York: Cambridge University Press, 1994.

———. *The English Noble Household, 1250–1600: Good Governance and Politic Rule*. Oxford; New York: Blackwell, 1988.

Meyer, Marc Anthony. 'The Queen's "Demesne" in Later Anglo-Saxon England'. In *The Culture of Christendom: Essays in Medieval History in Commemoration of Denis L. T. Bethell*, edited by Marc Anthony Meyer, 75–113. London; Rio Grande: Hambledon Press, 1993.

Select Bibliography

Mileson, S. A. 'The Importance of Parks in Fifteenth-Century Society'. In *The Fifteenth Century V: Of Mice and Men: Image, Belief and Regulation in Late Medieval England*, edited by Linda Clark, 19–37. Woodbridge: Boydell Press, 2005.

Morgan, D. A. L. 'The King's Affinity in the Polity of Yorkist England'. *TRHS* 23 (1973): 1–25.

Myatt-Price, E. M. 'Cromwell Household Accounts, 1417–1476'. In *Studies in the History of Accounting*, edited by A. C. Littleton, 99–113. London: Sweet & Maxwell, 1956.

Myers, A. R. *Crown, Household and Parliament in Fifteenth Century England*. Edited by Cecil H. Clough. London: Hambledon Press, 1985.

——. *The Household of Edward IV: The Black Book and the Ordinance of 1478*. Manchester: Manchester University Press, 1959.

——. 'The Household of Queen Elizabeth Woodville, 1466-7'. *BJRL* 50, no. 1 (1967): 207–35 and *BJRL* 50, no. 2 (1968): 443–81. Reprinted in *Crown, Household and Parliament*, 251–318.

——. 'The Household of Queen Margaret of Anjou, 1452-3'. *BJRL* 40, no. 1 (1957): 79–113 and *BJRL* 40, no. 2 (1958): 391–451. Reprinted in *Crown, Household and Parliament*, 135–209.

——. 'The Jewels of Queen Margaret of Anjou'. *BJRL* 42, no. 1 (1959): 113–31. Reprinted in *Crown, Household and Parliament*, 211–30.

——. 'Some Household Ordinances of Henry VI'. *BJRL*, 36, no. 2 (1954): 449–67 and *BJRL*, 37, no. 1 (1954): 11–13. Reprinted in *Crown, Household and Parliament*, 231–49.

Narbona-Cárceles, Maria. 'Woman at Court: A Prosopographic Study of the Court of Carlos III of Navarre (1387–1485)'. *Medieval Prosopography* 22 (2001): 31–64.

Nash, Penelope. 'Jane Austen and Medieval Women: What on Earth Do They Have in Common?'. *Sensibilities* 56 (June 2018): 49–67.

——. 'Shifting Terrain – Italy and Germany Dancing in Their Own Tapestry'. *Journal of the Australian Early Medieval Association* 6 (2010): 53–73.

Neal, Derek. 'The Queen's Grace: English Queenship, 1464–1503'. Unpublished MA thesis, McMaster University, 1996.

Nelson, Janet L. 'The Wary Widow'. In *Property and Power in the Early Middle Ages*, edited by W. Davies and P. Fouracre, 82–113. Cambridge: Cambridge University Press, 1995.

Norrie, Aidan, Carolyn Harris, J. L. Laynesmith, Danna R. Messer and Elena Woodacre, eds. *Later Plantagenet and the Wars of the Roses Consorts: Power, Influence and Dynasty*. Cham: Palgrave Macmillan, 2023.

Norrie, Aidan, Carolyn Harris, J. L. Laynesmith, Danna R. Messer and Elena Woodacre, eds. *Tudor and Stuart Consorts: Power, Influence, and Dynasty*. Cham: Palgrave Macmillan, 2022.

Okerlund, Arlene. *Elizabeth of York*. New York: Palgrave Macmillan, 2009.

——. *Elizabeth Wydeville: The Slandered Queen*. Stroud: Tempus, 2005.

Select Bibliography

Parsons, John Carmi. *Eleanor of Castile: Queen and Society in Thirteenth-Century England*. New York: St Martin's Press, 1995.

——. '"Never was a body buried in England with such solemnity and honour": The Burials and Posthumous Commemorations of English Queens to 1500'. In *Queens and Queenship in Medieval Europe: Proceedings of a Conference Held at King's College London, April 1995*, edited by Anne J. Duggan, 317–37. Woodbridge: Boydell Press, 1997.

Penn, Thomas. *Winter King: The Dawn of Tudor England*. London: Allen Lane, 2011.

Pollock, Sir Frederick, and Frederic William Maitland. *The History of English Law before the Time of Edward I*. London: Cambridge University Press, 1968.

Poos, L. R. *A Rural Society after the Black Death: Essex 1350–1525*. Cambridge: Cambridge University Press, 1991.

Poska, Allyson M. 'The Case for Agentic Gender Norms for Women in Early Modern Europe', *Gender & History* 30, no. 2 (2018): 354–65.

Rawcliffe, Carole. 'Baronial Councils in the Later Middle Ages'. In *Patronage, Pedigree and Power in Later Medieval England*, edited by Charles Ross, 87–108. Gloucester: Sutton, 1979.

——. *The Staffords, Earls of Stafford and Dukes of Buckingham 1394–1521*. Cambridge: Cambridge University Press, 1978.

Razi, Zvi. 'The Struggles between the Abbots of Halesowen and their Tenants in the Thirteenth and Fourteenth Centuries'. In *Social Relations and Ideas: Essays in Honour of R. H. Hilton*, edited by T. H. Aston, et al., 151–67. Cambridge: Cambridge University Press, 1983.

Richmond, C. F. 'Fauconberg's Kentish Rising of May 1471'. *EHR* 85, no. 337 (Oct. 1970): 673–92.

Robert, Rudolph. 'A Short History of Tallies'. In *Studies in the History of Accounting*, edited by A. C. Littleton, 75–85. London: Sweet & Maxwell, 1956.

Rodrigues, Ana Maria S. A., and Manuela Santos Silva. 'Private Properties, Seigniorial Tributes, and Jurisdictional Rents: The Income of the Queens of Portugal in the Late Middle Ages'. In *Women and Wealth in Late Medieval Europe*, edited by Theresa Earenfight, 209–28. New York: Palgrave Macmillan, 2010.

Rohr, Zita. *Yolande of Aragon (1381–1442) Family and Power: The Reverse of the Tapestry*. Basingstoke: Palgrave Macmillan, 2016.

Rosaldo, Michelle Zimbalist. 'Woman, Culture and Society: A Theoretical Overview'. In *Woman, Culture and Society*, edited by Michelle Zimbalist Rosaldo and Louise Lamphere, 17–42. Stanford: Stanford University Press, 1974.

Rosenthal, Joel T. 'The Estates and Finances of Richard, Duke of York (1411–1460)'. *Studies in Medieval and Renaissance History* 2 (1965): 116–204.

Ross, Charles. *Edward IV*. London: Methuen, 1974.

Ross, C. D., and T. B. Pugh. 'Materials for the Study of Baronial Incomes in Fifteenth-Century England'. *EcHR* 6, no. 2 (1953): 185–94.

Select Bibliography

Ross, James. 'A Governing Elite? The Higher Nobility in the Yorkist and Early Tudor Period'. In *The Yorkist Age*, edited by H. W. Kleineke and C. Steer, 95–115. Donington: Shaun Tyas, 2013.

———. 'The Noble Household as a Political Centre in the Early Tudor Period'. In *The Elite Household in England, 1100–1550: Proceedings of the 2016 Harlaxton Symposium*, edited by C. M. Woolgar, 75–92. Donington: Shaun Tyas, 2018.

Routh, Pauline E. 'Princess Bridget'. *The Ricardian* 3 (1975): 13–14.

Saul, Nigel. *Richard II*. New Haven: Yale University Press, 2008.

Schofield, R. S. 'The Geographical Distribution of Wealth in England, 1334–1649'. *EcHR* 18, no. 3 (1965): 483–510.

Scott, Joan W. 'Gender: A Useful Category of Historical Analysis'. *The American Historical Review* 91, no. 5 (1986): 1053–75.

Seah, Michele. 'Gifts and Rewards: Exploring the Expenditure of Late Medieval English Queens', *Journal of Medieval History* 50, no. 5 (2024): 581–97, https://doi.org/10.1080/03044181.2024.2415637.

Silen-McMillin, Andrea C. 'Assessing the Lands of the Six Wives of Henry VIII with Particular Focus on Wiltshire'. Unpublished MA thesis, University of Winchester, 2024.

Somerville, Robert. *The History of the Duchy of Lancaster*. Vol. I. London: Chancellor and Council of the Duchy of Lancaster, 1953.

St John, Lisa Benz. *Three Medieval Queens: Queenship and the Crown in Fourteenth-Century England*. New York: Palgrave Macmillan, 2012.

Stretton, Tim, and Krista J. Kesselring, eds. *Married Women and the Law: Couverture in England and the Common Law World*. London: McGill-Queen's University Press, 2013.

Stuart, Denis. *Manorial Records: An Introduction to Their Transcription and Translation*. Chichester: Phillimore, 1992.

Sutton, Anne F., and Livia Visser-Fuchs. 'The Royal Burials of the House of York at Windsor: II. Princess Mary, May 1482 and Queen Elizabeth Woodville, June 1492'. *The Ricardian* 11 (1999): 446–51.

Sykes, N. J. 'The Impact of the Normans on Hunting Practices in England'. In *Food in Medieval England: Diet and Nutrition*, edited by C. M. Woolgar, D. Sergeantson and T. Waldron, 162–75. Oxford; New York: Oxford University Press, 2006.

Tallis, Nicola. *All the Queen's Jewels 1445–1548: Power, Majesty and Display*. London; New York: Routledge, 2023.

Tanner, Heather J. 'Queenship: Office, Custom, or Ad Hoc? The Case of Queen Matilda III of England (1135–1152)'. In *Eleanor of Aquitaine: Lord and Lady*, edited by Bonnie Wheeler and John Carmi Parsons, 133–58. Basingstoke: Palgrave Macmillan, 2003.

Tanner, Heather J., Laura L. Gathagan, and Lois L. Huneycutt. 'Introduction'. In *Medieval Elite Women and the Exercise of Power, 1100–1400: Moving Beyond the Exceptionalist Debate*, edited by Heather J. Tanner, 1–18. Cham: Palgrave Macmillan, 2019.

Select Bibliography

Thorstad, Audrey M. 'There and Back Again: The Hospitality and Consumption of a Sixteenth-Century English Travelling Household'. In *Royal and Elite Households in Medieval and Early Modern Europe: More Than Just a Castle*, edited by Theresa Earenfight, 357–77. Leiden: Brill, 2018.

Thurley, Simon. *The Royal Palaces of Tudor England: Architecture and Court Life 1460–1547*. New Haven, CT: Yale University Press, 1993.

Tingle, Louise. '*Aurum Reginae*: Queen's Gold in Late Fourteenth-Century England'. *Royal Studies Journal* 7, no. 1 (2020): 77–90.

——. *Chaucer's Queens: Royal Women, Intercession and Patronage in England, 1328–1394*. Basingstoke: Palgrave Macmillan, 2021.

Tout, T. F. *Chapters in the Administrative History of Mediaeval England: The Wardrobe, the Chamber and the Small Seals*. Vol. I, Manchester: Manchester University Press, 1930.

Underwood, Malcolm. 'The Pope, the Queen and the King's Mother: or, the Rise and Fall of Adriano Castellesi'. In *The Reign of Henry VII: Proceedings of the 1993 Harlaxton Symposium*, edited by Benjamin Thompson, 65–81. Stamford: Paul Watkins, 1995.

Walker, Simon. *The Lancastrian Affinity, 1361–1399*. Oxford: Clarendon Press, 1990.

Walker, Sue Sheridan. 'Royal Wardship in Medieval England'. Unpublished PhD dissertation, University of Chicago, 1966.

Ward, Jennifer. *English Noblewomen in the Later Middle Ages*. London; New York: Longman, 1992.

Ward, Matthew J. *The Livery Collar in Late Medieval England and Wales: Politics, Identity and Affinity*. Woodbridge: Boydell Press, 2016.

Warner, Kathryn. *Edward II's Nieces, The Clare Sisters: Power Pawns of the Crown*. Barnsley: Pen and Sword, 2020.

Warnicke, Retha. *Elizabeth of York and Her Six Daughters-in-Law: Fashioning Tudor Queenship, 1485–1547*. Cham: Palgrave Macmillan, 2017.

——. *The Marrying of Anne of Cleves: Royal Protocol in Tudor England*. Cambridge: Cambridge University Press, 2000.

Waugh, Scott L. *The Lordship of England: Royal Wardships and Marriages in English Society and Politics, 1217–1327*. Princeton: Princeton University Press, 1988.

Wedgwood, Josiah. *History of Parliament: Biographies of the Members of the Commons House, 1439–1509*. London: His Majesty's Stationery Office, 1936.

Whelan, Fiona. 'Administering the Household, 1180–1250: From Daniel of Beccles to Robert Grosseteste'. In *The Elite Household in England, 1100–1550: Proceedings of the 2016 Harlaxton Symposium*, edited by C. M. Woolgar, 185–203. Donington: Shaun Tyas, 2018.

Wickham, Chris. 'European Forests in the Early Middle Ages: Landscape and Land Clearance'. Reproduced in *Land and Power: Studies in Italian and European Social History, 400–1200*, edited by Chris Wickham, 155–99. London: British School at Rome, 1994.

Select Bibliography

Wiesner-Hanks, Merry E. 'Women's Agency: Then and Now'. *Parergon* 40, no. 2 (2023): 9–25.

Wilkinson, Louise J., ed. and trans. *The Household Roll of Eleanor de Montfort, Countess of Leicester and Pembroke, 1265: British Library, Additional MS 8877.* Woodbridge: Boydell Press for the Pipe Roll Society, 2020.

——. 'The Rules of Robert Grosseteste Reconsidered: The Lady as Estate and Household Manager in Thirteenth-Century England'. In *The Medieval Household in Christian Europe, c.850–1550*, edited by Cordelia Beattie, Anna Maslakovic and Sarah Rees Jones, 293–306. Turnhout: Brepols, 2003.

Wolffe, B. P. 'The Management of the English Royal Estates under the Yorkist Kings'. *EHR* 71 (1956): 1–27.

——. *The Royal Demesne in English History: The Crown Estate in the Governance of the Realm from the Conquest to 1509.* London: Allen and Unwin, 1971.

Woodacre, Elena. *Joan of Navarre: Infanta, Duchess, Queen, Witch?* Abingdon; New York: Routledge, 2022.

Woolgar, C. M. *The Great Household in Late Medieval England.* New Haven, CT: Yale University Press, 1999.

——. *Household Accounts from Medieval England, Part 1.* Oxford; New York: Oxford University Press, 1992.

——. *The Senses in Late Medieval England.* New Haven, CT; London: Yale University Press, 2006.

Wright, Katia. 'A Dower for Life: Understanding the Dowers of England's Medieval Queens'. In *Later Plantagenet and the Wars of the Roses Consorts: Power, Influence, Dynasty*, edited by Aidan Norrie, Carolyn Harris, J. L. Laynesmith, Danna Messer, and Elena Woodacre, 145–63. New York: Palgrave Macmillan, 2022.

——. 'The Queen's Lands: Examining the Role of Queens as Female Lords in Fourteenth Century England'. Unpublished PhD thesis, University of Winchester, 2022.

Young, Charles R. *The Royal Forests of Medieval England.* Leicester: Leicester University Press, 1979.

Zelizer, Viviana A. 'The Social Meaning of Money: "Special Monies"'. *American Journal of Sociology* 95, no. 2 (1989): 342–77.

zum Kolk, Caroline. 'The Household of the Queen of France in the Sixteenth Century'. *The Court Historian* 14, no. 1 (2009): 3–22.

INDEX

acattery 140, 167
accounts 26, 29, 37, 38, 40, 45, 82, 84, 92, 93, 97, 100, 102, 113, 120, 121, 136, 140, 141, 143, 150, 151, 153, 165, 166, 184 n.28, 190, 204, 205 n.117
  of arrears 10, 39, 41, 42, 115
  bailiff's 60, 94, 98, 99, 101, 188 n.40
  farmer's 97, 99
  jewel 5, 9, 184, 189, 190, 192 n.65
  Privy Purse expense 9, 10, 29, 30, 35, 36, 44, 45, 84, 122, 147, 150, 154, 155, 156, 171, 172 n.134, 190, 198
  receiver's 11, 64, 94, 95 n.28, 98 n.43, 117, 118, 139, 151–2, 188, 190
  receiver-general's 9, 10, 30, 39, 150
  reeve's 99 n.51, 100, 101
  types of 8 n.30, 9, 10
ad terminum vite 17 *see also* 'lifetime' grant; 'term of life' grant
affinity 25, 77, 173, 182, 185, 189, 191, 193, 206
  definition 179–80
  multiple connections 188
  king's 181, 188, 202
  purpose 181, 196, 197
  queen's 12, 13, 202, 206, 207, 208, 210, 213, 214
    benefits to 189–96
    conceptual model 181–2, 206
    end of service 203–6
    establishing 185–8
    military aspect 197
    purpose 181, 196
    service provided by 196, 197–206 *see also* christening; funerals; Woodville, Elizabeth, churching

    structure 181–5, 206
Agard, John 101
agentic gender norms 212
Altheworthe, John 188
amobr 16
amobrage 16
Anne of Bohemia 19, 39, 71, 72
Anne of Brittany 185, 205–6
Anne of Cleves 76, 206
Anne, duchess of Exeter 28, 34
Anne, Lady Bourchier 169, 171, 172, 184
Ardern, Thomas 101
armigerus 167 *see also* esquires
Arthur (son of Henry VII and Elizabeth of York) 136, 149, 199–200, 200 n.93, 202
Ashby, George 32 n.81, 175
attorney-general 116, 117, 120, 122
auditors 24, 26, 27 n.56, 96, 115, 116, 117, 124, 128, 156, 164, 174
  duties 115, 120
  fees 116
Aurum Regine 44 *see also* queen's gold

bailiff of fees 98 *see also* feodary
bailiffs 96, 97, 98, 99, 100, 101, 102, 114, 122, 124 151, 173, 188 *see also* accounts, bailiff's
Baker, Alan 74
Baldwin, David 4
ballivus feodorum 98 *see also* feodary
Bárány, Attila 3
Barnwood forest 58, 125
Baron, John 100
Bawlde, Thomas 124
Bean, J. M. W. 94
Beauchamp, Anne 32
Beauchamp, Henry, duke of Warwick 32

273

Index

Beaufort, Edmund, duke of Somerset 120, 184, 191
Beaufort, Margaret 56, 59, 118, 123, 140, 149, 169, 171, 195, 198, 199
Bedell, Richard 116
Bedell, William 116
Beer, Michelle 201
Berdfield, John 115
Bermondsey Abbey 20, 23, 66, 204
Birchley, Richard 190, 198 n.88
Black Book of Edward IV *see under* Edward IV
Blaunch Appelton 64
Bliaunt, Simon 125, 193
Bluemantle Pursuivant 198, 202
Bothe, Laurence 164, 184, 195
Bothe, William 184
Bourchier, Henry Viscount 124–5
Bourchier, Humphrey 165, 186
Bourchier, John, Lord Berners 164, 186
Bourchier, William 186
Bourdieu, Pierre 6
Bradowe, Beatrix 168
Bragges, Emma 168
Brettes, lordship of 28
Bridget (daughter of Edward IV and Elizabeth Woodville) 199
Brington, manor of 62, 68
Brown, A. L. 120
Browne, Robert 116
Bryan, Margaret 186
Buckatzsch, E. J. 74
Bulkley, Reynold 194
Burgh, Edith 185, 198 n.88
Burton, Thomas 195
Butler, Thomas, earl of Ormonde 175, 205
buttery 140, 151

Caister castle 123
capital 6, 213
capitalis ballivus 102
carvers 120, 166, 172, 173, 175, 186
Castellesi, Adriano 195
castles 25 n.49, 62, 67, 78, 83, 94, 96
  appearance of 81
  as status symbols 81
  benefit of 80–2
  definition 80
  licence to crenellate 81
  queens' favourites 82
Catherine of Aragon 8, 76, 149, 156, 175, 176, 186, 201, 202. 203, 207
cellar 140
Chaderton, Edmund 117–18, 175, 184, 195
chamber 26, 29, 32 n.81, 34, 36, 118, 139, 141, 144, 147, 150, 151, 153, 154, 166, 167, 169 n.124, 173, 174, 175, 176, 187, 191, 196, 198, 199, 202
chamberlain 116, 120, 151, 156, 164, 165, 175, 186, 190, 201, 205
chancellor 120, 151, 156, 164, 165, 175, 195
chandlery 140
Chaucer, Alice, Lady Suffolk 182, 183
Cherneys, Jamona 171, 185
Cherry, Martin 185
christening 149, 199, 200 n.93, 202 *see also* Arthur (son of Henry VII and Elizabeth of York)
churching *see under* Woodville, Elizabeth
Clere, Edmund 192
clerks 39 n.122, 100, 115, 139, 140, 143, 149, 166, 192, 195
  of the avenary 150, 151, 166, 167
  of the chancery register 143, 150, 166
  of the council 121
  of the hanaper 117, 175
  of the queen's closet 150, 166
  of queen's gold 45
  of the queen's jewels 166
  of receipts 150, 166
  of the signet 32 n.81, 143, 166, 174, 175
  of the stables 151, 166, 167, 173
  of works 82
Coke, Sir Philip 123
collector of receipts 96, 97, 100, 101
correspondence 11, 124, 125, 126, 131,

274

Index

181, 192, 193, 194, 195, 213 *see also* Margaret of Anjou, letters
Corsham   99, 113, 114
Cotton, Anthony   173
Cotton, Richard   173
Cotton, Roger   173
Cotton, William   9, 25–6, 39, 40, 117, 118, 121, 122, 139, 165, 174, 175, 184
councils   119, 120, 129, 130, 206
 issues handled by   121–3
 members of   120–1
court perquisites   92, 99, 213
court rolls   10, 29 n.69, 58, 188 n.40
Courtenay, Edward   168
Courtenay, Henry   168
Courtenay, Katherine   168, 204, 205
Courtenay, Margaret   168
Courtenay, Thomas   182
Coventry   68 n.49, 81, 194, 201
Coventry Leet Book   201
Crawford, Anne   122, 125–6, 127, 193, 194
Croke, John   39
Croke, Richard   121
Crowmer, William   175, 187, 205 n.119
Curry, Anne   180

Darcy, Elizabeth   198 n.88
de Braose, William   89
de Clare, Eleanor   53
de Clare, Elizabeth   53
de Clare, Gilbert   53
de Clare, Margaret   53
de la Pole, William, earl, marquess and duke of Suffolk   32, 182, 183, 184, 187
de Lacy, Margaret, countess of Lincoln   89
de Montfort, Eleanor, countess of Leicester and Pembroke   137 n.9
de Pisan, Christine   90, 189
De Republica Anglorum   135
de St Pol, Marie   182
de Saint Valery, Matilda   89
de Valence, Joan   168
de Vere, John, earl of Oxford   125, 193

Decons, Richard   44, 46, 118, 150, 154, 164, 165, 174, 175
Denton, William   175
Dialogus de Scaccario   15, 37
Domesday Book   91–2
Donohue, Carolyn   200
dower   16, 19, 21, 22, 23, 25, 38, 51, 55, 57, 59, 60, 70, 79, 81, 83, 87, 130, 209 *see also* Elizabeth of York, dower; Margaret of Anjou, dower; Woodville, Elizabeth, dower
 changes   21, 30, 48, 71, 72
 definition   56
 factors affecting   72–3, 74, 75, 76, 77, 78
 provision for multiple queens   20–1, 70
 queen's access to   56–8, 59
 terminology   17–18
dower lands, queen's   64, 66, 68, 70, 75, 83, 86, 118, 188, 210, 211, 212 *see also* Elizabeth of York, lands; Margaret of Anjou, lands; Woodville, Elizabeth, lands
dowry   16, 17, 19, 55
Draper, John   98, 100, 101
Draper, William   101
Duffield Frith   83
Dunn, Diana   4

Earenfight, Theresa   5, 8, 156, 182
Edward IV   1, 11, 17 n.9, 20, 22, 43, 60, 72, 77, 82, 115, 119 n.100, 135, 146, 173, 183, 188, 202, 205
 Black Book of   138, 141, 142, 144, 148, 152
 family members   2, 135, 136, 149, 199, 200
 marriage to Elizabeth Woodville   2, 16, 62, 72, 172
 providing for Elizabeth Woodville   19, 73, 75, 76, 78
 service to   121, 175, 187, 190, 191, 198 n.88
Eleanor of Castile   21, 25, 39, 46, 48, 57, 70, 209

275

Index

Eleanor of Provence   21, 24, 38, 39, 46, 48, 57, 71, 137, 209
Elizabeth, Lady Scales   171, 172, 184
Elizabeth of York   1, 2, 4, 9, 45, 47, 48, 71, 73, 80, 81, 82, 146, 147, 153, 165, 186, 195, 197–8, 199, 201, 202, 209, 210
  background   76–7, 183
  death   203, 204
  debts   36, 37, 129, 154–5
  dower   17, 18, 20, 21, 22, 23, 28, 30, 36, 37, 66, 68, 73, 74, 95, 101, 129, 155
  dowry   17
  as estate and household administrator   68, 126, 128–9, 156
  family members   1 n.2, 22 n.35, 52, 136, 149, 171, 172, 183, 184, 186, 192, 199, 207
  funeral   140, 143, 144 n.35, 167, 171, 204–5
  gifts   36, 37, 84, 116 n.82, 190, 198
  historiography   3–5
  household   29, 116, 117, 118, 122, 123, 143, 144 n.35, 150, 164, 165, 168, 171, 173, 174, 175, 176, 184, 187, 190 *see also* household, queen's
  household finances   151, 152 n.75, 153, 154–5
  household ladies   169, 170 n.127, 171, 172, 176, 186, 196, 204
  inherited properties   28
  land purchases   28
  lands   28, 29, 60, 66, 67, 68, 71, 75–6, 83, 86, 87, 95, 209–10 *see also* landholdings, queen's
  letters   125 n.134, 194
  loans from Henry VII   36, 37
  Privy Purse   150, 164, 166 n.101, 191 *see also* accounts, Privy Purse expense; keeper of the Privy Purse
  queen's gold   21, 22, 44–6
Ellesmere, Edward   150, 166, 174, 184, 190
Elrington, Thomas   126, 127

Enfield   58
Erickson, Amy   53
esquires   9, 114, 139, 140, 143, 153, 167, 168, 173, 174, 183, 185, 191, 192, 204
Essex, William   39
estate treatises   11, 89, 90, 96, 97, 100, 102 n.67
estates, queen's   16, 18, 19, 20, 22, 24 n.43, 30 n.72, 58, 129, 130, 131
  accounts   10, 11 *see also* accounts
  legality of ownership   57, 58, 59
  management   12, 91, 93, 94, 102
  officials   94, 96–115 *see also* auditors; bailiffs; farmers; receiver-general; receivers; reeves; stewards of lands
  oversight   115–19
  policy-making   119–23
extra hospicium   136
Eyre, Thomas   32 n.81

farmers   97, 98, 99, 100, 188 *see also* accounts, farmer's
Fastolf, Sir John   51–2, 192
Feckenham   24, 25, 62, 66, 80, 91, 95, 98, 99, 113, 114
  forest of   66, 83, 95
fee-farms   20, 21, 23, 24, 25, 26, 27, 28, 29, 30, 33, 45, 62, 64, 73, 97–8 n.42, 102 n.70, 210
femme couvert   54, 56
femme sole   54, 56, 59
feodary   97, 98, 116
fieri facias   39
Fitzalan, Thomas, Lord Maltravers   199
Fitzlewis manors   27, 64
FitzNigel, Richard   15, 37
Fogge, Alice   184
forests   35, 36, 58, 66, 67, 78, 85, 95, 125, 175, 194, 195
  benefits   83, 84
  courts *see* swanimotes; wodemotes
  definition   82–3
  included in grants   81, 83
  legal   82–3
  physical   83

276

Index

Forster, John   43, 44, 117, 118, 121, 122, 151, 165, 184
Fößel, Amalie   16
Fotheringhay   28, 95
Foucault, Michel   5
funerals   200, 201, 203, 204, 205, 206
    see also Elizabeth of York, funeral
Fynaunce, Jacob/James   166

garcio   167 see also grooms
Geaman, Kristen   46
George, duke of Clarence   67 n.47, 77
Gerald of Wales   89
gifts   23, 31, 36, 37, 84, 116, 117, 166, 183, 189, 190, 191, 192 n.65, 198, 206
Gigli, Giovanni   195
Gillingham   24, 25, 36, 66, 70, 79, 83, 91 n.11, 96, 99, 100, 113
Godmanchester   20, 27, 64, 122
'good ladyship'   189, 190, 192, 193, 194, 207, 214
'good lordship'   189
Greenwich see Pleasaunce, manor of
Grey, Edward   187
Grey, John   62, 187
Grey, Katherine   201
Griffiths, Ralph   32, 34
grooms   9, 32 n.81, 139, 143, 147, 153, 167, 169 n.124, 173, 190
Grosseteste, Robert, bishop of Lincoln   89, 90, 198 n.88
Guildford, Jane   186-7, 196

Hall, Edward   203
Hamerton, George   147, 173
Hamerton, John   173
Hamerton, William   147, 173
Harleton, William   125
Harreys, Richard   114
Harvey, P. D. A.   12
Hatcliffe, John   167
Haute, Anne   191
Haute, Henry   173
Haute, James(Jaques)   165, 173, 186
Haute, Martin   173
Haute, Nicholas   172

Haute, Richard   172-3, 194
Haute, William   186
Havering-atte-Bower   58, 62, 66, 70, 79, 91, 97, 99, 113-14, 123, 126, 127, 129
Henry VI   1, 11, 43, 52, 70, 72, 84, 115, 144, 146, 175, 197, 201
    marriage to Margaret of Anjou   1, 18, 182
    Readeption of   1, 22, 59-60, 130
Henry VII   1, 2, 11, 21, 56, 67, 74, 75, 76, 77, 78, 82, 115, 140 n.26, 155, 195
    family members   52, 56, 76, 118, 136, 199
    granting lands of Cecily Neville to Elizabeth of York   66
    marriage to Elizabeth of York   2, 17, 73
    providing for Elizabeth of York   20-1, 66
    re-granting dower to Elizabeth Woodville   17-18 n.15, 20, 22, 28, 75
    service to   173, 175
Henry, duke of Buckingham   34
Herberquyne, Barbaline   171
Herman, Osanna   171
Hertingfordbury   81, 91, 98, 99, 100-1, 124
Honour of Tutbury   67, 81 n.94, 83, 84, 91 n.11, 94, 97 n.41, 98, 99, 101
Horrox, Rosemary   180, 187, 189
household, queen's:
    accounts   19, 20, 24, 25, 27, 32, 34, 42, 43, 95 n.31, 115, 116 n.83, 122, 125, 138, 139, 142, 183 see also accounts
    departments   139, 140, 141, 143, 148, 150, 151, 153 see also buttery; chamber; kitchen; marshalsea; pantry; wardrobe
    management   4, 22, 75, 89, 147, 177, 180, 210, 213
    financial   149-51
    operational   148-9
    ordinances   11, 119 n.100, 136, 138,

277

140, 144, 145, 148, 149, 169 n.124, 171, 176, 198, 199 n.91
organisation   4, 5, 9, 136, 138–41, 176, 177
personnel   5, 9, 136, 147, 153, 156, 176, 185, 196, 207 *see also* auditors; carvers; chamberlain; chancellor; clerks; esquires; grooms; marshal of the hall; marshal of the stables; master of horse; master of the queen's jewels; pages; receiver-general; sewers; stewards of households; treasurer; ushers; yeomen
  background   114, 156
  'below stairs'   167, 168
  gender of   168, 169, 199
  'middle management'   166, 167, 168–9
  numbers of   142, 144, 148
  social hierarchy   167
  wages   9, 113, 153, 164, 165
separation of households   136–8, 147, 152, 153
size   141–6, 176
Howard, John, duke of Norfolk   125–6, 193
Howard, Thomas   30, 192
Howell, Margaret   38, 39
Hull, Edward   165
Humphrey, brother of Henry, duke of Buckingham   34
Humphrey, duke of Gloucester   24, 25, 58
Huneycutt, Lois   7
Hungate, William   154
Huntingdon   20, 27, 80
Husbandry   96, 102
Huse quitclaim   27, 64, 67
Huse, William   64

in dotem   17
in dotis   17–18
income, queen's   5, 10, 12, 16 n.5, 48, 55, 57, 73, 76, 83, 93, 94, 151, 174, 210
  fee-farms   27, 29, 30

  landed sources   20, 23, 24, 25, 26, 27, 28, 29, 30, 75
  non-landed sources   31, 32, 33, 34, 37, 72
  queen's gold *see* queen's gold
infra hospicium   136
Ingaldesthorp, Elizabeth   32
Isabella of France   5, 19, 67, 70, 139, 145, 197, 205
Isabella of Valois   19, 70
Iseham, Robert   187
Ismanie, Lady Scales   183

jewel account *see* accounts, jewel
Joan, Lady Dacre   201
Joan of Navarre   19, 32 n.77, 43, 70, 71, 182
Joan, Lady Strange   201
John, duke of Bedford   182
John of Gaunt   81, 124, 182
John, Viscount Beaumont   114, 115, 164, 184
Johnstone, Hilda   5, 15, 16, 19, 22, 38, 47, 57, 96, 121, 136, 138
jointure   17, 56, 57, 59, 76
  definition   18, 55
  Elizabeth of York's   18
Josselyn, Rauf   192

Katherine of Valois   19, 24, 70, 77, 182
keeper of the wardrobe   150, 151, 165, 166, 174, 185, 195, 205
keeper of the park   32, 96, 195
keeper of the Privy Purse   44 n.138, 46, 150, 154 n.79, 164, 165, 166, 174, 175
keeper of the queen's jewels   150, 166, 191
Kelleher, Marie   7
Kenilworth   62, 81, 94, 173
Kerver, William   174, 187
Kettlewell, Robert   82
Kidwelly, Maurice   95, 114
Kidwelly, Morgan   114
kitchen   140, 143 n.34, 151, 152, 153, 166, 190
  funding records   151
  subdivisions:

278

acattery 140, 167
cellar 140
chandlery 140
larder 140
saucery 140, 153, 190
scaldinghouse 140
scullery 140, 153
spicery 140
stores 140

land organisation:
  bailiwick 92–3
  barony 92–3
  county 91
  honour 92–3
  hundred 91
  manor 78–9, 91, 92
  wapentake 91
land valors 10, 26, 27, 29, 30, 42 n.131, 43, 44, 45, 95 n.28, 115, 116 n.87
Lander, J. R. 120–1
landholdings, queen's 4–5, 24, 28, 47, 52, 56–8, 59, 71
  comparison of 66–71
  organisation *see* land organisation
  purchases of 59, 64
  shifting locus of 75, 77, 78
  types 78–85 *see also* castles; forests; manors; parks
Langley Marish 80, 114
larder 140
Laynesmith, J. L. 136, 205 n.117
Leo of Rozmittal, Baron 200
Liber regie capelle 203–4
'lifetime' grant 17, 18, 211
Liseux, Thomas 195
Louis of Bruges, Lord Gruthuse 202
Lovell, Geoffrey 193
Lovell, John 193
Lovell, Thomas 166, 175, 187

magna garderoba 139
manor court 58, 92, 99, 127, 213
manors:
  benefits 79–80, 81
  definition 78–9, 92–3, 94
  legal 79
  physical 78–9
  purpose 91–2
  queens' favourites 82
Margaret of Anjou 1, 4, 16, 22, 31, 52, 60, 77, 80, 81, 94, 95, 115, 116, 119, 120, 121, 127, 128, 152, 153, 164, 165, 177, 182, 187, 188, 189, 191, 197, 204, 209, 210, 211, 214
  dower 17, 18, 19, 21, 22, 23–4, 73, 87
  dowry 16
  as estate and household administrator 124–5, 127, 131, 155–6
  gifts 116, 117, 183, 189, 190, 192 n.65
  historiography 3–5
  household 117, 122, 139, 142, 143, 144, 147, 150, 151, 153, 154, 168, 171, 174 *see also* household, queen's
  household accounts 5, 8, 9, 24, 37, 84, 100, 101, 115, 138, 139, 150
  household ladies 169, 171, 185, 191, 196
  land purchases 27
  lands 58, 60, 62, 64, 67, 71, 75, 91 n.11 *see also* landholdings, queen's
  letters 58–9, 82, 84, 102, 124–5, 125 n.129, 146, 187 n.35, 192–3
  queen's gold 22, 39–40, 43, 47, 155
  visit to Coventry 201
Margaret of France 19, 70
Marlborough 62, 67, 70, 82, 94, 95, 100
marshal of the hall 166
marshal of the stables 166
marshalsea 140, 143, 144 n.35, 150 n.61, 166
Mashbury 91 n.11, 97–8 n.42, 99 n.48, 188
Massy, Alice 190–1
master of horse 166, 167, 172 n.135, 173
master of the queen's jewels 9, 166, 174
Matilda of Boulogne 57, 76
Matilda of Scotland 76, 137

279

Index

Matthew, Elizabeth   180
Mauncell, Thomas   95
Maurer, Helen   4, 16, 192
Mayer, John   45
McFarlane, K. B.   51–2
McIntosh, Marjorie   97, 126
Melksham, forest of   67, 83
Merden   94–5
Merston, John   191
Merston Meysy   99–100
Merston, Rose   191
Mertes, Kate   135, 145, 167, 168
Mervyn, John   100
messor   100
Meyer, Marc Anthony   70 n.54
Middleton   94, 95
Monro, Cecil   193
Montgomery, John   58
Mountgomery, Thomas   113
Mouseherst, Thomas   190
Myers, A. R.   5, 9, 40, 124, 125, 142, 144–5, 155–6, 164, 165, 175

Neal, Derek   4, 5, 38, 44, 168, 194
Needwood Forest   83
Neville, Anne   2, 3, 73, 76, 177
Neville, Cecily   18, 28, 29, 66, 68, 73, 95, 118, 123, 149, 199
Neville, John, earl of Northumberland   80
Neville, Richard, earl of Warwick   1, 114
Norrys, John   140, 166, 174, 184, 190
Norwich   30, 201

Odiham   24, 25, 62, 66, 70, 96
Ogard, Andrew   32, 165
Ogard, Henry   32
Okerlund, Arlene   155
Orchard, Thomas   101
Osgodby, William   95 n.29

pages   9, 139, 142, 143, 147, 153, 156, 167, 184–5 n.28
pagettus   167 *see also* pages
pantry   140, 151
Parker, Thomas   174, 187
parks   78, 80, 81, 82, 83, 84–5, 121

parva garderoba   139
Paston, John   191
Paston, John II   123
Paston, John III   123
Pembroke   24, 25, 33, 62, 96
Penyson, Katherine   183
Pesemersh, Cecily   168
Pewsham, forest of   36, 67, 83
Philippa of Hainault   5, 18, 19, 38, 39, 57, 138, 139, 141, 145, 164, 165
  lands of   67, 68, 69, 70–1
Pleasaunce, manor of   24, 25, 67, 82, 127, 128
Pleshey   60, 82, 91, 101, 102, 146
Poska, Allyson   212
power, hard   6, 7
power, soft   6, 7
Privy Purse expense account *see* accounts, Privy Purse expense
Prynne, William   38, 39, 42, 44
Pyrcan, Edmund   124

queen's council *see* councils
queen's gold   16, 19, 20, 22, 23, 38, 39, 43, 47, 48, 71, 209, 210, 213, 214 *see also* Elizabeth of York, queen's gold; Margaret of Anjou, queen's gold; Woodville, Elizabeth, queen's gold
  arrears of   24, 39, 41 n.127, 42 n.130
  Aurum Regine   44
  clerk of   45
  collector of   44, 46 *see also* receivers
  definition   15, 37–8, 46
  fieri facias   39
  importance of   39, 46–7, 48
  income from   39, 43, 46, 71–2
  origins   38–9
  receiver of *see under* receivers
  writs   38, 39, 40, 41 n.127 and 128, 42, 43, 44, 45, 46, 48
queens' households *see* household, queen's
queens' ladies *see* Elizabeth of York, household ladies; Margaret of Anjou, household ladies; Woodville, Elizabeth, household ladies

280

Index

queens' lands *see* landholdings, queen's

Radcliff, Roger   164, 184
Rawcliffe, Carole   102, 122
receiver-general   10, 25–6, 32, 34, 45, 93, 116, 117, 118, 119, 120, 124, 130, 139, 149–50, 151, 156, 164, 165, 174, 175 *see also* accounts, receiver-general's
receivers   10, 44 n.137, 60, 93, 94, 95, 96, 99, 102, 113, 114, 115, 116, 117, 118, 124, 130, 150, 151, 173, 174 *see also* accounts, receiver's
of queen's gold   43, 45, 46, 102 n.70
receivership   93, 94, 95, 96 n.32, 113
Ree, Roger   60, 115, 118
reeves   96, 97, 98, 99, 100, 101, 114, 122, 188 *see also* accounts, reeve's
Richard III   2, 20, 22, 73, 77
affinity   180, 187, 189
riding household   147
Rockingham   62, 67, 70, 81–2, 83
Roos, Richard   191
Rosenthal, Joel   93, 94, 117
Ross, James   77, 145
Rotherham, John   95 n.29
royal authority, shifting of   77, 78
royal residences, shifting of   78
Rules of Robert Grosseteste   89–90

St John, Lisa Benz   5–6, 136, 137, 138, 141, 145, 169
St Pol, Jacquetta *see* Woodville, Jacquetta, dowager duchess of Bedford
Saintlowe, Giles   168, 185, 195, 197 n.83, 198 n.88
Sandeland, Thomas   191
saucery   140, 153, 190
Savernake, forest of   67, 83
scaldinghouse   140
Schofield, R. S.   74
Scott, Joan Wallace   7
scullery   140, 153
Seneschaucy   96, 102
sewers   166

Sharnborne, Jamona *see* Cherneys, Jamona
Sharnborne, Thomas   168, 185, 192
Sharp, Christopher   113
Sharp, Nicholas   26, 116, 174, 187, 190
Sheen, manor of   82
Shelford, Thomas   187, 192
Smith, Sir Thomas   135
Somerville, Robert   62, 124
Southwode, William   100, 124
spicery   140
stables *see* marshalsea
Stafford, Edward, duke of Buckingham   146–7
Stafford, Elizabeth   184, 204
Stanford, John   116, 174
Stanley, Thomas, 3rd earl of Derby   56
stewards of households   140, 164–5, 184
stewards of lands   32 n.81, 36, 102, 113, 114, 115, 120, 125, 164, 172 n.135, 173, 184, 187, 211
Stidolf, Thomas   43, 45 n.143, 102 n.70
Stonor, Sir William   58, 125
stores   140
surveys   10
swanimotes   83

Talbot, Sir Gilbert   114
tallies   33
Tanfield, Robert   117, 121
'term of life' grant   17, 18
Tetzel, Gabriel   200, 202
Thomas, duke of Clarence   182
Thomas, Lord Scales   120
Thomson, Gilbert   100
Thurley, Simon   78, 146
Tingle, Louise   38 n.114, 138 n.15
travelling household   146, 147
Treasure of the City of Ladies   90, 189
treasurer   9, 15, 36, 117, 120, 140, 149, 151, 154, 155, 156, 165, 166, 174, 175, 191
treatise   11, 15, 89, 90, 96, 97, 100, 102 n.67
Treaty of Troyes   19
Tregory, Michael   192
Tresham holdings   27, 67, 68

281

Tudor, Edmund   182
Tudor, Jasper   62 n.39, 182
Tudor, Owen   182 n.19
Twyday, Thomas   187

ushers   32 n.81, 120, 166, 169 n.124, 173, 174, 175, 205

valettus   167 *see also* yeomen
Vaux, Henry   196
Vaux, Katherine   183, 187
Vaux, William   183
Verney, Eleanor   176
vill   91–2

Walden   124, 125
Walker, Simon   180
Walsh, John   26, 116, 174
Walter of Henley   96
Ward, William   102
wardrobe   8 n.30, 38, 39 n.118, 137–8, 139, 151 *see also* keeper of the wardrobe
  great   139–40, 141
  privy   139
wardships   31, 32, 35, 48, 64, 209
Warnicke, Retha   4, 76, 201, 205 n.117
Wenlock, John   32 n.81, 164, 175, 184, 190, 197 n.83
Weston, Anne   176
Whittingham, Katherine   185
Whittingham, Robert   185, 197 n.83
Wiesner-Hanks, Merry   8, 212
William, Geoffrey   190
Williams, Alice   168
wodemotes   83
Woodham Ferrers   17 n.9, 62
Woodville, Anthony   113, 172
Woodville, Elizabeth   1, 2, 4, 16, 34, 43, 48, 58, 60, 62, 68, 72, 81, 82, 83, 94, 102 n.70, 113, 119, 120, 121, 127, 128, 152 n.75, 153, 172, 179, 186, 191, 194, 199, 202, 204, 205, 209, 211
  background   76–7, 183
  churching   199, 200, 202
  dower   17, 18, 19–20, 23, 26, 73, 75

  as estate and household administrator   155–6
  family members   1, 135, 136, 169, 171, 172, 199, 200
  gifts   116 n.82, 190
  historiography   3–5
  household   116, 117, 119, 120, 122, 140, 142, 143, 147, 150, 151, 154, 164, 165, 168, 172, 173, 174, 175, 184 *see also* household, queen's
  household accounts   5, 9, 11, 27, 37, 84, 101, 115, 116 n.83, 125, 139, 143, 150, 151, 153, 156, 165, 191
  household ladies   169, 171
  land purchases   27–8, 64, 66
  lands   28, 29, 30, 67, 71, 75, 79, 80, 87, 91 n.11, 95, 96, 114, 118, 187, 188 *see also* landholdings, queen's
  letters   58, 125 n.134, 126, 193–4
  queen's gold   22, 42–4, 45, 46, 47
  re-grant of lands by Henry VII   21, 22, 29, 66, 75
  retirement to Bermondsey Abbey   20, 23, 66, 204
  visit to Norwich   201
Woodville, Jacquetta, dowager duchess of Bedford   183, 186, 199
Woodville, Jane   172 n.138, 186, 201
Woodville, John   172
Woodville, Katherine   168
Woodville, Margaret, Lady Maltravers   199
Woodville, Richard   186
Woolgar, C. M.   145, 147, 148, 151 n.68, 152
Wraysbury   114
Wright, Katia   18 n.16, 21 n.33, 57, 68
writs *see under* queen's gold

yeomen   9, 139, 140, 143, 147, 153, 167, 173, 174, 190, 191, 195

zum Kolk, Caroline   136–7

GENDER IN THE MIDDLE AGES

I *Gender and Medieval Drama*, Katie Normington, 2006
II *Gender and Petty Crime in Late Medieval England: The Local Courts in Kent, 1460–1560*, Karen Jones, 2006
III *The Pastoral Care of Women in Late Medieval England*, Beth Allison Barr, 2008
IV *Gender, Nation and Conquest in the Works of William of Malmesbury*, Kirsten A. Fenton, 2008
V *Monsters, Gender and Sexuality in Medieval English Literature*, Dana M. Oswald, 2010
VI *Medieval Anchoritisms: Gender, Space and the Solitary Life*, Liz Herbert McAvoy, 2011
VII *Middle-Aged Women in the Middle Ages*, edited by Sue Niebrzydowski, 2011
VIII *Married Women and the Law in Premodern Northwest Europe*, edited by Cordelia Beattie and Matthew Frank Stevens, 2013
IX *Religious Men and Masculine Identity in the Middle Ages*, edited by P. H. Cullum and Katherine J. Lewis, 2013
X *Reconsidering Gender, Time and Memory in Medieval Culture*, edited by Elizabeth Cox, Liz Herbert McAvoy and Roberta Magnani, 2015
XI *Medicine, Religion and Gender in Medieval Culture*, edited by Naoë Kukita Yoshikawa, 2015
XII *The Unspeakable, Gender and Sexuality in Medieval Literature, 1000–1400*, Victoria Blud, 2017
XIII *Popular Memory and Gender in Medieval England: Men, Women, and Testimony in the Church Courts, c.1200–1500*, Bronach C. Kane, 2019
XIV *Authority, Gender and Space in the Anglo-Norman World, 900–1200*, Katherine Weikert, 2020
XV *Female Desire in Chaucer's* Legend of Good Women *and Middle English Romance*, Lucy M. Allen-Goss, 2020
XVI *Treason and Masculinity in Medieval England: Gender, Law and Political Culture*, E. Amanda McVitty, 2020
XVII *Holy Harlots in Medieval English Religious Literature: Authority, Exemplarity and Femininity*, Juliette Vuille, 2021
XVIII *Addressing Women in Early Medieval Religious Texts*, Kathryn Maude, 2021

XIX	*Women, Dance and Parish Religion in England, 1300–1640: Negotiating the Steps of Faith,* Lynneth Miller Renberg, 2022
XX	*Women's Literary Cultures in the Global Middle Ages: Speaking Internationally,* edited by Kathryn Loveridge, Liz Herbert McAvoy, Sue Niebrzydowski and Vicki Kay Price, 2023
XXI	*Women and Devotional Literature in the Middle Ages: Giving Voice to Silence. Essays in Honour of Catherine Innes-Parker,* edited by Cate Gunn, Liz Herbert McAvoy and Naoë Kukita Yoshikawa, 2023
XXII	*Female Devotion and Textile Imagery in Medieval English Literature,* Anna McKay, 2024
XXIII	*Premodern Masculinities in Transition,* edited by Konrad Eisenbichler and Jacqueline Murray, 2024
XXIV	*The Queenship of Mathilda of Flanders: Embodying Conquest,* Laura L. Gathagan, 2025

Printed in the United States
by Baker & Taylor Publisher Services